T0381980

THE ENCYCLOPEDIA OF
PASTA

THE ENCYCLOPEDIA OF
PASTA

OVER 350 RECIPES FOR
THE ULTIMATE COMFORT FOOD

CIDER MILL PRESS

BOOK PUBLISHERS

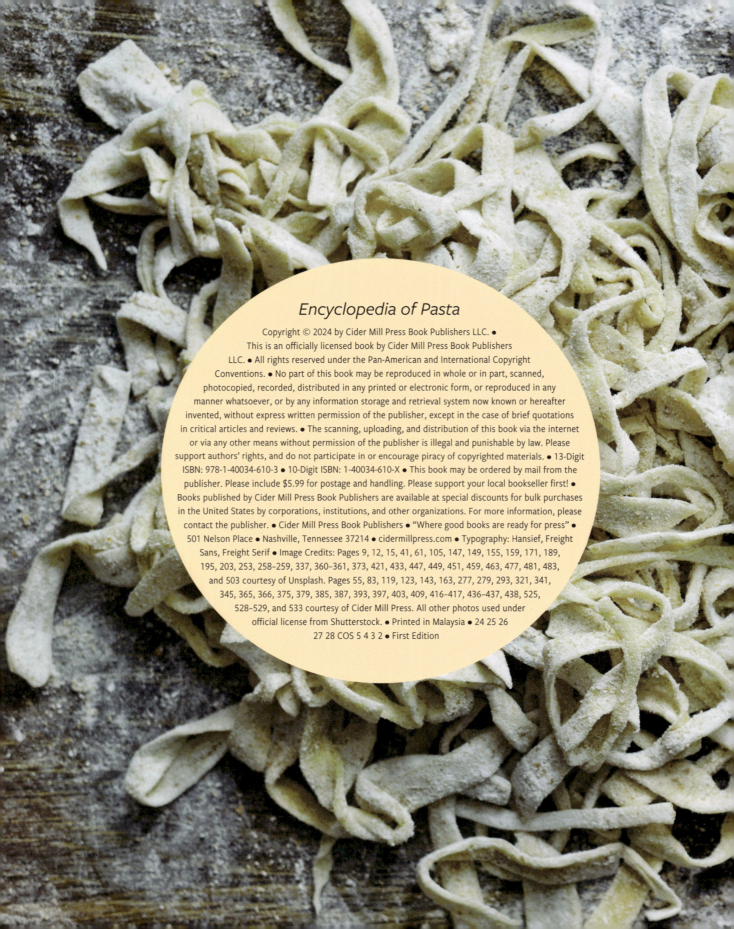

Encyclopedia of Pasta

Books published by Cider Mill Press Book Publishers are available at special discounts for bulk purchases
in the United States by corporations, institutions, and other organizations. For more information, please
contact the publisher. ● Cider Mill Press Book Publishers ● "Where good books are ready for press" ●
501 Nelson Place ● Nashville, Tennessee 37214 ● cidermillpress.com ● Typography: Hansief, Freight
Sans, Freight Serif ● Image Credits: Pages 9, 12, 15, 41, 61, 105, 147, 149, 155, 159, 171, 189,
195, 203, 253, 258–259, 337, 360–361, 373, 421, 433, 447, 449, 451, 459, 463, 477, 481, 483,
and 503 courtesy of Unsplash. Pages 55, 83, 119, 123, 143, 163, 277, 279, 293, 321, 341,
345, 365, 366, 375, 379, 385, 387, 393, 397, 403, 409, 416–417, 436–437, 438, 525,
528–529, and 533 courtesy of Cider Mill Press. All other photos used under
official license from Shutterstock. ● Printed in Malaysia ● 24 25 26
27 28 COS 5 4 3 2 ● First Edition

CONTENTS

INTRODUCTION

Versatile, wholesome, and inexpensive, pasta and noodles were destined to become beloved. Providing the proverbial blank canvas upon which some of the world's most popular dishes are crafted, they are the rare items that can withstand any shift in taste and accommodate every culinary trend. Blessing each plate or bowl they grace with feelings of comfort and care, pasta and noodles have transcended their humble compositions (flour, eggs, and, sometimes, water) to become cornerstones of the modern diet.

As the increasingly hectic pace of the world beckons us away from the kitchen, pasta and noodles are ties to the vital act of taking a step back to provide sustenance for our loved ones and ourselves. There are days when concocting a meal is the last thing one wants to think about, but thanks to pasta and noodles' adaptability and ease of preparation, they always provide a way past this apprehension.

Since the affection for all things pasta and noodles is undeniable, we thought it would be well worth fueling the fire. This book makes it easy for anyone to whip up fresh noodles, comforting soups, indulgent dishes, and silky sauces. That doesn't mean it's basic though—we're certain that even the most zealous pasta and noodle enthusiast will find something to warm their heart.

Dig in. You'll soon see why we believe that pasta and noodles are some of the best testaments to humanity's limitless creativity and ingenuity.

MAKING YOUR OWN PASTA & NOODLES

Making your own pasta and noodles is not rocket science. At the end of the day, it can be as simple as combining two ingredients, eggs and flour, or flour and water. Should you decide to use the all-purpose flour in your pantry and high-quality eggs, you'll make pasta and noodles more delicious than anything you could purchase fresh from the market, even those from high-end grocers.

If, on the other hand, you would like to delve deeper into understanding the subtleties of the ingredients that go into making pasta and noodles, read on. Once you begin experimenting with different types of flour and ingredients you will quickly be able to discern the slightest of differences, which is a profoundly satisfying development.

FLOUR: THE FOUNDATION OF PASTA & NOODLES

A passion for making great pasta and noodles translates into a knowledge of flour. There's no way around it. Otherwise, it's akin to trying to master the piano without understanding anything about chord structure.

To understand how flour will aid in your noodle-making exploits, it is important to recognize the role protein plays in flour and how it affects our dough. Once water is added to flour and the kneading process begins, proteins come into contact and form a bond that creates a network of fine strands in the dough known as gluten. This network is what gives dough its structure and strength.

In the seminal book *On Food and Cooking*, author and food scientist Harold McGee relates that the Chinese call gluten "the muscle of flour." It is an apt description, as gluten gives dough its elasticity and plasticity, which is the ability to take on a shape and keep it. The right amount of gluten results in a dough that is easier to knead, put through the pasta maker, and stretch without tearing when handled. This explains why bread flour contains higher amounts of protein and why pasta and noodles, which need to be more malleable, require less.

For thousands of years the wheat plant crossbred arbitrarily with other plants and grasses, evolving into several different species. One of them, *Triticum aestivum*, proved particularly desirable because it contains glutenin, which produced a more elastic and malleable dough that was easier to shape. Humans began to cultivate this particular species more than 8,000 years ago and it now accounts for 90 percent of the wheat grown around the world.

Within the *T. aestivum* genus, wheat is generally categorized by whether it is hard or soft, red or white, winter or spring. For the purposes of this book, we will focus on flours that tend to fall within the red (more flavorful, or "wheatier"), soft (less gluten, resulting in more malleable dough), and winter (slightly less gluten than spring) categories, as they tend to produce pasta and noodles that have a slightly chewy yet tender texture.

Accounting for most of the remaining 10 percent of world's wheat production is *Triticum durum*, also known as durum wheat. Similar to *T. aestivum*, it originated in the Middle East and spread to many parts of the Mediterranean Basin before the spread of the Roman Empire. Deep amber in color and rich in protein, durum wheat is ground into semolina flour and used to make almost all of the dried pasta that is sold commercially. Durum wheat is considerably different from other grains because its flour contains the gluten protein gliadin, which is extensible rather than elastic. This means that its dough can be rolled easily into sheets, that the resulting pasta dries without breaking, and can reliably hold intricate shapes.

Before we begin exploring the different flours used in making pasta and noodles, it is worth noting that flour is not a static product. If "a rose is a rose is a rose" in Gertrude Stein's world, then "flour is not flour is not flour" in ours. In other words, the bag of flour in your pantry is probably very different from your next-door neighbor's. In fact, flour varies greatly depending on whether it comes from a nearby mill, a regional manufacturer, or a nationally recognized one. That's because when flour is milled, its composition, and thus performance, depends on the wheat grain variety, growing season, the soil in which it is grown, protein content, milling technique, temperature of the grain at the time of milling, and storage. National brands are the exception. Blended specifically for consistency, they combine different hard and soft wheat varieties to guarantee certain protein-level compositions. Because of this, they are often the flour of choice among professional bakers, who value predictability and consistency above all else.

Ultimately, the decision is yours. As I mentioned earlier, fresh pasta and noodles made with a national brand of flour and good quality eggs will be delicious. Its only shortcoming will be its neutral flavor, which will contain none of the aromatic notes of nuts, tobacco, and even grass that you would find in a freshly milled flour.

Unbleached All-Purpose Flour: Typically produced from a blend of hard, high-protein bread flours and soft, low-protein pastry flours, all-purpose flour contains a moderate level of protein that ranges from 9 percent to 12 percent in national flour brands but that can go as low as 7.5 percent in small regional brands. Blended and milled to be versatile, it is strong enough to make bread and soft enough to create tender, delicate scones, cakes, and biscuits. It also makes perfectly tender pasta and noodles, though combining it with other flours such as semolina results in a tastier and slightly firmer result. Avoid bleached flour whenever possible, as it is treated with chemicals like benzoyl peroxide and chlorine gas to speed up the flour's aging process. The unbleached version is aged naturally, through oxidation.

"oo" Flour: Produced from soft wheat, and ground so fine it is almost talcum-like, "oo" flour is fairly low in protein content. It is the flour of choice in most Italian homes because it produces soft dough that is easy to roll and yields pastas and noodles that are smooth and silky. Tender egg pastas such tagliatelle, garganelli, and corzetti have most likely been prepared with a dough made from "oo" flour and eggs. Occasionally the categorization of "oo" flour causes some confusion because despite always being finely milled into powdery form, it can be made from soft or hard varieties of wheat and consequently contains different percentages of protein by weight. Soft wheat is lower in protein and creates soft and tender pasta that readily absorbs and takes on the flavor of a tasty sauce. Hard wheat is higher in protein content and creates a sturdy dough that is ideal for trapping air bubbles, like bread dough, but that quality makes it almost impossible to roll out into sheets for pasta and noodles. When purchasing it, you will find "oo" flour designated for bread and pizza or for pasta, with protein contents ranging from 5 percent to 12 percent. Be sure to select a "oo" flour toward the lower end in terms of protein content (or one specifically designated for making pasta). If this flour is not readily available in your area, it is only a click away on the internet.

Semolina Flour: This comes from milling durum wheat berries, which have the highest protein content of any flour. Semolina comes from milling the innermost layer, called the endosperm, of the berry. It is characteristically coarse and golden in color as a result of its high concentration of carotenoids (the same compounds responsible for the carrot's bright orange color). It creates a strong pasta dough that holds any shape and strengthens when heated. Experienced pasta makers often add small amounts of semolina flour to pasta dough made predominantly with "oo" flour to add a pleasant chewiness and subtle nutty flavor, as well as increase the dough's elasticity during rolling. Semolina flour also makes an excellent alternative to cornmeal, and can be used to dust formed pasta and work surfaces intended for pasta making. As the word *semolina* is also used to describe the innermost layer of any grain, such as corn and rice, some confusion can arise when people encounter this term.

Whole Wheat Flour: This flour is ground from the entire wheat berry of either hard red spring or winter wheat: the endosperm, germ, and bran. Brown in color and lightly speckled, whole wheat adds a full-bodied wheaty flavor that, due to the tannins in the outer bran, can at times verge on bitterness. Chock-full of naturally occurring vitamins, minerals, and fiber, it is a viable option for health-oriented individuals who don't mind its potent flavor. For better results, it is advisable to add some all-purpose flour to your dough to make it more pliable and the pasta or noodles more tender. Whole wheat flour also tends to absorb more moisture than white flour, so you'll need to adjust for that if you're substituting it in a recipe. There is also white whole wheat flour, which is ground from hard white spring or winter wheat berries; it possesses the same nutritional profile as whole wheat flour but is milder in flavor and lighter in color.

EGGS: TENDER PASTA & NOODLES' SECRET WEAPON

For the purposes of making pasta and noodles, and eating the most wholesome food possible, it is best to secure the highest quality eggs available to you.

Eggs play a vital role in many fresh pasta and noodle recipes. Not only do they enrich the noodles from a nutritional standpoint, they also add an appealing pale yellow color and a subtle flavor to the dough. Eggs also contribute two additional elements that may perhaps be more important. First, they provide more protein, which, when combined with the gluten in the dough, enhances its structure, making the dough elastic, soft, and easier to roll out thin without tearing. Secondly, the egg whites provide additional heft and firmness to the dough while preventing the loss of starch as the pasta cooks.

It is important to use eggs that have a vibrantly orange yolk, as it is a sign of a healthy, happy, and well-fed chicken. Egg yolks get their color from carotenoids, which are also responsible for strengthening the chicken's immune system. Because chickens only lay eggs if they have sufficient levels of carotenoids, the yolks possess deep hues of dark gold and orange. Paler yolks are often a result of chickens feeding on barley or white cornmeal, foods that don't nourish them as thoroughly as a carotenoid-enhancing diet based on yellow corn and marigold petals.

Using brown or white eggs is up to the discretion of the individual, since they both share the same nutritional profiles and taste the same. Pasta connoisseur—and author of the wonderful book *Making Artisan Pasta*—Aliza Green makes a good argument for buying brown eggs. First, brown eggs come from larger breeds that eat more, take longer to produce their eggs, and produce eggs with thicker protective shells, which prevents internal moisture loss over time and helps maintain freshness. Also, because brown eggs are considered a specialty product, she adds, their quality tends to be higher.

Eggs in the United States are graded according to the thickness of their shell and the firmness of their egg whites. Agricultural advances have made it possible for large egg producers to assess the quality of each individual egg and to efficiently sort them by size, weight, and quality. With almost scientific precision, eggs are graded AA (top quality), A (good quality found in most supermarkets), and B (substandard eggs with thin shells and watery whites that don't reach consumers, but are used commercially and industrially). They are also further categorized by size: medium, large (the most common size), and extra large.

The past decade or so has also seen a rise in popularity of free-range and organic eggs. The product of smaller-scale enterprises, these chickens are given organic feed and are caged with slightly more space at their disposal than what is available on industrial-scale chicken farms. While the jury is still out on whether this last category tastes better, it nonetheless constitutes an additional, and perhaps politically oriented, option for pasta and noodle makers.

For the purposes of making pasta and noodles at home, it is best to secure the freshest eggs available, so check the expiration dates before buying them and buy them when they are well within that window.

WATER

The water you use, its mineral content, and its temperature can impact the quality of your pasta dough.

Mineral-rich water from your tap is best for making pasta and noodles. The only exception is if your water is particularly hard, or excessively high in minerals like magnesium and calcium. In that case, you may be better off using spring water, as the presence of too much of these minerals can produce a tighter gluten network in the dough and result in a firmer, and sometimes too firm, dough. Always use warm water, around 105°F (or two parts cold water to one part boiling water), as it makes it easier for the flour to absorb the liquid.

USING A PASTA MAKER

First, since you're enough of a pasta and noodle fan to purchase a book dedicated to them, we're assuming that you already have a pasta maker. But if not, better-than-satisfactory versions are available for around $40.

Once you have cut and rolled your dough, set the pasta maker for the flat roller (no teeth) on the widest setting (typically notch 1). Now feed the dough into the rollers. As a rather rough, thick sheet comes out the other end, make sure to support it with a hand. Fold the sheet of dough over itself twice, as you would a letter, and then turn the folded dough 90 degrees and feed it back through the pasta maker. Repeat this folding and feeding technique three more times. This process is called "laminating" and it makes the dough more sturdy and manageable to handle.

Set the pasta maker to the second-widest setting (typically notch 2) and feed the dough into the rollers. Again, support the pasta as it comes out the other side. Fold it as you would a letter and feed it into the rollers. Repeat three additional times.

Set the pasta maker to the third-widest setting (typically notch 3) and feed the dough into the rollers. Again, support the sheet as it comes out the other side. Fold it as you would a letter and feed it into the rollers. Repeat three additional times.

Set the pasta maker to the second-smallest setting (typically notch 4). Feed the dough into the rollers. Again, support the dough as it comes out the other side. At this point, there is no need to laminate the dough.

Stop rolling at this point if making sheets that are ⅛ inch thick (for pasta such as pansoti, agnolotti, maltagliati, farfalle, and cappellacci dei briganti). If you like your fettuccine, pappardelle, and tagliatelle a little thicker, then this is the setting for you.

If thinner sheets of dough are desired, set the pasta maker to the smallest setting (typically notch 5). Cut the sheet in half and feed it into the rollers. Again, support the dough as it comes out the other side.

This last setting makes pasta sheets that are about 1/16 inch thick—that's so thin you can see right through them. It is ideal for filled pastas like ravioli, ravioloni, tortellini, anolini, cappellacci di zucca, and caramelle, whose fillings can easily be overshadowed by too much surrounding dough, as well as fazzoletti and quadretti. If you like your fettuccine, pappardelle, and tagliatelle very thin, then this is the setting for you.

The just-rolled dough will be very delicate, so be gentle handling it. If the sheet is too long to easily handle, carefully cut it in half. Lightly dust each sheet with flour and lay it on a surface lined with wax or parchment paper. Repeat all the above steps with the remaining pieces of dough.

The dough needs to dry for at least 15 minutes after it has been rolled out and before it is cut into strands or other shapes. This drying time makes the dough less sticky and easier to handle. Keep in mind that when the dough is very thick or wide it will need to be turned over to ensure thorough and even drying (not necessary for thinner noodles). The notable exception to this rule is if you are making stuffed pasta. In this case, not letting the dough dry is best because the slight stickiness helps the pasta adhere better and creates a better seal.

Once fresh pasta has been cut, toss it with some semolina flour, place it on a semolina flour–dusted surface, and allow it to dry for at least 15 minutes before cooking. This drying period is important because it allows the noodles to become firmer and less sticky, which prevents them from sticking together as they cook (noodles also hold their shape better when allowed to dry slightly before cooking). More specific drying times are indicated in individual recipes. Just note that the drying process can be fickle. Depending on temperature, humidity levels, and the size of the noodles or pasta, the process may take a longer or shorter period of time than stated in the recipes. Also, it is probably best to avoid making pasta or noodles on very humid days. If you can't avoid it, turn on the air conditioning or even an oscillating fan to help the air circulate more effectively.

DOUGHS & FORMATS

Scialatielli

YIELD: 1½ LBS. / **ACTIVE TIME:** 30 MINUTES / **TOTAL TIME:** 1 HOUR

15.8 OZ. FINELY GROUND SEMOLINA FLOUR, PLUS MORE AS NEEDED

7 OZ. WHOLE MILK

1 LARGE EGG, LIGHTLY BEATEN

HANDFUL OF FRESH BASIL, FINELY CHOPPED

1 OZ. PECORINO CHEESE, GRATED

⅓ OZ. EXTRA-VIRGIN OLIVE OIL

SALT, TO TASTE

1. Place the flour, milk, egg, basil, and pecorino in a large bowl and work the mixture until it starts to come together as a dough.

2. Add the olive oil and work the dough until it has been incorporated.

3. Transfer the dough to a flour-dusted work surface and knead it energetically until it is a smooth and homogeneous dough, about 10 minutes.

4. Cover the dough with plastic wrap and let it rest at room temperature for 30 minutes.

5. Divide the dough into 2 pieces. Cover 1 piece with plastic wrap and place the other piece on a flour-dusted work surface.

6. Roll the dough out into a rectangle that is about ⅕ inch thick. Sprinkle flour over the dough and, working from the long sides, roll up the dough from the edges so that they meet in the center.

7. Cut the dough into ⅖-inch-thick rings, unroll them, and dust them with flour. Let them dry until they are ready to be boiled.

8. Repeat Steps 6 and 7 with the other piece of dough.

9. To cook the scialatielli, bring water to a boil in a large saucepan. Add salt, let the water return to a boil, and add the scialatielli. Cook until they are al dente, about 5 minutes.

Cavatelli

YIELD: 1½ LBS. / **ACTIVE TIME:** 1 HOUR / **TOTAL TIME:** 1 HOUR AND 30 MINUTES

15.8 OZ. FINELY GROUND SEMOLINA FLOUR, PLUS MORE AS NEEDED

7.9 OZ. WATER, AT ROOM TEMPERATURE

PINCH OF FINE SEA SALT, PLUS MORE TO TASTE

1. Place all of the ingredients in a large bowl and work the mixture until it starts to come together as a dough.

2. Transfer the dough to a flour-dusted work surface and knead it energetically until it is a smooth and homogeneous dough, about 10 minutes.

3. Cover the dough with plastic wrap and let it rest at room temperature for 30 minutes.

4. Tear the dough into small pieces and form them into logs that are about ¼ inch thick. Cut the logs into 1-inch-long pieces.

5. Press down on one side of the cavatelli with the tips of your index and middle fingers, making a movement that first pushes it forward and then comes back, rolling the pasta so that it forms a hollow in the middle. Transfer the cavatelli to a flour-dusted baking sheet and let them dry.

6. To cook the cavatelli, bring water to a boil in a large saucepan. Add salt, let the water return to a boil, and add the cavatelli. Cook until they are al dente, about 8 minutes.

Fusilli al Ferro

YIELD: 1½ LBS. / **ACTIVE TIME:** 1 HOUR / **TOTAL TIME:** 1 HOUR AND 30 MINUTES

15.8 OZ. FINELY GROUND SEMOLINA FLOUR, PLUS MORE AS NEEDED

7.9 OZ. WATER, AT ROOM TEMPERATURE

PINCH OF FINE SEA SALT, PLUS MORE TO TASTE

1. Place all of the ingredients in a large bowl and work the mixture until it starts to come together as a dough.

2. Transfer the dough to a flour-dusted work surface and knead it energetically until it is a smooth and homogeneous dough, about 10 minutes.

3. Cover the dough with plastic wrap and let it rest at room temperature for 30 minutes.

4. Tear the dough into small pieces and form them into logs that are about ⅕ inch thick. Cut the logs into 3-inch-long pieces.

5. Coat a long, thin metal rod or a wooden skewer with flour. Working with 1 piece of pasta at a time, wrap it around the implement to form it into a spiral. Gently remove the fusilli from the implement, taking care not to undo the spiral. Transfer the fusilli to a flour-dusted baking sheet and let them dry.

6. To cook the fusilli, bring water to a boil in a large saucepan. Add salt, let the water return to a boil, and add the fusilli. Let them float to the surface and cook for another 3 minutes.

Maccheroni al Ferretto

YIELD: 1½ LBS. / **ACTIVE TIME:** 1 HOUR / **TOTAL TIME:** 1 HOUR AND 30 MINUTES

15.8 OZ. FINELY GROUND
SEMOLINA FLOUR, PLUS
MORE AS NEEDED

7.9 OZ. WATER, AT ROOM
TEMPERATURE

PINCH OF FINE SEA SALT,
PLUS MORE TO TASTE

1. Place all of the ingredients in a large bowl and work the mixture until it starts to come together as a dough.

2. Transfer the dough to a flour-dusted work surface and knead it energetically until it is a smooth and homogeneous dough, about 10 minutes.

3. Cover the dough with plastic wrap and let it rest at room temperature for 30 minutes.

4. Tear the dough into small pieces and form them into logs that are about ⅓ inch thick. Cut the logs into 2-inch-long pieces.

5. Coat a long, thin metal rod or a wooden skewer with flour. Working with one piece of pasta at a time, press the implement into the center of the log, creating a hollow. Roll the implement back and forth until the pasta closes around it. Gently remove the maccheroni from the implement, taking care not to unfold it. Transfer the maccheroni to a flour-dusted baking sheet and let them dry.

6. To cook the maccheroni, bring water to a boil in a large saucepan. Add salt, let the water return to a boil, and add the maccheroni. Let them float to the surface and cook for another 5 minutes.

Lagane

YIELD: 1 LB. / **ACTIVE TIME:** 1 HOUR / **TOTAL TIME:** 5 HOURS

5.3 OZ. FINELY GROUND
SEMOLINA FLOUR, PLUS
MORE AS NEEDED

5.3 OZ. ALL-PURPOSE FLOUR

5.3 OZ. WATER, AT ROOM
TEMPERATURE

PINCH OF FINE SEA SALT,
PLUS MORE TO TASTE

1. Place all of the ingredients in a large bowl and work the mixture until it starts to come together as a dough.

2. Transfer the dough to a flour-dusted work surface and knead it energetically until it is a smooth and homogeneous dough, about 10 minutes.

3. Cover the dough with plastic wrap and let it rest at room temperature for 30 minutes.

4. Divide the dough into 2 pieces. Cover 1 piece with plastic wrap and place the other piece on a flour-dusted work surface.

5. Roll the dough out into a ⅛-inch-thick sheet. Roll the dough up around the rolling pin, gently slide it off, and cut it into 1-inch-thick strips. Unroll the strips and place them on a flour-dusted baking sheet. Repeat with the remaining piece of dough.

6. Dust the lagane with flour, cover with kitchen towels, and let them rest for 2 to 3 hours before cooking.

7. To cook the lagane, bring water to a boil in a large saucepan. Add salt, let the water return to a boil, and add the lagane. Cook until they are al dente, about 5 minutes.

Busiate

YIELD: 1½ LBS. / **ACTIVE TIME:** 1 HOUR / **TOTAL TIME:** 1 HOUR AND 30 MINUTES

15.8 OZ. FINELY GROUND SEMOLINA FLOUR, PLUS MORE AS NEEDED

7.9 OZ. WATER, AT ROOM TEMPERATURE

PINCH OF FINE SEA SALT, PLUS MORE TO TASTE

1. Place all of the ingredients in a large bowl and work the mixture until it starts to come together as a dough.

2. Transfer the dough to a flour-dusted work surface and knead it energetically until it is a smooth and homogeneous dough, about 10 minutes.

3. Cover the dough with plastic wrap and let it rest at room temperature for 30 minutes.

4. Place the dough on a flour-dusted work surface, tear small pieces from it, and shape them into ¼-inch-thick logs. Cut the logs into 6-inch-long strands.

5. Coat a long, thin metal rod or a wooden skewer with flour. Working with one piece of pasta at a time, wrap it around the implement to form it into a long spiral. Gently remove the busiate from the implement, taking care not to undo the spiral. Transfer it to a flour-dusted baking sheet and let it dry.

6. To cook the busiate, bring water to a boil in a large saucepan. Add salt, let the water return to a boil, and add the busiate. Cook until they are al dente, 7 to 8 minutes.

Sagne Ncannulate

YIELD: 1½ LBS. / **ACTIVE TIME:** 1 HOUR / **TOTAL TIME:** 3 HOURS AND 30 MINUTES

15.8 OZ. FINELY GROUND SEMOLINA FLOUR, PLUS MORE AS NEEDED

7.9 OZ. WATER, AT ROOM TEMPERATURE

2 PINCHES OF FINE SEA SALT, PLUS MORE TO TASTE

1. Place all of the ingredients in a large bowl and work the mixture until it starts to come together as a dough.

2. Transfer the dough to a flour-dusted work surface and knead it energetically until it is a smooth and homogeneous dough, about 10 minutes.

3. Cover the dough with plastic wrap and let it rest at room temperature for 15 minutes.

4. Place the dough on a flour-dusted work surface and roll into a ¹⁄₁₀-inch-thick sheet.

5. Cut the dough in half with a pasta wheel, and then cut it into 10-inch-long strips that are about ½ inch wide.

6. Dust the sagne with flour, pull the ends in opposite directions to twist them, and then bring the ends together so that the pasta has a horseshoe shape.

7. Place the sagne on a flour-dusted baking sheet and let them dry for 2 to 3 hours.

8. To cook the sagne, bring water to a boil in a large saucepan. Add salt, let the water return to a boil, and add the sagne. Cook until they are al dente, 7 to 8 minutes.

Orecchiette

YIELD: 1½ LBS. / **ACTIVE TIME:** 1 HOUR / **TOTAL TIME:** 1 HOUR AND 30 MINUTES

15.8 OZ. FINELY GROUND SEMOLINA FLOUR, PLUS MORE AS NEEDED

7.9 OZ. WATER, AT ROOM TEMPERATURE

2 PINCHES OF FINE SEA SALT, PLUS MORE TO TASTE

1. Place all of the ingredients in a large bowl and work the mixture until it starts to come together as a dough.

2. Transfer the dough to a flour-dusted work surface and knead it energetically until it is a smooth and homogeneous dough, about 10 minutes.

3. Cover the dough with plastic wrap and let it rest at room temperature for 30 minutes.

4. Divide the dough into 3 pieces. Cover 2 pieces with plastic wrap and place the other on a flour-dusted work surface.

5. Shape the dough into a ⅖-inch-thick log and cut it into ⅖-inch-long pieces.

6. Using a knife with a smooth blade, shape the pieces into orecchiette by running the knife over their tops to drag them toward you. Use your thumb to turn the orecchiette over. Transfer them to flour-dusted baking sheets.

7. Repeat Steps 5 and 6 with the remaining pieces of dough.

8. To cook the orecchiette, bring water to a boil in a large saucepan. Add salt, let the water return to a full boil, and add the orecchiette. Cook until they are al dente, about 5 minutes.

Fregola

YIELD: 1½ LBS. / **ACTIVE TIME:** 1 HOUR / **TOTAL TIME:** 1 HOUR AND 30 MINUTES

¾ TEASPOON SAFFRON

9½ OZ. LUKEWARM WATER (90°F)

15.8 OZ. COARSE SEMOLINA FLOUR

1. Line a baking sheet with parchment paper. Place the saffron and water in a bowl and let the mixture steep for 30 minutes.

2. Place 2 tablespoons of flour and a tablespoon of saffron water in a terracotta dish or shallow, ceramic bowl. Rub the moistened flour continuously against the bottom of the dish until it comes together in ⅛-inch balls. Transfer the fregola to the baking sheet.

3. Repeat Steps 1 and 2 until all of the flour has been used up.

4. To cook the fregola, preheat the oven to 390°F. Place it in the oven and bake until it is lightly browned, about 20 minutes.

Culurgiones

YIELD: 40 CULURGIONES / **ACTIVE TIME:** 2 HOURS / **TOTAL TIME:** 24 HOURS

FOR THE FILLING

2 TABLESPOONS EXTRA-VIRGIN OLIVE OIL

2 GARLIC CLOVES, PEELED

SALT, TO TASTE

1½ LBS. POTATOES, PEELED

20 FRESH MINT LEAVES

1½ CUPS GRATED PECORINO CHEESE

FOR THE DOUGH

8.8 OZ. FINELY GROUND SEMOLINA FLOUR, PLUS MORE AS NEEDED

4½ OZ. ALL-PURPOSE FLOUR

5.8 OZ. LUKEWARM WATER (90°F)

1 TABLESPOON EXTRA-VIRGIN OLIVE OIL

¼ TEASPOON FINE SEA SALT, PLUS MORE TO TASTE

1. The day before you are going to prepare the culurgiones, prepare the filling. Place the olive oil and garlic in an airtight container and let the mixture steep for 6 hours.

2. Bring water to a boil in a large saucepan. Add salt and the potatoes and cook until they are tender. Drain the potatoes, place them in a bowl, and mash until they are smooth. Add the mint and pecorino and stir to incorporate. Strain the olive oil into the filling and stir to incorporate. Chill the filling in the refrigerator overnight.

3. Remove the filling from the refrigerator and let it rest at room temperature.

4. To begin preparations for the dough, place all of the ingredients in a large bowl and work the mixture until it starts to come together as a dough.

5. Transfer the dough to a flour-dusted work surface and knead it energetically until it is a smooth and homogeneous dough, about 10 minutes.

6. Cover the dough with plastic wrap and let it rest at room temperature for 30 minutes.

7. Place the dough on a flour-dusted work surface and roll it into a ¹⁄₁₀-inch-thick sheet (you can also use a pasta maker to do this). Cut the dough into 5-inch rounds.

8. Form tablespoons of the filling into patties and place them in the center of the rounds. Fold the dough over the filling to form half-moons.

9. To seal the culurgiones and give them the correct shape, it's best to watch a video, of which there are many online. You want to fold in one end of each culurgiones, and then fold one side over the other, making pleats as you do to seal in the filling.

10. To cook the culurgiones, bring water to a boil in a large saucepan. Add salt, let the water return to a boil, and add the culurgiones. Cook for about 6 minutes.

Malloreddus

YIELD: 1½ LBS. / **ACTIVE TIME:** 1 HOUR / **TOTAL TIME:** 3 HOURS

15.8 OZ. FINELY GROUND
SEMOLINA FLOUR, PLUS
MORE AS NEEDED

7.9 OZ. LUKEWARM WATER
(90°F)

PINCH OF FINE SEA SALT,
PLUS MORE TO TASTE

1. Place all of the ingredients in a large bowl and work the mixture until it starts to come together as a dough.

2. Transfer the dough to a flour-dusted work surface and knead it energetically until it is a smooth and homogeneous dough, about 10 minutes.

3. Cover the dough with plastic wrap and let it rest at room temperature for 15 minutes.

4. Divide the dough into 3 pieces. Cover 2 pieces with plastic wrap and place the other on a flour-dusted work surface.

5. Shape the dough into a ⅖-inch-thick log and cut it into ⅖-inch-long pieces.

6. Roll the pieces over a gnocchi board or a fork while gently pressing down on them to shape the malloreddus. Place them on a flour-dusted baking sheet, cover with a kitchen towel, and let them rest for 1 hour.

7. Repeat Steps 5 and 6 with the remaining pieces of dough.

8. To cook the malloreddus, bring water to a boil in a large saucepan. Add salt, let the water return to a boil, and add the malloreddus. Let them rise to the surface and cook for 1 more minute.

Strangozzi

YIELD: 1 LB. / **ACTIVE TIME:** 30 MINUTES / **TOTAL TIME:** 1 HOUR

5.3 OZ. FINELY GROUND SEMOLINA FLOUR, PLUS MORE AS NEEDED

5.3 OZ. ALL-PURPOSE FLOUR

5.3 OZ. WATER, AT ROOM TEMPERATURE

PINCH OF FINE SEA SALT, PLUS MORE TO TASTE

1. Place all of the ingredients in a large bowl and work the mixture until it starts to come together as a dough.

2. Transfer the dough to a flour-dusted work surface and knead it energetically until it is a smooth and homogeneous dough, about 10 minutes.

3. Cover the dough with plastic wrap and let it rest at room temperature for 30 minutes.

4. Place the dough on a flour-dusted work surface and roll it into a $\frac{1}{10}$-inch-thick sheet (you can also use a pasta maker to do this).

5. Roll the dough up around the rolling pin, gently slide it off, and cut it into $\frac{1}{10}$-inch-thick strips. Unroll the strips and place them on a flour-dusted baking sheet.

6. To cook the strangozzi, bring water to a boil in a large saucepan. Add salt, let the water return to a boil, and add the strangozzi. Cook until they are al dente, 3 to 5 minutes.

Tonnarelli

YIELD: 1 LB. / **ACTIVE TIME:** 30 MINUTES / **TOTAL TIME:** 1 HOUR

5.3 OZ. FINELY GROUND SEMOLINA FLOUR, PLUS MORE AS NEEDED

5.3 OZ. ALL-PURPOSE FLOUR

3 EGGS

2 PINCHES OF FINE SEA SALT, PLUS MORE TO TASTE

1. Place all of the ingredients in a large bowl and work the mixture until it starts to come together as a dough.

2. Transfer the dough to a flour-dusted work surface and knead it energetically until it is a smooth and homogeneous dough, about 10 minutes.

3. Cover the dough with plastic wrap and let it rest at room temperature for 30 minutes.

4. Place the dough on a flour-dusted work surface and roll it into a ¹⁄₁₀-inch-thick sheet (you can also use a pasta maker to do this).

5. Roll the dough up around the rolling pin, gently slide it off, and cut it into ¹⁄₁₀-inch-thick strips. Unroll the strips and place them on a flour-dusted baking sheet.

6. To cook the tonnarelli, bring water to a boil in a large saucepan. Add salt, let the water return to a boil, and add the tonnarelli. Cook until they are al dente, 3 to 5 minutes.

Spaghetti alla Chitarra

YIELD: 4 SERVINGS / **ACTIVE TIME:** 40 MINUTES / **TOTAL TIME:** 2 HOURS AND 30 MINUTES

14 OZ. SUPER-FINE SEMOLINA FLOUR, PLUS MORE AS NEEDED

4 EGGS

2 PINCHES OF FINE SEA SALT, PLUS MORE TO TASTE

1. Pile the flour on a clean work surface. Make a well in the center, crack the eggs into the well, and beat the eggs with a fork until scrambled.

2. Incorporate the flour, a little at a time, until the dough starts to come together.

3. Check the dough to see if the consistency is right. Depending on a number of factors (size of the eggs, strength of the flour, and ambient humidity), you may need to incorporate 1 or 2 tablespoons of water, or more flour.

4. Work the dough until it is elastic and smooth, about 10 minutes.

5. Cover the dough with plastic wrap and let it rest for 30 minutes before rolling it out.

6. Place the dough on a flour-dusted work surface and divide it into 6 pieces. Roll out each piece of dough into a ⅕-inch-thick sheet that will fit your chitarra.

7. Let the dough dry, uncovered, for 30 minutes.

8. Turn the dough over and let the other side dry, uncovered, for 30 minutes.

9. Place a sheet of pasta on the chitarra and pass the rolling pin over the sheet to cut it. Dust the strands with flour, form them into nests, and let them dry.

10. To cook spaghetti alla chitarra, bring water to a boil in a large saucepan. Add salt, let the water return to a full boil, and add the pasta. Cook until it is al dente, about 5 minutes.

Casonsei

YIELD: 4 SERVINGS / **ACTIVE TIME:** 1 HOUR / **TOTAL TIME:** 2 HOURS

1 TABLESPOON UNSALTED BUTTER

1 PEAR, PEELED, CORED, AND DICED

4½ OZ. SALAMI

3½ OZ. GROUND BEEF

1 TABLESPOON FRESHLY CHOPPED PARSLEY

½ GARLIC CLOVE, MINCED

ZEST OF ½ LEMON

1 OZ. GOLDEN RAISINS, SOAKED, DRIED, AND MINCED

1 SMALL EGG

2 AMARETTI, FINELY CRUMBLED

1 CUP BREAD CRUMBS

1 CUP GRATED GRANA PADANO CHEESE

SALT AND PEPPER, TO TASTE

2 PINCHES OF CINNAMON

2 PINCHES OF FRESHLY GRATED NUTMEG

PASTA ALL'UOVO (SEE PAGE 47)

1. Place the butter in a large skillet and melt it over medium heat. Add the pear and cook, stirring, until it is browned, about 6 minutes. Remove the pan from heat and let the pear cool.

2. Place the salami in a food processor and blitz until it is a paste.

3. Place the salami in a large bowl and add all of the remaining ingredients, except for the pasta dough. Stir to combine, add the pears, and stir to incorporate. Set the filling aside.

4. Divide the dough into 2 pieces and cover 1 piece with plastic wrap.

5. Run the other piece of dough through a pasta maker until it is ⅕₂₅ inch thick.

6. Cut the dough into 2-inch rounds and cover them with a kitchen towel.

7. Knead the scraps into a ball and let it rest for 15 minutes before running it through the pasta maker until it is ⅕₂₅ inch thick and cutting it into 2-inch rounds.

8. Repeat Steps 5, 6, and 7 with the other piece of dough.

9. Form tablespoons of the filling into balls and place one in the center of each round. Moisten the edge of the dough with water, fold the dough over the filling, and press down on the edge to seal the casonsei.

10. Place the casonsei seam side down and press your thumb in the center, making a slight depression and forming them into crescents.

11. To cook the casonsei, bring water to a boil in a large saucepan. Add salt, let the water return to a boil, and add the casonsei. Cook them for 6 minutes.

Pici

YIELD: 1 LB. / **ACTIVE TIME:** 30 MINUTES / **TOTAL TIME:** 4 HOURS

15.8 OZ. ALL-PURPOSE FLOUR, PLUS MORE AS NEEDED

9½ OZ. LUKEWARM WATER (90°F)

PINCH OF FINE SEA SALT, PLUS MORE TO TASTE

2 TABLESPOONS EXTRA-VIRGIN OLIVE OIL

SEMOLINA FLOUR, AS NEEDED

1. Place the all-purpose flour, water, and salt in a large bowl and work the mixture until it starts to come together as a dough. Add the olive oil and work the dough to incorporate it.

2. Transfer the dough to a work surface dusted with all-purpose flour and knead it energetically until it is a smooth and homogeneous dough, about 10 minutes.

3. Cover the dough with plastic wrap and let it rest at room temperature for 30 minutes.

4. Place the dough on a work surface dusted with all-purpose flour and roll it into a ⅖-inch-thick sheet.

5. Roll the dough up around the rolling pin, gently slide it off, and cut it into ⅖-inch-thick strips.

6. Working with a few strands at a time, hold each end and pull in opposite directions to elongate the pici, taking care not to break them.

7. Dust the pici with semolina, place them on a baking sheet, and let them dry for 3 hours.

8. To cook the pici, bring water to a boil in a large saucepan. Add salt, let the water return to a boil, and add the pici. Cook until they are al dente, 6 to 8 minutes.

Gnocchi di Grano Saraceno

YIELD: 4 SERVINGS / **ACTIVE TIME:** 40 MINUTES / **TOTAL TIME:** 1 HOUR

11.6 OZ. ALL-PURPOSE
FLOUR, PLUS MORE
AS NEEDED

8.8 OZ. BUCKWHEAT FLOUR

1 EGG YOLK

PINCH OF FINE SEA SALT,
PLUS MORE TO TASTE

9½ OZ. WATER, PLUS MORE
AS NEEDED

1. Place the flours in a mixing bowl and stir to combine. Add the egg yolk and salt and work the mixture to incorporate them. Gradually add the water and work the mixture until it comes together as a dough.

2. Place the dough on a flour-dusted work surface and knead it until it is smooth and not sticky, incorporating more water or flour as necessary.

3. Form the dough into a loaf, cover it with plastic wrap, and chill it in the refrigerator for 1 hour.

4. Cut the dough into pieces and form them into long, ⅗-inch-thick logs. Cut them into 1-inch-long pieces.

5. Dust a fork or a gnocchi board with flour and roll the pieces of dough over it, gently pressing down to shape the gnocchi.

6. Place the gnocchi on a flour-dusted baking sheet.

7. To cook the gnocchi, bring water to a boil in a large saucepan. Add salt, let the water return to a boil, and add the gnocchi. Cook until they rise to the surface and remove with a pasta fork.

Pasta All'uovo

YIELD: 1 LB. / **ACTIVE TIME:** 30 MINUTES / **TOTAL TIME:** 1 HOUR

14 OZ. ALL-PURPOSE FLOUR
4 MEDIUM EGGS
WATER, AS NEEDED

1. Pile the flour on a clean work surface. Make a well in the center, crack the eggs into the well, and beat the eggs with a fork until scrambled.

2. Incorporate the flour, a little at a time, until the dough starts to come together.

3. Check the dough to see if the consistency is right. Depending on a number of factors (size of the eggs, strength of the flour, and ambient humidity), you may need to incorporate 1 or 2 tablespoons of water or more flour.

4. Work the dough until it is elastic and smooth, about 10 minutes.

5. Cover the dough with plastic wrap and let it rest for 30 minutes before rolling it out and cutting it into the desired format.

Pasta All'uovo
SEE PAGE 47

Pasta All'uovo Verde

YIELD: 4 SERVINGS / **ACTIVE TIME:** 30 MINUTES / **TOTAL TIME:** 1 HOUR

5½ OZ. FRESH SPINACH, RINSED WELL

14 OZ. ALL-PURPOSE FLOUR, PLUS MORE AS NEEDED

3 MEDIUM EGGS

PINCH OF FINE SEA SALT

1. Place the spinach in a large skillet, add a little bit of water, and cover the pan. Steam the spinach over low heat until it has wilted, about 5 minutes. Remove the pan from heat and let the spinach cool completely.

2. Squeeze the spinach to remove any excess water and chop it fine or blitz it in a food processor until it is pureed. Set the spinach aside.

3. Pile the flour on a clean work surface. Make a well in the center, crack the eggs into the well, and beat the eggs with a fork until scrambled.

4. Incorporate the flour, a little at a time, until the dough starts to come together. Add the spinach and salt and work the mixture to incorporate them.

5. Check the dough to see if the consistency is right. Depending on a number of factors (size of the eggs, amount of water remaining in the spinach, strength of the flour, and ambient humidity), you may need to incorporate more flour.

6. Work the dough until it is elastic and smooth, about 10 minutes.

7. Cover the dough with plastic wrap and let it rest for 30 minutes before rolling it out and cutting it into the desired format.

Tagliatelle

YIELD: 1 LB. / **ACTIVE TIME:** 30 MINUTES / **TOTAL TIME:** 1 HOUR

SEMOLINA FLOUR,
AS NEEDED

PASTA ALL'UOVO
(SEE PAGE 47)

ALL-PURPOSE FLOUR,
AS NEEDED

SALT, TO TASTE

1. Dust a work surface with semolina and place the pasta dough on it. Roll it out into a 1/13-inch-thick sheet (you can also use a pasta maker to do this).

2. Dust a rolling pin with all-purpose flour. Roll the dough up around the rolling pin, gently slide it off, and flatten it slightly. Cut the dough into 1/3-inch-thick strips.

3. Unroll the tagliatelle and place them on a baking sheet dusted with semolina flour.

4. If you do not intend to cook the tagliatelle right away, form them into nests and let them dry completely before storing them in a cool, dry place until ready to cook.

5. To cook the tagliatelle, bring water to a boil in a large saucepan. Add salt, let the water return to a boil, and add the tagliatelle. Cook until they are al dente, about 4 minutes.

All-Yolk Pasta Dough

YIELD: ¾ LB. / **ACTIVE TIME:** 20 MINUTES / **TOTAL TIME:** 2 HOURS AND 30 MINUTES

1½ CUPS ALL-PURPOSE FLOUR

⅓ CUP "00" FLOUR, PLUS MORE AS NEEDED

8 LARGE EGG YOLKS

1 TO 2 TABLESPOONS WARM WATER (105°F), PLUS MORE AS NEEDED

1. Pile the flours on a clean work surface. Make a well in the center, place the egg yolks into the well, and beat the eggs with a fork until scrambled.

2. Incorporate the flour mixture, a little at a time, until the dough starts to come together.

3. Incorporate the warm water, a little bit at a time, until the consistency of the dough is right. Depending on a number of factors (size of the egg yolks, strength of the flour, and ambient humidity), you may need to incorporate more water or flour.

4. Work the dough until it is elastic and smooth, about 10 minutes.

5. Cover the dough with plastic wrap and let it rest for 30 minutes before rolling it out and cutting it into the desired format.

Whole Wheat Pasta Dough

YIELD: ¾ LB. / **ACTIVE TIME:** 20 MINUTES / **TOTAL TIME:** 2 HOURS AND 30 MINUTES

4 CUPS FINELY GROUND WHOLE WHEAT FLOUR, PLUS MORE AS NEEDED

1½ TEASPOONS FINE SEA SALT

4 LARGE EGG YOLKS

1 TABLESPOON EXTRA-VIRGIN OLIVE OIL

2 TABLESPOONS WATER, PLUS MORE AS NEEDED

1. Pile the flour on a clean work surface, add the salt, and whisk to combine. Make a well in the center of the flour, place the egg yolks, olive oil, and water in the well, and beat with a fork until scrambled.

2. Incorporate the flour mixture, a little at a time, until the dough starts to come together.

3. Check the consistency of the dough. Depending on a number of factors (size of the egg yolks, strength of the flour, and ambient humidity), you may need to incorporate more water or flour.

4. Work the dough until it is elastic and smooth, about 10 minutes.

5. Cover the dough with plastic wrap and let it rest for 30 minutes before rolling it out and cutting it into the desired format.

Fazzoletti

YIELD: 1 LB. / **ACTIVE TIME:** 45 MINUTES / **TOTAL TIME:** 4 HOURS

PASTA ALL'UOVO
(SEE PAGE 47)

ALL-PURPOSE FLOUR,
AS NEEDED

SEMOLINA FLOUR,
AS NEEDED

SALT, TO TASTE

1. Divide the dough into 3 pieces. Cover 2 pieces with plastic wrap and place the other on a flour-dusted work surface. Roll it into a ¹⁄₁₆-inch-thick sheet (you can also use a pasta maker to do this). Dust the sheet with flour, place it on a parchment-lined baking sheet, and cover it with plastic wrap. Repeat with the remaining pieces of dough.

2. Working with 1 pasta sheet at a time, place it on an all-purpose flour-dusted work surface and cut it into 2½-inch squares. Place the fazzoletti on parchment-lined baking sheets so they are not touching, dust them with semolina flour, and let them dry for 1 hour, turning them over halfway through. Repeat with the remaining sheets of pasta.

3. To cook the fazzoletti, bring water to a boil in a large saucepan. Add salt, let the water return to a full boil, and add the pasta. Cook until the pasta is al dente, 2 to 3 minutes.

Tortellini

YIELD: 1 LB. / **ACTIVE TIME:** 1 HOUR / **TOTAL TIME:** 5 HOURS

PASTA ALL'UOVO
(SEE PAGE 47)

SEMOLINA FLOUR,
AS NEEDED

SALT, TO TASTE

1. Divide the dough into 3 pieces. Cover 2 pieces with plastic wrap and place the other on a flour-dusted work surface. Roll it into a 1/16-inch-thick sheet (you can also use a pasta maker to do this). Dust the sheet with flour, place it on a flour-dusted, parchment-lined baking sheet, and cover it with plastic wrap. Repeat with the remaining pieces of dough.

2. Working with 1 sheet of pasta at a time, place it on a flour-dusted work surface and, using a round stamp or pastry cutter, cut as many 1¼-inch rounds or squares out of it as possible. Transfer the rounds or squares to flour-dusted, parchment-lined baking sheets and cover with plastic wrap. Repeat with all the pasta sheets. Gather the scraps together into a ball, roll them out into an additional pasta sheet, and cut those as well.

3. Place ½ teaspoon of your desired filling in the center of each round or square. Lightly moisten the edge of the pasta with a fingertip dipped in water. Fold the dough over to form a half-moon or a triangle. Now draw the two corners together; if using a pasta round, this will form a nurse's cap; for a square, it will have a kerchief shape. Press down around the joined sides to create a tight seal. As you do this, try to push out any air from around the filling, which prevents the tortellini from coming apart in the water when boiling due to vapor pressure. Press one more time to ensure you have a tight seal. Dust the tortellini with semolina flour, place the tortellini on parchment-lined baking sheets, and let them dry for 2 hours.

4. To cook the tortellini, bring water to a boil in a large saucepan. Add salt, let the water return to a boil, and add the tortellini. Cook until they are al dente, 2 to 4 minutes.

Pumpkin Gnocchi

YIELD: 4 SERVINGS / **ACTIVE TIME:** 40 MINUTES / **TOTAL TIME:** 1 HOUR AND 30 MINUTES

2.2 LBS. PUMPKIN, HALVED, SEEDED, AND CUT INTO WEDGES

1 EGG WHITE

7 OZ. ALL-PURPOSE FLOUR, PLUS MORE AS NEEDED

SALT, TO TASTE

1. Preheat the oven to 390°F. Wrap the pumpkin in aluminum foil, place it in a baking dish, and place it in the oven. Bake until the flesh is tender, about 1 hour.

2. Remove the pumpkin from the oven and scrape the flesh into a mixing bowl. Mash the pumpkin until smooth.

3. Add the egg white, flour, and a couple of pinches of salt to the pumpkin and work the mixture until it comes together as a smooth dough. If the dough is a little too loose for your liking, incorporate a little more flour until it has the desired consistency.

4. Place the dough on a flour-dusted work surface and divide it into 6 pieces. Roll each piece into a 1-inch-thick log. Cut each log into 1-inch gnocchi and gently press down on them with the tines of a fork to give the traditional gnocchi shape.

5. To cook the gnocchi, bring water to a boil in a large saucepan. Add salt, let the water return to a boil, and add the gnocchi. Let the gnocchi rise to the surface and cook for another minute once they do.

Tortelli

YIELD: 8 SERVINGS / **ACTIVE TIME:** 2 HOURS / **TOTAL TIME:** 3 DAYS

2 BATCHES OF PASTA
ALL'UOVO (SEE PAGE 47)

ALL-PURPOSE FLOUR,
AS NEEDED

SALT, TO TASTE

1. Divide the dough into 2 pieces. Cover 1 piece with plastic wrap and place the other on a flour-dusted work surface. Roll the dough into a 1/16-inch-thick sheet (you can also use a pasta maker to do this). Repeat with the other piece of dough and cover 1 piece with plastic wrap.

2. Using a pastry wheel, cut the sheet into 2½-inch squares. To fill the tortelli, place a generous teaspoon of the filling in the center of every square and fold each square over the filling. Press down on the edges to seal the tortelli. If the pasta dough feels a bit too dry, moisten the edges of the squares before sealing.

3. To cook the tortelli, bring water to a boil in a large saucepan. Add salt, let the water return to a full boil, and add the pasta. Cook until the tortelli rise to the surface.

Cicelievitati

YIELD: 4 SERVINGS / **ACTIVE TIME:** 1 HOUR / **TOTAL TIME:** 3 HOURS

17.6 OZ. ALL-PURPOSE
FLOUR

1 PACKET OF ACTIVE DRY
YEAST

2 EGGS

2 PINCHES OF FINE SEA
SALT, PLUS MORE TO TASTE

1 CUP WATER

SEMOLINA FLOUR,
AS NEEDED

1. Place the flour, yeast, and eggs in the work bowl of a stand mixer fitted with the dough hook and work the mixture until combined. Add the salt, work the mixture until it has been incorporated, and then add the water, 1 tablespoon at a time. Work the mixture until it comes together as a dry dough.

2. Cover the work bowl with plastic wrap and let the dough rise until it has doubled in size, about 1½ hours.

3. Dust a work surface with semolina flour, place the dough on it, and tear off a small piece of the dough. Roll the small piece of dough into a 3-inch-long stick that is about the thickness of a ballpoint pen. Repeat with the remaining dough.

4. To cook the cicelievitati, bring water to a boil in a large saucepan. Add salt, let the water return to a full boil, and add the pasta. Cook until the pasta has the consistency of properly cooked gnocchi, light and slightly chewy, 3 to 5 minutes.

Farfalle

YIELD: ¾ LB. / **ACTIVE TIME:** 1 HOUR / **TOTAL TIME:** 3 HOURS AND 30 MINUTES

PASTA ALL'UOVO
(SEE PAGE 47)

SEMOLINA FLOUR,
AS NEEDED

SALT, TO TASTE

1. Divide the dough into 3 pieces. Cover 2 pieces with plastic wrap and place the other on a flour-dusted work surface. Roll it into a ⅛-inch-thick sheet (you can also use a pasta maker to do this). Dust the sheet with flour, place it on a flour-dusted, parchment-lined baking sheet, and cover it with plastic wrap. Repeat with the remaining pieces of dough.

2. Working with 1 pasta sheet at a time, place it on a flour-dusted work surface and trim both ends to create a rectangle. Using a sharp knife, cut the pasta sheet into 1- to 1¼-inch-thick ribbons. Carefully separate the ribbons from each other, then, using a pastry wheel, cut the ribbons into 2-inch pieces. To form the butterfly shape, place the index finger of your weaker hand on the center of the piece of pasta. Then place the thumb and index finger of your dominant hand on the short sides of the rectangle and pinch the dough toward the center to create a butterfly shape. Firmly pinch the center again to help it hold its shape. Leave the ruffled ends of the farfalle untouched. Place the farfalle on parchment-lined baking sheets so they are not touching and let them air-dry for at least 30 minutes. Repeat with the remaining sheets of pasta.

3. To cook the farfalle, bring water to a boil in a large saucepan. Add salt, let the water return to a full boil, and add the pasta. Cook until the pasta is al dente, 2 to 4 minutes.

Pizzoccheri

YIELD: 1 LB. / **ACTIVE TIME:** 30 MINUTES / **TOTAL TIME:** 2 HOURS AND 15 MINUTES

1 CUP BUCKWHEAT FLOUR

1 CUP ALL-PURPOSE FLOUR

½ TEASPOON FINE SEA SALT, PLUS MORE TO TASTE

¼ CUP VERY WARM WATER (160°F), PLUS MORE AS NEEDED

2 LARGE EGGS

SEMOLINA FLOUR, AS NEEDED

1. Pile the buckwheat flour, all-purpose flour, and salt on a clean work surface and whisk to combine. Make a well in the center, place the water and eggs in the well, and beat with a fork until scrambled.

2. Incorporate the flour mixture, a little at a time, until the dough starts to come together.

3. Check the consistency of the dough. Depending on a number of factors (size of the egg yolks, strength of the flour, and ambient humidity), you may need to incorporate more water or flour.

4. Work the dough until it is elastic and smooth, about 10 minutes.

5. Divide the dough into 4 pieces. Cover 3 pieces with plastic wrap, place the other on a semolina flour–dusted work surface, and roll it into a ⅟₁₀-inch-thick sheet (you can also use a pasta maker to do this). Hang the dough across a wooden drying rack and let it dry for 30 minutes, turning the sheets over twice during that time. Repeat with the remaining pieces of dough.

6. Lightly dust one sheet of dough with semolina flour and gently roll it up. Gently slice the roll across into ⅓-inch-wide ribbons, taking care not to compress the roll too much as you slice through it. Repeat with the remaining pieces of dough.

7. Lightly dust the pasta with semolina flour, unroll it, and place it on parchment-lined baking sheets. Let them rest for 30 minutes.

8. To cook the pizzoccheri, bring water to a boil in a large saucepan. Add salt, let the water return to a full boil, and add the pasta. Cook until the pasta is al dente, 4 to 7 minutes.

Nodi

YIELD: 1 LB. / **ACTIVE TIME:** 45 MINUTES / **TOTAL TIME:** 5 HOURS

1¾ CUPS FINELY GROUND SEMOLINA FLOUR, PLUS MORE AS NEEDED

1 TEASPOON FINE SEA SALT, PLUS MORE TO TASTE

½ TEASPOON FENNEL SEEDS, FINELY GROUND

⅔ CUP WARM WATER (105°F)

1. Place all of the ingredients in a large bowl and work the mixture until it starts to come together as a dough.

2. Transfer the dough to a flour-dusted work surface and knead it energetically until it is a smooth and homogeneous dough, about 10 minutes.

3. Cover the dough with plastic wrap and let it rest at room temperature for 30 minutes.

4. Place the dough on a flour-dusted work surface and roll it into a 2-inch-thick log. Cut it into 18 rounds, leave 1 round out, and cover the rest with plastic wrap.

5. Roll the piece of dough into a long rope that is about ⅛ inch thick. Starting at one end of the rope, tie a simple knot, gently pull on both ends to tighten the knot slightly, then cut the knot off the rope, leaving a tail on each side of about ⅜ inch long. Keep making and cutting off knots in this manner until you use up all of the rope. Set the finished knots on flour-dusted, parchment-lined baking sheets, making sure they are not touching, and let them dry, turning them over once. Repeat with the remaining pieces of dough.

6. To cook the nodi, bring water to a boil in a large saucepan. Add salt, let the water return to a full boil, and add the pasta. Cook until the pasta is al dente, 8 to 10 minutes.

Garganelli

YIELD: 1½ LBS. / **ACTIVE TIME:** 1 HOUR / **TOTAL TIME:** 4 HOURS

2¼ CUPS FINELY GROUND SEMOLINA FLOUR, PLUS MORE AS NEEDED

1½ TEASPOONS FINE SEA SALT, PLUS MORE TO TASTE

3 LARGE EGGS

2 TABLESPOONS EXTRA-VIRGIN OLIVE OIL

2 TABLESPOONS WATER

1. Pile the flour on a clean work surface, add the salt, and whisk to combine. Make a well in the center of the flour, place the egg yolks, olive oil, and water in the well, and beat with a fork until scrambled.

2. Incorporate the flour mixture, a little at a time, until the dough starts to come together.

3. Check the consistency of the dough. Depending on a number of factors (size of the egg yolks, strength of the flour, and ambient humidity), you may need to incorporate more water or flour.

4. Work the dough until it is elastic and smooth, about 10 minutes. Wrap the ball of dough tightly in plastic wrap and let it rest for 30 minutes.

5. Cut the dough into 4 even pieces. Place 1 piece of dough on a flour-dusted work surface and roll it into a ⅒-inch-thick sheet (you can also use a pasta maker to do this). Cut it into 1½-inch-wide strips and then cut the strips into 1½-inch squares. Place the squares on a parchment-lined baking sheet and cover with plastic wrap. Repeat with the remaining pieces of dough.

6. Coat a long, thin metal rod or a wooden skewer with flour. Working with 1 square of pasta at a time, wrap it around the implement to form it into a spiral. Gently press down on the ends to shape the garganello into a tight spiral and then gently remove it from the implement, taking care not to undo the spiral. Transfer to a flour-dusted baking sheet and let the garganelli dry for 1 hour, turning them over halfway through.

7. To cook the garganelli, bring water to a boil in a large saucepan. Add salt, let the water return to a full boil, and add the pasta. Cook until the pasta is al dente, 8 to 10 minutes.

Tajarin

YIELD: ½ LB. / **ACTIVE TIME:** 45 MINUTES / **TOTAL TIME:** 3 HOURS AND 30 MINUTES

PASTA ALL'UOVO
(SEE PAGE 47)

SEMOLINA FLOUR,
AS NEEDED

SALT, TO TASTE

1. Divide the dough into 3 pieces. Cover 2 pieces with plastic wrap and place the other on a flour-dusted work surface. Roll it into a ⅟₁₆-inch-thick sheet (you can also use a pasta maker to do this). Cut the sheet into 8-inch-long pieces, place them on a parchment-lined baking sheet, and cover it with plastic wrap. Repeat with the remaining pieces of dough.

2. Working with 1 pasta sheet at a time, roll the dough up around a rolling pin, gently slide it off, and cut it into ⅟₁₂-inch-thick strips. Unroll the strips and place them on a flour-dusted baking sheet. Repeat with the remaining sheets of dough. When you have cut all of the tajarin, let it dry.

3. To cook the tajarin, bring water to a boil in a large saucepan. Add salt, let the water return to a full boil, and add the pasta. Cook until the pasta is al dente, 2 to 4 minutes.

Trofie

YIELD: 1 LB. / **ACTIVE TIME:** 45 MINUTES / **TOTAL TIME:** 5 HOURS

2¾ CUPS ALL-PURPOSE FLOUR

1 TEASPOON FINE SEA SALT, PLUS MORE TO TASTE

1 CUP WATER

SEMOLINA FLOUR, AS NEEDED

1. Place all of the ingredients, except for the semolina, in a large bowl and work the mixture until it starts to come together as a dough.

2. Transfer the dough to a flour-dusted work surface and knead it energetically until it is a smooth and homogeneous dough, about 10 minutes.

3. Cover the dough with plastic wrap and let it rest at room temperature for 30 minutes.

4. Place the dough on a semolina flour–dusted work surface and roll it into a 2-inch-thick log. Cut it into 8 pieces, leave 1 piece out, and cover the rest with plastic wrap.

5. Roll the piece of dough into a long rope that is about ½ inch thick. Cut the rope into ½-inch-long pieces and dust them with flour. Working with one piece at a time, press down on the dough with your fingertips and roll it down the palm of your other hand. This will cause the piece of dough to turn into a narrow spiral with tapered ends. Dust the spirals with semolina flour, place them on parchment-lined baking sheets, and let them dry, turning them over once. Repeat with the remaining pieces of dough.

6. To cook the trofie, bring water to a boil in a large saucepan. Add salt, let the water return to a full boil, and add the pasta. Cook until the pasta is al dente, 2 to 4 minutes.

Sweet Potato Gnocchi

YIELD: 1 LB. / **ACTIVE TIME:** 1 HOUR / **TOTAL TIME:** 2 HOURS AND 30 MINUTES

4 LBS. SWEET POTATOES

¾ CUP RICOTTA CHEESE

3 EGG YOLKS

1 TABLESPOON SLICED
FRESH CHIVES

1 TABLESPOON FINELY
CHOPPED FRESH PARSLEY

2 TEASPOONS FINE SEA
SALT, PLUS MORE TO TASTE

2 CUPS ALL-PURPOSE
FLOUR, PLUS MORE
AS NEEDED

1 CUP FINELY GROUND
SEMOLINA FLOUR

EXTRA-VIRGIN OLIVE OIL,
AS NEEDED

1. Preheat the oven to 400°F. Wash the sweet potatoes, place them on a parchment-lined baking sheet, and use a knife to poke several holes in their tops. Place in the oven and cook until they are soft all the way through, 45 minutes to 1 hour.

2. Remove the sweet potatoes from the oven, slice them open, and let them cool completely.

3. Scrape the cooled sweet potato flesh into a mixing bowl until you have about 2 cups and mash until it is smooth. Add the ricotta, egg yolks, chives, parsley, and salt, and stir until thoroughly combined.

4. Add the flours 1 cup at a time and work the mixture with your hands until they have been incorporated. When touched, the dough should hold its shape and not stick to your hand. If it is too moist, add more all-purpose flour until the proper consistency has been achieved.

5. Transfer the dough to a flour-dusted work surface and cut it into 10 even pieces. Roll each piece into a long rope and cut the ropes into ¾-inch pieces. Use a fork or a gnocchi board to shape the gnocchi and place them on a lightly floured baking sheet.

6. Bring water to a boil in a large saucepan. Working in small batches, add salt and the gnocchi and stir to keep them from sticking to the bottom. The gnocchi will eventually float to the surface. Cook for 1 more minute and then remove them with a pasta fork.

Chickpea Gnocchetti

YIELD: ¾ LB. / **ACTIVE TIME:** 1 HOUR / **TOTAL TIME:** 1 HOUR

1 (14 OZ.) CAN OF CHICKPEAS, DRAINED AND RINSED

4 LARGE EGG YOLKS

1 TABLESPOON WATER

1½ CUPS ALL-PURPOSE FLOUR, PLUS MORE AS NEEDED

1½ TEASPOONS FINE SEA SALT, PLUS MORE TO TASTE

1. Remove the outer skin from each chickpea. Place the chickpeas, egg yolks, and water in a food processor and puree until smooth. Transfer the puree to a mixing bowl and add the flour and salt. Knead until a soft, tacky dough forms, about 8 minutes. The dough should have no elasticity whatsoever. If you poke it with a finger, the indentation should remain.

2. Tear off a handful of the dough and cover the remainder with plastic wrap to keep it from drying out. Place the piece of dough on a flour-dusted work surface, roll it into a long rope that is about ½ inch thick, and cut the rope into ½-inch pieces. Use a fork or a gnocchi board to shape the gnocchetti and place them on a lightly floured baking sheet. Repeat with the remaining dough.

3. To cook the gnocchetti, bring water to a boil in a large saucepan. Working in small batches, add salt and the gnocchetti and stir to keep them from sticking to the bottom. The gnocchetti will eventually float to the surface. Cook for 1 more minute and then remove them with a pasta fork.

Passatelli

YIELD: 1 LB. / **ACTIVE TIME:** 20 MINUTES / **TOTAL TIME:** 2 HOURS AND 30 MINUTES

1¼ CUPS VERY FINE BREAD CRUMBS

1¼ CUPS GRATED PARMESAN CHEESE

2 TABLESPOONS UNSALTED BUTTER, MELTED

HANDFUL OF FRESH PARSLEY, FINELY CHOPPED

3 LARGE EGGS, PLUS MORE AS NEEDED

1 TEASPOON FRESHLY GRATED NUTMEG OR LEMON ZEST

1 TEASPOON FINE SEA SALT, PLUS MORE TO TASTE

½ TEASPOON WHITE PEPPER

1. Place all of the ingredients in a large bowl and work the mixture until it comes together as a firm, slightly tacky dough. If the mixture feels too wet, incorporate more bread crumbs, 1 tablespoon at a time. Cover the dough with plastic wrap and let it rest at room temperature for 15 minutes.

2. Bring water to a boil in a small saucepan. Coat the cup of a spätzle maker with nonstick cooking spray. Form a pinch of dough into a ball and drop it in the water. If it falls apart, add another egg to the dough and stir to incorporate. Working in batches, place handfuls of dough into the cup of the spätzle maker and press down to squeeze long ropes of dough out the other side. Cut the ropes into 1½-inch-long pieces, transfer them to a parchment-lined baking sheet, and let them dry.

3. Bring water to a boil in a large saucepan. Working in small batches, add salt and the passatelli and stir to keep them from sticking to the bottom. The passatelli will eventually float to the surface. Cook for 1 more minute, remove them with a pasta fork, and transfer to a bowl.

Pizzicotti

YIELD: 1 LB. / **ACTIVE TIME:** 30 MINUTES / **TOTAL TIME:** 2 HOURS AND 45 MINUTES

4 CUPS ALL-PURPOSE FLOUR

2½ TEASPOONS ACTIVE DRY YEAST

2 TEASPOONS FINE SEA SALT, PLUS MORE TO TASTE

1¼ CUPS WARM WATER (105°F)

SEMOLINA FLOUR, AS NEEDED

1. Place all of the ingredients, except for the semolina, in a large bowl and work the mixture until it starts to come together as a dough.

2. Transfer the dough to a flour-dusted work surface and knead it energetically until it is a smooth and homogeneous dough, about 10 minutes. Place the dough in a large bowl, cover it with plastic wrap, and let it rise in a naturally warm place until it doubles in size, about 1 hour.

3. To cook the pizzicotti, bring water to a boil in a large saucepan. Add salt to the water and let it return to a boil. Knead the dough to remove any air, pinch off peanut-sized pieces of it, and drop them into the boiling water, working in batches if necessary.

4. Cook the pizzicotti until they float to the surface, 2 to 3 minutes.

Lorighittas

YIELD: 6 SERVINGS / **ACTIVE TIME:** 2 HOURS AND 30 MINUTES / **TOTAL TIME:** 26 HOURS

2¾ CUPS FINELY GROUND SEMOLINA FLOUR, PLUS MORE AS NEEDED

1 TEASPOON FINE SEA SALT, PLUS MORE TO TASTE

1 CUP PLUS 1 TABLESPOON WATER

1. Place all of the ingredients in a large bowl and work the mixture until it starts to come together as a dough.

2. Transfer the dough to a flour-dusted work surface and knead it energetically until it is a smooth and homogeneous dough, about 10 minutes.

3. Cover the dough with plastic wrap and let it rest at room temperature for 1 hour.

4. Place the dough on a flour-dusted work surface and roll it into a long, 2-inch-thick log. Cut the log into 20 pieces, leave 1 out, and cover the rest with plastic wrap.

5. Roll the piece of dough into a long rope that is no thicker than ⅛ inch. Wrap the dough around four fingers of one hand twice, forming two loops, and then break the string of dough off, letting it fall to the work surface. Using your thumb and index finger, twirl the two loops around each other to form a braided ring. Place them on flour-dusted, parchment paper–lined baking sheets and repeat until all of the dough has been formed into lorighittas. Let the lorighittas dry for 24 hours, turning them over halfway through.

6. To cook the lorighittas, bring water to a boil in a large saucepan. Add salt, let the water return to a full boil, and add the pasta. Cook until the pasta is al dente, 15 to 25 minutes.

Rye Mafalde

YIELD: 1¼ LBS. / **ACTIVE TIME:** 45 MINUTES / **TOTAL TIME:** 2 HOURS AND 30 MINUTES

1¾ CUPS FINELY GROUND SEMOLINA FLOUR, PLUS MORE AS NEEDED

1 CUP PLUS 2 TABLESPOONS DARK RYE FLOUR

1½ TEASPOONS GROUND CARAWAY SEEDS

½ TEASPOON FINE SEA SALT, PLUS MORE TO TASTE

3 LARGE EGGS

3 TABLESPOONS LUKEWARM WATER (90°F)

1. Place all of the ingredients in a large bowl and work the mixture until it starts to come together as a dough.

2. Transfer the dough to a flour-dusted work surface and knead it energetically until it is a smooth and homogeneous dough, about 10 minutes.

3. Cover the dough with plastic wrap and let it rest at room temperature for 30 minutes.

4. Divide the dough into 3 pieces. Cover 2 pieces with plastic wrap and place the other on a flour-dusted work surface. Roll the dough into a ⅛ -inch-thick sheet (you can also use a pasta maker to do this) and place it on a parchment-lined baking sheet. Repeat with the other pieces of dough.

5. Working with one pasta sheet at a time, lay it on a flour-dusted work surface and trim the ends to create a rectangle. Using a pastry wheel, cut the pasta crosswise into 1-inch-thick strips. Lightly dust the ribbons with flour and set on a parchment paper–lined baking sheet so they aren't touching. Let the mafalde dry, turning them over once. Repeat with the remaining sheets of dough.

6. To cook the mafalde, bring water to a boil in a large saucepan. Add salt, let the water return to a full boil, and add the pasta. Cook until the pasta is al dente, 8 to 10 minutes.

Umbricelli

YIELD: 6 SERVINGS / **ACTIVE TIME:** 1 HOUR / **TOTAL TIME:** 3 HOURS AND 15 MINUTES

3 CUPS ALL-PURPOSE FLOUR, PLUS MORE AS NEEDED

1½ TEASPOONS FINE SEA SALT, PLUS MORE TO TASTE

1 CUP LUKEWARM WATER (90°F)

SEMOLINA FLOUR, AS NEEDED

1. Place all of the ingredients, except for the semolina, in a large bowl and work the mixture until it starts to come together as a dough.

2. Transfer the dough to an all-purpose flour–dusted work surface and knead it energetically until it is a smooth and homogeneous dough, about 10 minutes.

3. Cover the dough with plastic wrap and let it rest at room temperature for 30 minutes.

4. Divide the dough into 3 pieces. Cover 2 pieces with plastic wrap and place the other on an all-purpose flour–dusted work surface. Roll the dough into a ¼-inch-thick sheet and place it on a parchment-lined baking sheet. Repeat with the other pieces of dough. Let the sheets dry for 15 minutes.

5. Working with 1 pasta sheet at a time, cut the pasta into ½-inch-thick strips. Working with your hands, gently roll the strips into 9-inch-long ropes with tapered ends. Generously dust the ropes with semolina, transfer them to parchment-lined baking sheets, and cover with plastic wrap. Repeat with the remaining pieces of dough.

6. To cook the umbricelli, bring water to a boil in a large saucepan. Add salt, let the water return to a full boil, and add the pasta. Cook until the pasta is al dente, 4 to 6 minutes.

Corzetti

YIELD: 6 SERVINGS / **ACTIVE TIME:** 1 HOUR / **TOTAL TIME:** 2 HOURS

2 CUPS "00" FLOUR, PLUS MORE AS NEEDED

1½ TEASPOONS FINE SEA SALT, PLUS MORE TO TASTE

1 LARGE EGG

1 TABLESPOON EXTRA-VIRGIN OLIVE OIL

½ CUP WATER

1. Place all of the ingredients in a large bowl and work the mixture until it starts to come together as a dough.

2. Transfer the dough to a flour-dusted work surface and knead it energetically until it is a smooth and homogeneous dough, about 10 minutes.

3. Cover the dough with plastic wrap and let it rest at room temperature for 30 minutes.

4. Divide the dough into 3 pieces. Cover 2 pieces with plastic wrap and place the other on a flour-dusted work surface. Roll the dough into a ⅟₁₆-inch-thick sheet (you can also use a pasta maker to do this) and place it on a parchment-lined baking sheet. Repeat with the other pieces of dough.

5. Working with 1 pasta sheet at a time, place it on a flour-dusted work surface. Using the hollow side of a corzetti stamp, cut the dough into rounds. Place the rounds on top of the stamping section of the corzetti stamp and gently press down to impress the design into them. Place the corzetti on parchment-lined baking sheets and let them dry. Repeat with the remaining sheets of pasta.

6. To cook the corzetti, bring water to a boil in a large saucepan. Add salt, let the water return to a full boil, and add the pasta. Cook until the pasta is al dente, 2 to 4 minutes.

Ricotta Cavatelli

YIELD: 6 SERVINGS / **ACTIVE TIME:** 1 HOUR / **TOTAL TIME:** 1 HOUR AND 30 MINUTES

3½ CUPS ALL-PURPOSE FLOUR, PLUS MORE AS NEEDED

1 TEASPOON FINE SEA SALT, PLUS MORE TO TASTE

15 OZ. WHOLE-MILK RICOTTA CHEESE

2 LARGE EGGS

1. Place all of the ingredients in a large bowl and work the mixture until it starts to come together as a dough.

2. Transfer the dough to a flour-dusted work surface and knead it energetically until it is a smooth and homogeneous dough, about 10 minutes.

3. Cover the dough with plastic wrap and let it rest at room temperature for 30 minutes.

4. Tear the dough into small pieces and form them into logs that are about ¼ inch thick. Cut the logs into 1-inch-long pieces.

5. Press down on one side of the cavatelli with the tips of your index and middle fingers, making a movement that first pushes it forward and then comes back, rolling the pasta so that it forms a hollow in the middle. Transfer the cavatelli to a flour-dusted baking sheet and let them dry.

6. To cook the cavatelli, bring water to a boil in a large saucepan. Add salt, let the water return to a boil, and add the cavatelli. Cook until they are al dente, 2 to 4 minutes.

Maltagliati

YIELD: 6 SERVINGS / **ACTIVE TIME:** 1 HOUR / **TOTAL TIME:** 1 ½ HOURS, PLUS 2 HOURS TO DRY

PASTA ALL'UOVO
(SEE PAGE 47)

ALL-PURPOSE FLOUR,
AS NEEDED

SALT, TO TASTE

1. Divide the dough into 3 pieces. Cover 2 pieces with plastic wrap and place the other on a flour-dusted work surface. Roll the dough into a ⅒-inch-thick sheet (you can also use a pasta maker to do this) and place it on a parchment-lined baking sheet. Repeat with the other pieces of dough and then let them dry for 15 minutes.

2. Working with 1 pasta sheet at a time, place it on a flour-dusted work surface. Dust the sheet with more flour and then fold it into thirds, as you would a letter. Using a pastry cutter, cut the folded sheet into rough diamond- and triangle-shaped pieces. Place the pieces on a parchment-lined baking sheet and let them dry, turning them over once. Repeat with the remaining sheets of pasta.

3. To cook the maltagliati, bring water to a boil in a large saucepan. Add salt, let the water return to a boil, and add the pasta. Cook until the pasta is al dente, 5 to 7 minutes.

Cappellacci dei Briganti

YIELD: 1 LB. / **ACTIVE TIME:** 1 HOUR / **TOTAL TIME:** 3 HOURS AND 30 MINUTES

PASTA ALL'UOVO
(SEE PAGE 47)

ALL-PURPOSE FLOUR, FOR
DUSTING

SALT, TO TASTE

1. Divide the dough into 3 pieces. Cover 2 pieces with plastic wrap and place the other on a flour-dusted work surface. Roll the dough into a 1/16-inch-thick sheet (you can also use a pasta maker to do this) and place it on a parchment-lined baking sheet. Repeat with the other pieces of dough and then let them dry for 15 minutes.

2. Working with 1 pasta sheet at a time, place it on a flour-dusted work surface. Use a 2-inch ring mold or glass to cut the pasta into rounds. Transfer the rounds to a parchment-lined baking sheet and cover them loosely with plastic wrap. Repeat with the remaining sheets of pasta.

3. To shape the cappellacci, wrap a round around an index finger, starting about ½ inch down from the fingertip and making sure one side of the round overlaps the other. Apply pressure to seal the two sides where they overlap and then gently fold up the piece of dough at the bottom of the round to create what resembles the wide brim of a hat; this resemblance is where the pasta gets its name, as it translates to "bringands' hats" in English.

4. Transfer the cappellacci to parchment-lined baking sheets, dust them with flour, and let them dry for 30 minutes.

5. To cook the cappellacci, bring water to a boil in a large saucepan. Add salt, let the water return to a boil, and add the pasta. Cook until the pasta is al dente, 2 to 4 minutes.

Quadretti

YIELD: ¾ LB. / **ACTIVE TIME:** 45 MINUTES / **TOTAL TIME:** 2 DAYS

PASTA ALL'UOVO
(SEE PAGE 47)

ALL-PURPOSE FLOUR, FOR
DUSTING

SALT, TO TASTE

1. Divide the dough into 3 pieces. Cover 2 pieces with plastic wrap and place the other on a flour-dusted work surface. Roll the dough into a ¹⁄₁₆-inch-thick sheet (you can also use a pasta maker to do this), cut the sheet into 24-inch-long rectangles, and place them on a parchment-lined baking sheet. Repeat with the other pieces of dough and then let them dry for 15 minutes.

2. Working with 1 rectangle at a time, place it on a flour-dusted work surface. Fold it in half lengthwise three times and then cut the roll into ⅛ -inch-thick strips. Cut those strips into ⅛ -inch squares. Dust the pasta squares with flour and transfer them to a parchment-lined baking sheet. Repeat with the remaining rectangles and then let the quadretti dry for 2 days.

3. To cook the quadretti, add them to a soup that is close to finished. Cook until the pasta is al dente, 2 to 4 minutes.

Cappellacci

YIELD: 4 SERVINGS / **ACTIVE TIME:** 1 HOUR / **TOTAL TIME:** 2 HOURS

PASTA ALL'UOVO
(SEE PAGE 47)

ALL-PURPOSE FLOUR,
AS NEEDED

SALT, TO TASTE

1. Divide the dough into 2 pieces. Cover 1 piece with plastic wrap and place the other on a flour-dusted work surface. Roll the dough into a 1/16-inch-thick sheet (you can also use a pasta maker to do this). Repeat with the other piece of dough and cover 1 piece with plastic wrap.

2. Using a pastry wheel, cut the sheet into 2½-inch squares. To fill the cappellacci, place a generous teaspoon of the filling in the center of every square and fold one corner of the square over the filling, creating a triangle. Press down on the edges to seal the cappellacci. If the pasta dough feels a bit too dry, moisten the edges of the squares before sealing. Join the two ends of the base of the triangle together and gently press to seal.

3. Place the cappellacci on flour-dusted baking sheets and let them dry for 30 minutes.

4. To cook the cappellacci, bring water to a boil in a large saucepan. Add salt to the boiling water and let the water return to a full boil. Add the cappellacci to the boiling water and cook until they rise to the surface.

Agnolotti

YIELD: 8 SERVINGS / **ACTIVE TIME:** 1 HOUR AND 20 MINUTES / **TOTAL TIME:** 27 HOURS

2 BATCHES OF PASTA ALL'UOVO (SEE PAGE 47)

ALL-PURPOSE FLOUR, AS NEEDED

SALT, TO TASTE

1. Divide the dough into 2 pieces. Cover 1 piece with plastic wrap and place the other on a flour-dusted work surface. Roll the dough into a $\frac{1}{16}$-inch-thick sheet (you can also use a pasta maker to do this). Repeat with the other piece of dough and cover 1 piece with plastic wrap.

2. Using a pastry wheel, cut the sheet into 2½-inch squares. To fill the agnolotti, place a generous teaspoon of the filling in the center of every square and fold one side over the filling. Press down on the edges to seal the agnolotti. If the pasta dough feels a bit too dry, moisten the edges of the squares before sealing.

3. To cook the agnolotti, bring water to a boil in a large saucepan. Add salt to the boiling water and let the water return to a full boil. Add the agnolotti to the boiling water and cook until they rise to the surface.

Cappelletti

YIELD: 6 SERVINGS / **ACTIVE TIME:** 1 HOUR / **TOTAL TIME:** 5 HOURS

1½ BATCHES OF PASTA
ALL'UOVO (SEE PAGE 47)

ALL-PURPOSE FLOUR,
AS NEEDED

CHICKEN STOCK
(SEE PAGE 536)

SALT, TO TASTE

1. Divide the dough into 2 pieces. Cover 1 piece with plastic wrap and place the other on a flour-dusted work surface. Roll the dough into a ⅟₁₆-inch-thick sheet (you can also use a pasta maker to do this). Repeat with the other piece of dough and cover 1 piece with plastic wrap.

2. Using a pastry wheel, cut the sheet into 1⅓-inch squares. To fill the cappelletti, form the filling into small balls. Place a ball in the center of each square and fold one corner of the square over the filling, creating a triangle. Press down on the edges to seal the cappelletti. If the pasta dough feels a bit too dry, moisten the edges of the squares before sealing. Join the two ends of the base of the triangle together and gently press to seal.

3. Place the cappelletti on flour-dusted baking sheets and let them dry for 30 minutes.

4. To cook the cappelletti, place the stock in a large saucepan and warm it over medium heat. Add salt and let the stock return to a full boil. Add the cappelletti to the stock and cook until they rise to the surface.

Testaroli

YIELD: 1 LB. / **ACTIVE TIME:** 1 HOUR / **TOTAL TIME:** 1 HOUR

2½ CUPS PLUS 2 TABLESPOONS FINELY GROUND SEMOLINA FLOUR, PLUS MORE AS NEEDED

2 TEASPOONS FINE SEA SALT, PLUS MORE TO TASTE

2⅔ CUPS WATER

2 TABLESPOONS EXTRA-VIRGIN OLIVE OIL, PLUS MORE AS NEEDED

1. Place the flour and salt in a large bowl and whisk to combine. Slowly stream in the water while whisking continually until the mixture comes together as a very thin batter.

2. Place the olive oil in a small bowl and set it near the stove. Warm a small nonstick skillet over medium-low heat and then brush it with some of the olive oil, just enough to lightly coat the pan.

3. Pour a scant ¼ cup of batter into the center of the pan and tilt the pan to evenly distribute the batter over the entire pan. Cook the testaroli for 30 seconds and gently lift the edge of it to assess the color. If it is browned, gently turn it over and cook until it is browned on that side, 15 to 20 seconds.

4. Transfer the testaroli to a wire rack to cool and repeat with the remaining batter. Do not stack the cooked testaroli, as they will get soggy.

5. To shape the pasta, cut the cooled testaroli into rhombi.

6. To cook the testaroli, bring water to a boil in a large saucepan. Add salt, let the water return to a boil, and add the pasta. Cook until the pasta is al dente, about 3 minutes.

Saffron Pasta Dough

YIELD: 1 LB. / **ACTIVE TIME:** 15 MINUTES / **TOTAL TIME:** 1 HOUR

3 TABLESPOONS BOILING WATER

1 TEASPOON SAFFRON THREADS

1 CUP PLUS 3 TABLESPOONS "00" FLOUR

7 TABLESPOONS FINELY GROUND SEMOLINA FLOUR

1½ TEASPOONS FINE SEA SALT

8 LARGE EGG YOLKS

2 TABLESPOONS EXTRA-VIRGIN OLIVE OIL

1. Place the water and saffron in a bowl and let the mixture steep for 15 minutes.

2. Place the flours and salt in a large bowl and whisk to combine. Make a well in the center and add the egg yolks and olive oil. Strain the saffron water, add 2 tablespoons of it to the well, and set the rest aside.

3. Beat the mixture in the well with a fork until scrambled. Incorporate the flour mixture, a little at a time, until the dough starts to come together.

4. Check the consistency of the dough. Depending on a number of factors (size of the egg yolks, strength of the flour, and ambient humidity), you may need to incorporate more of the saffron water or flour.

5. Work the dough until it is elastic and smooth, about 10 minutes. Wrap the ball of dough tightly in plastic wrap and let it rest for 30 minutes before rolling it out.

Chestnut Pasta Dough

YIELD: 1 LB. / **ACTIVE TIME:** 15 MINUTES / **TOTAL TIME:** 1 HOUR

1¼ CUPS CHESTNUT FLOUR

¾ CUP "00" FLOUR

⅔ CUP FINELY GROUND SEMOLINA FLOUR

½ TEASPOON FINE SEA SALT

4 LARGE EGGS

2 EGG YOLKS

1 TABLESPOON EXTRA-VIRGIN OLIVE OIL

1. Place the flours and salt in a large bowl and whisk to combine. Make a well in the center and add the eggs, egg yolks, and olive oil.

2. Beat the mixture in the well with a fork until scrambled. Incorporate the flour mixture, a little at a time, until the dough starts to come together.

3. Check the consistency of the dough. Depending on a number of factors (size of the egg yolks, strength of the flour, and ambient humidity), you may need to incorporate some water or more flour.

4. Work the dough until it is elastic and smooth, about 10 minutes. Wrap the ball of dough tightly in plastic wrap and let it rest for 30 minutes before rolling it out.

Spiced Pasta Dough

YIELD: ¾ LB. / **ACTIVE TIME:** 15 MINUTES / **TOTAL TIME:** 1 HOUR

1¼ CUPS FINELY GROUND SEMOLINA FLOUR

⅓ CUP PLUS 2 TABLESPOONS "00" FLOUR

1 TABLESPOON BLACK PEPPER

1 TEASPOON SMOKED PAPRIKA

1 TEASPOON CUMIN

½ TEASPOON CINNAMON

1½ TEASPOONS FINE SEA SALT

9 LARGE EGG YOLKS

2 TABLESPOONS EXTRA-VIRGIN OLIVE OIL

1. Place the flours, pepper, paprika, cumin, cinnamon, and salt in a large bowl and whisk to combine. Make a well in the center and add the egg yolks and olive oil.

2. Beat the mixture in the well with a fork until scrambled. Incorporate the flour mixture, a little at a time, until the dough starts to come together.

3. Check the consistency of the dough. Depending on a number of factors (size of the egg yolks, strength of the flour, and ambient humidity), you may need to incorporate some water or more flour.

4. Work the dough until it is elastic and smooth, about 10 minutes. Wrap the ball of dough tightly in plastic wrap and let it rest for 30 minutes before rolling it out.

Citrus Pasta Dough

YIELD: ¾ LB. / **ACTIVE TIME:** 15 MINUTES / **TOTAL TIME:** 1 HOUR

1¼ CUPS "00" FLOUR

½ CUP FINELY GROUND SEMOLINA FLOUR

1½ TEASPOONS FINE SEA SALT

9 LARGE EGG YOLKS

2 TABLESPOONS EXTRA-VIRGIN OLIVE OIL

ZEST OF 1 LEMON OR LIME (OR OF ½ ORANGE)

1. Place the flours and salt in a large bowl and whisk to combine. Make a well in the center and add the egg yolks, olive oil, and citrus zest.

2. Beat the mixture in the well with a fork until scrambled. Incorporate the flour mixture, a little at a time, until the dough starts to come together.

3. Check the consistency of the dough. Depending on a number of factors (size of the egg yolks, strength of the flour, and ambient humidity), you may need to incorporate some water or more flour.

4. Work the dough until it is elastic and smooth, about 10 minutes. Wrap the ball of dough tightly in plastic wrap and let it rest for 30 minutes before rolling it out.

Fresh Herb Pasta Dough

YIELD: 1 LB. / **ACTIVE TIME:** 15 MINUTES / **TOTAL TIME:** 1 HOUR AND 30 MINUTES

¼ CUP FRESH HERBS (BASIL, CILANTRO, CHIVES, PARSLEY, OR MINT; OR A MIXTURE)

1¼ CUPS "00" WHEAT FLOUR

1½ CUPS ALL-PURPOSE FLOUR

½ CUP FINELY GROUND SEMOLINA FLOUR

1½ TEASPOONS FINE SEA SALT

9 LARGE EGG YOLKS

2 TABLESPOONS EXTRA-VIRGIN OLIVE OIL

1. Bring water to a boil in a small saucepan. Add the herbs and blanch for just 10 seconds. Drain, reserving the water, and let the herbs and water cool.

2. Transfer the herbs and 3 tablespoons of the water to a food processor and blitz until the puree is very smooth.

3. Place the flours and salt in a large bowl and whisk to combine. Make a well in the center and add the egg yolks, olive oil, and herb puree.

4. Beat the mixture in the well with a fork until scrambled. Incorporate the flour mixture, a little at a time, until the dough starts to come together.

5. Check the consistency of the dough. Depending on a number of factors (size of the egg yolks, strength of the flour, and ambient humidity), you may need to incorporate some of the reserved water or more flour.

6. Work the dough until it is elastic and smooth, about 10 minutes. Wrap the ball of dough tightly in plastic wrap and let it rest for 30 minutes before rolling it out.

Fresh Herb Pasta Dough
SEE PAGE 91

Arugula & Boursin Gnocchi

YIELD: 1½ LBS. / **ACTIVE TIME:** 1 HOUR / **TOTAL TIME:** 2 HOURS

½ LB. ARUGULA

1½ LBS. YUKON GOLD OR RUSSET POTATOES, PEELED AND CHOPPED

1⅔ CUPS ALL-PURPOSE FLOUR, PLUS MORE AS NEEDED

1 LARGE EGG

2 TABLESPOONS EXTRA-VIRGIN OLIVE OIL

2 TEASPOONS FINE SEA SALT, PLUS MORE TO TASTE

WHITE PEPPER, TO TASTE

3 TABLESPOONS BOURSIN CHEESE

¼ CUP GRATED PARMESAN CHEESE

1. Warm a medium skillet over medium heat. Rinse the arugula and add it to the pan wet. Cook until it has just softened. Remove the arugula and let it cool. When it is cool enough to handle, squeeze the arugula to remove excess water and then mince it. Set it aside.

2. Place the potatoes in a large saucepan and cover them with cold water. Bring to a boil and cook until a knife inserted into the potatoes passes easily to their centers. Drain the potatoes.

3. Sift the flour onto a work surface, place the potatoes over it, and mash the potatoes.

4. Place the arugula, egg, olive oil, and salt in a food processor, season with pepper, and blitz until smooth.

5. Add the mixture to the potato mixture along with the Boursin and Parmesan. Work the mixture with your hands until it comes together as a soft, smooth dough. Be careful not to incorporate too much additional flour into the dough, otherwise the gnocchi will harden too much during cooking.

6. Cut the dough into pieces and form them into long, ⅜-inch-thick logs. Cut them into 1-inch-long pieces.

7. Dust a fork or a gnocchi board with flour and roll the pieces of dough over it, gently pressing down to shape the gnocchi.

8. Place the gnocchi on a flour-dusted baking sheet.

9. To cook the gnocchi, bring water to a boil in a large saucepan. Add salt, let the water return to a boil, and add the gnocchi. Cook until they rise to the surface and then remove them with a pasta fork.

Baccalà Gnocchi

YIELD: 2 LBS. / **ACTIVE TIME:** 1½ HOURS / **TOTAL TIME:** 3 DAYS

5 OZ. BACCALÀ (DRIED, SALTED COD)

1⅓ LBS. YUKON GOLD POTATOES

¾ CUP ALL-PURPOSE FLOUR, PLUS MORE AS NEEDED

⅓ CUP GRATED MANCHEGO CHEESE

ZEST OF 1 LEMON

1 LARGE EGG, BEATEN

SALT AND WHITE PEPPER, TO TASTE

1. Three days before you intend to make the gnocchi, place the baccalà in a large baking dish and cover with water. Cover with plastic wrap and refrigerate for 3 days, changing the water twice a day. After 3 days, drain the baccalà, remove any remaining skin or bones, pat it dry with paper towels, and mince. Set aside.

2. Place the potatoes in a large saucepan and cover them with cold water. Bring to a boil and cook until a knife inserted into the potatoes passes easily to their centers. Drain the potatoes.

3. Sift the flour onto a work surface, place the potatoes over it, and mash the potatoes.

4. Place the cheese, lemon zest, ⅓ cup of baccalà, and egg in a food processor, season with salt and pepper, and pulse until smooth.

5. Add the mixture to the potato mixture. Work the mixture with your hands until it comes together as a soft, smooth dough. Be careful not to incorporate too much additional flour into the dough, otherwise the gnocchi will harden too much during cooking.

6. Cut the dough into pieces and form them into long, ⅖-inch-thick logs. Cut them into 1-inch-long pieces.

7. Dust a fork or a gnocchi board with flour and roll the pieces of dough over it, gently pressing down to shape the gnocchi.

8. Place the gnocchi on a flour-dusted baking sheet.

9. To cook the gnocchi, bring water to a boil in a large saucepan. Add salt, let the water return to a boil, and add the gnocchi. Cook until they rise to the surface and then remove them with a pasta fork.

Chocolate & Cheese Gnocchi

YIELD: 2 LBS. / **ACTIVE TIME:** 45 MINUTES / **TOTAL TIME:** 2 HOURS

1½ LBS. YUKON GOLD POTATOES

1¾ CUPS ALL-PURPOSE FLOUR, PLUS MORE AS NEEDED

2 TABLESPOONS UNSWEETENED COCOA POWDER

2 TEASPOONS SUGAR

½ TEASPOON CINNAMON

5 OZ. BRIE CHEESE, RIND REMOVED, AT ROOM TEMPERATURE

2 LARGE EGGS

2 TEASPOONS FINE SEA SALT, PLUS MORE TO TASTE

WHITE PEPPER, TO TASTE

1. Place the potatoes in a large saucepan and cover them with cold water. Bring to a boil and cook until a knife inserted into the potatoes passes easily to their centers. Drain the potatoes.

2. Sift the flour, cocoa powder, sugar, and cinnamon onto a work surface, place the potatoes over the mixture, and mash the potatoes.

3. Place the Brie, eggs, and salt in a food processor, season with pepper, and pulse until smooth.

4. Add the mixture to the potato mixture. Work the mixture with your hands until it comes together as a soft, smooth dough. Be careful not to incorporate too much additional flour into the dough, otherwise the gnocchi will harden too much during cooking.

5. Cut the dough into pieces and form them into long, ⅗-inch-thick logs. Cut them into 1-inch-long pieces.

6. Dust a fork or a gnocchi board with flour and roll the pieces of dough over it, gently pressing down to shape the gnocchi.

7. Place the gnocchi on a flour-dusted baking sheet.

8. To cook the gnocchi, bring water to a boil in a large saucepan. Add salt, let the water return to a boil, and add the gnocchi. The gnocchi will eventually float to the surface. Cook for 1 more minute and then remove them with a pasta fork.

Gnudi Toscana

YIELD: ¾ LB. / **ACTIVE TIME:** 30 MINUTES / **TOTAL TIME:** 1 HOUR AND 30 MINUTES

SALT AND PEPPER, TO TASTE

8 CUPS FRESH SPINACH

1 CUP RICOTTA CHEESE, DRAINED IN THE REFRIGERATOR FOR AT LEAST 1 HOUR

1 SMALL EGG

½ CUP GRATED PARMESAN CHEESE

ALL-PURPOSE FLOUR, AS NEEDED

1. Bring water to a boil in a large saucepan. Add salt and the spinach and cook for 3 minutes. Drain the spinach and let it cool. When it is cool enough to handle, squeeze the spinach to remove as much water as possible.

2. Place the spinach in a bowl, add the ricotta, egg, and Parmesan, and season the mixture with salt and pepper. Stir until well combined.

3. Check to see if the mixture is dry enough to shape. If it is not, incorporate 1 teaspoon of flour at a time until the mixture has the right consistency.

4. Dust your hands with flour and shape the mixture into rounds or ovals.

5. To cook the gnudi, bring water to a boil in a large saucepan. Add salt and let the water return to a boil. Working with a few gnudi at a time, add them to the water. Once they rise to the surface, cook the gnudi for another minute and then remove them with a pasta fork.

Gnudi Toscana
SEE PAGE 97

Pantrucas

YIELD: 1 LB. / **ACTIVE TIME:** 30 MINUTES / **TOTAL TIME:** 30 MINUTES

2 CUPS ALL-PURPOSE FLOUR, PLUS MORE AS NEEDED

1 TEASPOON FINE SEA SALT, PLUS MORE TO TASTE

⅔ CUP LUKEWARM WATER (90°F), PLUS MORE AS NEEDED

2 LARGE EGGS

1 TABLESPOON VEGETABLE OIL

1. Place the flour and salt in a large bowl and stir to combine. Add the water, eggs, and vegetable oil and work the mixture with a wooden spoon until it starts to stick together. Work the dough with your hands and knead it until it becomes uniform, soft, and smooth, about 10 minutes. If the dough is too dry, incorporate more water, 1 teaspoon at a time.

2. Place the dough on a flour-dusted work surface and roll it into a thick log. Cut the log into 10 rounds, leave one piece out, and cover the rest with plastic wrap. Shape the piece of dough into a ball and press down to flatten it into a patty. Start rolling the dough with a flour-dusted rolling pin, turning it 45 degrees following each pass to ensure that it remains round. Once the dough is ⅛ inch thick, cut it into 1½-inch-wide strips. Cut the strips into 1½-inch squares.

3. Arrange the squares in a single layer on a parchment-lined, flour-dusted baking sheet. Once you run out of room on that piece of parchment paper, cover the squares with another sheet of parchment paper, lightly dust it with flour, and repeat the process until all of the pieces of dough have been turned into pantrucas.

4. To cook the pantrucas, bring water to a boil in a large saucepan. Add salt, let the water return to a boil, and add the pasta. Cook until it is al dente, 4 to 6 minutes.

THE ENCYCLOPEDIA OF PASTA

Baked Spinach & Ricotta Gnocchi

YIELD: 4 SERVINGS / **ACTIVE TIME:** 45 MINUTES / **TOTAL TIME:** 1 HOUR

2½ CUPS WHOLE-MILK RICOTTA CHEESE

4 GARLIC CLOVES, UNPEELED

20 OZ. BABY SPINACH

HANDFUL OF FRESH BASIL, TORN

½ CUP ALL-PURPOSE FLOUR

1 TEASPOON FRESHLY GRATED NUTMEG

¾ CUP GRATED PARMESAN CHEESE

4 LARGE EGG YOLKS

SALT AND WHITE PEPPER, TO TASTE

2 TABLESPOONS UNSALTED BUTTER, MELTED

1. Preheat the oven to 350°F. Line a fine-mesh sieve with cheesecloth and place the ricotta in it. Place the sieve over a bowl and let the ricotta drain for 30 minutes.

2. Gather the cheesecloth in a bundle and turn it to squeeze excess water from the ricotta. Place the cheese in a large bowl and set it aside.

3. Bring water to a boil in a small saucepan. Add the garlic, cook for 4 minutes, and drain; this mellows out the flavor just a bit. Let the garlic cool and then peel it. Set it aside.

4. Warm a large skillet over medium-high heat. Add the spinach to the pan by the handful and cook until it has softened slightly. Remove the spinach and let it cool. When it is cool enough to handle, squeeze the spinach to remove excess water and then mince it. Set it aside.

5. Using a mortar and pestle, grind the basil and garlic until it is a chunky paste. Add the paste to the ricotta along with the spinach, flour, nutmeg, Parmesan, and egg yolks. Season with salt and pepper and work until the mixture is well combined.

6. Form the mixture into spheres that are slightly smaller than golf balls and arrange them on foil-lined baking sheets. Brush the gnocchi with the butter, place them in the oven, and bake until they are a light golden brown, about 15 minutes.

Ricotta Gnocchetti

YIELD: ¾ LB. / **ACTIVE TIME:** 40 MINUTES / **TOTAL TIME:** 50 MINUTES

15 OZ. WHOLE-MILK
RICOTTA CHEESE

2 LARGE EGGS

1½ CUPS GRATED
PARMESAN CHEESE

1 TEASPOON FRESHLY
GRATED NUTMEG

¼ TEASPOON FRESH THYME

SALT AND WHITE PEPPER,
TO TASTE

1¼ CUPS ALL-PURPOSE
FLOUR, PLUS MORE
AS NEEDED

1. Place the ricotta, eggs, Parmesan, nutmeg, and thyme in a food processor, season with salt and pepper, and puree until smooth. Transfer the puree to a mixing bowl and add the flour. Knead until a soft, tacky dough forms, about 8 minutes. The dough should have no elasticity whatsoever. If you poke it with a finger, the indentation should remain.

2. Tear off a handful of the dough and cover the remainder with plastic wrap to keep it from drying out. Place the piece of dough on a flour-dusted work surface, roll it into a long rope that is about ½ inch thick, and cut the rope into ½-inch pieces. Use a fork or a gnocchi board to shape the gnocchetti and place them on a lightly floured baking sheet. Repeat with the remaining dough.

3. Bring water to a boil in a large saucepan. Working in small batches, add salt and the gnocchetti and stir to keep them from sticking to the bottom. The gnocchetti will eventually float to the surface. Cook for 1 more minute and then remove them with a pasta fork.

Spinach Malfatti

YIELD: 4 SERVINGS / **ACTIVE TIME:** 40 MINUTES / **TOTAL TIME:** 50 MINUTES

2 LBS. FRESH SPINACH, STEMS REMOVED

4 LARGE EGGS, LIGHTLY BEATEN

1¼ CUPS ALL-PURPOSE FLOUR

1 TEASPOON FRESHLY GRATED NUTMEG

SALT AND WHITE PEPPER, TO TASTE

1. Warm a large skillet over medium-high heat. Add the spinach to the pan by the handful and cook until it has softened slightly. Remove the spinach and let it cool. When it is cool enough to handle, squeeze the spinach to remove excess water and then mince it. Set it aside.

2. Place the eggs in a bowl, add the spinach, and stir to combine. Add the flour and nutmeg, season with salt and pepper, and stir until the mixture comes together as a thick batter.

3. Bring water to a boil in a large saucepan. Add salt and let the water return to a boil. Working in batches to avoid crowding the pot, add teaspoons of the batter to the water and cook until they float to the surface.

Chinese Egg Noodles

YIELD: 1 LB. / **ACTIVE TIME:** 20 MINUTES / **TOTAL TIME:** 1 HOUR AND 30 MINUTES

2 CUPS ALL-PURPOSE
FLOUR, PLUS MORE
AS NEEDED

1 TEASPOON FINE SEA SALT

2 LARGE EGGS, LIGHTLY
BEATEN

3 TO 4 TABLESPOONS
WATER, PLUS MORE
AS NEEDED

1. Place the flour and salt in a large bowl and stir to combine. Add the eggs and work the mixture until it comes together as a dough. Add 3 tablespoons of water and continue to work the dough until you almost can't see any remaining traces of flour. If you find that after incorporating the water the dough is still very floury, add more water, 1 tablespoon at a time, and continue mixing it with your hand until the dough starts coming together.

2. Knead the dough until it is smooth, about 10 minutes. Cover the dough with plastic wrap and let it rest at room temperature for 45 minutes.

3. Place the dough on a flour-dusted work surface. Using a rolling pin, beat the dough, turning it over after every 10 whacks or so. Continue doing this for 6 minutes. Shape the dough into a ball, cover it with plastic wrap, and let it rest at room temperature for 30 minutes.

4. Place the dough on the flour-dusted work surface, cut it into 2 pieces, and cover 1 with plastic wrap. Roll the other half into a large, thin sheet; you should be able to almost see your hand through it. Dust both sides of the sheet with flour and then fold the sheet of dough in thirds, as you would a letter.

5. Using a very sharp knife, slice the roll into noodles, making them as thin or thick as you'd like. Dust the noodles with flour and transfer them to a parchment-lined baking sheet. Repeat with the other piece of dough.

6. To cook the noodles, bring water to a boil in a large saucepan. Add the noodles and cook until they are al dente, 2 to 4 minutes.

Udon Noodles

YIELD: 1 LB. / **ACTIVE TIME:** 30 MINUTES / **TOTAL TIME:** 3 HOURS

¼ CUP WARM WATER
(110°F), PLUS MORE
AS NEEDED

1 TEASPOON FINE SEA SALT

2¼ CUPS CAKE FLOUR OR
"00" FLOUR

POTATO STARCH,
AS NEEDED

1. Place the water and salt in a small bowl and stir until the salt dissolves. Place the flour in a large bowl and make a well in the center. Add the salted water in a slow stream while stirring. Once all of the water has been added, begin working the mixture with your hands until it comes together as a dough. If the mixture is too dry, add water in 1-teaspoon increments until it comes together as a dough.

2. Lightly dust a work surface with potato starch. Place the dough on the surface and knead it until it is smooth and elastic, about 10 minutes. Cover the dough with plastic wrap and let it rest for 2 hours.

3. Bring water to a boil in a large saucepan.

4. Cut the dough into 2 pieces. Place 1 on a lightly floured work surface and cover the other with plastic. Pat the dough into a rectangle, dust a rolling pin with potato starch, and roll the dough into a ⅛-inch-thick rectangle. Lightly dust the dough with potato starch and then fold it in thirds, as you would a letter.

5. Using a very sharp knife, cut the dough into ⅛-inch-wide strips. Dust the noodles with potato starch and immediately add them to the boiling water. Cook until they are al dente, 2 to 3 minutes.

6. Repeat with the remaining piece of dough.

Pisarei

YIELD: 6 SERVINGS / **ACTIVE TIME:** 1 HOUR / **TOTAL TIME:** 1 HOUR AND 30 MINUTES

2 CUPS DRY BREAD CRUMBS

3½ CUPS ALL-PURPOSE FLOUR, PLUS MORE AS NEEDED

2 TEASPOONS FINE SEA SALT, PLUS MORE TO TASTE

1 CUP PLUS 2 TABLESPOONS BOILING WATER, PLUS MORE AS NEEDED

1. Place the bread crumbs in a food processor and pulse until they are very finely ground. Transfer them to a large bowl and add the flour and salt. Mix well. Incorporate the water a little bit at a time, stirring to incorporate each increment.

2. When the dough is cool enough to handle, knead the dough until it stops feeling granular and starts feeling silky, 5 to 6 minutes. Cover the dough with plastic wrap and let it rest at room temperature for 30 minutes.

3. Tear off a chunk of dough, keeping the rest of the dough covered with plastic wrap. Using the palms of your hands, roll the dough back and forth on an unfloured work surface until it is a long, ¾-inch-thick rope. Cut the rope across into ¼-inch-wide pieces. To shape the pisarei, place the side of one thumb on each piece of pasta and roll it along the work surface while flicking your thumb up slightly, creating a shallow indentation that will help ensure that the pisarei cook evenly. Place the pisarei on a parchment-lined baking sheet and repeat with the remaining dough.

4. To cook the pisarei, bring water to a boil in a large saucepan. Add salt, let the water return to a full boil, and add the pisarei. Cook until they are al dente, about 5 minutes.

Pansoti

YIELD: 4 SERVINGS / **ACTIVE TIME:** 1 HOUR / **TOTAL TIME:** 1 HOUR AND 30 MINUTES

FOR THE PASTA

1.1 LBS. ALL-PURPOSE FLOUR, PLUS MORE AS NEEDED

2 EGGS

¼ CUP DRY WHITE WINE

¼ CUP WATER, PLUS MORE AS NEEDED

PINCH OF FINE SEA SALT, PLUS MORE TO TASTE

1. Pile the flour on a clean work surface. Make a well in the center, place the eggs in the well, and beat the eggs with a fork until scrambled.

2. Add the wine, water, and salt and incorporate the flour, a little at a time, until the dough starts to come together.

3. Work the dough vigorously until it is smooth and elastic. If the dough feels too dry, incorporate a small amount of water.

4. Form the dough into a ball, cover it with plastic wrap, and place it in the refrigerator.

5. Place the dough on a flour-dusted work surface and roll it into a ¹⁄₁₆-inch-thick sheet (you can also use a pasta maker to do this). Using a pastry wheel, cut the sheet into 3-inch squares.

6. To fill the pansoti, place a spoonful of the filling in the center of each square and moisten the edges of the square with water. Fold one corner of the square over the filling, creating a triangle. Press down on the edges to seal the pansoti. Join the two ends of the base of the triangle together and gently press to seal.

7. Place the pansoti on flour-dusted baking sheets and dust them with flour.

8. To cook the pansoti, bring water to a boil in a large saucepan. Add salt and let the water return to a full boil. Add the pansoti and cook until they are al dente, about 8 minutes.

Menietti

YIELD: 6 SERVINGS / **ACTIVE TIME:** 1 HOUR / **TOTAL TIME:** 2 HOURS

1¾ CUPS ALL-PURPOSE FLOUR

1 TEASPOON FINE SEA SALT, PLUS MORE TO TASTE

⅓ CUP WHOLE MILK, AT ROOM TEMPERATURE

2 TABLESPOONS EXTRA-VIRGIN OLIVE OIL

SEMOLINA FLOUR, AS NEEDED

1. Place the flour and salt in a large bowl and stir to combine. Add the milk and olive oil and work the mixture until it comes together as a rough dough.

2. Transfer the dough to a semolina flour–dusted work surface and knead until it is smooth and elastic, about 10 minutes. Working with a teaspoon of dough at a time, roll it between the palms of your hands until it is a narrow, 1¾ -inch-long rope with tapered ends. Place them on a parchment-lined baking sheet, dust them with semolina flour, and let them dry for 1 hour, turning them over halfway through.

3. To cook the menietti, bring water to a boil in a large saucepan. Add salt, let the water return to a full boil, and add the pasta. Cook until it is al dente, 6 to 8 minutes.

Trahana

YIELD: 1 LB. / **ACTIVE TIME:** 1 HOUR / **TOTAL TIME:** 6 HOURS

3 VERY RIPE PLUM TOMATOES

1 RED BELL PEPPER, STEMMED, SEEDED, AND MINCED

1 LARGE ONION, CHOPPED

¾ TABLESPOON DRIED THYME

SALT AND PEPPER, TO TASTE

2 CUPS SEMOLINA FLOUR, PLUS MORE AS NEEDED

½ CUP FULL-FAT PLAIN GREEK YOGURT

1¾ CUPS BREAD FLOUR, PLUS 1½ TEASPOONS

1. Bring water to a boil in a medium saucepan. Add the tomatoes and cook for 1 minute. Use tongs to transfer them to a cutting board and let them cool. When the tomatoes are cool enough to handle, peel the tomatoes, cut them into quarters, remove the seeds, and chop the remaining flesh. Set the tomatoes aside.

2. Warm a large skillet over medium-low heat for 2 to 3 minutes. Raise the heat to medium, add the tomatoes, bell pepper, onion, and thyme, season with salt and pepper, and stir to combine. Bring the mixture to a boil, reduce the heat to low, cover the pan, and cook for 40 minutes, stirring occasionally, until the mixture resembles a watery, chunky tomato sauce. Remove the pan from heat and let the mixture cool.

3. Place the mixture in a food processor and blitz until pureed. Strain through a fine-mesh sieve into a bowl, add the semolina flour and a generous pinch of salt, and stir to combine. Cover the bowl with plastic wrap and let it rest at room temperature for 1 hour.

4. Line two rimmed baking sheets with parchment paper. Preheat the oven to 200°F and position a rack in the center. Stir the yogurt into the semolina mixture, add the bread flour, and stir until the mixture comes together as a dough. Transfer the dough to a semolina flour–dusted work surface, dust the dough with semolina, and knead until it is smooth and elastic.

5. Divide the dough into 3 pieces and pat each of them into a ¼-inch-thick round. Place the rounds on the prepared baking sheets and place them in the oven. Lower the oven's temperature to 175°F and bake for 1 hour.

6. Remove the baking sheets from the oven, flip the rounds over, return them to the oven, and bake for another hour. Remove from the oven and leave it at 175°F. The rounds should be quite firm but not rock hard. Let the rounds cool completely.

7. Break each round in half and, using the large holes on a box grater, grate them into large crumbs. Spread the crumbs on the baking sheets, place them in the oven, and bake until the trahana are rock hard, which will take about 1½ hours. Remove the trahana from the oven and let them cool completely.

8. To cook the trahana, bring water to a boil in a large saucepan. Add salt, reduce the heat to medium-low, and add the trahana. Cook until they are al dente, about 20 minutes.

Spätzle

YIELD: 1 LB. / **ACTIVE TIME:** 30 MINUTES / **TOTAL TIME:** 1 HOUR AND 30 MINUTES

2½ CUPS ALL-PURPOSE FLOUR

1 TABLESPOON FINE SEA SALT, PLUS MORE TO TASTE

2 LARGE EGGS

1¼ CUPS WHOLE MILK, PLUS MORE AS NEEDED

1. Place the flour, salt, eggs, and milk in a mixing bowl and stir until the dough becomes somewhat shiny and resembles pancake batter, 7 to 8 minutes. If the dough seems too thick, incorporate more milk, 1 teaspoon at a time. Cover the bowl with plastic wrap and let it rest at room temperature for 1 hour.

2. Bring water to a boil in a large saucepan and prepare an ice bath. Reduce the heat so the water is gently boiling and add salt.

3. Working in batches, place handfuls of dough into the cup of a spätzle maker that has been coated with nonstick cooking spray. While pressing down, grate the dough into the boiling water and cook until the spätzle floats to the top.

4. Remove the cooked spätzle with a slotted spoon and transfer them to the ice bath. When all of the spätzle are cooked, drain and place them on paper towels to dry.

Sweet Potato Spätzle

YIELD: 1¼ LBS. / **ACTIVE TIME:** 45 MINUTES / **TOTAL TIME:** 2 HOURS

3 LBS. SWEET POTATOES

1 CUP ALL-PURPOSE FLOUR

1 TEASPOON FINE SEA SALT, PLUS MORE TO TASTE

2 EGGS, SEPARATED INTO YOLKS AND WHITES

1. Preheat the oven to 400°F. Place the sweet potatoes on a baking sheet, prick them several times with a fork, and bake until they are soft all the way through, 45 minutes to 1 hour.

2. Remove the potatoes from the oven, slice them open, and let cool completely.

3. When the sweet potatoes are cool enough to handle, scoop the flesh into the work bowl of a food processor and puree until smooth. Place the sweet potato puree in a saucepan and cook, stirring frequently, over low heat until the puree has reduced to 2 cups, about 30 minutes. This will help concentrate the flavor. Transfer the reduced puree to a mixing bowl and let cool for 10 minutes.

4. Bring water to a boil in a large saucepan and prepare an ice bath. Add the flour and salt to the puree and fold to incorporate. Add the egg yolks and whisk to combine. Place the egg whites in a separate bowl and beat until soft peaks form. Fold the beaten egg whites into the sweet potato mixture.

5. Reduce the heat so the water is gently boiling and add salt. Working in batches, place handfuls of dough into the cup of a spätzle maker that has been coated with nonstick cooking spray. While pressing down, grate the dough into the boiling water and cook until the spätzle floats to the top.

6. Remove the cooked spätzle with a slotted spoon and transfer them to the ice bath. When all of the spätzle are cooked, drain and place them on paper towels to dry.

Chard Spätzle

YIELD: 1 LB. / **ACTIVE TIME:** 1 HOUR / **TOTAL TIME:** 2 HOURS

1½ TABLESPOONS FINE SEA SALT, PLUS MORE TO TASTE

2 LBS. SWISS CHARD, STEMMED

4 LARGE EGGS

1 TEASPOON FRESHLY GRATED NUTMEG

2 CUPS ALL-PURPOSE FLOUR, PLUS MORE AS NEEDED

¼ CUP WATER

WHOLE MILK, AT ROOM TEMPERATURE, AS NEEDED

1. Bring water to a boil in a large saucepan. Add salt, let the water return to a full boil, and add the chard. Cook until the chard has wilted, about 3 minutes. Drain and rinse the chard under cold water. Drain again and squeeze the chard to remove as much liquid as possible. Transfer the chard to a clean kitchen towel and pat it dry.

2. Place the chard, eggs, nutmeg, and salt in a food processor and pulse until the greens are mostly shredded. Add the flour and water and puree until the mixture is smooth, scraping down the work bowl as needed. The dough should resemble pancake batter. If it seems too thick, incorporate milk, 1 teaspoon at a time. Cover the dough with plastic wrap and let sit for 1 hour.

3. Bring water to a boil in a large saucepan and prepare an ice bath. Reduce the heat so the water is gently boiling and add salt.

4. Working in batches, place handfuls of dough into the cup of a spätzle maker that has been coated with nonstick cooking spray. While pressing down, grate the dough into the boiling water and cook until the spätzle floats to the top.

5. Remove the cooked spätzle with a slotted spoon and transfer them to the ice bath. When all of the spätzle are cooked, drain and place them on paper towels to dry.

DISHES

Rigatoni au Gratin

YIELD: 4 TO 6 SERVINGS / **ACTIVE TIME:** 20 MINUTES / **TOTAL TIME:** 45 MINUTES

SALT, TO TASTE

1 LB. RIGATONI

½ CUP UNSALTED BUTTER

2 SHALLOTS, DICED

½ CUP DICED BELL PEPPER

3 CUPS EVAPORATED MILK

1½ CUPS GRATED PARMESAN CHEESE

1½ CUPS GRATED GOUDA CHEESE

½ CUP MAYONNAISE

2 TEASPOONS GARLIC POWDER

2 TEASPOONS ADOBO SEASONING

1. Bring water to a boil in a large saucepan. Add salt, let the water return to a full boil, and add the pasta. Cook until the pasta is very al dente, 6 to 8 minutes. Drain the pasta and let it cool.

2. Preheat the oven to 375°F.

3. Place the butter in a large skillet and melt it over medium heat. Add the shallots and pepper and cook, stirring occasionally, until the shallots are translucent, about 3 minutes.

4. Add the evaporated milk, three-quarters of the cheeses, the mayonnaise, garlic powder, and adobo and stir continually until the cheeses have melted. Taste and adjust the seasoning as necessary.

5. Add the pasta and stir to combine.

6. Coat a baking dish with nonstick cooking spray. Pour the rigatoni mixture into the dish, making sure it is spread in an even layer.

7. Top with the remaining cheeses and place the dish in the oven. Bake until the top is golden brown, about 20 minutes.

8. Remove the dish from the oven and let it cool slightly before serving.

Pasta with Halibut & Artichokes

YIELD: 4 TO 6 SERVINGS / **ACTIVE TIME:** 40 MINUTES / **TOTAL TIME:** 1 HOUR

2 TABLESPOONS AVOCADO OIL

½ LB. HALIBUT FILLETS, CHOPPED

SALT AND PEPPER, TO TASTE

3 GARLIC CLOVES, MINCED

1 SMALL YELLOW ONION, MINCED

⅛ TEASPOON RED PEPPER FLAKES

¼ CUP PANKO

1 LB. SPAGHETTI

JUICE OF 2 LEMONS

MARINATED ARTICHOKES (SEE PAGE 536)

FRESH BASIL, CHOPPED, FOR GARNISH

1. Place the avocado oil in a large skillet and warm it over medium-high heat. Season the halibut with salt, add it to the pan, and cook, stirring occasionally, until it is browned on both sides and just cooked through, about 4 minutes. Remove the halibut from the pan and set it aside.

2. Add the garlic and onion to the pan, reduce the heat to medium-low, and cook, stirring frequently, until the onion just starts to soften, about 5 minutes.

3. Add the red pepper flakes and panko, season with salt and pepper, and stir until well combined. Remove the pan from heat and set it aside.

4. Bring a large pot of water to a boil. Add salt, let the water return to a boil, add the pasta, and cook until it is al dente, 8 to 10 minutes. Drain the pasta and set it aside.

5. Place the skillet over medium heat. Add the halibut, lemon juice, artichokes, and pasta and cook until everything is warmed through, tossing to combine. Garnish the dish with basil and enjoy.

Cicelievitati with Duck Ragù

YIELD: 4 SERVINGS / **ACTIVE TIME:** 1 HOUR / **TOTAL TIME:** 3 HOURS

1 CUP DRY RED WINE

2½ TABLESPOONS PLUS 1 TEASPOON EXTRA-VIRGIN OLIVE OIL

1 TABLESPOON UNSALTED BUTTER

4 DUCK LEGS

SALT AND PEPPER, TO TASTE

2 GARLIC CLOVES, MINCED

1 SMALL ONION, CHOPPED

2 CUPS CHICKEN STOCK (SEE PAGE 536)

2 TEASPOONS CINNAMON

2 BAY LEAVES

1 TEASPOON FINELY CHOPPED FRESH ROSEMARY

1 (28 OZ.) CAN OF PEELED WHOLE TOMATOES, GENTLY CRUSHED BY HAND, WITH THEIR LIQUID

CICELIEVITATI (SEE PAGE 59)

½ CUP GRATED PECORINO CHEESE

1. Place the wine in a small saucepan and bring it to a boil. Cook until the wine has reduced by half, about 5 minutes. Remove the pan from heat and set the wine aside.

2. Place the olive oil, butter, and duck legs, skin side down, in a large, deep skillet and cook over medium heat. Season the duck with salt and pepper and cook until it is golden brown on both sides and the fat has rendered, 10 to 12 minutes, turning it over once. Transfer the duck to a plate.

3. Drain just enough of the duck fat from the skillet that you only see a thin film covering the bottom of the skillet. Add the garlic and onion, season with salt, and cook for 1 minute. Reduce the heat to low, cover the pan, and cook, stirring occasionally, until the onion is very tender, about 20 minutes.

4. Stir the reduced wine into the pan, raise the heat to medium-high, and cook for 2 minutes. Return the duck to the skillet, along with any juices that might have accumulated on the plate. Add the stock, cinnamon, bay leaves, rosemary, and tomatoes, season with salt, and bring the sauce to a boil. Reduce the heat to low, cover the pan, and gently simmer until the sauce has visibly thickened and the fat has separated and is bubbling on the surface.

5. Remove the duck legs from the sauce and transfer them to a cutting board. Remove the rosemary and discard it. Puree the sauce with an immersion blender, raise the heat to medium-high, and cook until the sauce has reduced, stirring occasionally, 8 to 10 minutes.

6. Shred the duck meat with forks, return it to the sauce, and turn off the heat below the sauce.

7. Bring water to a boil in a large saucepan. Add salt, let the water return to a full boil, and add the pasta. Cook until the pasta has the consistency of properly cooked gnocchi, light and slightly chewy.

8. Drain the pasta and place it in a serving dish. Top with the sauce and pecorino and serve.

Baked Orzo

YIELD: 6 SERVINGS / **ACTIVE TIME:** 30 MINUTES / **TOTAL TIME:** 1 HOUR AND 30 MINUTES

2 CUPS ORZO

3 TABLESPOONS EXTRA-VIRGIN OLIVE OIL

1 EGGPLANT, SEEDED AND CHOPPED INTO ½-INCH CUBES

1 ONION, CHOPPED

4 GARLIC CLOVES, MINCED

2 TEASPOONS DRIED OREGANO

1 TABLESPOON TOMATO PASTE

3 CUPS CHICKEN STOCK (SEE PAGE 536)

1 CUP GRATED PARMESAN CHEESE

2 TABLESPOONS CAPERS, DRAINED AND CHOPPED

SALT AND PEPPER, TO TASTE

2 TOMATOES, SLICED THIN

2 ZUCCHINI, SLICED THIN

1 CUP CRUMBLED FETA CHEESE

1. Preheat the oven to 350°F. Place the orzo in a medium saucepan and toast it, stirring frequently, over medium heat until it is lightly browned, about 10 minutes. Transfer the orzo to a bowl.

2. Place 2 tablespoons of the olive oil in the saucepan and warm it over medium heat. Add the eggplant and cook, stirring occasionally, until it has browned, about 10 minutes. Remove the eggplant from the pan and place it in the bowl with the orzo.

3. Add the remaining olive oil to the saucepan and warm it over medium heat. Add the onion and cook, stirring occasionally, until it has softened, about 5 minutes. Add the garlic, oregano, and tomato paste and cook, stirring continually, for 1 minute.

4. Remove the pan from heat, add the stock, Parmesan, capers, orzo, and eggplant, season the mixture with salt and pepper, and stir to combine. Pour the mixture into a 10 x 8–inch baking dish.

5. Alternating rows, layer the tomatoes and zucchini on top of the orzo mixture. Season with salt and pepper.

6. Place the baking dish in the oven and bake until the orzo is tender, about 30 minutes. Remove the dish from the oven, sprinkle the feta on top, and enjoy.

Spaghetti alla Nerano

YIELD: 4 SERVINGS / **ACTIVE TIME:** 15 MINUTES / **TOTAL TIME:** 30 MINUTES

½ CUP PLUS 3 TABLESPOONS EXTRA-VIRGIN OLIVE OIL

1½ LBS. ZUCCHINI, THINLY SLICED

SALT AND PEPPER, TO TASTE

14 OZ. SPAGHETTI

2 GARLIC CLOVES

7 OZ. PROVOLONE CHEESE, GRATED

2 OZ. PARMIGIANO REGGIANO CHEESE, GRATED

20 FRESH BASIL LEAVES

1. Place ½ cup of olive oil in a large, deep skillet and warm it to 350°F. Add the zucchini to the hot oil and fry until they are starting to brown, turning as necessary. Transfer the fried zucchini to a paper towel–lined plate to drain and season it with salt.

2. Bring water to a boil in a large saucepan. Add salt, let the water return to a full boil, and add the pasta. Cook until the pasta is very al dente. Reserve 1½ cups pasta water and drain the spaghetti.

3. Place the remaining olive oil in a large skillet and warm it over medium heat. Add the garlic, cook for 2 minutes, and then remove it from the pan.

4. Add the pasta to the garlic oil and toss to combine.

5. Add some of the pasta water and the cheeses and toss until well combined and the pasta is al dente.

6. Add the fried zucchini, half of the basil, and more pasta water if it is needed and gently toss to combine.

7. Stir in the remaining basil, season the dish with black pepper, and enjoy.

Spaghetti allo Scoglio

YIELD: 4 SERVINGS / **ACTIVE TIME:** 1 HOUR / **TOTAL TIME:** 2 HOURS

¼ CUP EXTRA-VIRGIN OLIVE OIL

2 GARLIC CLOVES

2 LBS. CLAMS, RINSED

2 LBS. MUSSELS, RINSED AND DEBEARDED

10 OZ. SQUID, CLEANED AND CUT INTO RINGS

SALT, TO TASTE

1 CUP DRY WHITE WINE

1 CUP HALVED CHERRY TOMATOES

10 OZ. SHRIMP, DEVEINED

1 LB. SPAGHETTI

FRESH PARSLEY, FINELY CHOPPED, FOR GARNISH

1. Place half of the olive oil in a large skillet and warm it over medium heat. Add 1 garlic clove and cook, stirring occasionally, for 2 minutes.

2. Add the clams and mussels, raise the heat to medium-high, and cover the pan with a lid. Cook until the majority of the clams and mussels have opened, about 5 minutes.

3. Discard any clams and/or mussels that did not open. Remove the remaining clams and mussels from the pan, remove the meat from most of the shells, and set it aside. Leave the meat in some of the mussels and clams and reserve them for garnish. Strain any liquid in the pan and set it aside.

4. Add the remaining olive oil to the pan and warm it over medium heat. Add the remaining garlic clove and cook, stirring occasionally, for 2 minutes. Add the squid, season it lightly with salt, and cook for 2 minutes.

5. Add the wine and cook until it has evaporated. Remove the garlic clove, discard it, and add the tomatoes. Cook for 5 minutes.

6. Add the shrimp and cook until they turn pink, 2 to 3 minutes. Peel the shrimp, pressing down on their heads to release the juices. Reserve these juices.

7. Add the shrimp, their juices, mussels, and clams to the sauce, season it with salt, and remove the pan from heat.

8. Bring water to a boil in a large saucepan. Add salt, let the water return to a full boil, and add the pasta. Cook until the pasta is very al dente. Drain the spaghetti and add it to the skillet.

9. Cook the pasta and sauce over medium-high heat, tossing to combine and gradually adding the reserved liquid from cooking the mussels and clams.

10. When the pasta is al dente, garnish the dish with the parsley and reserved mussels and clams and enjoy.

Chicken Lo Mein

YIELD: 4 TO 6 SERVINGS / **ACTIVE TIME:** 45 MINUTES / **TOTAL TIME:** 45 MINUTES

2 TEASPOONS CORNSTARCH

2 TEASPOONS WATER

4½ TABLESPOONS PLUS 2 TEASPOONS PEANUT OIL

½ LB. BONELESS, SKINLESS CHICKEN BREAST, SLICED THIN

2 CUPS MUNG BEAN SPROUTS, PICKED OVER

¾ LB. CHINESE EGG NOODLES (SEE PAGE 104)

2 GARLIC CLOVES, MINCED

4 CUPS CABBAGE, SHREDDED

2 MEDIUM CARROTS, JULIENNED

SALT, TO TASTE

1 TABLESPOON SHAOXING RICE WINE OR DRY SHERRY

2½ TABLESPOONS DARK SOY SAUCE

1 TEASPOON TOASTED SESAME OIL

½ TEASPOON SUGAR

4 SCALLIONS, TRIMMED AND THINLY SLICED

1. Whisk the cornstarch, water, and 2 teaspoons of peanut oil together in a medium bowl until combined. Add the chicken and toss until the chicken is evenly coated.

2. Bring water to a boil in a large saucepan. Add the sprouts and cook for 2 minutes. Remove them with a strainer, run them under cold water, and set them aside.

3. Add the noodles to the boiling water and cook until they are al dente, 2 to 3 minutes. Drain and transfer them to a medium bowl. Drizzle ½ tablespoon of the peanut oil over them and toss to coat. Set the noodles aside.

4. Warm a large wok or skillet over medium heat for 2 to 3 minutes. Add 2 tablespoons of peanut oil and raise the heat to medium-high. Add the chicken and cook, stir-frying, until it is golden brown, 2 to 3 minutes. Transfer the chicken to a warmed plate and cover it loosely with aluminum foil to keep warm.

5. Add the remaining peanut oil and the garlic, stir-fry for 20 seconds, and then add the cabbage, carrots, and a couple pinches of salt. Stir-fry for 2 minutes, stir in the rice wine, and then add the noodles and chicken. Cook, tossing to combine, for 1 minute. Cover and let steam for 1 minute.

6. Remove the lid, add the soy sauce, sesame oil, and sugar, and stir. Cook for 1 minute, add the bean sprouts and scallions, and stir-fry for 1 minute. Serve immediately.

Chinese Egg Noodles
with Pork & Black Bean Sauce

YIELD: 4 SERVINGS / **ACTIVE TIME:** 25 MINUTES / **TOTAL TIME:** 40 MINUTES

½ LB. PORK LOIN, DICED

2 TABLESPOONS SHAOXING RICE WINE, MIRIN, OR SHERRY

1-INCH PIECE OF FRESH GINGER, PEELED AND GRATED

SALT, TO TASTE

½ TEASPOON BLACK PEPPER

½ CUP BLACK BEAN PASTE

¼ CUP CANOLA OIL

2 TABLESPOONS SUGAR

CHINESE EGG NOODLES (SEE PAGE 104)

1 LARGE ONION, DICED

1½ CUPS CHOPPED CABBAGE

1 LARGE ZUCCHINI, CUBED

2 CUPS CHICKEN STOCK (SEE PAGE 536)

2 TABLESPOONS CORNSTARCH, DISSOLVED IN ¼ CUP WATER

1 SMALL CUCUMBER, PEELED, SEEDED, AND JULIENNED, FOR GARNISH

1. Place the pork, rice wine, ginger, a couple pinches of salt, and pepper in a medium bowl and mix well. Let the pork marinate at room temperature for 15 minutes.

2. Place the black bean paste, 2 tablespoons of canola oil, and the sugar in a small saucepan and cook, stirring continually, over medium heat until the mixture is a runny paste, 2 to 3 minutes. Remove the pan from heat and set the sauce aside.

3. Bring water to a boil in a large saucepan. Add the noodles and cook until they are al dente, 2 to 3 minutes. Drain and set the noodles aside.

4. Place the remaining canola oil in a large wok or skillet and warm it over medium-high heat. Add the pork and cook, stirring frequently, until it starts to brown, 3 to 4 minutes. Transfer the pork to a bowl and cover it loosely with aluminum foil.

5. Add the onion, cabbage, and zucchini to the pan, season with salt, and cook, stirring occasionally, until the vegetables have softened, 5 to 6 minutes.

6. Add the pork and the black bean sauce to the pan and toss to combine. Add the stock, bring to a boil, and cook until the pork is cooked through, 3 to 4 minutes.

7. Stir in the cornstarch and cook until the sauce thickens, 1 to 2 minutes. Taste, adjust the seasoning as necessary, and remove the pan from heat.

8. Divide the noodles among the serving plates, top with the contents of the pan, garnish with the cucumber, and serve.

Spaghetti alla Puttanesca

YIELD: 4 SERVINGS / **ACTIVE TIME:** 10 MINUTES / **TOTAL TIME:** 25 MINUTES

1.1 LBS. TOMATOES

¼ CUP EXTRA-VIRGIN OLIVE OIL

1 GARLIC CLOVE, CHOPPED

8 SALT-PACKED ANCHOVIES, RINSED AND CHOPPED

RED PEPPER FLAKES, TO TASTE

1 CUP PITTED BLACK OLIVES, CHOPPED

1 TABLESPOON SALT-PACKED CAPERS, SOAKED, DRAINED, DRIED, AND CHOPPED

2 TABLESPOONS FINELY CHOPPED FRESH ITALIAN PARSLEY

SALT, TO TASTE

14 OZ. SPAGHETTI

1. Bring water to a boil in a large saucepan. Add the tomatoes and boil them for 2 minutes. Drain the tomatoes and let them cool. When they are cool enough to handle, peel the tomatoes, remove the seeds, and chop the remaining flesh. Set the tomatoes aside.

2. Place the olive oil in a large skillet and warm it over medium-low heat. Add the garlic and cook for 2 minutes. Add the anchovies and red pepper flakes and cook for 1 minute.

3. Stir in the olives and capers and cook, stirring frequently, for 3 minutes.

4. Add the tomatoes and half of the parsley and cook, stirring occasionally, until the tomatoes start to break down, about 20 minutes.

5. Bring water to a boil in a large saucepan. Add salt, let the water return to a full boil, and add the pasta. Cook until the pasta is very al dente. Reserve ¼ cup of pasta water and drain the spaghetti.

6. Add the spaghetti and pasta water to the skillet, raise the heat to medium-high, and toss to combine. Cook until the pasta is al dente.

7. Stir in the remaining parsley and serve.

Ants Climbing a Tree

YIELD: 6 SERVINGS / **ACTIVE TIME:** 20 MINUTES / **TOTAL TIME:** 45 MINUTES

½ LB. CELLOPHANE NOODLES

2½ TABLESPOONS PEANUT OIL

4 OZ. GROUND PORK

4 OZ. GROUND BEEF

1½ TABLESPOONS LIGHT SOY SAUCE

⅛ TEASPOON KOSHER SALT

1½ TABLESPOONS DOUBANJIANG

¾ CUP CHICKEN STOCK (SEE PAGE 536), WARM

3 SCALLIONS, TRIMMED AND SLICED THIN, FOR GARNISH

1. Place the noodles in a baking dish and cover them with hot water. Let the noodles sit until they are al dente, about 15 minutes. Drain the noodles, rinse them under cold water, and drain them again. Place the noodles in a bowl, add ½ tablespoon of peanut oil, and toss to combine. Set the noodles aside.

2. Combine the pork, beef, ½ tablespoon of soy sauce, and the salt in a bowl and stir until well combined.

3. Place the remaining peanut oil in a large wok or skillet and warm it over medium-high heat. Add the ground meat mixture and cook, breaking it up with a wooden spoon, until it starts to brown, 5 to 7 minutes.

4. Add the doubanjiang, remaining soy sauce, the noodles, and stock and toss to combine. Reduce the heat to medium-low, cover the pan, and simmer until the ground meat is cooked through and the liquid has reduced, 8 to 10 minutes. Garnish the dish with the scallions and serve.

Lobster Ravioli

YIELD: 4 SERVINGS / **ACTIVE TIME:** 20 MINUTES / **TOTAL TIME:** 2 HOURS AND 15 MINUTES

FOR THE RAVIOLI

1 LB. FRESH LOBSTER

2 TABLESPOONS UNSALTED BUTTER, MELTED

1 TABLESPOON FRESH LEMON JUICE

¼ TEASPOON BLACK PEPPER

SALT, TO TASTE

RAVIOLI (SEE PAGE 40)

FOR THE SAUCE

2 TABLESPOONS UNSALTED BUTTER, CUBED

1 TABLESPOON EXTRA-VIRGIN OLIVE OIL

⅔ CUP HEAVY CREAM

⅓ CUP GRATED PARMESAN CHEESE

1. Prepare an ice bath. To begin preparations for the ravioli, place 3 inches of water in a large saucepan and bring it to a rolling boil. Add the lobster, headfirst. Cover the pan with a tight-fitting lid and steam the lobster until it turns bright red and is cooked through, about 8 minutes.

2. Remove the lobster from the pan and plunge it into the ice bath. Let the lobster cool for 5 minutes.

3. Transfer the lobster to a cutting board and pat it dry with paper towels. Remove the tail, cut it in half, and remove the meat. Crack the claws and remove the meat.

4. Roughly chop the lobster meat and transfer it to a mixing bowl. Stir in the melted butter, lemon juice, and pepper and season with salt.

5. Bring a large saucepan of water to a boil and make the ravioli as instructed, filling the depressions with the lobster mixture.

6. When the water is boiling, add salt, let the water return to a full boil, and add the ravioli. Cook until they are just al dente, about 2 minutes.

7. Drain the ravioli, divide them among the serving plates, and drizzle the sauce over the top. Garnish with additional Parmesan and serve.

8. To prepare the sauce, place the butter and olive oil in a large skillet and warm the mixture over medium heat. Add the ravioli and cream to the skillet and cook for 2 minutes, stirring occasionally. Stir in the Parmesan and enjoy.

Spaghetti d'o Puveriello

YIELD: 4 SERVINGS / **ACTIVE TIME:** 10 MINUTES / **TOTAL TIME:** 15 MINUTES

3½ OZ. LARD

4 EGGS

SALT AND PEPPER, TO TASTE

14 OZ. SPAGHETTI

¼ CUP GRATED PECORINO ROMANO CHEESE

1. Place the lard in a large skillet and melt it over medium heat. Add the eggs and fry until the whites are set and the yolks are runny, turning them just once and taking care not to overcook them. Transfer the eggs to a plate and set them aside.

2. Bring water to a boil in a large saucepan. Add salt to the boiling water, let the water return to a full boil, and add the pasta. Cook until the pasta is very al dente. Reserve ½ cup pasta water and drain the spaghetti.

3. Add the pasta to the skillet and toss to combine.

4. Add the pasta water and toss to combine.

5. When the pasta is al dente, add the pecorino and eggs, season the dish generously with pepper, toss until combined and the pasta is al dente, and enjoy.

Pasta e Patate

YIELD: 4 SERVINGS / **ACTIVE TIME:** 15 MINUTES / **TOTAL TIME:** 1 HOUR

2 OZ. LARD, DICED

2 TABLESPOONS EXTRA-VIRGIN OLIVE OIL

½ MEDIUM WHITE ONION, FINELY DICED

1 LARGE CARROT, PEELED AND FINELY DICED

1 CELERY STALK, FINELY DICED

1 CUP DICED CHERRY TOMATOES

1⅓ LBS. POTATOES, PEELED AND DICED

2 CUPS VEGETABLE STOCK (SEE PAGE 537)

2 PARMESAN RINDS, EXTERIORS REMOVED

1½ CUPS WATER

6 OZ. SHORT PASTA (TUBETTI OR RUOTE)

SALT, TO TASTE

5 OZ. PROVOLA CHEESE, CUBED (OPTIONAL)

1. Place the lard and olive oil in a medium saucepan and warm the mixture over low heat. Add the onion, carrot, celery, and tomatoes and cook, stirring occasionally, until they have softened, about 6 minutes.

2. Add the potatoes and cook, stirring occasionally, for 6 minutes.

3. Add the stock, raise the heat to medium, and bring to a boil. Reduce the heat to low, cover the pan, and cook until the potatoes are tender, about 40 minutes, gently stirring occasionally.

4. Add the Parmesan rinds, water, and pasta, raise the heat to medium, and cook until the pasta is al dente. If there is too much liquid, raise the heat to reduce it to the desired amount.

5. Remove the Parmesan rinds, discard them, season the dish with salt, and remove the pan from heat.

6. Stir in the provola (if desired) and enjoy.

Pasta e Piselli

YIELD: 4 SERVINGS / **ACTIVE TIME:** 10 MINUTES / **TOTAL TIME:** 25 MINUTES

2 TABLESPOONS EXTRA-VIRGIN OLIVE OIL

1 ONION, FINELY DICED

6 OZ. PANCETTA, DICED (OPTIONAL)

2 CUPS PEAS

2 CUPS WATER

SALT AND PEPPER, TO TASTE

9 OZ. PASTA (MACARONI OR BROKEN SPAGHETTI RECOMMENDED)

PARMESAN OR PECORINO CHEESE, GRATED, TO TASTE

1. Place the olive oil in a large skillet and warm it over medium heat. Add the onion and cook, stirring occasionally, until it has softened, about 5 minutes.

2. Add the pancetta (if desired), reduce the heat to medium-low, and cook until the fat starts to render, about 5 minutes.

3. Add the peas, raise the heat to medium, and cook, stirring occasionally, until they are tender, 3 to 5 minutes.

4. Add the water and bring to a boil. Add salt, let the water return to a full boil, and add the pasta. Cook until the pasta is al dente and has absorbed the water.

5. Season the dish with Parmesan and pepper and enjoy.

Calamarata

YIELD: 4 SERVINGS / **ACTIVE TIME:** 15 MINUTES / **TOTAL TIME:** 40 MINUTES

¼ CUP EXTRA-VIRGIN OLIVE OIL

1 GARLIC CLOVE

1 RED CHILE PEPPER, STEMMED, SEEDED, AND MINCED

10 OZ. SQUID, CLEANED AND CUT INTO RINGS

½ CUP DRY WHITE WINE

2½ CUPS HALVED CHERRY TOMATOES

SALT, TO TASTE

14 OZ. MEZZI PACCHERI PASTA

FRESH PARSLEY, CHOPPED, FOR GARNISH

1. Place the olive oil in a large skillet and warm it over medium heat. Add the garlic and chile and cook, stirring occasionally, for 2 minutes.

2. Remove the garlic from the pan and discard it. Add the squid and cook for 2 minutes.

3. Add the wine and cook until it has evaporated. Add the tomatoes and cook, stirring occasionally, for 5 minutes.

4. Reduce the heat to low, cover the pan, and cook until the tomatoes have collapsed, about 20 minutes.

5. Bring water to a boil in a large saucepan. Add salt, let the water return to a full boil, and add the pasta. Cook until the pasta is very al dente.

6. Drain the pasta and add it to the skillet. Season the dish with salt, raise the heat to medium-high, and toss to combine. Cook until the pasta is al dente.

7. Garnish the dish with parsley and enjoy.

Pici with Crispy Anchovy Bread Crumbs

YIELD: 4 SERVINGS / **ACTIVE TIME:** 10 MINUTES / **TOTAL TIME:** 25 MINUTES

⅓ CUP PLUS 2½ TABLESPOONS EXTRA-VIRGIN OLIVE OIL

10 ANCHOVY FILLETS IN OLIVE OIL, DRAINED

2 CUPS BREAD CRUMBS

SALT AND PEPPER, TO TASTE

¾ LB. PICI (SEE PAGE 44)

FRESH PARSLEY, CHOPPED, FOR GARNISH

1. Bring water to a boil in a large saucepan. Place the ⅓ cup of olive oil in a large skillet and warm it over medium heat. Add the anchovies, mash them with a fork, and cook until they almost disintegrate, about 3 minutes.

2. Raise the heat to medium-high and stir in the bread crumbs. Cook until they are golden brown, about 3 minutes, and remove the skillet from heat. Season the mixture with salt and pepper and set it aside.

3. Add salt to the boiling water, let the water return to a full boil, and add the pasta. Cook until it is very al dente, 6 to 8 minutes. Reserve ½ cup of pasta water and drain the pasta.

4. Place the saucepan over high heat. Add the remaining olive oil and pasta water and stir to combine. Add the drained pasta and cook, tossing continually, until the pasta is al dente, about 2 minutes. Transfer the pasta to a large bowl.

5. Top the pasta with the warm anchovy-and-bread crumb mixture and toss to combine. Garnish with parsley and serve.

THE ENCYCLOPEDIA OF PASTA

Pasta allo Scarpariello

YIELD: 4 SERVINGS / **ACTIVE TIME:** 10 MINUTES / **TOTAL TIME:** 20 MINUTES

¼ CUP EXTRA-VIRGIN OLIVE OIL

1 GARLIC CLOVE

½ MILD CHILE PEPPER, STEMMED, SEEDED, AND MINCED

1 LB. CHERRY TOMATOES, HALVED

SALT, TO TASTE

14 OZ. SPAGHETTI

LARGE HANDFUL OF FRESH BASIL

6 TABLESPOONS GRATED PECORINO ROMANO CHEESE

6 TABLESPOONS GRATED PARMIGIANO REGGIANO CHEESE

1. Bring water to a boil in a large saucepan.

2. Place the olive oil in a large skillet and warm it over medium-low heat. Add the garlic and cook for 2 minutes. Add the chile and cook for 1 minute.

3. Add the tomatoes, raise the heat to medium, and cook, stirring occasionally, until the tomatoes start to collapse, about 10 minutes.

4. Add salt to the boiling water, let the water return to a full boil, and add the pasta. Cook until the pasta is very al dente. Reserve 2 cups of pasta water and drain the spaghetti.

5. Add the basil and some of the pasta water to the skillet, season the sauce with salt, and remove the garlic clove.

6. Add the pasta and more pasta water (if desired) and toss until combined and the pasta is al dente.

7. Turn off the heat, add the cheeses, and toss to combine. Serve immediately.

Pasta Fagioli e Cozze

YIELD: 4 SERVINGS / **ACTIVE TIME:** 20 MINUTES / **TOTAL TIME:** 24 HOURS

SALT AND PEPPER, TO TASTE

¾ LB. DRIED CANNELLINI BEANS, SOAKED OVERNIGHT AND DRAINED

¼ CUP EXTRA-VIRGIN OLIVE OIL

2 GARLIC CLOVES

½ RED CHILE PEPPER, STEMMED, SEEDED, AND MINCED

2 LBS. MUSSELS, RINSED AND DEBEARDED

8 CHERRY TOMATOES

¾ LB. MIXED SHORT-FORM PASTA

FRESH PARSLEY, CHOPPED, FOR GARNISH

1. Bring water to a boil in a large saucepan. Add salt and the beans and cook until they are tender, about 45 minutes. Drain the beans, reserving the cooking liquid. Strain the cooking liquid and set it and the beans aside.

2. Place half of the olive oil in a large skillet and warm it over medium heat. Add half of the garlic and chile and cook, stirring occasionally, for 2 minutes.

3. Add the mussels, raise the heat to medium-high, and cover the pan with a lid. Cook until the majority of the mussels have opened, about 5 minutes. Discard any mussels that did not open. Remove the remaining mussels from the pan, remove the meat from most of the shells, and set it aside. Leave the meat in some of the mussels and reserve them for garnish. Strain any liquid in the pan and set it aside.

4. Add the remaining olive oil to the pan and warm it over medium heat. Add the remaining garlic clove and chile and cook, stirring occasionally, for 2 minutes. Add the tomatoes and cook, stirring occasionally, for 5 minutes.

5. Add the beans, half of their cooking liquid, and half of the liquid reserved from cooking the mussels. Add the pasta, cover the pan, and cook until the pasta has absorbed most of the liquid, stirring occasionally.

6. Add the remaining cooking liquid from the mussels and some more of the cooking liquid from the beans. Cook until the pasta is al dente and the sauce is creamy.

7. Add the meat from the mussels, remove the pan from heat, and season the dish with salt and pepper.

8. Garnish the dish with parsley and the reserved mussels and enjoy.

Scialatielli All'amalfitana

YIELD: 4 SERVINGS / **ACTIVE TIME:** 40 MINUTES / **TOTAL TIME:** 1 HOUR AND 15 MINUTES

¼ CUP EXTRA-VIRGIN OLIVE OIL

1 GARLIC CLOVE, MINCED

5 MEDIUM TOMATOES, CHOPPED

HANDFUL OF FRESH BASIL

1 LB. MUSSELS, RINSED AND DEBEARDED

½ LB. CLAMS, RINSED

½ LB. SQUID, CLEANED AND CHOPPED

½ LB. SHRIMP, SHELLS REMOVED, DEVEINED

SALT, TO TASTE

½ CUP DRY WHITE WINE

1 LB. SCIALATIELLI (SEE PAGE 20)

FRESH PARSLEY, CHOPPED, FOR GARNISH

1. Place the olive oil in a large skillet and warm it over medium-high heat. Add the garlic and cook for 1 minute.

2. Add the tomatoes and basil and cook, stirring occasionally, for 10 minutes.

3. Add the seafood, season the dish with salt, and cook until the majority of the clams and mussels have opened, about 5 minutes.

4. Remove the mussels and clams from the pan and set them aside. Discard any mussels and/or clams that did not open.

5. Add the wine, cook until it has evaporated, and remove the pan from heat.

6. Bring water to a boil in a large saucepan. Add salt, let the water return to a full boil, and add the pasta. Cook until the pasta is al dente.

7. While the pasta water is coming to a boil, remove the meat from two-thirds of the mussels and clams and reserve the remaining one-third for garnish.

8. Drain the pasta and add it to the sauce along with the mussels and clams. Cook over medium-high heat until everything is warmed through, tossing to combine.

9. Garnish the dish with parsley and the reserved mussels and clams and enjoy.

Toasted Pasta with Crab

YIELD: 4 SERVINGS / **ACTIVE TIME:** 15 MINUTES / **TOTAL TIME:** 45 MINUTES

¼ CUP EXTRA-VIRGIN
OLIVE OIL

½ LB. ANGEL HAIR PASTA,
BROKEN INTO 2-INCH
PIECES

1 ONION, CHOPPED

3 GARLIC CLOVES, MINCED

¼ CUP WHITE WINE

4 CUPS CHICKEN STOCK
(SEE PAGE 536)

1 BAY LEAF

1 (14 OZ.) CAN OF DICED
TOMATOES, DRAINED

1 TEASPOON PAPRIKA

SALT AND PEPPER, TO TASTE

1 LB. LUMP CRABMEAT

FRESH PARSLEY, CHOPPED,
FOR GARNISH

1. Preheat the oven to 425°F. Place 1 tablespoon of the olive oil and the pasta in a large cast-iron skillet and toast the pasta over medium-high heat until it is browned, about 8 minutes. Transfer the pasta to a bowl.

2. Wipe out the skillet, add the remaining olive oil, and warm it over medium heat. Add the onion and cook, stirring occasionally, until it has softened, about 5 minutes. Add the garlic and cook, stirring continually, for 1 minute.

3. Add the wine and cook until the alcohol has been cooked off, 2 to 3 minutes. Add the stock, bay leaf, tomatoes, and paprika and bring the mixture to a boil. Reduce the heat, add the pasta, and simmer until the pasta is tender, about 10 minutes.

4. Season the dish with salt and pepper, add the crab, place the pan in the oven, and bake until the pasta is crispy, 5 to 10 minutes.

5. Remove the pan from the oven, garnish the dish with parsley, and enjoy.

Pasta alla Genovese

YIELD: 4 SERVINGS / **ACTIVE TIME:** 40 MINUTES / **TOTAL TIME:** 5 HOURS

2½ LBS. BEEF

⅔ CUP EXTRA-VIRGIN OLIVE OIL

5 LBS. YELLOW OR WHITE ONIONS, SLICED THIN

SALT, TO TASTE

14 OZ. ZITI SPEZZATI OR RIGATONI

2 OZ. PECORINO CHEESE, GRATED

1. Leave one piece of beef as is and cut the rest of it into chunks.

2. Place some of the olive oil in a large saucepan and warm it over medium-high heat. Working in batches to avoid crowding the pan, add the beef and sear until it is browned all over, turning it as necessary.

3. Place all of the beef in the pan and cover it with the onions. Reduce the heat to low, cover the pan, and cook, stirring occasionally, until the onions start to soften.

4. Uncover the pan and cook until the meat is tender but not yet falling apart, 2 to 3 hours.

5. Season the mixture with salt, remove the biggest piece of beef from the pan, and set it aside. Cover the pan and continue cooking the sauce until the onions have almost dissolved and the sauce becomes juicy, 1 to 2 hours.

6. Bring water to a boil in a large saucepan. Add salt, let the water return to a full boil, and add the pasta. Cook until the pasta is al dente.

7. Drain the pasta, place it in a serving dish, and add some of the sauce and half of the pecorino. Toss to combine and top with the remaining pecorino.

8. Pour the remaining sauce over the large piece of beef and serve it following the pasta dish.

Pasta al Forno Napoletana

YIELD: 6 SERVINGS / **ACTIVE TIME:** 40 MINUTES / **TOTAL TIME:** 1 HOUR AND 30 MINUTES

FOR THE MEATBALLS

½ LB. GROUND PORK

½ LB. GROUND BEEF

4 EGGS

½ LB. FRESH BREAD CRUMBS

1 CUP GRATED PECORINO
OR PARMESAN CHEESE

SALT AND PEPPER, TO TASTE

EXTRA-VIRGIN OLIVE OIL,
AS NEEDED

FOR THE PASTA

KOSHER SALT, TO TASTE

1 LB. ZITI, MEZZE MANICHE,
OR RIGATONI

1 LB. RICOTTA CHEESE

6 CUPS RAGÙ NAPOLETANO
(SEE PAGE 252)

9 OZ. PROVOLA CHEESE,
CUBED

3 HARD-BOILED EGGS,
SLICED (OPTIONAL)

¼ LB. ITALIAN SALAMI,
CHOPPED (OPTIONAL)

1 LB. FRESH MOZZARELLA
CHEESE, DRAINED AND
SHREDDED

1⅓ CUPS GRATED PECORINO
OR PARMESAN CHEESE

1. To begin preparations for the meatballs, place all of the ingredients, except for the olive oil, in a mixing bowl and work the mixture until it is well combined. Form the mixture into small, walnut-sized meatballs.

2. Add olive oil to a large, deep skillet until it is about 1 inch deep and warm it over medium heat. Add the meatballs and cook until they are browned all over, turning them as necessary. Place the meatballs on paper towel–lined plates and let them drain.

3. Preheat the oven to 360°F. To begin preparations for the pasta, bring water to a boil in a large saucepan. Add salt, let the water return to a full boil, and add the pasta. Cook until the pasta is al dente. Drain the pasta and set it aside.

4. Place the ricotta and 1 cup of the ragù in a large mixing bowl and stir to combine. Add the mixture to the pasta along with 2 more cups of ragù and stir to combine.

5. Spread some ragù over the bottom of a 13 x 9–inch baking dish. Arrange half of the pasta, half of the provola, half of the meatballs, half of the eggs and salami (if desired), half of the mozzarella, and half of the pecorino in separate layers. Repeat the layering process with the remaining ingredients.

6. Place the dish in the oven and bake until the top is crispy, about 30 minutes.

7. Remove the dish from the oven and let it rest for 10 to 15 minutes before serving.

Beef & Broccoli

YIELD: 4 SERVINGS / **ACTIVE TIME:** 15 MINUTES / **TOTAL TIME:** 30 MINUTES

¾ LB. WIDE RICE NOODLES

1 TABLESPOON AVOCADO OIL

2 GARLIC CLOVES, MINCED

1 LB. BROCCOLI, CUT INTO FLORETS

¼ CUP THINLY SLICED EGGPLANT

SALT, TO TASTE

1 LB. RIB EYE, SLICED THIN AGAINST THE GRAIN

¼ CUP OYSTER SAUCE

2 TABLESPOONS SOY SAUCE

CHILE PEPPERS, SLICED THIN, FOR GARNISH

1. Bring water to a boil in a large saucepan. Add the noodles and cook until they are al dente, 6 to 8 minutes. Drain the noodles and set them aside.

2. Coat a large skillet with the avocado oil and warm it over high heat. Add the garlic, broccoli, and eggplant and cook, stirring frequently, until the broccoli has softened and the eggplant has collapsed, about 8 minutes.

3. Season the rib eye with salt and add it to the pan. Cook, stirring frequently, until it has the desired level of doneness, 3 to 4 minutes for medium-rare.

4. Add the oyster sauce, soy sauce, and noodles and toss to combine. Garnish the dish with the chile peppers and serve.

Lasagne alla Napoletana

YIELD: 6 SERVINGS / **ACTIVE TIME:** 1 HOUR / **TOTAL TIME:** 2 HOURS

FOR THE MEATBALLS

5½ OZ. GROUND BEEF

5½ OZ. GROUND PORK

2 EGGS

¼ LB. FRESH BREAD CRUMBS

2 OZ. PECORINO OR PARMESAN CHEESE, GRATED

SALT AND PEPPER, TO TASTE

EXTRA-VIRGIN OLIVE OIL, AS NEEDED

FOR THE LASAGNA

SALT, TO TASTE

1½ LBS. LASAGNA SHEETS

1 LB. RICOTTA CHEESE

4 CUPS RAGÙ NAPOLETANO (SEE PAGE 252), PLUS MORE FOR TOPPING

14 OZ. PROVOLA CHEESE, CUBED

3 HARD-BOILED EGGS, SLICED (OPTIONAL)

3 OZ. GRATED PECORINO OR PARMESAN CHEESE, PLUS MORE FOR TOPPING

1. To begin preparations for the meatballs, place all of the ingredients, except for the olive oil, in a mixing bowl and work the mixture until it is well combined. Form the mixture into small, walnut-sized meatballs.

2. Add olive oil to a large, deep skillet until it is about 1 inch deep and warm it over medium heat. Add the meatballs and cook until they are browned all over, turning them as necessary. Place the meatballs on paper towel–lined plates and let them drain.

3. Preheat the oven to 360°F. To begin preparations for the lasagna, bring water to a boil in a large saucepan. Add salt, let the water return to a full boil, and add a few of the lasagna sheets at a time to avoid overcrowding the pot. Cook until the lasagna sheets are al dente. Drain the lasagna sheets and set them on kitchen towels to dry.

4. Place the ricotta and 1 cup of the ragù in a large mixing bowl and stir to combine.

5. Spread some ragù over the bottom of a 13 x 9–inch baking dish. Arrange one-third of the lasagna sheets, one-third of the ricotta mixture, one-third of the provola, one-third of the meatballs, one-third of the eggs (if desired), and one-third of the pecorino in separate layers. Repeat the layering process two more times with the remaining ingredients.

6. Top the lasagna with additional ragù and pecorino, place it in the oven, and bake for 50 minutes.

7. Remove the lasagna from the oven and let it rest for 10 to 15 minutes before serving.

Pasta alla Mugnaia

YIELD: 4 SERVINGS / **ACTIVE TIME:** 40 MINUTES / **TOTAL TIME:** 2 HOURS

¼ CUP EXTRA-VIRGIN OLIVE OIL

1 GREEN BELL PEPPER, STEMMED, SEEDED, AND FINELY DICED

1 ONION, THINLY SLICED

½ CARROT, PEELED AND DICED

½ LB. PIECE OF BONE-IN BEEF OR PORK

SALT, TO TASTE

1 RED BELL PEPPER, STEMMED, SEEDED, AND FINELY DICED

1 EGGPLANT, CUBED

1 LB. WHOLE PEELED TOMATOES, PUREED

1 CUP WATER

1 LB. TAGLIATELLE (SEE PAGE 52) OR FETTUCCINE

PECORINO CHEESE, GRATED, FOR GARNISH

1. Place the olive oil in a large skillet and warm it over medium heat. Add the green bell pepper, onion, and carrot and cook, stirring occasionally, until they have softened, about 5 minutes.

2. Season the beef with salt, add it to the pan, and sear it until it is browned all over, turning it as necessary.

3. Add the red bell pepper and eggplant and cook until they are browned.

4. Reduce the heat to low, add the tomatoes and water, and season the sauce with salt. Cover the pan and cook the sauce until the meat is tender, about 1 hour. Remove the sauce from heat and set it aside.

5. Bring water to a boil in a large saucepan. Add salt, let the water return to a full boil, and add the pasta. Cook until the pasta is al dente. Drain the pasta and place it in a serving dish.

6. Add the sauce to the pasta and toss to combine. Garnish the dish with pecorino and enjoy.

Bucatini con Asparagi e Salsiccia

YIELD: 4 SERVINGS / **ACTIVE TIME:** 30 MINUTES / **TOTAL TIME:** 50 MINUTES

10 OZ. FRESH ASPARAGUS, TRIMMED

SALT AND PEPPER, TO TASTE

¼ CUP EXTRA-VIRGIN OLIVE OIL

1 ONION, FINELY DICED

11 OZ. ITALIAN SAUSAGE, CASING REMOVED AND CRUMBLED

1 CUP WHITE WINE

1 LB. BUCATINI

⅔ CUP GRATED PECORINO CHEESE

1. Bring water to a boil in a medium saucepan. Separate the stems from the tips of the asparagus and add salt and the asparagus stems to the boiling water. Cook until the asparagus stems are tender, about 4 minutes, drain, and set them aside.

2. Place 2 tablespoons of olive oil in a large skillet and warm it over medium heat. Add the onion and cook, stirring occasionally, until it has softened, about 5 minutes.

3. Add the sausage and cook, stirring occasionally, until it has browned, about 8 minutes.

4. Add the wine, reduce the heat to low, and cook for 15 minutes.

5. Place the remaining olive oil in a large skillet and warm it over medium heat. Add the asparagus tips and cook, stirring frequently, until they are tender, 3 to 4 minutes. Season the asparagus tips with salt and pepper, remove the pan from heat, and set the asparagus tips aside.

6. Bring water to a boil in a large saucepan. Chop the asparagus stems, add them to the sauce, and cook for 10 minutes.

7. Add salt to the boiling water, let the water return to a full boil, and add the pasta. Cook until the pasta is al dente. Drain the pasta, add it to the sauce, and toss to combine.

8. Top the dish with the asparagus tips and pecorino and enjoy.

Egg Noodles with Chicken & Cashew Butter

YIELD: 4 SERVINGS / **ACTIVE TIME:** 40 MINUTES / **TOTAL TIME:** 45 MINUTES

½ TEASPOON KOSHER SALT, PLUS MORE TO TASTE

½ TEASPOON CAYENNE PEPPER, PLUS MORE TO TASTE

½ TEASPOON BROWN SUGAR

½ TEASPOON CHILI POWDER

⅓ CUP CASHEW BUTTER

¼ CUP SOY SAUCE

1½ TABLESPOONS RICE VINEGAR

2½ TEASPOONS TOASTED SESAME OIL

2 TEASPOONS CHILI OIL

¾ TEASPOON SUGAR

2 GARLIC CLOVES, MINCED

3 TABLESPOONS CANOLA OIL

2 MEDIUM BONE-IN CHICKEN BREASTS

CHINESE EGG NOODLES (SEE PAGE 104)

1 LB. SWISS CHARD, STEMMED AND SLICED INTO RIBBONS

SCALLIONS, SLICED THIN, FOR GARNISH

1. Preheat the oven to 400°F. Bring water to a boil in a large saucepan.

2. Place the salt, cayenne pepper, brown sugar, and chili powder in a small bowl and stir until well combined. Place the cashew butter, soy sauce, rice vinegar, sesame oil, chili oil, sugar, and garlic in a medium bowl and stir until well combined.

3. Place the canola oil in a large cast-iron skillet and warm it over medium-high heat. Rub the spice mixture over the chicken, place it in the pan, and cook until it is nicely browned on both sides, 6 to 8 minutes, turning it over halfway through.

4. Transfer the skillet to the oven and roast the chicken until it is cooked through (the interior is 165°F), about 10 minutes. Remove the skillet from the oven, transfer the chicken to a plate, and let it cool. When the chicken is cool enough to handle, shred it and set aside.

5. Add salt to the boiling water, let it return to a boil, and add the noodles. Cook for 1 minute. Add the chard and cook until the noodles are al dente, 1 to 2 minutes.

6. Drain the noodles and chard and transfer the mixture to a large bowl. Add the shredded chicken and the cashew butter mixture and toss to coat. Garnish with scallions and serve.

Mongolian Beef with Crispy Chow Mein Noodles

YIELD: 4 SERVINGS / **ACTIVE TIME:** 45 MINUTES / **TOTAL TIME:** 4 HOURS

1 LB. FLANK STEAK

1 (12 OZ.) BOTTLE OF BEER

SALT, TO TASTE

8 BABY BOK CHOY, QUARTERED

1 TABLESPOON TOASTED SESAME OIL

3 GARLIC CLOVES, SLICED THIN

2-INCH PIECE OF FRESH GINGER, PEELED AND GRATED

½ CUP SOY SAUCE

½ CUP WATER

1½ TABLESPOONS MOLASSES

1 TEASPOON SRIRACHA, PLUS MORE TO TASTE

⅔ CUP BROWN SUGAR

CHINESE EGG NOODLES (SEE PAGE 104)

2¼ CUPS PEANUT OIL

2 TABLESPOONS CORNSTARCH

1. Place the steak and beer in a large resealable plastic bag. Place the bag in the refrigerator and marinate the steak for 3 hours, turning the bag over a few times.

2. Bring water to a boil in a large saucepan. Add salt, let the water return to a full boil, and add the bok choy. Cook for 1 minute, remove the bok choy with a strainer, and set it aside. Keep the water at a gentle simmer.

3. Place the sesame oil in a small saucepan and warm it over medium heat. Add the garlic and ginger and cook, stirring continually, for 1 minute. Add the soy sauce and water and bring to a boil. Add the molasses, sriracha, and brown sugar and cook, stirring frequently, until the sauce has thickened, about 5 minutes. Remove the pan from the heat and set aside.

4. Bring the water back to a boil. Add the noodles and cook until they are al dente, 2 to 3 minutes. Drain and pat the noodles dry.

5. Place 2 tablespoons of peanut oil in a large, deep skillet and warm it over medium-high heat. Add half of the noodles and fry, without touching them, until they are golden brown and crispy on the bottom, 3 to 4 minutes. Carefully flip the cake of noodles over and fry for another 3 minutes. Transfer the fried noodles to a paper towel–lined plate to drain. Repeat with 2 more tablespoons of the peanut oil and the remaining noodles.

6. Slice the steak into thin strips, cutting against the grain. Place the steak in a medium bowl with the cornstarch and toss until the steak is completely coated.

7. Place the remaining peanut oil in a Dutch oven and warm it 350°F. Working in batches to avoid crowding the pot, gently slip the steak into the hot oil and fry until it is crispy and cooked to the desired level of doneness. Remove the steak with a slotted spoon and transfer it to a paper towel–lined plate.

8. Transfer the cooked steak to a medium bowl, add ¾ cup of the sauce, and toss to coat. Cut the crispy noodle cakes in half and place one piece on each serving plate. Top the noodle cake with some steak and bok choy, drizzle some of the remaining sauce over the top, and serve.

Penne with Rabbit Ragù

YIELD: 4 SERVINGS / **ACTIVE TIME:** 30 MINUTES / **TOTAL TIME:** 2 HOURS

¼ CUP EXTRA-VIRGIN OLIVE OIL

2½ TO 3½ LB. RABBIT, CUT INTO 8 PIECES

SALT AND PEPPER, TO TASTE

1 CUP ALL-PURPOSE FLOUR

1 YELLOW ONION, DICED

2 CELERY STALKS, DICED

2 CARROTS, PEELED AND DICED

1 GARLIC CLOVE, MINCED

2 TABLESPOONS TOMATO PASTE

½ CUP RED WINE

1 (28 OZ.) CAN OF CRUSHED TOMATOES

1 CUP CHICKEN STOCK (SEE PAGE 536)

2 BAY LEAVES

2 SPRIGS OF FRESH ROSEMARY

4 SPRIGS OF FRESH THYME

2 CUPS WATER

2 TABLESPOONS UNSALTED BUTTER, CUBED

1 LB. PENNE

PARMESAN CHEESE, GRATED, FOR GARNISH

1. Place the olive oil in a cast-iron Dutch oven and warm it over medium heat. Season the pieces of rabbit with salt and pepper, dredge them in the flour, and shake to remove any excess. Add the rabbit and cook until the pieces are browned all over, 8 to 10 minutes, turning as necessary.

2. Use a slotted spoon to remove the rabbit from the pot and set it aside. Add the onion, celery, carrots, and garlic and cook, stirring frequently, until browned. Add the tomato paste, stir to coat, and cook for approximately 4 minutes.

3. Add the wine and let the mixture come to a boil. Reduce the heat and cook until the wine has reduced by half, about 10 minutes.

4. Add the tomatoes, stock, bay leaves, rosemary, and thyme and simmer for 2 minutes before returning the rabbit. Simmer until the sauce has thickened and the rabbit is very tender, about 1½ hours.

5. Use a slotted spoon to remove the rabbit from the sauce and set it aside. Remove the bay leaves, rosemary, and thyme from the sauce and discard them. When the rabbit is cool enough to handle, pick the meat off the bones and shred it. Discard the bones and return the meat to the sauce.

6. Bring water to a boil in a large pot. Add salt, let the water return to a boil, and add the pasta. Cook until the pasta is al dente, 8 to 10 minutes. Drain the pasta.

7. To serve, ladle the ragù over the pasta and garnish with the Parmesan.

Cavatelli alla Ventricina

YIELD: 4 SERVINGS / **ACTIVE TIME:** 10 MINUTES / **TOTAL TIME:** 50 MINUTES

3 TABLESPOONS EXTRA-VIRGIN OLIVE OIL

½ ONION, FINELY DICED

2 GARLIC CLOVES, HALVED

1 LB. PEELED TOMATOES, CRUSHED

SALT, TO TASTE

⅔ CUP CHOPPED VENTRICINA

1 LB. CAVATELLI (SEE PAGE 21)

HANDFUL OF FRESH BASIL, SHREDDED

2 OZ. PECORINO CHEESE, GRATED

1. Place the olive oil in a large skillet and warm it over medium heat. Add the onion and garlic and cook, stirring frequently, until the onion has softened, about 5 minutes.

2. Add the tomatoes, reduce the heat to low, and cook for 20 minutes.

3. Remove the garlic, season the sauce with salt, and stir in the ventricina. Cook for 20 minutes, stirring occasionally.

4. Bring water to a boil in a large saucepan. Add salt, let the water return to a full boil, and add the pasta. Cook until the pasta is al dente.

5. Drain the pasta and place it in a serving dish.

6. Stir the basil into the sauce. Top the pasta with the sauce and pecorino and serve.

Cavatelli al Sugo Vedovo

YIELD: 4 SERVINGS / **ACTIVE TIME:** 40 MINUTES / **TOTAL TIME:** 40 MINUTES

6 OZ. LARD, FINELY DICED

1 GARLIC CLOVE, HALVED

6 SPRIGS OF FRESH PARSLEY

2 LBS. TOMATOES, CHOPPED

SALT AND PEPPER, TO TASTE

1 LB. CAVATELLI (SEE PAGE 21)

HANDFUL OF FRESH BASIL

⅔ CUP GRATED PECORINO CHEESE

1. Place the lard in a large skillet and warm it over medium heat. Add the garlic and parsley and cook, stirring frequently, for 2 minutes.

2. Add the tomatoes and cook, stirring occasionally, until the tomatoes collapse, about 20 minutes.

3. Bring water to a boil in a large saucepan. Add salt, let the water return to a full boil, and add the pasta. Cook until the pasta is al dente.

4. Drain the pasta and place it in a serving dish.

5. Stir the basil into the sauce. Top the pasta with the sauce and pecorino, season it with salt and pepper, and serve.

Fusilli alla Molisana

YIELD: 4 SERVINGS / **ACTIVE TIME:** 30 MINUTES / **TOTAL TIME:** 3 HOURS

¼ CUP EXTRA-VIRGIN OLIVE OIL

1 ONION, FINELY DICED

1 CARROT, PEELED AND FINELY DICED

1 CELERY STALK, FINELY DICED

½ LB. LAMB, CHOPPED

½ LB. VEAL, CHOPPED

2 ITALIAN SAUSAGES, CASINGS REMOVED AND CRUMBLED

½ CUP WHITE WINE

2 LBS. WHOLE PEELED TOMATOES, CRUSHED

SALT, TO TASTE

1 LB. FUSILLI AL FERRO (SEE PAGE 22)

PECORINO CHEESE, GRATED, FOR GARNISH

1. Place the olive oil in a large saucepan and warm it over medium heat. Add the onion, carrot, and celery and cook, stirring occasionally, until the onion has softened, about 5 minutes.

2. Add the lamb, veal, and sausages and cook over medium-high heat until they are browned, 8 to 10 minutes.

3. Deglaze the pan with the white wine, scraping up any browned bits from the bottom. Cook until the wine has evaporated.

4. Add the tomatoes, season the sauce with salt, and reduce the heat to low. Cook until the meat starts falling apart, 2 to 3 hours.

5. Bring water to a boil in a large saucepan. Add salt, let the water return to a full boil, and add the pasta. Cook until the pasta is al dente, about 3 minutes after they rise to the surface.

6. Drain the pasta and stir it into the sauce. Garnish the dish with pecorino and serve.

Pasta al Pesto Calabrese

YIELD: 4 SERVINGS / **ACTIVE TIME:** 20 MINUTES / **TOTAL TIME:** 1 HOUR

¼ CUP EXTRA-VIRGIN OLIVE OIL

1 RED ONION, FINELY DICED

2 RED BELL PEPPERS, STEMMED, SEEDED, AND SLICED THIN

5 OZ. WHOLE PEELED TOMATOES, CRUSHED

RED PEPPER FLAKES, TO TASTE

SALT, TO TASTE

½ CUP RICOTTA CHEESE

⅔ CUP GRATED CACIOCAVALLO OR PECORINO CHEESE

1 LB. PENNE OR DRIED FUSILLI

1. Place the olive oil in a large skillet and warm it over medium-low heat. Add the onion and cook, stirring occasionally, until it has softened, about 6 minutes.

2. Add the peppers, cover the pan, and cook, stirring occasionally, until they are tender, about 20 minutes.

3. Add the tomatoes and season the sauce with red pepper flakes and salt. Cover the pan and cook the sauce, stirring occasionally, for 20 minutes.

4. Stir in the ricotta and caciocavallo and use an immersion blender to puree the sauce until it is smooth.

5. Bring water to a boil in a large saucepan. Add salt, let the water return to a full boil, and add the pasta. Cook until the pasta is al dente.

6. Reserve 1 cup pasta water, drain the pasta, and stir it into the sauce.

7. Toss to combine, adding pasta water as needed to get the right consistency. Serve immediately.

Fusilli alla Silana

YIELD: 6 SERVINGS / **ACTIVE TIME:** 10 MINUTES / **TOTAL TIME:** 50 MINUTES

¼ CUP EXTRA-VIRGIN OLIVE OIL

1 SMALL ONION, FINELY DICED

2 OZ. GUANCIALE, SKINLESS AND CUT INTO STRIPS

5 OZ. SOPPRESSATA, SLICED

1 CHILE PEPPER, STEMMED, SEEDED, AND CHOPPED

1 OZ. COGNAC OR WHISKEY

1 LB. WHOLE PEELED TOMATOES, CRUSHED

SALT AND PEPPER, TO TASTE

1 LB. DRIED FUSILLI

7 OZ. CACIOCAVALLO CHEESE, CUBED

HANDFUL OF FRESH PARSLEY, CHOPPED

⅔ CUP GRATED PECORINO CHEESE

1. Place the olive oil in a large, deep skillet and warm it over medium heat. Add the onion, guanciale, soppressata, and chile and cook, stirring occasionally, until the guanciale's fat starts to render and the onion has softened, about 5 minutes.

2. Remove the pan from heat, add the cognac, and place the pan over medium-low heat. Cook until the cognac has evaporated.

3. Add the tomatoes and cook for 30 minutes, stirring occasionally.

4. Bring water to a boil in a large saucepan. Add salt, let the water return to a full boil, and add the pasta. Cook until the pasta is al dente.

5. Drain the pasta and stir it into the sauce.

6. Add the caciocavallo and parsley, cover the pan, and cook until the caciocavallo has melted.

7. Top the dish with the pecorino, season it with salt and pepper, and serve.

Linguine with Clam Sauce

YIELD: 4 SERVINGS / **ACTIVE TIME:** 20 MINUTES / **TOTAL TIME:** 40 MINUTES

½ CUP EXTRA-VIRGIN OLIVE OIL

3 GARLIC CLOVES, SLICED THIN

32 LITTLENECK CLAMS, SCRUBBED AND RINSED WELL

1 CUP WHITE WINE

SALT AND PEPPER, TO TASTE

1 LB. LINGUINE

1 CUP CLAM JUICE

1 CUP CHOPPED FRESH PARSLEY

¼ CUP FRESHLY GRATED PARMESAN CHEESE

1. Bring water to a boil in a large saucepan.

2. Place a Dutch oven over medium heat. Add half of the olive oil and the garlic and cook, stirring continually, until the garlic starts to brown, about 2 minutes. Add the clams and wine, cover the pot, and cook until the majority of the clams have opened, 5 to 7 minutes. Use a slotted spoon to transfer the clams to a colander. Discard any clams that did not open.

3. Add salt to the boiling water, let it return to a full boil, and add the pasta. Cook until the linguine is al dente, 2 to 4 minutes for fresh pasta, and 8 to 10 minutes for dried pasta. Reserve ¼ cup of pasta water, drain the pasta, and set it aside.

4. Add the clam juice, parsley, and pasta water to the Dutch oven. Cook, stirring occasionally, until the sauce starts to thicken, about 10 minutes. Remove all the clams from their shells and mince one-quarter of them.

5. Add the linguine to the pot, along with the Parmesan. Season with salt and pepper and stir until the cheese begins to melt. Fold in all of the clams, drizzle the remaining olive oil over the dish, and serve.

Maccheroni with 'Nduja & Soppressata

YIELD: 4 SERVINGS / **ACTIVE TIME:** 20 MINUTES / **TOTAL TIME:** 24 HOURS

½ LB. DRIED CHICKPEAS, SOAKED OVERNIGHT

1 SPRIG OF FRESH ROSEMARY

1 GARLIC CLOVE

2 TABLESPOONS EXTRA-VIRGIN OLIVE OIL

1 RED ONION, FINELY DICED

¼ LB. SOPPRESSATA, FINELY DICED

1 LB. WHOLE PEELED TOMATOES, CRUSHED

2 TABLESPOONS 'NDUJA

SALT, TO TASTE

1 LB. MACCHERONI AL FERRETTO (SEE PAGE 24)

⅔ CUP GRATED PECORINO CHEESE

1. Drain the chickpeas, place them in a large saucepan, and cover them with cold water. Add the rosemary and garlic, bring to a boil, and cook until the chickpeas are tender, about 45 minutes. Drain the chickpeas, reserve the cooking liquid, and set both aside.

2. Place the olive oil in a large, deep skillet and warm it over medium heat. Add the onion and soppressata and cook, stirring occasionally, until the onion has softened, about 5 minutes.

3. Add the tomatoes, reduce the heat to medium-low, and cook for 20 minutes, stirring occasionally.

4. Stir in the 'nduja and cook for 20 minutes.

5. Place half of the chickpeas in a blender and puree until smooth. Add the puree and remaining chickpeas to the sauce, season it with salt, and stir to combine.

6. Bring water to a boil in a large saucepan. Add salt, let the water return to a full boil, and add the pasta. Cook until the pasta is al dente.

7. Drain the pasta and stir it into the sauce along with some of the reserved cooking liquid. Toss to combine, top the dish with the pecorino, and enjoy.

Maccheroni con Sugo di Salsiccia

YIELD: 4 SERVINGS / **ACTIVE TIME:** 15 MINUTES / **TOTAL TIME:** 1 HOUR AND 30 MINUTES

¼ CUP EXTRA-VIRGIN OLIVE OIL

1 RED ONION, FINELY DICED

4 ITALIAN SAUSAGES WITH FENNEL, CASINGS REMOVED AND CRUMBLED

1 LB. WHOLE PEELED TOMATOES, CRUSHED

1 MILD CHILE PEPPER, STEMMED, SEEDED, AND CHOPPED

SALT, TO TASTE

1 LB. MACCHERONI AL FERRETTO (SEE PAGE 24)

HANDFUL OF FRESH BASIL

⅔ CUP GRATED SMOKED AND AGED RICOTTA CHEESE

1. Place the olive oil in a large skillet and warm it over medium-low heat. Add the onion and cook, stirring occasionally, until it has softened, about 6 minutes.

2. Add the sausages and cook, stirring occasionally, until they are browned, 8 to 10 minutes.

3. Add the tomatoes and chile, season the sauce with salt, and reduce the heat to low. Cover the pan and cook the sauce until the flavor has developed to your liking, about 1 hour.

4. Bring water to a boil in a large saucepan. Add salt, let the water return to a full boil, and add the pasta. Cook until the pasta is al dente.

5. Drain the pasta and stir it into the sauce along with the basil. Toss to combine, top the dish with the smoked ricotta, and serve.

Pappardelle All'aquilana

YIELD: 4 SERVINGS / **ACTIVE TIME:** 20 MINUTES / **TOTAL TIME:** 50 MINUTES

1⅓ CUPS DRIED PORCINI MUSHROOMS

SALT, TO TASTE

¾ CUP PEAS

2 TABLESPOONS EXTRA-VIRGIN OLIVE OIL

½ ONION, DICED

⅔ CUP DICED ITALIAN COTTO OR PARMA HAM

1 SLICE OF GUANCIALE, SKINLESS AND DICED

1 ITALIAN SAUSAGE, CASING REMOVED AND CRUMBLED

1 LB. PAPPARDELLE

1½ TEASPOONS SAFFRON THREADS

½ CUP GRATED PECORINO CHEESE

1. Place the porcini mushrooms in a bowl, cover them with warm water, and let them soak for 30 minutes.

2. Drain the mushrooms, reserve the soaking liquid, and squeeze the mushrooms to remove as much moisture as possible. Chop the mushrooms and set them aside. Strain the soaking liquid and set it aside.

3. Bring water to a boil in a medium saucepan. Add salt and the peas and cook for 2 minutes. Drain the peas and set them aside.

4. Place the olive oil in a large skillet and warm it over medium heat. Add the onion, cotto, and guanciale and cook, stirring occasionally, until the onion has softened, about 5 minutes.

5. Add the sausage and cook, stirring occasionally, until it has browned, about 8 minutes.

6. Add the peas, mushrooms, and some of the reserved soaking liquid. Season the dish with salt, reduce the heat to low, and cook for 15 minutes.

7. Bring water to a boil in a large saucepan. Add salt, let the water return to a full boil, and add the pasta. Cook until the pasta is very al dente. Reserve ½ cup of pasta water, drain the pasta, and set it aside.

8. Place the saffron in the pasta water and let it steep for 10 minutes.

9. Add the pasta, saffron, and some of the saffron water to the skillet and toss until well combined. You want the sauce to be thick instead of soupy, and for the pasta to be al dente.

10. Stir in the pecorino and serve.

Maccheroni with 'Nduja & Ricotta

YIELD: 4 SERVINGS / **ACTIVE TIME:** 10 MINUTES / **TOTAL TIME:** 20 MINUTES

¼ CUP EXTRA-VIRGIN OLIVE OIL

1 RED ONION, FINELY DICED

1 SHALLOT, FINELY DICED

7 OZ. 'NDUJA, CHOPPED

11 OZ. RICOTTA CHEESE

3 OZ. PARMESAN CHEESE, GRATED

SALT, TO TASTE

1 LB. MACCHERONI AL FERRETTO (SEE PAGE 24)

1. Bring water to a boil in a large saucepan. Place the olive oil in a large, deep skillet and warm it over medium heat. Add the onion and shallot and cook, stirring occasionally, until they have softened, about 5 minutes.

2. Add the 'nduja and cook, stirring frequently, for 5 minutes.

3. Place the ricotta and Parmesan in a bowl and stir to combine.

4. Add salt, let the water return to a full boil, and add the pasta. Cook until the pasta is al dente. Add ½ cup of pasta water to the ricotta mixture and stir to incorporate.

5. Drain the pasta and stir it into the sauce along with the ricotta mixture. Toss quickly to combine and serve.

Pasta alla Ionica

YIELD: 4 SERVINGS / **ACTIVE TIME:** 30 MINUTES / **TOTAL TIME:** 50 MINUTES

4 TOMATOES

2 MEDIUM BELL PEPPERS

2 TABLESPOONS EXTRA-VIRGIN OLIVE OIL

2 GARLIC CLOVES, HALVED

¾ LB. GUANCIALE, SKIN REMOVED AND CUT INTO STRIPS

2 HANDFULS OF FRESH BASIL

SALT, TO TASTE

1 LB. MACCHERONI AL FERRETTO (SEE PAGE 24)

1 CUP GRATED PECORINO CHEESE

1. Bring water to a boil in a large saucepan and prepare an ice bath. Add the tomatoes and peppers, boil for 1 minute, and drain. Plunge them into the ice bath, drain them, and remove the skins.

2. Remove the stem and seeds from the peppers and discard them. Place the tomatoes and peppers in a food processor, puree until smooth, and set the mixture aside.

3. Place the olive oil in a large, deep skillet and warm it over medium-low heat. Add the garlic and cook, stirring frequently, for 2 minutes.

4. Add the guanciale and cook, stirring frequently, until its fat has rendered.

5. Add the tomato-and-pepper puree and cook for 20 minutes, stirring occasionally.

6. Remove the garlic and discard it. Add the basil, season the sauce with salt, and continue cooking it over low heat.

7. Bring water to a boil in a large saucepan. Add salt, let the water return to a full boil, and add the pasta. Cook until the pasta is al dente.

8. Drain the pasta, add it to the sauce, and toss to combine. Stir in the pecorino and serve.

Penne alla Vodka

YIELD: 6 SERVINGS / **ACTIVE TIME:** 40 MINUTES / **TOTAL TIME:** 1 HOUR

2½ TABLESPOONS UNSALTED BUTTER

4 OZ. PANCETTA, DICED

3 SHALLOTS, MINCED

SALT, TO TASTE

1 (28 OZ.) CAN OF CRUSHED TOMATOES

1 TEASPOON RED PEPPER FLAKES

1 CUP HEAVY CREAM

1¼ LBS. PENNE

½ CUP VODKA, AT ROOM TEMPERATURE

1 CUP FRESHLY GRATED PARMESAN CHEESE, PLUS MORE FOR GARNISH

FRESH PARSLEY, CHOPPED, FOR GARNISH

1. Bring water to a boil in a large saucepan.

2. Place 2 tablespoons of the butter in a large skillet and melt it over medium heat. Add the pancetta and cook, stirring occasionally, until it is browned and crispy, 8 to 10 minutes. Transfer the pancetta to a small bowl and set aside.

3. Add the shallots to the skillet, season with salt, reduce the heat to low, cover the pan, and cook, stirring occasionally, until the shallots are tender, about 10 minutes.

4. Add the tomatoes and red pepper flakes to the skillet, season with salt, and raise the heat to medium-high. Once the mixture begins to boil, reduce the heat to low, partially cover the pan, and cook until the sauce thickens slightly, 15 to 20 minutes. Add the cream and heat through until the sauce gently bubbles. Remove from heat and cover the pan.

5. Add salt to the boiling water, let it return to a full boil, and add the pasta. Cook until it is very al dente, 6 to 8 minutes. Reserve ¼ cup of pasta water and drain the pasta.

6. Place the saucepan over high heat. Add the vodka, reserved pasta water, and remaining butter and stir to combine. Add the pasta and cook, tossing continually, until it is al dente, about 2 minutes. Add the sauce and Parmesan to the pan and toss to combine. Top the dish with the pancetta, garnish with parsley and additional Parmesan, and serve.

Pasta Chjina

YIELD: 6 SERVINGS / **ACTIVE TIME:** 1 HOUR / **TOTAL TIME:** 1 HOUR AND 30 MINUTES

3½ OZ. DAY-OLD BREAD, CHOPPED

2 TABLESPOONS MILK

¾ LB. GROUND BEEF

1 EGG

1 EGG YOLK

1½ CUPS GRATED PECORINO OR PARMESAN CHEESE

SALT, TO TASTE

1 CUP BREAD CRUMBS

2 TABLESPOONS EXTRA-VIRGIN OLIVE OIL, PLUS MORE AS NEEDED

½ RED ONION, FINELY DICED

2 LBS. WHOLE PEELED TOMATOES, LIGHTLY CRUSHED

FRESH BASIL, SHREDDED, TO TASTE

1 LB. RIGATONI

3 HARD-BOILED EGGS, CUT INTO WEDGES

6 OZ. SOPPRESSATA, CHOPPED

6 OZ. CACIOCAVALLO CHEESE, CUBED

1. Place the bread and milk in a bowl and let the bread soak for 15 minutes.

2. Drain the bread, squeeze it to remove as much liquid as possible, and place it in a large mixing bowl. Add the beef, egg, egg yolk, and ¼ cup of pecorino, season the mixture with salt, and work the mixture until it is well combined. Form the mixture into 1 oz. balls.

3. Place the bread crumbs in a shallow bowl and dredge the meatballs in them until the meatballs are evenly coated.

4. Add olive oil to a large, deep skillet until it is about 1 inch deep and warm it over medium heat. Add the meatballs and cook them until they are browned all over, turning them as necessary. Transfer the cooked meatballs to a paper towel–lined plate to drain.

5. Place the olive oil in a large skillet and warm it over medium-low heat. Add the onion and cook, stirring frequently, until it has softened, about 6 minutes.

6. Add the tomatoes and basil, partially cover the pan, and cook, stirring occasionally, for 20 minutes. Season the sauce with salt and set it aside.

7. Preheat the oven to 390°F. Bring water to a boil in a large saucepan. Add salt, let the water return to a full boil, and add the pasta. Cook until the pasta is very al dente.

8. Drain the pasta, place it in a large bowl, and add the meatballs, eggs, soppressata, caciocavallo, two-thirds of the sauce, and two-thirds of the remaining pecorino. Gently stir to combine.

9. Transfer the mixture to a 13 x 9–inch baking pan and top it with the remaining sauce and pecorino. Place the pan in the oven and bake until the filling is bubbly, 15 to 20 minutes.

10. Remove from the oven and let it rest for 15 minutes before slicing and serving.

'Ndruppeche

YIELD: 4 SERVINGS / **ACTIVE TIME:** 30 MINUTES / **TOTAL TIME:** 1 HOUR AND 30 MINUTES

3 TABLESPOONS EXTRA-VIRGIN OLIVE OIL

1 GARLIC CLOVE, HALVED

5 OZ. GROUND BEEF

⅔ CUP DICED ITALIAN SALAMI

½ CUP DRY WHITE WINE

1 LB. WHOLE PEELED TOMATOES, LIGHTLY CRUSHED

2 BAY LEAVES

SALT, TO TASTE

1 LB. MACCHERONI AL FERRETTO (SEE PAGE 24) OR STROZZAPRETI

FRESH HORSERADISH, GRATED, FOR GARNISH

1. Place the olive oil in a large, deep skillet and warm it over medium heat. Add the garlic and cook, stirring frequently, for 2 minutes.

2. Add the beef and salami and cook, stirring occasionally, until the meat is browned, about 8 minutes.

3. Add the wine and cook until it has evaporated.

4. Add the tomatoes and bay leaves, reduce the heat to low, partially cover the pan, and cook for 1 hour.

5. Bring water to a boil in a large saucepan. Add salt, let the water return to a full boil, and add the pasta. Cook until the pasta is al dente.

6. Remove the bay leaves from the sauce and discard them. Drain the pasta, stir it into the sauce, and toss to combine. Garnish the dish with horseradish and serve.

Green Linguine with Roasted Sunchokes

YIELD: 4 SERVINGS / **ACTIVE TIME:** 10 MINUTES / **TOTAL TIME:** 40 MINUTES

PASTA ALL'UOVO VERDE
(SEE PAGE 50)

ALL-PURPOSE FLOUR,
AS NEEDED

2 LBS. SUNCHOKES,
SCRUBBED

1 TABLESPOON EXTRA-
VIRGIN OLIVE OIL

SALT, TO TASTE

¼ CUP WATER

1. Preheat the oven to 500°F. Place the dough on a flour-dusted work surface and roll it into a ⅒-inch-thick sheet (you can also use a pasta maker to do this).

2. Roll the dough up around the rolling pin, gently slide it off, and cut it into ⅛-inch-thick strips. Unroll the strips and place them on a flour-dusted baking sheet.

3. Place the sunchokes and olive oil in a large bowl and toss to coat. Season with salt and toss to coat.

4. Warm a large cast-iron skillet over high heat. When it is hot, add the sunchokes and water, place it in the oven, and roast for 20 minutes.

5. Stir the sunchokes and then cook until the sunchokes are well-browned and tender, about 15 minutes.

6. While the sunchokes are in the oven, bring water to a boil in a large saucepan. Add salt, let the water return to a boil, and add the pasta. Cook until it is al dente, 2 to 4 minutes.

7. Remove the sunchokes from the oven and serve.

Spaghetti with Green Beans & Bacon

YIELD: 4 SERVINGS / **ACTIVE TIME:** 10 MINUTES / **TOTAL TIME:** 30 MINUTES

6 SLICES OF UNCURED BACON

2 CUPS TRIMMED GREEN BEANS

SALT AND PEPPER, TO TASTE

14 OZ. SPAGHETTI

2 TABLESPOONS UNSALTED BUTTER, CHOPPED

¼ CUP GRATED PARMESAN CHEESE

DRIED OREGANO, TO TASTE

1. Bring water to a boil in a large saucepan.

2. Warm a large cast-iron skillet over medium heat for 5 minutes. Add the bacon and cook until it is crispy and browned, about 8 minutes, turning it as necessary. Transfer the bacon to a paper towel–lined plate to drain. When it is cool enough to handle, crumble the bacon into bite-sized pieces.

3. Remove all but 2 tablespoons of the bacon fat from the skillet. Add the green beans and cook, tossing to coat, until they are just tender, about 4 minutes. Transfer the green beans to a large bowl and season with salt and pepper.

4. Add salt to the boiling water, let it return to a full boil, and add the pasta. Cook until it is al dente, 8 to 10 minutes.

5. Drain the pasta and add it to the bowl containing the green beans, along with the butter, Parmesan, and bacon. Season with salt, pepper, and oregano, toss to combine, and serve.

Orecchiette alla Materana

YIELD: 4 SERVINGS / **ACTIVE TIME:** 30 MINUTES / **TOTAL TIME:** 1 HOUR AND 40 MINUTES

3 TABLESPOONS EXTRA-VIRGIN OLIVE OIL

¾ LB. LEAN LAMB, FINELY DICED

½ CUP DRY WHITE WINE

1½ LBS. WHOLE PEELED TOMATOES, LIGHTLY CRUSHED

SALT, TO TASTE

1 LB. ORECCHIETTE (SEE PAGE 30)

1⅔ CUPS DICED MOZZARELLA CHEESE

1⅔ CUPS GRATED PECORINO CHEESE

1. Place the olive oil in a large, deep skillet and warm it over medium heat. Add the lamb and cook, stirring occasionally, until it is browned, about 8 minutes.

2. Add the wine and cook until it has evaporated.

3. Add the tomatoes, reduce the heat to low, partially cover the pan, and cook for 1 hour.

4. Bring water to a boil in a large saucepan. Add salt, let the water return to a full boil, and add the pasta. Cook until the pasta is very al dente.

5. Drain the pasta, place it in a large mixing bowl, and add the sauce. Stir to combine.

6. Preheat the oven to 360°F. Place one-third of the pasta in a layer on the bottom of a 13 x 9–inch baking pan and top it with a layer of the mozzarella and pecorino. Repeat the layering process two more times.

7. Place the dish in the oven and bake until the cheese is bubbling, 20 to 25 minutes.

8. Remove the dish from the oven and let it rest for 10 minutes before serving.

Strascinati alla Menta

YIELD: 4 SERVINGS / **ACTIVE TIME:** 10 MINUTES / **TOTAL TIME:** 25 MINUTES

3½ OZ. LARD, CHOPPED

1 DRIED CRUSCO PEPPER, STEMMED, SEEDED, AND FINELY CHOPPED

SALT, TO TASTE

1 LB. STRASCINATI

3 TABLESPOONS FRESHLY CHOPPED MINT

FRESH HORSERADISH, GRATED, FOR GARNISH

1. Place the lard and pepper in a large skillet and warm the mixture over medium-low heat for 5 minutes.

2. Bring water to a boil in a large saucepan. Add salt, let the water return to a full boil, and add the pasta. Cook until the pasta is al dente.

3. Drain the pasta, add it to the skillet along with the mint, and toss to coat.

4. Garnish the dish with horseradish and enjoy.

Pasta al Ragù con Rafano e Mollica

YIELD: 4 SERVINGS / **ACTIVE TIME:** 30 MINUTES / **TOTAL TIME:** 1 HOUR AND 40 MINUTES

3 TABLESPOONS EXTRA-VIRGIN OLIVE OIL

1 ITALIAN SAUSAGE, CASING REMOVED AND CRUMBLED

6 OZ. LEAN PORK, CUBED

1 LB. WHOLE PEELED TOMATOES, LIGHTLY CRUSHED

¼ CUP BREAD CRUMBS

SALT, TO TASTE

1 LB. FUSILLI AL FERRO (SEE PAGE 22)

FRESH HORSERADISH, GRATED, FOR GARNISH

GRATED PECORINO CHEESE, FOR GARNISH

1. Place 2 tablespoons of olive oil in a large, deep skillet and warm it over medium heat. Add the sausage and pork and cook, stirring occasionally, until they are browned, about 8 minutes.

2. Add the tomatoes, reduce the heat to low, partially cover the pan, and cook for 1 hour.

3. Place the remaining olive oil in a small skillet and warm it over medium heat. Add the bread crumbs and cook, stirring occasionally, until they have browned. Remove the pan from heat and set it aside.

4. Bring water to a boil in a large saucepan. Add salt, let the water return to a full boil, and add the pasta. Cook until the pasta is al dente.

5. Drain the pasta, place it in a large serving dish, and add the sauce and bread crumbs. Toss to combine, garnish with horseradish and pecorino, and enjoy.

Strangozzi with Sherry Mushrooms & Pine Nuts

YIELD: 4 SERVINGS / **ACTIVE TIME:** 10 MINUTES / **TOTAL TIME:** 25 MINUTES

2 CUPS PINE NUTS

5 TABLESPOONS EXTRA-VIRGIN OLIVE OIL

PINCH OF KOSHER SALT, PLUS MORE TO TASTE

PINCH OF SUGAR

1 LARGE SHALLOT, MINCED

1 CUP SHERRY

¼ CUP SHERRY VINEGAR

ZEST OF 1 ORANGE

6 CUPS ASSORTED WILD MUSHROOMS

¼ CUP UNSALTED BUTTER

STRANGOZZI (SEE PAGE 36)

1 CUP THINLY SLICED DAIKON RADISH, FOR GARNISH

FRESH PARSLEY, CHOPPED, FOR GARNISH

1. Warm a large cast-iron skillet over medium heat. Add the pine nuts and toast until lightly browned, shaking the pan frequently. Remove from the pan and let the pine nuts cool. When they are cool enough to handle, finely chop them and set them aside.

2. Add 1 tablespoon of the olive oil, the salt, sugar, and shallot to the skillet and cook, stirring occasionally, until the shallot is translucent, about 3 minutes. Add the sherry and vinegar and cook for 5 minutes, until the liquid has reduced. Add the orange zest and then transfer the mixture to a bowl.

3. Add the remaining olive oil to the skillet and warm it over medium heat. Add the mushrooms and cook, without stirring, for 3 minutes. Add the butter, stir, and cook until the mushrooms are browned all over. Remove the mushrooms from the pan, add them to the shallot-and-sherry mixture, and toss to coat. Set the mixture aside.

4. Bring water to a boil in a large saucepan. Add salt, let the water return to a boil, and add the Strangozzi. Cook until they are al dente, 3 to 5 minutes.

5. Drain the pasta and place it in a large bowl. Add the mushroom mixture and toss to combine.

6. Garnish with the daikon radish, parsley, and toasted pine nuts and serve.

THE ENCYCLOPEDIA OF PASTA

Spaghetti alla san Giuannin

YIELD: 4 SERVINGS / **ACTIVE TIME:** 30 MINUTES / **TOTAL TIME:** 1 HOUR AND 40 MINUTES

¼ CUP EXTRA-VIRGIN OLIVE OIL

1 GARLIC CLOVE, HALVED

1 HOT CHILE PEPPER, STEMMED, SEEDED, AND MINCED

6 ANCHOVIES IN OLIVE OIL, DRAINED AND CHOPPED

19½ OZ. CHERRY TOMATOES, HALVED

SALT, TO TASTE

2 TABLESPOONS CAPERS IN BRINE, DRAINED AND RINSED

1 LB. SPAGHETTI

FRESH BASIL, SHREDDED, FOR GARNISH

PECORINO CHEESE, GRATED, FOR GARNISH

1. Place the olive oil in a large, deep skillet and warm it over medium heat. Add the garlic, chile, and anchovies and cook, stirring frequently, for 2 minutes.

2. Add the tomatoes, remove the garlic, and discard it. Season the tomatoes with salt and cook for 10 minutes.

3. Add the capers and a bit of water to the pan, reduce the heat to low, and let the sauce simmer gently.

4. Bring water to a boil in a large saucepan. Add salt, let the water return to a full boil, and add the pasta. Cook until the pasta is al dente.

5. Drain the pasta, add it to the sauce, and cook for 2 to 3 minutes, tossing to combine.

6. Garnish the dish with basil and pecorino and serve.

Pasta al Ragù di Polpo

YIELD: 4 SERVINGS / **ACTIVE TIME:** 50 MINUTES / **TOTAL TIME:** 1 HOUR AND 20 MINUTES

2 LBS. FRESH OCTOPUS

¼ CUP EXTRA-VIRGIN OLIVE OIL

1 GARLIC CLOVE

½ YELLOW ONION, FINELY DICED

⅓ HOT CHILE PEPPER, MINCED

½ CUP DRY WHITE WINE

2 LBS. PEELED TOMATOES, LIGHTLY CRUSHED

1 BAY LEAF

SALT, TO TASTE

1 LB. SCIALATIELLI (SEE PAGE 20)

FRESH PARSLEY, CHOPPED, FOR GARNISH

1. Rinse the octopus thoroughly under cold water and let it drain.

2. Cut the octopus into large pieces, leaving 4 tentacles whole.

3. Place the olive oil in a large, deep skillet and warm it over medium heat. Add the garlic, onion, and chile and cook, stirring frequently, for 5 minutes.

4. Add the octopus and cook, stirring frequently, until it is browned.

5. Add the white wine, raise the heat to medium-high, and cook until the wine has evaporated.

6. Remove the garlic and discard it. Add the tomatoes and bay leaf, reduce the heat to low, and season the sauce with salt. Cook until the sauce has thickened and the octopus is tender, 30 to 35 minutes.

7. Bring water to a boil in a large saucepan. Add salt, let the water return to a full boil, and add the pasta. Cook until the pasta is al dente.

8. Drain the pasta, add it to the sauce, and toss to combine.

9. To serve, top each portion with a long octopus tentacle and garnish with parsley.

Orecchiette con Cime di Rapa

YIELD: 4 SERVINGS / **ACTIVE TIME:** 40 MINUTES / **TOTAL TIME:** 1 HOUR

SALT, TO TASTE

2.2 LBS. TURNIP GREENS, STEMMED AND RINSED WELL

¼ CUP EXTRA-VIRGIN OLIVE OIL, PLUS MORE AS NEEDED

2 GARLIC CLOVES, HALVED

1 HOT CHILE PEPPER, STEMMED, SEEDED, AND FINELY DICED

8 ANCHOVIES IN OLIVE OIL, DRAINED AND CHOPPED

¼ CUP BREAD CRUMBS

1 LB. ORECCHIETTE (SEE PAGE 30)

1. Bring salted water to a boil in a large saucepan. Add the turnip greens and cook until just tender, about 5 minutes. Drain the turnip greens and set them aside.

2. Place the olive oil in a large, deep skillet and warm it over medium heat. Add the garlic, chile, and anchovies and cook, stirring frequently, for 2 minutes. Remove the pan from heat and set it aside.

3. Lightly coat a small skillet with olive oil and warm it over medium heat. Add the bread crumbs and cook, stirring occasionally, until they are browned, about 5 minutes.

4. Bring water to a boil in a large saucepan. Add salt, let the water return to a full boil, and add the pasta. Cook until the pasta is al dente.

5. Add the turnip greens to the garlic mixture and cook over medium heat for 2 to 3 minutes, tossing to combine.

6. Drain the pasta, add it to the sauce, and toss to combine.

7. Top the dish with the toasted bread crumbs and serve.

Orecchiette con Cime di Rapa
SEE PAGE 183

Pasta con le Sarde

YIELD: 4 SERVINGS / **ACTIVE TIME:** 50 MINUTES / **TOTAL TIME:** 2 HOURS

1 LB. FRESH SARDINES

SALT AND PEPPER, TO TASTE

7 OZ. WILD FENNEL, RINSED WELL

PINCH OF SAFFRON THREADS

¼ CUP EXTRA-VIRGIN OLIVE OIL

1 LARGE WHITE ONION, FINELY DICED

5 ANCHOVIES IN OLIVE OIL, RINSED AND CHOPPED

3 TABLESPOONS RAISINS, SOAKED IN WARM WATER

3 TABLESPOONS BREAD CRUMBS

1 LB. BUCATINI

3 TABLESPOONS PINE NUTS

3 TABLESPOONS FINELY CHOPPED BLANCHED ALMONDS

1. Clean the sardines: scrub them, remove the heads, entrails, and spines, and open them completely. Rinse the sardines under running water and pat them dry with paper towels.

2. Bring water to a boil in a large saucepan. Add salt and the fennel and cook until the fennel is tender, about 10 minutes. Remove the fennel from the boiling water with a strainer or slotted spoon and set it aside. When the fennel has cooled slightly, chop it. Keep the water at a gentle boil.

3. Place the saffron in ½ cup water and let it steep.

4. Place the olive oil in a large skillet and warm it over medium heat. Add the onion and anchovies and cook, stirring occasionally, until the onion has softened and the anchovies have dissolved, about 5 minutes.

5. Add the saffron, saffron water, sardines, and fennel. Drain the raisins, squeeze them to remove any excess liquid, and add them to the pan. Cook until the sardines are cooked through and the sauce has thickened, about 10 minutes.

6. While the sauce is cooking, place the bread crumbs in a skillet and toast them over medium heat until they are browned, shaking the pan occasionally.

7. Add the pasta to the boiling water and cook until it is al dente.

8. Drain the pasta and add it to the sauce along with the bread crumbs, pine nuts, and almonds. Toss to combine, season with salt and pepper, remove the pan from heat, and let the dish sit for a few minutes before serving.

Pasta alla Norma

YIELD: 4 SERVINGS / **ACTIVE TIME:** 50 MINUTES / **TOTAL TIME:** 2 HOURS

2 LARGE EGGPLANTS, CUT INTO CHUNKS

¼ CUP COARSE SALT

2 LBS. TOMATOES

6 TABLESPOONS EXTRA-VIRGIN OLIVE OIL

1 GARLIC CLOVE, HALVED

FINE SEA SALT AND PEPPER, TO TASTE

1 LB. RIGATONI

¼ CUP GRATED RICOTTA SALATA CHEESE, FOR GARNISH

FRESH BASIL, SHREDDED, FOR GARNISH

1. Place the eggplants in a colander and season them with the coarse salt. Fill a large saucepan with water and place it on top of the eggplants. Let the eggplants drain for 1 hour.

2. Rinse the eggplants and squeeze them to remove as much water as possible. Place the eggplants on kitchen towels and let them dry.

3. Bring water to a boil in a large saucepan. Add the tomatoes and cook for 1 minute. Remove the tomatoes, peel them, and remove the seeds. Chop the remaining flesh and set them aside.

4. Place 2 tablespoons of olive oil in a medium saucepan and warm it over medium heat. Add the garlic and cook, stirring frequently, for 2 minutes.

5. Remove the garlic and discard it. Add the tomatoes, season with salt and pepper, and cook until the sauce starts to thicken, 20 to 30 minutes.

6. Place the remaining olive oil in a large skillet and warm it over medium-high heat. Add the eggplants and cook, stirring occasionally, until they are golden brown, 5 to 7 minutes. Transfer the eggplants to a paper towel–lined plate to drain.

7. Add the eggplants to the sauce and cook for a few minutes, stirring occasionally.

8. Bring water to a boil in a large saucepan. Add salt, let the water return to a full boil, and add the pasta. Cook until the pasta is very al dente.

9. Drain the pasta, add it to the sauce, and cook for 2 to 3 minutes, tossing to combine.

10. Garnish the dish with the ricotta salata and basil and serve.

Pad Thai

YIELD: 4 SERVINGS / **ACTIVE TIME:** 15 MINUTES / **TOTAL TIME:** 35 MINUTES

6 OZ. THIN RICE NOODLES

3 TABLESPOONS CANOLA OIL

2 LARGE BONELESS, SKINLESS CHICKEN BREASTS, SLICED THIN

1 LARGE EGG

¼ CUP TAMARIND PASTE

2 TABLESPOONS WATER

1½ TABLESPOONS FISH SAUCE

2 TABLESPOONS RICE VINEGAR

1½ TABLESPOONS BROWN SUGAR

4 SCALLIONS, GREEN PARTS ONLY, SLICED

1 CUP BEAN SPROUTS

½ TEASPOON CAYENNE PEPPER

¼ CUP CRUSHED PEANUTS

LIME WEDGES, FOR SERVING

1. Place the noodles in a wide, shallow bowl and cover them with boiling water. Stir and let the noodles rest until they have softened, about 15 minutes.

2. Place the canola oil in a large cast-iron wok or skillet and warm it over medium-high heat.

3. Add the chicken and stir-fry until it is cooked through, about 5 minutes. Remove the chicken from the pan and set it aside.

4. Add the egg to the pan and stir. Add the noodles and return the chicken to the pan. Stir to incorporate and then add the tamarind paste, water, fish sauce, vinegar, brown sugar, scallions, bean sprouts, cayenne pepper, and peanuts. Stir to combine and cook until the flavors have developed to your liking, 2 to 3 minutes. Serve with lime wedges.

Pasta con i Pomodori Secchi

YIELD: 4 SERVINGS / **ACTIVE TIME:** 20 MINUTES / **TOTAL TIME:** 40 MINUTES

6 TABLESPOONS EXTRA-VIRGIN OLIVE OIL

1 GARLIC CLOVE, HALVED

12 SUN-DRIED TOMATOES IN OLIVE OIL, DRAINED AND CHOPPED

3 TABLESPOONS BREAD CRUMBS

SALT, TO TASTE

1 LB. SPAGHETTI

3 TABLESPOONS FRESHLY CHOPPED PARSLEY

PECORINO CHEESE, GRATED, FOR GARNISH

1. Place ¼ cup of olive oil in a large, deep skillet and warm it over medium heat. Add the garlic and cook, stirring frequently, for 2 minutes.

2. Remove the garlic and discard it. Add the tomatoes and cook for 5 minutes.

3. Place the remaining olive oil in a small skillet and warm it over medium heat. Add the bread crumbs and cook, stirring occasionally, until they are browned, about 5 minutes.

4. Bring water to a boil in a large saucepan. Add salt, let the water return to a full boil, and add the pasta. Cook until the pasta is very al dente.

5. Drain the pasta, add it to the sauce along with the parsley, and cook for 2 to 3 minutes, tossing to combine.

6. Garnish the dish with the bread crumbs and pecorino and serve.

Pasta chi Vruoccoli Arrriminati

YIELD: 4 SERVINGS / **ACTIVE TIME:** 50 MINUTES / **TOTAL TIME:** 2 HOURS

SALT AND PEPPER, TO TASTE

1 HEAD OF CAULIFLOWER, CUT INTO FLORETS

5 TABLESPOONS EXTRA-VIRGIN OLIVE OIL

1 CUP BREAD CRUMBS

2 SMALL ONIONS, FINELY DICED

4 ANCHOVIES IN OLIVE OIL, DRAINED AND CHOPPED

2 PINCHES OF SAFFRON THREADS

⅓ CUP RAISINS, SOAKED IN WARM WATER

⅓ CUP PINE NUTS

1 LB. BUCATINI

1. Bring water to a boil in a large saucepan. Add salt and the cauliflower and cook until the cauliflower is tender, about 10 minutes. Remove the cauliflower from the boiling water with a strainer or slotted spoon and set it aside. Keep the water at a gentle boil.

2. Place 1 tablespoon of olive oil in a small skillet and warm it over medium heat. Add the bread crumbs, season them with salt, and cook, stirring occasionally, until they have browned, about 4 minutes. Remove the pan from heat and set it aside.

3. Place the remaining olive oil in a large skillet and warm it over medium heat. Add the onions and anchovies and cook, stirring occasionally, until the onions have softened and the anchovies have dissolved, about 5 minutes.

4. Place the saffron in a cup, add a bit of the boiling water, and let the saffron steep.

5. Drain the raisins, squeeze them to remove any excess liquid, and add them to the skillet along with the pine nuts. Cook for 5 minutes.

6. Add the cauliflower, season with salt and pepper, and cook for 2 minutes. Add the saffron and saffron water and cook, stirring frequently, until the sauce becomes creamy.

7. Add the pasta to the boiling water and cook until it is al dente.

8. Drain the pasta and add it to the sauce along with the bread crumbs. Toss to combine and serve.

Pasta 'Ncasciata

YIELD: 4 SERVINGS / **ACTIVE TIME:** 1 HOUR / **TOTAL TIME:** 2 HOURS AND 30 MINUTES

1 CUP EXTRA-VIRGIN OLIVE OIL, PLUS MORE AS NEEDED

1 WHITE ONION, FINELY DICED

6½ OZ. GROUND BEEF

6½ OZ. GROUND PORK

½ CUP DRY WHITE WINE

1½ LBS. PEELED TOMATOES, LIGHTLY CRUSHED

2 HANDFULS OF FRESH BASIL LEAVES

SALT AND PEPPER, TO TASTE

2 LARGE EGGPLANTS, CUT INTO ½-INCH-THICK SLICES

1 LB. SHORT-FORM PASTA

9 OZ. CACIOCAVALLO CHEESE, CUBED

1 CUP GRATED PECORINO CHEESE

1. Place 2 tablespoons of olive oil in a large, deep skillet and warm it over medium-low heat. Add the onion and cook, stirring occasionally, until it has softened, about 6 minutes.

2. Add the beef and pork, raise the heat to medium-high, and cook, breaking the meat up with a wooden spoon, until it is browned, about 8 minutes.

3. Add the wine and cook until it has evaporated.

4. Add the tomatoes and basil, season with salt and pepper, and reduce the heat to medium-low. Partially cover the pan and cook the sauce for about 40 minutes.

5. Place the eggplants in a colander and season them with salt. Fill a large saucepan with water and place it on top of the eggplants. Let the eggplants drain for 30 minutes.

6. Rinse the eggplants and squeeze them to remove as much water as possible. Place the eggplants on kitchen towels and let them dry.

7. Place the remaining olive oil in a large skillet and warm it over medium-high heat. Add the eggplants and cook, stirring occasionally, until they are golden brown, 5 to 7 minutes. Transfer the eggplants to a paper towel–lined plate to drain.

8. Bring water to a boil in a large saucepan. Add salt, let the water return to a full boil, and add the pasta. Cook until the pasta is very al dente.

9. Drain the pasta and place it in a bowl. Add half of the sauce to the bowl and toss to combine.

10. Preheat the oven to 360°F. Coat a 13 x 9–inch baking pan with olive oil and place one-half of the pasta on the bottom. Top the pasta with a layer consisting of half of the eggplant, one-third of the caciocavallo, a few tablespoons of sauce, and one-third of the pecorino. Repeat this layering process and then top with a layer of the remaining caciocavallo and pecorino. Place the 'ncasciata in the oven and bake until the cheese is melted and bubbling, about 20 minutes. Remove the 'ncasciata from the oven and let it rest for 10 minutes before serving.

Baked Shells with Zucchini, Ham & Béchamel

YIELD: 6 SERVINGS / **ACTIVE TIME:** 1 HOUR / **TOTAL TIME:** 1 HOUR AND 45 MINUTES

2 TABLESPOONS EXTRA-
VIRGIN OLIVE OIL

1 YELLOW ONION,
CHOPPED

SALT AND PEPPER, TO TASTE

3 ZUCCHINI, MINCED

14 OZ. LARGE SHELL PASTA

¼ CUP BREAD CRUMBS

½ LB. FRESH MOZZARELLA
CHEESE, GRATED

½ LB. LEFTOVER HAM,
MINCED

BÉCHAMEL SAUCE
(SEE PAGE 514)

1½ CUPS FRESHLY GRATED
PARMESAN CHEESE

1. Preheat the oven to 375°F. Bring water to a boil in a large saucepan.

2. Place the olive oil in a large skillet and warm it over medium heat. Add the onion, season with salt, and cook, stirring occasionally, until the onion starts to brown, about 10 minutes. Add the zucchini and cook, stirring occasionally, until the zucchini is tender, about 10 minutes. Remove the pan from heat and let the mixture cool.

3. Add salt to the boiling water, let it return to a full boil, and add the pasta. Cook until it just starts to soften, 5 to 7 minutes. Drain the pasta, rinse it under cold water, and place the shells on paper towels to dry.

4. Preheat the oven to 375°F. Combine the zucchini mixture, bread crumbs, cheese, ham, and 1 cup of the Béchamel Sauce in a large bowl, season to taste, and gently stir until combined. Divide the mixture between the cooked shells.

5. Spread ¾ cup of the Béchamel Sauce over the bottom of a baking dish large enough to accommodate the pasta in a single layer. Add the filled shells and pour the remaining Béchamel Sauce over the top. Sprinkle the Parmesan over the top and cover the dish with aluminum foil.

6. Place the dish in the oven and lower the oven's temperature to 350°F. Bake the shells for 20 minutes, remove the foil, and then bake until the tops of the shells just start to turn golden brown, about 10 minutes.

7. Remove the shells from the oven and let them cool briefly before serving.

Spaghetti all'Aragosta

YIELD: 4 SERVINGS / **ACTIVE TIME:** 30 MINUTES / **TOTAL TIME:** 1 HOUR

SALT, TO TASTE

2 MEDIUM LOBSTERS

¼ CUP EXTRA-VIRGIN OLIVE OIL

1 WHITE ONION, FINELY DICED

1 GARLIC CLOVE

1 LB. PEELED TOMATOES, LIGHTLY CRUSHED

1 LB. SPAGHETTI

FRESH PARSLEY, CHOPPED, FOR GARNISH

1. Bring water to a boil in a large pot. Add salt and then the lobsters, making sure they are head down, which will minimize their pain. Cover the pot, reduce the heat to low, and cook the lobsters for 15 minutes.

2. Drain the lobsters and let them cool. When they are cool enough to handle, extract the meat from the lobsters, chop it, and set it aside.

3. Place the olive oil in a large, deep skillet and warm it over medium heat. Add the onion and garlic and cook, stirring frequently, until the onion has softened, about 5 minutes.

4. Remove the garlic and discard it. Add the tomatoes, season with salt, and cook, stirring occasionally, for 20 minutes.

5. Bring water to a boil in a large saucepan. Add salt, let the water return to a full boil, and add the pasta. Cook until the pasta is very al dente.

6. Add the lobster to the sauce. Drain the pasta, add it to the sauce, and raise the heat to medium-high. Cook for 2 to 3 minutes, tossing to combine.

7. Garnish the dish with parsley and enjoy.

Busiate al Pesto alla Trapanese

YIELD: 4 SERVINGS / **ACTIVE TIME:** 30 MINUTES / **TOTAL TIME:** 45 MINUTES

½ LB. TOMATOES

⅓ CUP BLANCHED ALMONDS

2½ CUPS FRESH BASIL

1 GARLIC CLOVE

2 TABLESPOONS EXTRA-VIRGIN OLIVE OIL, PLUS MORE AS NEEDED

5 TABLESPOONS GRATED PECORINO CHEESE

SALT AND PEPPER, TO TASTE

RED PEPPER FLAKES, TO TASTE

1 LB. BUSIATE (SEE PAGE 27)

1. Bring water to a boil in a large saucepan. Cut a cross on the bottom of the tomatoes and add them to the boiling water. Cook for 2 minutes, remove the tomatoes with a slotted spoon, and peel them. Set the tomatoes aside. Keep the water at a boil.

2. Place the almonds, basil, and garlic in a blender and pulse until finely ground. Add the olive oil and puree until the mixture is a paste.

3. Add the tomatoes and 2 tablespoons of pecorino, season the mixture with salt, pepper, and red pepper flakes, and puree until the mixture is smooth and creamy, adding more olive oil if needed to get the desired texture.

4. Add salt to the boiling water, let the water return to a full boil, and add the pasta. Cook until the pasta is al dente.

5. Add a few tablespoons of pasta water to the sauce and stir to combine. Drain the pasta, place it in a bowl, and add the sauce. Toss to combine.

6. Top with the remaining pecorino and serve.

Anelletti al Forno

YIELD: 4 SERVINGS / **ACTIVE TIME:** 1 HOUR / **TOTAL TIME:** 2 HOURS AND 30 MINUTES

1 CUP EXTRA-VIRGIN OLIVE OIL, PLUS MORE AS NEEDED

1 RED ONION, FINELY DICED

9 OZ. GROUND PORK

1 OZ. GROUND BEEF

1 CUP RED WINE

9 OZ. PEELED TOMATOES, LIGHTLY CRUSHED

9 OZ. PEAS

SALT AND PEPPER, TO TASTE

1 LARGE EGGPLANT, CUBED

1 LB. ANELLETTI

3½ OZ. CACIOCAVALLO CHEESE, CUBED

3 HARD-BOILED EGGS, SLICED

7 OZ. TOMINO OR PECORINO CHEESE, GRATED

2 TABLESPOONS BREAD CRUMBS

1. Place 2 tablespoons of olive oil in a large, deep skillet and warm it over medium-low heat. Add the onion and cook, stirring occasionally, until it has softened, about 6 minutes.

2. Add the pork and beef, raise the heat to medium-high, and cook, breaking the meat up with a wooden spoon, until it is browned, about 8 minutes.

3. Add the wine and cook until it has evaporated.

4. Add the tomatoes and peas, season with salt and pepper, and reduce the heat to medium-low. Partially cover the pan and cook the sauce for about 40 minutes.

5. Place the eggplant in a colander and season it with salt. Fill a large saucepan with water and place it on top of the eggplant. Let the eggplant drain for 30 minutes.

6. Rinse the eggplant and squeeze it to remove as much water as possible. Place the eggplant on a kitchen towel and let it dry.

7. Place the remaining olive oil in a large skillet and warm it over medium-high heat. Add the eggplant and cook, stirring occasionally, until it is golden brown, 5 to 7 minutes. Transfer the eggplant to a paper towel–lined plate to drain.

8. Bring water to a boil in a large saucepan. Add salt, let the water return to a full boil, and add the pasta. Cook until the pasta is very al dente.

9. Drain the pasta and place it in a bowl. Add half of the sauce to the bowl and toss to combine. Preheat the oven to 360°F. Coat a 13 x 9–inch baking pan with olive oil and place half of the pasta on the bottom. Top the pasta with a layer consisting of half of the eggplant, one-third of the caciocavallo, one-third of the eggs, a few tablespoons of the sauce, and one-third of the tomino. Repeat this layering process and then top with a layer of the remaining caciocavallo and tomino, and the bread crumbs.

10. Place the anelletti al forno in the oven and bake until the cheese is melted and bubbling, about 35 minutes. Remove the anelletti al forno from the oven and let it rest for 10 minutes before serving.

Spaghetti alla Bottarga

YIELD: 4 SERVINGS / **ACTIVE TIME:** 10 MINUTES / **TOTAL TIME:** 30 MINUTES

SALT AND PEPPER, TO TASTE

1 LB. SPAGHETTI

¼ CUP EXTRA-VIRGIN OLIVE OIL

2 GARLIC CLOVES

3½ OZ. MULLET BOTTARGA, GRATED

¼ CUP FRESHLY CHOPPED PARSLEY

1. Bring water to a boil in a large saucepan. Add salt, let the water return to a full boil, and add the pasta. Cook until the pasta is very al dente.

2. Place the olive oil in a large skillet and warm it over medium heat. Add the garlic and cook, stirring frequently, for 2 minutes.

3. Add two-thirds of the bottarga and parsley, and a few tablespoons of the pasta water to the pan. Cook, gently stirring, for 2 minutes.

4. Reserve 1 cup of pasta water, drain the pasta, add it to the pan, and raise the heat to medium-high. Cook for 2 to 3 minutes, tossing to combine and adding pasta water as necessary to get the desired texture.

5. Top with the remaining bottarga and parsley, season with salt and pepper, and serve.

Malloreddus con Noci e Pangrattato

YIELD: 4 SERVINGS / **ACTIVE TIME:** 15 MINUTES / **TOTAL TIME:** 35 MINUTES

¼ CUP EXTRA-VIRGIN
OLIVE OIL

1 GARLIC CLOVE, MINCED

5½ OZ. WALNUTS, GROUND

2 TABLESPOONS FRESHLY
CHOPPED PARSLEY

1 CUP BREAD CRUMBS

1 LB. MALLOREDDUS
(SEE PAGE 34)

SALT AND PEPPER, TO TASTE

1. Place the olive oil in a large skillet and warm it over medium-low heat. Add the garlic and cook for 2 minutes.

2. Add the walnuts and parsley and cook, stirring frequently, for 2 minutes. Remove the pan from heat and set it aside.

3. Place the bread crumbs in a small skillet and toast over low heat until they are browned, shaking the pan occasionally. Remove the pan from heat and set it aside.

4. Bring water to a boil in a large saucepan. Add salt, let the water return to a full boil, and add the pasta. Cook until the pasta is al dente.

5. Reserve 1 cup of pasta water, drain the pasta, and add it to the pan containing the walnut mixture. Stir in the bread crumbs, place the pan over medium-high heat, and cook for 2 to 3 minutes, tossing to combine and adding pasta water as needed to get the desired texture. Season with salt and pepper and serve immediately.

Mushroom & Béchamel Lasagna

YIELD: 6 SERVINGS / **ACTIVE TIME:** 1 HOUR / **TOTAL TIME:** 2 HOURS

1 CUP DRY RED WINE

¾ LB. PASTA ALL'UOVO (SEE PAGE 47)

ALL-PURPOSE FLOUR, AS NEEDED

2 TABLESPOONS UNSALTED BUTTER

3 SHALLOTS, MINCED

SALT AND PEPPER, TO TASTE

2 GARLIC CLOVES, PEELED AND MINCED

1 LB. CREMINI MUSHROOMS, STEMMED AND SLICED THIN

1 OZ. DRIED PORCINI MUSHROOMS, REHYDRATED, DRAINED, AND CHOPPED, SOAKING LIQUID RESERVED

2 TABLESPOONS FRESH THYME, PLUS MORE FOR GARNISH

BÉCHAMEL SAUCE (SEE PAGE 514)

1½ CUPS GRATED PARMESAN CHEESE

1. Preheat the oven to 350°F. Place the wine in a small saucepan and bring to a boil. Cook until it has reduced almost by half, about 5 minutes. Remove the pan from heat and set the wine aside.

2. To begin preparations for the pasta, divide the dough into 3 pieces. Cover 2 pieces with plastic wrap and place the other on a flour-dusted work surface. Roll it into a ⅟₁₆-inch-thick sheet (you can also use a pasta maker to do this). Cut the sheet into 14-inch-long pieces and place the squares on flour-dusted, parchment-lined baking sheets. Repeat with the remaining pieces of dough.

3. Place the butter in a large, deep skillet and melt it over medium heat. Add the shallots, season with salt, and cook, stirring occasionally, until the shallots are translucent, about 3 minutes. Reduce the temperature to low, cover the pan, and cook, stirring occasionally, until the shallots are tender, about 10 minutes.

4. Add the garlic and cook for 30 seconds. Add the mushrooms and thyme, season with salt, and cook, stirring frequently, until the mushrooms begin to release their liquid. Add the reduced wine and the porcini soaking liquid, and bring to a gentle simmer. Cook, stirring occasionally, until the mushrooms are tender and the liquid has reduced by half, 12 to 15 minutes. Remove the pan from the heat, season to taste, and then stir the Béchamel Sauce into the mixture.

5. Cover the bottom of a deep 13 x 9–inch baking pan with some of the mushroom mixture. Cover this with a layer of noodles, making sure they are slightly overlapping. Cover with a layer of the mushroom mixture and sprinkle ½ cup of the Parmesan on top. Repeat this layering two more times, concluding with a layer of the mushroom mixture topped with the remaining Parmesan.

6. Cover the pan loosely with aluminum foil, place it in the oven, and bake for 35 minutes. Remove the foil and continue to bake until the edges of the lasagna sheets are lightly browned, about 12 minutes.

7. Remove the lasagna from the oven and let it rest for 15 minutes before serving.

Fregola con Salsiccia

YIELD: 4 SERVINGS / **ACTIVE TIME:** 30 MINUTES / **TOTAL TIME:** 50 MINUTES

¼ CUP EXTRA-VIRGIN
OLIVE OIL

1 ONION, FINELY DICED

5 OZ. ITALIAN SAUSAGE,
CASING REMOVED AND
CRUMBLED

¾ LB. FREGOLA
(SEE PAGE 32)

3 CUPS VEGETABLE STOCK
(SEE PAGE 537), WARM

PINCH OF SAFFRON
THREADS

SALT, TO TASTE

½ CUP GRATED SARDINIAN
CHEESE

FRESH PARSLEY, CHOPPED,
FOR GARNISH

1. Place the olive oil in a large skillet and warm it over medium-low heat. Add the onion and cook until it has softened, about 5 minutes.

2. Add the sausage and cook, stirring frequently, until it has browned, about 8 minutes.

3. Add the Fregola to the pan and lightly toast it. Add the stock and cook, stirring frequently, until the broth has evaporated and the dish is moist but not soupy, about 20 minutes.

4. Stir in the saffron, season the dish with salt, and cook for 1 minute. Add the grated cheese and fold to incorporate it.

5. Garnish the dish with parsley and serve.

Fregola con i Carciofi

YIELD: 4 SERVINGS / **ACTIVE TIME:** 40 MINUTES / **TOTAL TIME:** 1 HOUR

6 FRESH ARTICHOKE
HEARTS, SLICED

JUICE OF ½ LEMON

¼ CUP EXTRA-VIRGIN
OLIVE OIL

2 GARLIC CLOVES, MINCED

2 TABLESPOONS FRESHLY
CHOPPED PARSLEY

3 CUPS VEGETABLE STOCK
(SEE PAGE 537), WARM

¾ LB. FREGOLA
(SEE PAGE 32)

SALT AND PEPPER, TO TASTE

½ CUP GRATED PECORINO
CHEESE

1. Place the artichoke hearts and lemon juice in a bowl and cover with water.

2. Place the olive oil in a large, deep skillet and warm it over medium-low heat. Add the garlic and parsley and cook for 2 minutes.

3. Drain the artichoke hearts, add them to the pan, and cook for 3 minutes.

4. Add half of the stock and cook, stirring occasionally, for about 15 minutes.

5. Add the Fregola and cook for 20 minutes, gradually incorporating the remaining broth and letting the Fregola absorb each addition, as you would with risotto.

6. Season the dish with salt and pepper, stir in the pecorino, and serve.

Fregola con i Carciofi
SEE PAGE 205

Fregola con le Vongole

YIELD: 4 SERVINGS / **ACTIVE TIME:** 30 MINUTES / **TOTAL TIME:** 50 MINUTES

2 LBS. CLAMS

SALT AND PEPPER, TO TASTE

¼ CUP EXTRA-VIRGIN OLIVE OIL

1 GARLIC CLOVE

¾ LB. FREGOLA (SEE PAGE 32)

1 LB. CANNED PEELED TOMATOES, CRUSHED

FRESH PARSLEY, CHOPPED, FOR GARNISH

1. Place the clams in a large bowl, cover them with cold water, and stir in 4 handfuls of salt. Let them soak for 2 hours to remove the sand.

2. Drain the clams, rinse them, and set them aside.

3. Place 2 tablespoons of olive oil in a large, deep skillet and warm it over medium-low heat. Add the garlic and cook for 2 minutes.

4. Add the clams, cover the pan with a lid, and cook until the majority of the clams have opened, about 5 minutes. Discard any clams that did not open. Drain the clams and reserve the liquid they release. Strain the liquid and set it and the clams aside.

5. Place the remaining olive oil in the pan and warm it over medium heat. Add the Fregola and cook, stirring continually, for 2 minutes.

6. Add the tomatoes and the reserved liquid and cook for 20 minutes.

7. Remove half of the clams from their shells. Add these and the clams in their shells to the pan, season with salt and pepper, and stir to combine. Garnish the dish with parsley and serve.

Malloreddus alla Campidanese

YIELD: 4 SERVINGS / **ACTIVE TIME:** 20 MINUTES / **TOTAL TIME:** 50 MINUTES

¼ CUP EXTRA-VIRGIN OLIVE OIL

1 ONION, FINELY DICED

11 OZ. ITALIAN SAUSAGE, CASING REMOVED AND CRUMBLED

1⅓ CUPS PEELED AND CRUSHED TOMATOES

SALT, TO TASTE

7 OZ. PECORINO CHEESE, GRATED

¼ CUP WATER

1 LB. MALLOREDDUS (SEE PAGE 34)

1. Place the olive oil in a large skillet and warm it over medium-low heat. Add the onion and cook until it has softened, about 5 minutes.

2. Add the sausage and cook, stirring frequently, until it has browned, about 8 minutes.

3. Add the tomatoes, season with salt, and partially cover the pan. Cook for 30 minutes, stirring occasionally.

4. Place the pecorino and water in a bowl and whisk until the mixture is smooth and creamy.

5. Bring water to a boil in a large saucepan. Add salt, let the water return to a full boil, and add the pasta. Cook until the pasta is al dente.

6. Drain the pasta and add it to the sauce along with the pecorino cream. Raise the heat to medium-high and cook for 2 to 3 minutes, tossing to combine. Serve immediately.

Culurgiones al Pomodoro

YIELD: 4 SERVINGS / **ACTIVE TIME:** 10 MINUTES / **TOTAL TIME:** 20 MINUTES

2 CUPS SUGO AL BASILICO (SEE PAGE 448)

SALT, TO TASTE

1 LB. CULURGIONES (SEE PAGE 33)

½ CUP GRATED PECORINO CHEESE, FOR GARNISH

1. Place the tomato sauce in a medium saucepan and warm it over medium heat.

2. Bring water to a boil in a large saucepan. Add salt, let the water return to a full boil, and add the Culurgiones. Cook until they are al dente.

3. Drain the Culurgiones and add them to the sauce. Toss to combine, garnish with the pecorino, and serve.

Skillet Lasagna

YIELD: 6 SERVINGS / **ACTIVE TIME:** 30 MINUTES / **TOTAL TIME:** 45 MINUTES

2 TABLESPOONS EXTRA-VIRGIN OLIVE OIL

1 ONION, SLICED THIN

4 GARLIC CLOVES, SLICED THIN

2 ZUCCHINI, CHOPPED

1 CUP CHOPPED EGGPLANT

2 CUPS BABY SPINACH

1 (28 OZ.) CAN OF WHOLE PEELED SAN MARZANO TOMATOES, WITH THEIR LIQUID, CRUSHED BY HAND

SALT AND PEPPER, TO TASTE

8 SHEETS OF NO-COOK LASAGNA

1 CUP RICOTTA CHEESE

½ CUP GRATED PARMESAN CHEESE, PLUS MORE FOR GARNISH

½ LB. FRESH MOZZARELLA CHEESE, SLICED THIN

1. Place the olive oil in a large cast-iron skillet and warm it over medium-low heat. Add onion and cook, stirring occasionally, until it has softened, about 5 minutes.

2. Add the garlic and cook, stirring continually, for 1 minute. Raise the heat to medium, add the zucchini and eggplant and cook, stirring occasionally, until the zucchini has softened and the eggplant has collapsed, about 10 minutes.

3. Add the spinach and cook, stirring continually, until it has wilted, about 2 minutes. Transfer the vegetable mixture to a bowl.

4. Cover the bottom of the skillet with a thin layer of the tomatoes and season it with salt and pepper. Top with four sheets of lasagna, breaking off the edges as necessary to fit the pan. Spread half of the vegetable mixture over the lasagna and dot the mixture with dollops of ricotta. Top with one-third of the remaining tomatoes, season them with salt and pepper, and spread the remaining vegetable mixture over the top. Dot the vegetables with dollops of the remaining ricotta. Top with the remaining sheets of lasagna sheets, spread the remaining tomatoes over the top, and then layer the Parmesan and mozzarella over the tomatoes.

5. Season with salt and pepper, cover the skillet, and cook over medium-low heat until the pasta is tender and the cheese has completely melted, 5 to 10 minutes.

6. Uncover the skillet, raise the heat to medium-high, and cook until the sauce has thickened, about 5 minutes. Remove the pan from heat and let the lasagna cool slightly, 5 to 10 minutes, before cutting. Sprinkle basil and more Parmesan over the lasagna and serve.

Pici al Ragù Bianco

YIELD: 4 SERVINGS / **ACTIVE TIME:** 10 MINUTES / **TOTAL TIME:** 20 MINUTES

RAGÙ BIANCO (SEE PAGE 452)

SALT, TO TASTE

PICI (SEE PAGE 44)

1. Place the ragù in a large skillet and warm it over medium heat.

2. Bring water to a boil in a large saucepan. Add salt, let the water return to a full boil, and add the pasta. Cook the pasta until it is very al dente. Reserve ½ cup pasta water and drain the pasta.

3. Add the pasta to the ragù. Add pasta water until the sauce has the desired consistency and cook, tossing to combine, for 2 to 3 minutes. Serve immediately.

Pappardelle al Ragù di Cinghiale

YIELD: 4 SERVINGS / **ACTIVE TIME:** 10 MINUTES / **TOTAL TIME:** 20 MINUTES

RAGÙ DI CINGHIALE (SEE PAGE 453)

SALT, TO TASTE

14 OZ. PAPPARDELLE

1. Place the ragù in a large skillet and warm it over medium heat.

2. Bring water to a boil in a large saucepan. Add salt, let the water return to a full boil, and add the pasta. Cook the pasta until it is al dente. Reserve ½ cup pasta water and drain the pasta.

3. Add the pasta to the ragù. Add pasta water until the sauce has the desired consistency and cook, tossing to combine, for 2 to 3 minutes. Serve immediately.

Gnudi al Pommodoro

YIELD: 6 SERVINGS / **ACTIVE TIME:** 30 MINUTES / **TOTAL TIME:** 40 MINUTES

GNUDI TOSCANA
(SEE PAGE 97)

SALT, TO TASTE

SUGO AL BASILICO (SEE
PAGE 448), WARM

HANDFUL OF FRESH BASIL,
TORN, FOR GARNISH

EXTRA-VIRGIN OLIVE OIL,
FOR GARNISH

1. Bring water to a boil in a large saucepan. Add salt and let the water return to a boil. Working with a few gnudi at a time, add them to the water. Once they rise to the surface, cook the gnudi for another minute and then gently remove them with a strainer or pasta fork.

2. Place the cooked gnudi in a serving dish, add the tomato sauce, and gently toss to combine. Garnish with the basil and olive oil and serve.

Vincisgrassi

YIELD: 6 SERVINGS / **ACTIVE TIME:** 20 MINUTES / **TOTAL TIME:** 1 HOUR

SALT, TO TASTE

10 LARGE LASAGNA SHEETS
OR 40 SMALL ONES

RAGÙ RICCO (SEE PAGE 450)

1½ CUPS GRATED
PARMESAN CHEESE

1. Preheat the oven to 350°F. If using dried lasagna sheets, bring water to a boil in a large saucepan. Add salt, let the water return to a full boil, and add the lasagna. Cook until it is al dente. Drain the pasta.

2. Spread some ragù over the bottom of a large baking dish. Place some lasagna on top, spread a thin layer of ragù on top, and top this with a generous sprinkle of Parmesan. Repeat until you have 10 layers.

3. Place the lasagna in the oven and bake until it is bubbling, about 30 minutes. Remove the lasagna from the oven and let it rest for 20 minutes before slicing and serving.

Strangozzi al Tartufo Nero

YIELD: 4 SERVINGS / **ACTIVE TIME:** 15 MINUTES / **TOTAL TIME:** 25 MINUTES

3½ OZ. BLACK TRUFFLES

5 TABLESPOONS EXTRA-VIRGIN OLIVE OIL

2 GARLIC CLOVES, HALVED

SALT, TO TASTE

STRANGOZZI (SEE PAGE 36)

1. Bring water to a boil in a large saucepan. Using a kitchen brush, remove any soil from the truffles. Cut them into small, thin flakes and set them aside.

2. Place the olive oil in a large skillet and warm it over medium-low heat. Add the garlic and cook, stirring frequently, for 2 minutes.

3. Remove the pan from heat, remove the garlic, and discard it. Stir the truffles into the infused oil and set it aside.

4. Add salt, let the water return to a full boil, and add the pasta. Cook the pasta until it is al dente.

5. Drain the pasta, add it to the truffle oil, and toss to combine. Serve immediately.

Penne all'Arrabbiata

YIELD: 4 SERVINGS / **ACTIVE TIME:** 20 MINUTES / **TOTAL TIME:** 30 MINUTES

¼ CUP EXTRA-VIRGIN OLIVE OIL

2 GARLIC CLOVES, HALVED

2 HOT CHILE PEPPERS, STEMMED, SEEDED, AND SLICED THIN

1.1 LBS. PEELED TOMATOES, LIGHTLY CRUSHED

SALT, TO TASTE

1 LB. PENNE RIGATE

HANDFUL OF FRESHLY CHOPPED PARSLEY

1 CUP GRATED PECORINO CHEESE, PLUS MORE FOR SERVING

1. Place the olive oil in a large skillet and warm it over low heat. Add the garlic and chiles and cook until the garlic is lightly browned.

2. Add the tomatoes, season with salt, raise the heat to medium, and cook, stirring occasionally, for 10 to 15 minutes.

3. Remove the garlic from the pan, reduce the heat to medium-low, and gently simmer the sauce.

4. Bring water to a boil in a large saucepan. Add salt, let the water return to a full boil, and add the pasta. Cook the pasta until it is al dente. Drain the pasta and place it in a bowl.

5. Add the sauce, parsley, and pecorino to the bowl and toss to combine. Serve immediately with additional pecorino.

Spaghetti con Ricotta

YIELD: 4 SERVINGS / **ACTIVE TIME:** 10 MINUTES / **TOTAL TIME:** 20 MINUTES

SALT AND PEPPER, TO TASTE

1 LB. SPAGHETTI

1.1 LBS. RICOTTA CHEESE

1½ CUPS GRATED PECORINO CHEESE

1. Bring water to a boil in a large saucepan. Add salt, let the water return to a full boil, and add the pasta. Cook the pasta until it is al dente.

2. Place the ricotta and pecorino in a large bowl and add a few tablespoons of pasta water. Season with salt and pepper and whisk to combine.

3. Reserve 1 cup of pasta water, drain the pasta, and place it in the bowl.

4. Toss to combine, adding pasta water as needed to get the desired consistency. Serve immediately.

Skillet Tortellini

YIELD: 4 TO 6 SERVINGS / **ACTIVE TIME:** 20 MINUTES / **TOTAL TIME:** 45 MINUTES

10 OZ. PEAS

2 TABLESPOONS EXTRA-VIRGIN OLIVE OIL

1 LARGE YELLOW ONION, MINCED

SALT AND PEPPER, TO TASTE

½ LB. GROUND BEEF

½ LB. GROUND PORK

2 TABLESPOONS TOMATO PASTE

1½ TEASPOONS WORCESTERSHIRE SAUCE

1¼ CUPS CHICKEN STOCK (SEE PAGE 536)

1 LB. TORTELLINI (SEE PAGE 56)

1 CUP PARMESAN CHEESE, GRATED, PLUS MORE FOR GARNISH

1. Place the peas in a colander and run warm water over them for 1 minute. Drain and set aside.

2. Place the olive oil in a large, deep cast-iron skillet and warm it over medium heat. Add the onion, season with salt, and cook, stirring occasionally, until it is translucent, about 3 minutes. Reduce the heat to low, cover the skillet, and cook until the onion is very tender, about 30 minutes.

3. Uncover the skillet, raise the heat to medium-high, and add the ground beef and pork. Season generously with salt and cook, breaking the meats up with a wooden spoon, until they are browned, 8 to 10 minutes.

4. Add the tomato paste and Worcestershire sauce and cook for 1 minute. Add the stock and peas and bring to a boil. Add the tortellini and reduce the heat to medium. Cover the pan and cook, stirring occasionally, until the tortellini are al dente, 2 to 4 minutes.

5. Remove the pan from heat and stir in the Parmesan. Season with pepper, garnish with additional Parmesan, and serve.

Pasta Amatriciana

YIELD: 4 SERVINGS / **ACTIVE TIME:** 30 MINUTES / **TOTAL TIME:** 40 MINUTES

6 RIPE SAN MARZANO TOMATOES

1 TABLESPOON EXTRA-VIRGIN OLIVE OIL

4½ OZ. GUANCIALE, CUT INTO 1-INCH-LONG AND ¼-INCH-WIDE STRIPS

1 CHILE PEPPER

2 TABLESPOONS DRY WHITE WINE

SALT, TO TASTE

18 OZ. SPAGHETTI

1 CUP GRATED PECORINO CHEESE, PLUS MORE FOR SERVING

1. Bring water to a boil in a large saucepan. Add the tomatoes and boil them for 2 minutes. Drain the tomatoes and let them cool. When they are cool enough to handle, peel the tomatoes, remove the seeds, and chop the remaining flesh. Set the tomatoes aside.

2. Place the olive oil in a large cast-iron skillet and warm it over medium heat. Add the guanciale and chile and cook until the guanciale starts to render its fat. Raise the heat to medium-high and cook until the guanciale has browned.

3. Add the wine and cook until it has evaporated.

4. Remove the guanciale from the pan with a slotted spoon. Set it aside.

5. Add the tomatoes to the pan, season with salt, and reduce the heat to medium. Cook for 2 minutes.

6. Remove the chile, return the guanciale to the pan, and gently simmer the sauce.

7. Bring water to a boil in a large saucepan. Add salt, let the water return to a full boil, and add the pasta. Cook the pasta until it is al dente. Drain the pasta and place it in a bowl.

8. Add the pecorino to the bowl and toss to combine. Add the sauce, toss to combine, and serve with additional pecorino.

Pasta Amatriciana
SEE PAGE 219

Beef Stroganoff

YIELD: 4 SERVINGS / **ACTIVE TIME:** 40 MINUTES / **TOTAL TIME:** 1 HOUR AND 30 MINUTES

1 TABLESPOON EXTRA-VIRGIN OLIVE OIL

1 LB. BEEF CHUCK, CUT INTO STRIPS

1 SMALL ONION, MINCED

2 GARLIC CLOVES, PRESSED

½ CUP SLICED MUSHROOMS

1½ CUPS BEEF STOCK (SEE PAGE 538)

¼ CUP DRY SHERRY

1 TABLESPOON WORCESTERSHIRE SAUCE

¼ CUP ALL-PURPOSE FLOUR

SALT AND PEPPER, TO TASTE

½ LB. EGG NOODLES

½ CUP SOUR CREAM

1. Bring water to a boil in a large saucepan.

2. Place the olive oil in a large cast-iron skillet and warm it over medium-high heat. Working in batches if necessary to avoid crowding the pan, add the beef and cook until it is browned all over and cooked through, turning it as necessary. Transfer the beef to a plate and cover it with aluminum foil to keep it warm.

3. Add the onion, garlic, and mushrooms and cook, stirring frequently, until they start to soften, about 5 minutes.

4. Add the stock, sherry, and Worcestershire sauce and bring to a boil, scraping up any the browned bits from the bottom of the pan.

5. Place the flour in a bowl and add some of the warm sauce, whisking until the mixture is a paste. Add a bit more sauce to the bowl and stir until the mixture is smooth. Transfer the slurry to the skillet and stir to incorporate. Cook until the sauce has thickened, 10 to 15 minutes.

6. Add salt to the boiling water, let it return to a full boil, and add the noodles. Cook until they are al dente, 8 to 10 minutes. Drain and set the noodles aside.

7. Reduce the heat under the skillet to low and stir the sour cream into the sauce. Return the beef to the skillet and cooked until it is warmed through. Season the stroganoff with salt and pepper and serve over the egg noodles.

Goulash

YIELD: 6 SERVINGS / **ACTIVE TIME:** 30 MINUTES / **TOTAL TIME:** 2 HOURS AND 30 MINUTES

2 TABLESPOONS CANOLA OIL

3 LBS. BEEF CHUCK, TRIMMED AND CUBED

3 YELLOW ONIONS, CHOPPED

2 CARROTS, PEELED AND CHOPPED

2 BELL PEPPERS, STEMMED, SEEDED, AND CHOPPED

1 TEASPOON CARAWAY SEEDS

¼ CUP ALL-PURPOSE FLOUR

3 TABLESPOONS SWEET HUNGARIAN PAPRIKA

3 TABLESPOONS TOMATO PASTE

2 GARLIC CLOVES, MINCED

1 TEASPOON SUGAR

SALT AND PEPPER, TO TASTE

2 CUPS BEEF STOCK (SEE PAGE 538)

1 LB. WIDE EGG NOODLES

1 CUP SOUR CREAM

1. Place the canola oil in a cast-iron Dutch oven and warm it over medium heat. Working in batches to avoid crowding the pot, add the beef and cook until it is browned all over, turning it as necessary. Remove the browned beef from the pot and set it aside.

2. Reduce the heat to medium-low. Wait 2 minutes and then add the onions, carrots, and peppers. Stir to coat and cook, stirring occasionally, until the vegetables are browned, about 10 minutes.

3. Stir in the caraway seeds and cook until the seeds are fragrant, about 1 minute.

4. Add the flour, paprika, tomato paste, garlic, sugar, salt, and pepper and stir to incorporate. Add the stock and bring the mixture to a boil, scraping up any browned bits from the bottom of the pot.

5. Reduce the heat and let the goulash simmer until it thickens slightly, about 10 minutes. Return the beef to the Dutch oven, cover it, and simmer over low heat until the meat is very tender, about 2 hours.

6. Approximately 20 minutes before the goulash will be done, bring water to a boil in a large saucepan. Add salt, let the water return to a full boil, and add the noodles. Cook until they are al dente, 8 to 10 minutes. Drain and set the noodles aside.

7. To serve, stir the sour cream into the goulash and ladle it over the cooked egg noodles.

Agnolotti Alessandrini

YIELD: 8 SERVINGS / **ACTIVE TIME:** 1 HOUR AND 20 MINUTES / **TOTAL TIME:** 27 HOURS

2.2 LBS. STEW BEEF, CUT INTO LARGE CUBES

26.4 OZ. BARBERA OR OTHER MEDIUM-STRONG RED WINE

1 SMALL ONION, CHOPPED

2 GARLIC CLOVES, HALVED

1 CARROT, PEELED AND CHOPPED

1 CELERY STALK, PEELED AND CHOPPED

1 CINNAMON STICK

4 JUNIPER BERRIES

2 BAY LEAVES

2 OZ. UNSALTED BUTTER

3½ OZ. SPLEEN, CHOPPED (OPTIONAL)

5 OZ. ITALIAN SAUSAGE, CASING REMOVED AND CRUMBLED

SALT AND PEPPER, TO TASTE

1 HEAD OF ESCAROLE

3½ OZ. SALAMI, FINELY DICED

1 EGG (OPTIONAL)

AGNOLOTTI (SEE PAGE 85), CUT AND UNFILLED

ALL-PURPOSE FLOUR, AS NEEDED

1 CUP GRATED GRANA PADANO

1. Place the beef, wine, onion, garlic, carrot, celery, cinnamon stick, juniper berries, and bay leaves in a large bowl and stir to combine. Cover the bowl with plastic wrap and let the beef marinate in the refrigerator for 24 hours.

2. Drain the mixture, reserving the liquid. Remove the beef from the mixture and set the vegetables and aromatics aside.

3. Place the butter in a Dutch oven and melt it over medium heat. Pat the beef dry and add it to the pot along with the spleen (if desired) and sausage. Cook until the meats have browned, turning them as necessary.

4. Add the vegetables, season with salt and pepper, and cook, stirring occasionally, for 5 minutes.

5. Strain the wine into a small saucepan and warm it over medium heat.

6. Add the wine to the Dutch oven, reduce the heat to low, and cover the pot. Cook until the meat starts to fall apart, about 2 hours.

7. While the beef is braising, bring water to a boil in a large saucepan. Add salt and the escarole and cook for 2 minutes. Drain the escarole, finely chop it, and set it aside.

8. Remove one-third of the meat from the Dutch oven and finely chop it. Remove the ragù from heat.

9. Place the finely chopped meat, salami, and escarole in a bowl and stir to combine. If necessary, add the egg to bind the filling together. Set the filling aside.

10. Place a generous teaspoon of the filling in the center of every agnolotti square and fold one side over the filling. Press down on the edges to seal the agnolotti.

11. To cook the agnolotti, bring water to a boil in a large saucepan. Warm the ragù over medium-low heat.

12. Add salt to the boiling water and let the water return to a full boil. Add the agnolotti to the boiling water and cook until they rise to the surface.

13. Remove the agnolotti with a pasta fork and add them to the ragù. Top with the Grana Padano, gently toss to combine, and serve immediately.

Casonsei alla Bergamasca

YIELD: 4 SERVINGS / **ACTIVE TIME:** 30 MINUTES / **TOTAL TIME:** 30 MINUTES

3½ OZ. PANCETTA, CUT INTO STICKS (OPTIONAL)

SALT, TO TASTE

CASONSEI (SEE PAGE 43)

¼ CUP UNSALTED BUTTER

HANDFUL OF FRESH SAGE

3½ OZ. PARMESAN CHEESE, GRATED

1. Warm the oven to 200°F. Place the pancetta in a large skillet and cook it over medium heat until the fat renders, about 4 minutes. Remove the pancetta with a slotted spoon, place it in a crock, and place it in the oven to keep it warm.

2. Bring water to a boil in a large saucepan. Add salt and the Casonsei and cook until they float to the top and the meat is cooked through, about 4 minutes. Remove the Casonsei with a pasta fork and set them aside.

3. Place the butter in the skillet and melt it over medium heat. Add the sage and cook, stirring continually, for 2 minutes.

4. Add the Parmesan and some pasta water and stir until you have a creamy sauce.

5. Add the Casonsei and pancetta to the pan, toss to combine, and serve immediately.

Gnocchi di Patate al Gorgonzola e Noci

YIELD: 4 SERVINGS / **ACTIVE TIME:** 15 MINUTES / **TOTAL TIME:** 25 MINUTES

½ CUP MILK

6 OZ. GORGONZOLA CHEESE

SALT AND PEPPER, TO TASTE

1.1 LBS. GNOCCHI (SEE PAGE 42)

½ CUP WALNUTS, TOASTED AND CHOPPED

1 TABLESPOON FINELY CHOPPED FRESH PARSLEY

1. Place the milk and Gorgonzola in a large saucepan and warm over low heat until the Gorgonzola has melted. Remove the pan from heat and set the sauce aside.

2. Bring water to a boil in a large saucepan. Add salt and the gnocchi, let the gnocchi rise to the surface, and cook for another minute once they do.

3. Drain the gnocchi and add them to the sauce along with the walnuts and parsley. Season with pepper, toss to combine, and serve immediately.

Gnocchi alla Bava

YIELD: 4 SERVINGS / **ACTIVE TIME:** 20 MINUTES / **TOTAL TIME:** 30 MINUTES

1½ CUPS WHIPPING CREAM

9 OZ. FONTINA CHEESE, CUBED

SALT AND PEPPER, TO TASTE

GNOCCHI DI GRANO SARACENO (SEE PAGE 46)

1. Place the cream in a small saucepan and warm it over low heat.

2. Add the Fontina and let it melt very slowly over low heat.

3. Season the sauce with salt and pepper, remove the pan from heat, and cover it.

4. Bring water to a boil in a large saucepan. Add salt and the gnocchi, let the gnocchi rise to the surface, and cook for another minute once they do.

5. Drain the gnocchi and add them to the sauce. Toss to combine and serve immediately.

Gnocchi alla Bava
SEE PAGE 227

Tortellini Modenesi al Sugo

YIELD: 6 SERVINGS / **ACTIVE TIME:** 40 MINUTES / **TOTAL TIME:** 1 HOUR AND 30 MINUTES

2 TABLESPOONS UNSALTED BUTTER

5½ OZ. VEAL, MINCED

5½ OZ. PORK TENDERLOIN, MINCED

SALT AND PEPPER, TO TASTE

3½ OZ. MORTADELLA, FINELY DICED

3½ OZ. PARMA HAM, FINELY DICED

3 CUPS GRATED PARMESAN CHEESE, PLUS MORE FOR SERVING

2 PINCHES OF FRESHLY GRATED NUTMEG

TORTELLINI (SEE PAGE 56), CUT AND UNFILLED

ALL-PURPOSE FLOUR, AS NEEDED

SUGO AL BASILICO (SEE PAGE 448)

1. Place the butter in a Dutch oven and melt it over medium heat. Add the veal and pork and sear until they have browned, turning them as necessary. Remove the meats from the pot, season with salt and pepper, and set them aside.

2. Add the mortadella, ham, Parmesan, and nutmeg. Cook, stirring occasionally, until they have been incorporated. Remove the pan from heat and add the mixture to the pork and veal. Toss to combine and set the filling aside. If a smoother consistency is desired for the filling, place it in a food processor and blitz until it is a paste.

3. Form small amounts of the filling into balls. Place a ball in the center of each tortellini, fold them, and gently press on the edges to seal.

4. Place the tortellini on flour-dusted baking sheets and let them dry for 30 minutes.

5. Place the sauce in a large saucepan and warm it over medium-low heat.

6. Bring water to a boil in a large saucepan. Add salt, let the water return to a full boil, and add the tortellini. Cook until they rise to the surface.

7. Remove the tortellini with a slotted spoon and add them to the sauce. Gently toss to combine and serve with additional Parmesan.

Gnocchi alla Zucca

YIELD: 4 SERVINGS / **ACTIVE TIME:** 40 MINUTES / **TOTAL TIME:** 1 HOUR AND 30 MINUTES

PUMPKIN GNOCCHI
(SEE PAGE 57)

SALT, TO TASTE

6 TABLESPOONS UNSALTED
BUTTER

HANDFUL OF FRESH SAGE

½ CUP GRATED GRANA
PADANO CHEESE

1. Bring water to a boil in a large saucepan. Add salt, let the water return to a boil, and add the gnocchi. Let the gnocchi rise to the surface and cook for another minute once they do. Remove them with a pasta fork and transfer to a bowl.

2. Place the butter in a small skillet and melt it over medium heat. Add the sage, reduce the heat to medium-low, and cook for 2 to 3 minutes. Remove the sage butter from heat.

3. Add the gnocchi to the sauce. Top with the Grana Padano, gently toss to combine, and serve immediately.

Gnocchi alla Zucca
SEE PAGE 231

Tortelli di Zucca

YIELD: 8 SERVINGS / **ACTIVE TIME:** 2 HOURS / **TOTAL TIME:** 3 DAYS

2.2 LBS. PUMPKIN, HALVED, SEEDED, AND CUT INTO WEDGES

5 CUPS GRATED GRANA PADANO, PLUS MORE FOR TOPPING

11 OZ. AMARETTI, CRUMBLED

7 OZ. MOSTARDA MANTOVANA (SEE PAGE 543), MINCED

SALT, TO TASTE

FRESHLY GRATED NUTMEG, TO TASTE

TORTELLI (SEE PAGE 58), CUT AND UNFILLED

½ CUP UNSALTED BUTTER

2 HANDFULS OF FRESH SAGE

1. Preheat the oven to 390°F. Wrap the pumpkin in aluminum foil, place it in a baking dish, and bake until the flesh is tender, about 1 hour.

2. Remove the pumpkin from the oven and scrape the flesh into a mixing bowl. Mash the pumpkin until smooth.

3. Add the Grana Padano, Amaretti, and Mostarda Mantovana, season with salt and nutmeg, and stir until combined. Set the filling aside.

4. Place a generous teaspoon of the filling in the center of every square and fold each square over the filling. Press down on the edges to seal the tortelli.

5. Bring water to a boil in a large saucepan. Place the butter in a large skillet and melt it over medium heat. Add the sage and cook for 2 minutes. Remove the sage butter from heat.

6. Add salt, let the water return to a full boil, and add the pasta. Cook until the tortelli rise to the surface.

7. Remove the tortelli with a pasta fork and add them to the sage butter. Top with a generous amount of Grana Padano, shake the pan to distribute the sauce, and serve immediately.

Cappellacci di Zucca

YIELD: 4 SERVINGS / **ACTIVE TIME:** 1 HOUR / **TOTAL TIME:** 2 HOURS

1.3 LBS. BUTTERNUT SQUASH, HALVED, SEEDED, AND CUT INTO WEDGES

1½ CUPS GRATED PARMESAN CHEESE, PLUS MORE FOR TOPPING

1 EGG

SALT AND PEPPER, TO TASTE

FRESHLY GRATED NUTMEG, TO TASTE

BREAD CRUMBS, TO TASTE

CAPPELLACCI (SEE PAGE 84), CUT AND UNFILLED

ALL-PURPOSE FLOUR, AS NEEDED

¼ CUP UNSALTED BUTTER

HANDFUL OF FRESH SAGE

1. Preheat the oven to 390°F. Wrap the squash in aluminum foil, place it in a baking dish, and bake until the flesh is tender, about 40 minutes.

2. Remove the squash from the oven and scrape the flesh into a mixing bowl. Mash the squash until smooth.

3. Add the Parmesan and egg, season with salt, pepper, and nutmeg, and stir to combine. If the filling is too soft, incorporate some bread crumbs until it has the right consistency. Cover the bowl with plastic wrap and chill it in the refrigerator.

4. Place a generous teaspoon of the filling in the center of every square and fold one corner of the square over the filling, creating a triangle. Press down on the edges to seal the cappellacci. Join the two ends of the base of the triangle together and gently press to seal.

5. Place the cappellacci on flour-dusted baking sheets and let them dry for 30 minutes.

6. Bring water to a boil in a large saucepan. Place the butter in a large skillet and melt it over medium heat. Add the sage and cook for 2 minutes. Remove the sage butter from heat.

7. Add salt to the boiling water and let the water return to a full boil. Add the cappellacci to the boiling water and cook until they rise to the surface.

8. Remove the cappellacci with a pasta fork and add them to the sage butter. Top with a generous amount of Parmesan, shake the pan to distribute the sauce, and serve immediately.

Cappellacci di Zucca
SEE PAGE 235

Cappelletti in Brodo

YIELD: 6 SERVINGS / **ACTIVE TIME:** 1 HOUR / **TOTAL TIME:** 5 HOURS

½ CUP UNSALTED BUTTER

1 MEDIUM CARROT, PEELED AND FINELY DICED

1 CELERY STALK, FINELY DICED

1 SMALL YELLOW ONION, FINELY DICED

7 OZ. LEAN BEEF

5½ OZ. LEAN VEAL

5½ OZ. PORK TENDERLOIN

1 CUP RED WINE

2 CUPS BEEF STOCK (SEE PAGE 538)

A PINCH OF CINNAMON

2 PINCHES OF GROUND CLOVES

2 PINCHES OF FRESHLY GRATED NUTMEG

KOSHER SALT AND PEPPER, TO TASTE

3 OZ. PARMA HAM, FINELY DICED

2½ CUPS GRATED PARMESAN CHEESE, PLUS MORE FOR SERVING

CAPPELLETTI (SEE PAGE 86), CUT AND UNFILLED

ALL-PURPOSE FLOUR, AS NEEDED

6 CUPS CHICKEN STOCK (SEE PAGE 536)

1. Place the butter in a Dutch oven and melt it over medium heat. Add the carrot, celery, and onion and cook until they have browned, about 8 minutes.

2. Add the beef, veal, and pork and sear until they have browned, turning them as necessary.

3. Add the wine and cook until it has evaporated.

4. Add the Beef Stock, cinnamon, cloves, and nutmeg, season with salt and pepper, and reduce the heat to low. Braise until the meats start to fall apart, about 3 hours. Drain the meat and vegetables, place them in a bowl, and let them cool.

5. Mince the meat, return it to the bowl, stir in the ham and Parmesan, and cover with plastic wrap. Chill the filling in the refrigerator for 30 minutes.

6. Remove the filling from the refrigerator and form small amounts of it into balls. Place a ball in the center of each cappelletti square and fold one corner of the square over the filling, creating a triangle. Press down on the edges to seal the cappelletti. Join the two ends of the base of the triangle together and gently press to seal.

7. Place the cappelletti on flour-dusted baking sheets and let them dry for 30 minutes.

8. Place the Chicken Stock in a large saucepan and warm it over medium heat.

9. Add salt and let the stock return to a full boil. Add the cappelletti to the stock and cook until they rise to the surface.

10. Remove the cappelletti with a pasta fork and divide them among the serving bowls. Ladle some broth into each bowl and serve with additional Parmesan.

Ravioli Ricotta e Spinaci

YIELD: 4 SERVINGS / **ACTIVE TIME:** 40 MINUTES / **TOTAL TIME:** 2 HOURS

½ CUP PLUS 1 TABLESPOON UNSALTED BUTTER

14 OZ. FRESH SPINACH

7 OZ. RICOTTA CHEESE, DRAINED

7 OZ. PARMESAN CHEESE, GRATED

FRESHLY GRATED NUTMEG, TO TASTE

SALT AND PEPPER, TO TASTE

RAVIOLI (SEE PAGE 40), UNCUT

ALL-PURPOSE FLOUR, AS NEEDED

2 HANDFULS OF FRESH SAGE LEAVES

1. Place the 1 tablespoon of butter in a large skillet and melt it over medium heat. Add the spinach and cook until it has wilted, 2 to 3 minutes. Remove the spinach, place it in a colander, and let it drain and cool.

2. Squeeze the spinach to remove any excess liquid and chop it. Set the spinach aside.

3. Place the ricotta, half of the Parmesan, and the spinach in a bowl, season with nutmeg, salt, and pepper, and stir to combine. Set the filling aside.

4. Distribute dollops of the filling over one sheet of ravioli, leaving 1¼ inches between each dollop. Moisten the area around each dollop with water.

5. Lay the second sheet of ravioli over the first. Pinch the pasta around the filling so that the 2 sheets get sealed together. Using a pastry wheel, cut the ravioli.

6. Bring water to a boil in a large saucepan. Place the remaining butter in a large skillet and melt it over medium heat. Add the sage and cook for 2 minutes. Remove the sage butter from heat.

7. Add salt to the boiling water and let the water return to a full boil. Add the ravioli to the boiling water and cook until they rise to the surface.

8. Remove the ravioli with a pasta fork and add them to the sage butter. Top with the remaining Parmesan, shake the pan to distribute the sauce, and serve immediately.

Spaghetti Aglio Olio e Peperoncino

YIELD: 4 SERVINGS / **ACTIVE TIME:** 10 MINUTES / **TOTAL TIME:** 20 MINUTES

SALT, TO TASTE

6 TABLESPOONS EXTRA-VIRGIN OLIVE OIL

2 GARLIC CLOVES, HALVED

2 HOT CHILE PEPPERS, STEMMED, SEEDED, AND MINCED

1 LB. SPAGHETTI

HANDFUL OF FRESH PARSLEY, CHOPPED

1. Bring water to a boil in a large saucepan.

2. Place the olive oil in a large skillet and warm it over low heat. Add the garlic and chiles and cook until the garlic is lightly browned. Then remove the garlic from the pan and set aside.

3. Add salt to the boiling water, let it return to a full boil, and add the pasta. Cook until the pasta is al dente.

4. Drain the pasta and add it to the skillet along with the parsley. Raise the heat to medium-high and cook for 2 to 3 minutes, tossing to combine. Serve immediately.

Passatelli in Brodo

YIELD: 4 SERVINGS / **ACTIVE TIME:** 40 MINUTES / **TOTAL TIME:** 3 HOURS

6 CUPS BEEF STOCK, PLUS MORE AS NEEDED

PASSATELLI (SEE PAGE 71)

PARMESAN CHEESE, GRATED, FOR GARNISH

1. Place the stock in a large saucepan and bring it to a boil. Add the Passatelli to the stock and cook until they rise to the surface. Cook for another minute.

2. Divide the passatelli and stock among the serving bowls, garnish each portion with a generous sprinkle of Parmesan, and serve.

Tagliatelle Ragù alla Bolognese

YIELD: 4 SERVINGS / **ACTIVE TIME:** 40 MINUTES / **TOTAL TIME:** 3 HOURS AND 30 MINUTES

2 TABLESPOONS UNSALTED BUTTER

1 CARROT, PEELED AND MINCED

1 SMALL ONION, MINCED

1 CELERY STALK, PEELED AND MINCED

1 BAY LEAF

6 OZ. PANCETTA, MINCED

11 OZ. GROUND PORK

1.1 LBS. GROUND BEEF

⅔ CUP DRY WHITE WINE

1.3 LBS. PEELED TOMATOES, CRUSHED

2 TABLESPOONS TOMATO PASTE

BEEF STOCK (SEE PAGE 538), TO TASTE

⅔ CUP WHOLE MILK

SALT AND PEPPER, TO TASTE

TAGLIATELLE (SEE PAGE 52)

3½ OZ. PARMESAN CHEESE, GRATED

1. Place the butter in a Dutch oven and melt it over medium heat. Add the carrot, onion, celery, and bay leaf and cook until the vegetables have softened, about 5 minutes.

2. Add the pancetta and cook until it starts to brown, about 5 minutes.

3. Add the pork and beef and cook, breaking them up with a wooden spoon, until they have browned, about 6 minutes.

4. Add the wine and cook until it has evaporated.

5. Remove the bay leaf and discard it. Add the tomatoes and tomato paste, reduce the heat to low, and cover the pot. Cook until the sauce has thickened considerably, stirring occasionally and adding stock as necessary, about 3 hours.

6. Stir in the milk, season with salt and pepper, and raise the heat to medium-high. Let the sauce cook until it becomes creamy, then remove it from heat.

7. Bring water to a boil in a large saucepan. Add salt, let the water return to a full boil, and add the pasta. Cook until the pasta is al dente.

8. Drain the pasta and place it in a large serving bowl. Add the sauce and half of the Parmesan and toss to combine. Top each portion with the remaining Parmesan and serve.

Lasagne alla Bolognese

YIELD: 4 SERVINGS / **ACTIVE TIME:** 30 MINUTES / **TOTAL TIME:** 1 HOUR

PASTA ALL'UOVO VERDE
(SEE PAGE 50)

ALL-PURPOSE FLOUR,
AS NEEDED

SALT, TO TASTE

BÉCHAMEL SAUCE
(SEE PAGE 514)

BOLOGNESE SAUCE
(SEE PAGE 458)

7 OZ. PARMESAN CHEESE,
GRATED

2 TABLESPOONS UNSALTED
BUTTER, CHOPPED

1. Preheat the oven to 320°F. Place the pasta dough on a flour-dusted work surface and roll it into a ⅕-inch-thick rectangle. Cut the dough into 7 sheets that will fit your baking dish (8 x 10–inch sheets should be good for four generous portions).

2. Bring water to a boil in a large saucepan. Add salt, let the water return to a full boil, and add the pasta. Cook until the pasta has just softened.

3. Drain the pasta and place it on a kitchen towel to dry.

4. Spread a thin layer of béchamel over the baking dish. Top with a sheet of pasta, cover the pasta with a layer of béchamel, spread a layer of the ragù over the béchamel, and finish with a generous sprinkle of the Parmesan. Repeat until all of the pasta sheets have been used up.

5. Top the last pasta sheet with bèchamel, ragù, the butter, and the remaining Parmesan.

6. Place the lasagna in the oven and bake until the cheese has melted and the top is golden brown, about 30 minutes.

7. Remove the lasagna from the oven and let it rest for 20 minutes before slicing and serving.

Trofie al Pesto

YIELD: 4 SERVINGS / **ACTIVE TIME:** 20 MINUTES / **TOTAL TIME:** 40 MINUTES

SALT, TO TASTE

2 MEDIUM POTATOES, PEELED AND DICED

2 CUPS GREEN BEANS, TRIMMED

1 LB. TROFIE (SEE PAGE 67)

1 CUP BASIL PESTO (SEE PAGE 482)

HANDFUL OF FRESH BASIL

1. Bring water to a boil in a large saucepan. Add salt and the potatoes and boil for 7 minutes.

2. Add the green beans and boil for another 5 minutes.

3. Add the pasta and cook until it is al dente.

4. Drain the pasta and vegetables and place them in a large bowl. Add the pesto and toss to combine, trying not to break the potatoes.

5. Top the dish with the basil and serve.

Pansoti alla Genovese

YIELD: 4 SERVINGS / **ACTIVE TIME:** 1 HOUR / **TOTAL TIME:** 1 HOUR AND 30 MINUTES

2.2 LBS. PREBUGGIÙN (SEE NOTE BELOW)

1 EGG

3½ OZ. LIGURIAN PRESCINSÊUA OR RICOTTA CHEESE

3½ OZ. PARMESAN CHEESE, GRATED

1 TABLESPOON FINELY CHOPPED FRESH MARJORAM

PINCH OF FRESHLY GRATED NUTMEG

SALT AND PEPPER, TO TASTE

PANSOTI (SEE PAGE 108), CUT AND UNFILLED

ALL-PURPOSE FLOUR, AS NEEDED

SALSA DI NOCI (SEE PAGE 456)

1. Place the prebuggiùn, egg, cheeses, marjoram, and nutmeg in a bowl, season with salt and pepper, and stir until well combined. Set the filling aside.

2. Place a spoonful of the filling in the center of each Pansoti square and moisten the edges of the square with water. Fold one corner of the square over the filling, creating a triangle. Press down on the edges to seal the Pansoti. Join the two ends of the base of the triangle together and gently press to seal.

3. Place the Pansoti on flour-dusted baking sheets and dust them with flour.

4. Bring water to a boil in a large saucepan. Place the sauce in a large saucepan and warm it over medium-low heat.

5. Add salt to the boiling water and let the water return to a full boil. Add the Pansoti to the boiling water and cook for about 8 minutes.

6. Drain the pasta and place it in a large serving bowl. Add the sauce, toss to combine, and serve immediately.

Note: Prebuggiùn is a bouquet of wild leafy green vegetables such as borage, nettle, chard, dandelion, wild fennel, wild radicchio, wild poppy leaves, horseradish leaves, wild arugula, pimpinella, and/or chicory. In the absence of these wild greens, use baby spinach, small leaves of chard, arugula, and whatever other small leafy greens you prefer.

Linguine with Asparagus with Garlic Cream

YIELD: 4 SERVINGS / **ACTIVE TIME:** 20 MINUTES / **TOTAL TIME:** 35 MINUTES

SALT AND PEPPER, TO TASTE

2 BUNCHES OF ASPARAGUS, TRIMMED

3 GARLIC CLOVES, MINCED

2 CUPS HEAVY CREAM

3 TABLESPOONS UNSALTED BUTTER

1 CUP DICED PANCETTA

14 OZ. LINGUINE

1. Bring water to a boil in a large saucepan. Add salt and the asparagus and cook until the asparagus is tender, about 2 minutes. Drain the asparagus and let it cool. When it is cool enough to handle, chop the garlic into bite-size pieces.

2. Place the garlic, cream, and butter in a large cast-iron skillet and bring the mixture to a simmer over medium heat.

3. Place the pancetta in an small cast-iron skillet and cook over medium-high heat until it just starts to turn golden brown. Stir the pancetta into the garlic-and-cream sauce, taste the sauce, and adjust the seasoning as necessary. Remove the pan from heat and set the sauce aside.

4. Bring water to a boil in a large saucepan. Add salt, let the water return to a full boil, and add the pasta. Cook until it is al dente, about 8 minutes.

5. Drain the pasta and place it in a large serving bowl. Add the sauce and asparagus, toss to combine, and serve immediately.

Ziti with Charred Broccoli, Pine Nuts & Lemon

YIELD: 2 TO 4 SERVINGS / **ACTIVE TIME:** 20 MINUTES / **TOTAL TIME:** 20 MINUTES

SALT AND PEPPER, TO TASTE

2 CROWNS OF BROCCOLI, QUARTERED

1 EGG YOLK

¼ CUP GRATED PARMESAN CHEESE, PLUS MORE FOR GARNISH

2 TABLESPOONS FRESH LEMON JUICE

1 TEASPOON DIJON MUSTARD

1 CUP EXTRA-VIRGIN OLIVE OIL

14 OZ. ZITI

3 TABLESPOONS CANOLA OIL

½ CUP TOASTED PINE NUTS, FOR GARNISH

1. Bring water to a boil in a large saucepan and prepare an ice bath. Add salt to the boiling water until it tastes like seawater (about 3 tablespoons of salt) and let it return to a boil. Add the broccoli and cook for 1 minute. Remove the broccoli with a strainer and plunge it into the ice bath. Drain the broccoli and let it dry on a paper towel–lined plate.

2. Place the egg yolk, Parmesan, lemon juice, and mustard in a small bowl and stir to combine. While whisking continually, slowly stream in the olive oil until it has emulsified. Taste, adjust the seasoning as necessary, and set the dressing aside.

3. Bring water to a boil in a large saucepan. Add salt, let the water return to a full boil, and add the pasta. Cook until the pasta is al dente, 8 to 10 minutes.

4. While the pasta is cooking, place the canola oil in a large cast-iron skillet and warm it over high heat. Lightly season the broccoli with salt and pepper and place it in the pan, taking care not to crowd the pan. Sear the broccoli until it is lightly charred on both sides.

5. Drain the pasta and place it in a large bowl. Add the broccoli and lemon dressing and toss to combine. Garnish with the toasted pine nuts and serve.

Pasta Cacio e Pepe

YIELD: 4 SERVINGS / **ACTIVE TIME:** 20 MINUTES / **TOTAL TIME:** 25 MINUTES

2 TABLESPOONS BLACK PEPPERCORNS

SALT, TO TASTE

1 LB. TONNARELLI OR SPAGHETTI

3 CUPS GRATED PECORINO CHEESE, PLUS MORE TO TASTE

1. Use a spice grinder or mortar and pestle to coarsely grind the peppercorns. Set them aside.

2. Bring water to a boil in a large saucepan. Add salt, let the water return to a full boil, and add the pasta. Cook the pasta until it is very al dente. Reserve 1 cup of pasta water, drain the pasta, and set it aside.

3. Place 1 tablespoon of the ground pepper in a large skillet and toast it over medium heat for 1 minute. Add a few tablespoons of pasta water and stir to incorporate.

4. Place the pecorino and a few tablespoons of pasta water in a bowl and stir to combine. Set the mixture aside.

5. Add the pasta to the skillet, raise the heat to medium-high, and cook for 2 to 3 minutes, tossing to combine.

6. Pour the pasta into the bowl with the pecorino cream and toss to combine, adding more pasta water if needed to get the desired consistency.

7. Serve with the remaining ground pepper and additional pecorino on the side.

Spaghetti with Roasted Garlic Radicchio

YIELD: 4 SERVINGS / **ACTIVE TIME:** 10 MINUTES / **TOTAL TIME:** 1 HOUR AND 30 MINUTES

¼ CUP EXTRA-VIRGIN OLIVE OIL

8 GARLIC CLOVES, MINCED

2 TEASPOONS MINCED ROSEMARY LEAVES

¼ CUP BALSAMIC VINEGAR

1 ANCHOVY FILLET, SMASHED

SALT AND PEPPER, TO TASTE

4 HEADS OF RADICCHIO, EACH HALVED THROUGH THE ROOT

14 OZ. SPAGHETTI

PARMESAN CHEESE, GRATED, FOR GARNISH

1. Preheat the oven to 425°F. Place the olive oil, garlic, rosemary, vinegar, and anchovy in a large bowl, season with salt and pepper, and stir to combine.

2. Add the radicchio to the bowl and carefully toss to coat. Let the radicchio marinate for 1 hour.

3. Warm a large cast-iron skillet over high heat for 10 minutes, so that it is extremely hot. Using tongs, remove the radicchio from the marinade and arrange, cut side down, in the skillet. Sear the radicchio for a few minutes.

4. Reduce the heat and pour the marinade over the radicchio. Place the skillet in the oven and roast until the radicchio is tender, about 20 minutes.

5. While the radicchio is in the oven, bring water to a boil in a large saucepan. Add salt, let the water return to a full boil, and add the pasta. Cook until the pasta is al dente, 8 to 10 minutes.

6. Remove the radicchio from the oven. Drain the pasta and place it in a large bowl. Add the radicchio and toss to combine. Garnish with Parmesan and serve.

Balsamic Spinach & Shallots with Orecchiette

YIELD: 6 SERVINGS / **ACTIVE TIME:** 10 MINUTES / **TOTAL TIME:** 10 MINUTES

3 TABLESPOONS EXTRA-VIRGIN OLIVE OIL

4 LARGE SHALLOTS, SLICED THIN

2 LBS. FRESH SPINACH, STEMMED, RINSED WELL, AND PATTED DRY

1 TABLESPOON BALSAMIC VINEGAR

SALT AND PEPPER, TO TASTE

ORECCHIETTE (SEE PAGE 30)

1. Place the olive oil in a large cast-iron skillet and warm it over medium-high heat. Add the shallots and cook, stirring occasionally, until shallots are translucent, about 3 minutes.

2. Add the spinach and cook, stirring continually, until the leaves are completely covered by the olive oil and shallots, 2 or 3 minutes. The spinach will start to wilt quickly. Reduce the heat and keep stirring to ensure none of it burns.

3. When the spinach has wilted and is still bright green, splash it with the balsamic vinegar, shaking the pan to distribute it. Season with salt and pepper and remove the pan from heat.

4. Bring water to a boil in a large saucepan. Add salt, let the water return to a boil, and add the Orecchiette. Cook until they are al dente, 5 to 7 minutes.

5. Drain the pasta and place it in a large bowl. Add the spinach-and-shallot mixture, toss to combine, and serve.

Pasta al Ragù Napoletano

YIELD: 6 SERVINGS / **ACTIVE TIME:** 1 HOUR / **TOTAL TIME:** 7 TO 8 HOURS

1 CUP EXTRA-VIRGIN OLIVE OIL

2 YELLOW ONIONS, FINELY DICED

3 (1 LB.) PIECES OF STEW BEEF

6 PORK RIBS

1 CUP RED WINE

1 TABLESPOON TOMATO PASTE

4 LBS. WHOLE PEELED TOMATOES, LIGHTLY CRUSHED

SALT, TO TASTE

1½ LBS. ZITI OR RIGATONI

2 OZ. PECORINO OR PARMESAN CHEESE, GRATED

HANDFUL OF FRESH BASIL

1. Place the olive oil in a large saucepan and warm it over medium heat. Add the onions, beef, and pork ribs and cook until the onions have caramelized and the meat is browned all over, about 1½ hours. You will need to stay close to the pan, turning the meat as needed and increasing or decreasing the heat accordingly.

2. Add the wine and cook until it has nearly evaporated. Remove the meat from the pan and set it aside.

3. Reduce the heat to low, add the tomato paste, and cook, stirring occasionally, for 2 minutes.

4. Add the tomatoes, season with salt, partially cover the pan, and cook, stirring every 15 minutes, for 3 hours.

5. Return the meat to the pan and cook the sauce until it changes from bright red to a deep maroon and the flavor develops to your liking, 3 to 4 hours.

6. Bring water to a boil in a large saucepan. Add salt, let the water return to a full boil, and add the pasta. Cook until the pasta is al dente.

7. Drain the pasta, place it in a serving dish, and add some of the sauce and the smaller pieces of meat along with half of the pecorino and the basil. Toss to combine and top with the remaining pecorino.

8. Serve the larger pieces of meat and remaining sauce following the pasta.

Scialatielli with Smoky Seared Eggplant

YIELD: 4 SERVINGS / **ACTIVE TIME:** 10 MINUTES / **TOTAL TIME:** 30 MINUTES

1 CUP WOOD CHIPS

1 ONION, QUARTERED

2 TEASPOONS KOSHER SALT

¼ CUP AVOCADO OIL

1 SMALL EGGPLANT, TRIMMED AND CUBED

1 RED BELL PEPPER, STEMMED, SEEDED, AND DICED

¼ CUP BALSAMIC VINEGAR

SCIALATIELLI (SEE PAGE 30)

1. Place the wood chips in a small cast-iron skillet and light them on fire. Place the cast-iron pan in a roasting pan and place the onion beside the skillet. Cover the roasting pan with aluminum foil and smoke the onion for 20 minutes.

2. Transfer the onion to a food processor and puree until smooth. Add 1 teaspoon of the salt, stir to combine, and set the puree aside.

3. Place the avocado oil in a large cast-iron skillet and warm it over high heat. Add the eggplant, season it with the remaining salt, and sear it for 1 minute. Turn the eggplant over, add the bell pepper, and cook for another minute.

4. Add the balsamic vinegar and toss to coat. Set the mixture aside.

5. Bring water to a boil in a large saucepan. Add salt, let the water return to a boil, and add the Scalatielli. Cook until they are al dente, 5 to 7 minutes.

6. Drain the pasta and place it in a large bowl. Add the onion puree and eggplant, toss to combine, and serve.

Bucatini with Kale, Raisins & Lemon

YIELD: 4 SERVINGS / **ACTIVE TIME:** 10 MINUTES / **TOTAL TIME:** 25 MINUTES

- 1 TABLESPOON EXTRA-VIRGIN OLIVE OIL
- ½ LB. KALE, STEMMED AND CHOPPED
- 2 GARLIC CLOVES, MINCED
- ¼ CUP RAISINS
- 14 OZ. BUCATINI
- ¼ CUP GRATED PECORINO CHEESE
- SALT AND PEPPER, TO TASTE
- 2 LEMON WEDGES

1. Bring water to a boil in a large saucepan.

2. Place the olive oil in a large skillet and warm it over medium-high heat. Add the kale and cook, stirring occasionally, for 5 minutes.

3. Add the garlic and cook, stirring continually, for 1 minute. Add the raisins and then deglaze the pan with ¼ cup water, scraping up any browned bits from the bottom of the pan. Cook until the water has evaporated and the kale is tender, about 5 minutes. Transfer the mixture to a large bowl.

4. Add salt to the boiling water, let the water return to a boil, and add the bucatini. Cook until they are al dente, 8 to 10 minutes. Drain the pasta and add it to the bowl along with the pecorino.

5. Toss to combine, season the dish with salt and pepper, squeeze the lemon wedges over the top, and enjoy.

Il Cif e Ciaf with Pici

YIELD: 5 SERVINGS / **ACTIVE TIME:** 20 MINUTES / **TOTAL TIME:** 1 HOUR AND 40 MINUTES

½ CUP EXTRA-VIRGIN OLIVE OIL

1 SPRIG OF FRESH ROSEMARY

3 BAY LEAVES

2½ LBS. ASSORTED CUTS OF PORK (BACON, RIBS, LEAN CUTS, ETC.)

1 CUP DRY WHITE WINE

SALT AND PEPPER, TO TASTE

10 GARLIC CLOVES, PEELED

2 DRIED CHILE PEPPERS, STEMMED, SEEDED, AND TORN

PICI (SEE PAGE 44)

1. Place the olive oil in a large cast-iron skillet and warm it over medium-high heat. Add the rosemary and bay leaves and cook for 1 minute.

2. Add the pork to the pan and sear until it is browned all over, turning it as necessary.

3. Deglaze the pan with the wine, scraping up any browned bits from the bottom. Cook until the wine has evaporated, cover the pan, and reduce the heat to low. Cook, stirring occasionally, for 30 minutes.

4. Remove the bay leaves and discard them. Season the dish with salt and pepper and check to see if the pork is sticking to the pan. If it is, add 1 cup water, cover the pan, and cook for another 30 minutes.

5. Preheat the oven to 390°F.

6. Add the garlic and peppers, transfer the pan to the oven, and braise the pork until it is very tender, about 20 minutes.

7. While the pork is braising in the oven, bring water to a boil in a large saucepan. Add salt, let the water return to a boil, and add the Pici. Cook until they are al dente, 6 to 8 minutes.

8. Drain the pasta and remove the pan from the oven. Divide the Pici between the serving plates, top it with the Il Cif e Ciaf, and enjoy.

Spaghetti & Meatballs

YIELD: 4 TO 6 SERVINGS / **ACTIVE TIME:** 30 MINUTES / **TOTAL TIME:** 1 HOUR

¼ CUP EXTRA-VIRGIN OLIVE OIL, PLUS MORE AS NEEDED

2 GARLIC CLOVES, MINCED

1 WHITE ONION, MINCED

1 TABLESPOON KOSHER SALT, PLUS MORE TO TASTE

2 TABLESPOONS CHOPPED FRESH PARSLEY

1 LB. GROUND BEEF

1 LB. GROUND PORK

1 LB. GROUND VEAL

1 CUP LIGHT CREAM

5-INCH PIECE OF ITALIAN BREAD, CRUST REMOVED, MINCED

2 EGGS

¾ CUP GRATED PARMESAN CHEESE

1 TABLESPOON FINELY CHOPPED FRESH BASIL

BLACK PEPPER, TO TASTE

6 CUPS MARINARA SAUCE (SEE PAGE 480)

1 LB. SPAGHETTI

1. Place a Dutch oven over high heat and add 2 tablespoons of olive oil. Add the garlic, onion, and parsley and cook, stirring frequently, until the onion starts to brown, about 8 minutes. Remove the mixture from the pot and let it cool completely.

2. When the onion-and-garlic mixture has cooled, place it in a bowl with all of the meats, the cream, bread, eggs, Parmesan, and basil. Season with salt and pepper and gently stir to combine. Make sure not to overwork the mixture or the meatballs could get a little tough. Place a small piece of the mixture in the Dutch oven and cook until it is cooked through. Taste the cooked piece and adjust the seasoning in the mixture as necessary. Form the remaining mixture into meatballs.

3. Coat the bottom of the Dutch oven with olive oil and warm it over medium-high heat. Add half of the meatballs and cook until they are browned on two sides, about 6 minutes, turning them as necessary. Remove the meatballs from the pan, transfer them to a paper towel–lined plate, and add the uncooked meatballs. Cook them until they are also browned on both sides. Drain any grease from the Dutch oven and wipe it out.

4. Place the sauce in the Dutch oven and warm it over medium-low heat. Bring water to a boil in a large saucepan.

5. Add the meatballs to the sauce, cover the pot, and cook until the meatballs are cooked through, about 15 minutes.

6. Add salt to the boiling water, let the water return to a boil, and add the pasta. Cook until it is al dente, 8 to 10 minutes. Drain the pasta and transfer the pasta to a large bowl. Add the remaining olive oil, toss to coat, and set the pasta aside.

7. When the meatballs are nearly done cooking, add the pasta to the Dutch oven and stir until it is warmed through. Serve immediately.

Spaghetti & Meatballs
SEE PAGE 257

Tagliatelle with Spicy Sausage & Summer Vegetables

YIELD: 6 SERVINGS / **ACTIVE TIME:** 35 MINUTES / **TOTAL TIME:** 1 HOUR

2 TABLESPOONS UNSALTED BUTTER

1 ONION, DICED

2 GARLIC CLOVES, MINCED

1 LB. HOT ITALIAN SAUSAGE, SLICED

2 TEASPOONS CHILI POWDER

½ TEASPOON CAYENNE PEPPER

2 RED BELL PEPPERS, STEMMED, SEEDED, AND DICED

KERNELS FROM 3 EARS OF CORN

1 SMALL ZUCCHINI, CUT INTO THIN HALF-MOONS

4 TOMATOES, SEEDED AND CHOPPED

SALT AND PEPPER, TO TASTE

14 OZ. TAGLIATELLE (SEE PAGE 52)

FRESH PARSLEY, CHOPPED, FOR GARNISH

1. Place the butter in a large cast-iron skillet and melt it over medium-high heat. Add the onion and garlic and cook, stirring frequently, until they have softened, about 5 minutes.

2. Add the sausage and cook until it is browned all over, about 5 minutes, turning it as necessary.

3. Bring water to a boil in a large saucepan. Stir the chili powder and cayenne into the skillet and cook for 1 minute. Add the peppers, corn, zucchini, and tomatoes, stir to combine, and season with salt and pepper.

4. Cover the skillet, reduce the heat to medium, and cook until the sausage is cooked through and the vegetables are tender, about 20 minutes.

5. Add salt to the boiling water, let the water return to a boil, and add the pasta. Cook until it is al dente, 8 to 10 minutes. Drain the pasta and transfer the pasta to a large bowl.

6. Add the sausage-and-vegetable mixture to the bowl and toss to combine. Garnish with parsley and serve.

Mussels with Tomatoes & Orzo

YIELD: 6 SERVINGS / **ACTIVE TIME:** 30 MINUTES / **TOTAL TIME:** 45 MINUTES

3 TABLESPOONS EXTRA-VIRGIN OLIVE OIL, PLUS MORE AS NEEDED

2 GARLIC CLOVES, SLICED THIN

1 LARGE SHALLOT, SLICED THIN

4 SCALLIONS, TRIMMED AND SLICED THIN, GREENS RESERVED FOR GARNISH

1 CUP ORZO

¼ CUP SUN-DRIED TOMATOES IN OLIVE OIL, DRAINED AND SLICED THIN

4 CUPS CHERRY TOMATOES

1½ CUPS CHICKEN STOCK (SEE PAGE 536)

½ CUP WHITE WINE

SALT AND PEPPER, TO TASTE

3 LBS. P.E.I. MUSSELS, RINSED WELL AND DEBEARDED

FRESH BASIL, CHOPPED, FOR GARNISH

CRUSTY BREAD, FOR SERVING

1. Preheat the oven to 350°F. Place the olive oil in a large cast-iron skillet and warm it over medium-high heat. Add the garlic, shallot, and scallion whites and cook, stirring frequently, for 3 minutes. Stir in the orzo and sun-dried tomatoes and cook, stirring occasionally, until the orzo is lightly toasted, about 2 minutes.

2. Add the cherry tomatoes, stock, and white wine, season with salt and pepper, and transfer the skillet to the oven. Cook until the orzo is al dente and the tomatoes begin to burst, about 10 minutes.

3. Remove the skillet from the oven and place the hinge of each mussel into the orzo, ensuring that the openings of the mussels are facing upward. Return the pan to the oven and bake until the majority of the mussels have opened, 5 to 7 minutes.

4. Remove the pan from the oven and discard any unopened mussels. Drizzle olive oil over the dish, garnish with basil and the scallion greens, and serve with crusty bread.

Fettuccine with Garlic Shrimp

YIELD: 4 SERVINGS / **ACTIVE TIME:** 10 MINUTES / **TOTAL TIME:** 30 MINUTES

¼ CUP UNSALTED BUTTER, SOFTENED

1 LB. SHRIMP, SHELLS REMOVED, DEVEINED

8 GARLIC CLOVES, MINCED

½ TEASPOON LEMON-PEPPER SEASONING

1 LB. FETTUCCINE

1 TABLESPOON FRESH LEMON JUICE

1 TABLESPOON FINELY CHOPPED FRESH CHIVES OR PARSLEY, FOR GARNISH

1. Bring water to a boil in a large saucepan.

2. Place a large skillet over medium heat and add the butter. When the butter has melted and is foaming, add the shrimp and cook, without stirring, for 3 minutes. Remove the shrimp from the pan with a slotted spoon and set them aside.

3. Reduce the heat to medium-low and add the garlic and lemon-pepper seasoning. Cook until the garlic has softened, about 3 minutes. Remove the pan from heat.

4. Add salt to the boiling water, let the water return to a boil, and add the fettuccine. Cook until they are al dente, 8 to 10 minutes. Reserve ¼ cup pasta water and drain the pasta.

5. Add the shrimp, pasta, and pasta water to the skillet and cook until everything is warmed through and combined. Sprinkle the lemon juice over the dish, garnish with the chives or parsley, and serve.

Farfalle with Spicy Broccolini

YIELD: 4 SERVINGS / **ACTIVE TIME:** 15 MINUTES / **TOTAL TIME:** 15 MINUTES

½ LB. BROCCOLINI, TRIMMED

SALT AND PEPPER, TO TASTE

FARFALLE (SEE PAGE 60)

2 TABLESPOONS EXTRA-VIRGIN OLIVE OIL

6 GARLIC CLOVES, MINCED

1½ TABLESPOONS RED WINE VINEGAR

¼ TEASPOON RED PEPPER FLAKES, OR TO TASTE

SLIVERED ALMONDS, TOASTED, FOR GARNISH

1. Bring water to a boil in a large saucepan. Add salt until the water tastes like seawater and let it return to a full boil. Add the broccolini and cook for 30 seconds. Remove the broccolini with a strainer and transfer it to a paper towel–lined plate.

2. Add the Farfalle to the boiling water and cook until it is al dente, 2 to 4 minutes. Drain the pasta and set it aside.

3. Coat a large cast-iron skillet with olive oil and warm it over medium-high heat. Add the broccolini and cook until it is well browned on one side. Turn the broccolini over, season with salt and pepper, and cook until browned all over.

4. Add the garlic, vinegar, red pepper flakes, and pasta to the skillet and cook, tossing to combine. Garnish with toasted almonds and serve.

Pizzoccheri with Radicchio & Chickpeas

YIELD: 4 SERVINGS / **ACTIVE TIME:** 40 MINUTES / **TOTAL TIME:** 24 HOURS

⅔ CUP DRIED CHICKPEAS, SOAKED OVERNIGHT

1 TABLESPOON EXTRA-VIRGIN OLIVE OIL

1 SMALL HEAD OF RADICCHIO, CORED AND SLICED THIN

1 SHALLOT, MINCED

1 GARLIC CLOVE, MINCED

¼ CUP WHITE WINE

¼ CUP VEGETABLE STOCK (SEE PAGE 537)

SALT AND PEPPER, TO TASTE

PIZZOCCHERI (SEE PAGE 62)

½ TEASPOON FRESH THYME

PARMESAN CHEESE, GRATED, FOR GARNISH

BALSAMIC VINEGAR, FOR DRIZZLING

1. Drain the chickpeas. Place them in a large saucepan, cover them with water, and bring to a gentle simmer. Reduce the heat so that the chickpeas simmer and cook, stirring occasionally, until they are tender, 45 minutes to 1 hour. Drain and set the chickpeas aside.

2. Bring water to a boil in a large saucepan.

3. Place the olive oil in a large skillet and warm it over medium heat. Add the radicchio and cook, stirring frequently, until it starts to wilt and brown, about 5 minutes.

4. Stir in the shallot and garlic and cook, stirring continually, until the garlic starts to brown, about 1 minute. Deglaze the pan with the wine and stock and cook until the liquid has reduced by half.

5. Add salt to the boiling water, let the water return to a full boil, and add the pasta. Cook until the pasta is al dente, 4 to 6 minutes. Reserve ¼ cup pasta water and drain the pasta.

6. Add the chickpeas, pasta, and pasta water to the radicchio mixture along with the thyme. Season the mixture with salt and pepper, cook until the liquid has reduced slightly, and then remove the pan from heat. Garnish with Parmesan, drizzle balsamic vinegar over the top, and serve.

Frittata with Pasta

YIELD: 6 TO 8 SERVINGS / **ACTIVE TIME:** 15 MINUTES / **TOTAL TIME:** 2 HOURS AND 30 MINUTES

2 CUPS COOKED, LEFTOVER SPAGHETTI

3 EGGS, BEATEN

2 TABLESPOONS FRESHLY GRATED PARMESAN CHEESE

½ CUP CHOPPED FRESH HERBS

SALT AND PEPPER, TO TASTE

EXTRA-VIRGIN OLIVE OIL, AS NEEDED

1. Preheat the oven to 375°F. Place the pasta and eggs in a bowl, stir to combine, and then stir in the Parmesan and fresh herbs. Season with salt and pepper and set the mixture aside.

2. Add olive oil to a large, deep cast-iron skillet until it is about ½ inch deep and warm it over medium heat. Add the frittata mixture and cook until you can lift it up and look at the bottom of it. Place the frittata in the oven and bake until the frittata is just firm to the touch.

3. Remove the pan from the oven and let the frittata sit at room temperature for 2 hours before serving, or refrigerate, letting it return to room temperature before slicing and serving.

Garganelli with Roasted Asparagus, Fried Eggs & Lemon–Pepper Mayonnaise

YIELD: 4 TO 6 SERVINGS / **ACTIVE TIME:** 20 MINUTES / **TOTAL TIME:** 35 MINUTES

FOR THE PASTA

SALT AND PEPPER, TO TASTE

2 BUNCHES OF ASPARAGUS, TRIMMED

2 TABLESPOONS EXTRA-VIRGIN OLIVE OIL

GARGANELLI (SEE PAGE 64)

2 TABLESPOONS UNSALTED BUTTER

6 EGGS

PARMESAN CHEESE, GRATED, FOR GARNISH

FOR THE MAYONNAISE

1 CUP MAYONNAISE

3 TABLESPOONS FRESHLY GRATED PARMESAN CHEESE

1 TABLESPOON LEMON ZEST

3 TABLESPOONS FRESH LEMON JUICE

1½ TEASPOONS BLACK PEPPER

2 TEASPOONS KOSHER SALT

1. Preheat the oven to 400°F. To begin preparations for the pasta, bring a large pot of salted water to a boil and prepare an ice bath in a large bowl.

2. Place the asparagus in the boiling water and cook for 30 seconds. Remove the asparagus with a strainer and transfer it to the ice bath. Let it sit until it is completely cool, about 3 minutes. Transfer the asparagus to a kitchen towel and let it dry. Keep the water boiling.

3. To prepare the mayonnaise, place all of the ingredients in a mixing bowl and whisk to combine. Set aside.

4. Pat the asparagus dry. Place the olive oil in a large skillet and warm it over medium-high heat. Working in batches to avoid crowding the pan, add the asparagus and cook until it is browned all over, turning it as necessary. Transfer cooked asparagus to a plate and tent it with aluminum foil to keep it warm.

5. Add the pasta to the boiling water and cook until it is al dente, 8 to 10 minutes.

6. While the pasta is cooking, place the butter in a cast-iron skillet and melt it over medium heat. Crack the eggs into the pan, taking care not to break the yolks. Season the eggs with salt and pepper and place the skillet in the oven. Cook until the whites are cooked through, 2 to 3 minutes. Remove them from the oven.

7. Drain the pasta. To serve, spread some of the mayonnaise on each serving plate and lay some asparagus on top. Top with the pasta and an egg and garnish with the Parmesan.

Pappardelle with Roman-Style Fava Beans

YIELD: 4 SERVINGS / **ACTIVE TIME:** 25 MINUTES / **TOTAL TIME:** 50 MINUTES

2 TABLESPOONS EXTRA-VIRGIN OLIVE OIL

2 TABLESPOONS MINCED ONION

4 OZ. PANCETTA OR BACON, CHOPPED

¾ LB. SHELLED AND PEELED FAVA BEANS

SALT AND PEPPER, TO TASTE

1 LB. PAPPARDELLE

2 TABLESPOONS UNSALTED BUTTER

¼ CUP GRATED PECORINO CHEESE

1. Bring water to a boil in a large saucepan.

2. Place the olive oil in a large skillet and warm it over medium heat. Add the onion and cook, stirring frequently, until it is translucent, about 3 minutes.

3. Add the pancetta and cook, stirring occasionally, for 2 minutes. Add ⅓ cup of water and the beans, season the mixture with pepper, and bring to a gentle simmer. Cover the pan and cook until the fava beans are tender, 10 to 15 minutes.

4. Add the pasta to the boiling water and cook until it is al dente, 2 to 4 minutes for fresh pasta, and 8 to 10 for dried pasta. Reserve ¼ cup pasta water and drain the pasta.

5. Add the butter, pecorino, pasta, and pasta water to the fava bean mixture, season with salt, raise the heat to high, and cook until the liquid has reduced slightly. Serve immediately.

Bucatini alla Gricia

YIELD: 4 SERVINGS / **ACTIVE TIME:** 10 MINUTES / **TOTAL TIME:** 30 MINUTES

½ LB. GUANCIALE, DICED

½ TEASPOON BLACK PEPPER, PLUS MORE TO TASTE

SALT, TO TASTE

¾ LB. BUCATINI

1 TEASPOON EXTRA-VIRGIN OLIVE OIL

⅓ CUP GRATED PECORINO CHEESE, PLUS MORE FOR GARNISH

1. Bring water to a boil in a large saucepan.

2. Place the guanciale in a large, deep skillet and cook over medium heat, stirring occasionally, until the guanciale's fat renders and its edges start to brown, about 20 minutes. Stir in the pepper and remove the skillet from the heat.

3. Add salt to the boiling water, let it return to a full boil, and add the pasta. Cook until it is very al dente, 6 to 8 minutes. Reserve ¾ cup of pasta water, drain the pasta, and return the pot to the stove. Add the pasta water and the olive oil, raise the heat to high, add the pasta, and toss to combine.

4. Stir in the guanciale, its rendered fat, and the pecorino and cook, tossing to combine. Season the dish with salt and pepper, garnish with additional pecorino, and serve.

Bucatini alla Gricia
SEE PAGE 269

Orecchiette with Greens & Potatoes

YIELD: 4 SERVINGS / **ACTIVE TIME:** 20 MINUTES / **TOTAL TIME:** 30 MINUTES

6 TABLESPOONS EXTRA-VIRGIN OLIVE OIL, PLUS 1 TEASPOON

2 GARLIC CLOVES, HALVED

1 TEASPOON CAPERS, DRAINED, RINSED, AND MINCED

½ CUP GREEN OLIVES, PITTED AND MINCED

⅛ TEASPOON CAYENNE PEPPER

SALT AND BLACK PEPPER, TO TASTE

2 LARGE RUSSET POTATOES, PEELED AND CHOPPED

¾ LB. ORECCHIETTE (SEE PAGE 30)

½ LB. BITTER GREENS

¼ CUP GRATED PECORINO CHEESE, PLUS MORE FOR GARNISH

1. Bring water to a boil in a large saucepan.

2. Place 6 tablespoons of the olive oil in a large, deep skillet and warm it over low heat. Add the garlic, capers, olives, and cayenne and cook, stirring frequently, until the garlic starts to brown, about 3 minutes. Discard the garlic and remove the pan from heat.

3. Add salt and the potatoes to the boiling water. When the water returns to a boil, add the pasta and cook until it is al dente, 8 to 10 minutes, adding the greens 1 minute prior to the pasta being done.

4. Reserve ½ cup of the pasta water, drain, and return the saucepan to the stove.

5. Set the skillet containing the garlic-and-olive mixture over medium-high heat. Add reserved pasta water to the saucepan, turn heat to high, and add the pasta, potatoes, greens, and the remaining olive oil. Toss until the pasta water has been absorbed.

6. Transfer the mixture to the skillet and cook, tossing to combine. Add the pecorino and toss until it has melted.

7. Season the dish with salt and pepper and garnish with additional pecorino before serving.

Butternut Squash Ravioli

YIELD: 4 SERVINGS / **ACTIVE TIME:** 30 MINUTES / **TOTAL TIME:** 1 HOUR AND 30 MINUTES

1½ LBS. BUTTERNUT SQUASH, HALVED LENGTHWISE AND SEEDED

EXTRA-VIRGIN OLIVE OIL, AS NEEDED

¼ CUP FRESH BREAD CRUMBS

½ CUP GRATED PARMESAN CHEESE, PLUS MORE FOR GARNISH

¼ CUP CRUMBLED GORGONZOLA CHEESE

2 EGG YOLKS, BEATEN

1 TEASPOON FRESHLY GRATED NUTMEG

1 TEASPOON FINELY CHOPPED FRESH ROSEMARY

RAVIOLI (SEE PAGE 40), UNCUT

SALT, TO TASTE

CREAMY LEEK SAUCE (SEE PAGE 511), FOR SERVING

1. Preheat the oven to 375°F. Brush the flesh of the squash with olive oil and place them, cut side up, on parchment-lined baking sheets. Place the squash in the oven and roast until it is fork-tender, 40 to 45 minutes.

2. Remove the squash from the oven and let it cool, then scoop the flesh into a bowl and mash until it is smooth. Add the bread crumbs, cheeses, egg yolks, nutmeg, and rosemary to the mashed squash and stir until thoroughly combined.

3. Bring a large saucepan of water to a boil and make the ravioli as instructed, filling the depressions with the butternut squash mixture.

4. When the water is boiling, add salt, let the water return to a full boil, and add the ravioli. Cook until they are al dente, 2 to 4 minutes.

5. Drain the ravioli, divide them among the serving plates, and drizzle the sauce over the top. Garnish with additional Parmesan and serve.

Butternut Squash Ravioli
SEE PAGE 273

Vegetarian Rotolo

YIELD: 6 SERVINGS / **ACTIVE TIME:** 35 MINUTES / **TOTAL TIME:** 1 HOUR

1. Divide the dough into 3 pieces. Cover 2 pieces with plastic wrap and place the other on a flour-dusted work surface. Roll it into a ⅟₁₆-inch-thick sheet (you can also use a pasta maker to do this).

2. Cut the sheet into 15-inch-long pieces that are each about 4 inches wide. Dust the pieces with flour, place them on a flour-dusted, parchment-lined baking sheet, and cover them with plastic wrap. Repeat with the remaining pieces of dough.

3. Bring water to a boil in a large saucepan. Preheat the oven to 475°F.

4. Place the olive oil in a large skillet and warm it over medium heat. Add the scallions and a pinch of salt and cook, stirring occasionally, until the scallions are translucent, about 3 minutes. Raise the heat to medium-high, add the mushrooms, tofu, cabbage, and carrots and cook, stirring until all the vegetables start to soften, about 5 minutes.

5. Place 2 tablespoons of the water, the sugar, and pepper in a small bowl. Place the cornstarch and the remaining water in another bowl, whisk it until smooth, and then whisk it into the water-and-sugar mixture. Stir the resulting mixture into the skillet and raise the heat to high. Cook until the liquid has evaporated and the vegetables are cooked through, 2 to 4 minutes. Remove the pan from heat and let the mixture cool slightly. Transfer it to a food processor and pulse until it is a chunky puree. Season with salt and set it aside.

6. Add salt to the boiling water, let it return to a full boil, and add a single piece of pasta. Cook for 1 minute, retrieve the sheet using a pasta fork or two large slotted spoons, transfer it to a kitchen towel, and let it cool. Repeat until all the pasta sheets have been cooked.

7. Generously coat a 15 x 10–inch baking pan with olive oil. Working with one piece of pasta at a time, lay it on a work surface covered with parchment paper. Using a rubber spatula, spread some of the puree over the sheet and sprinkle some of the parsley on top. Starting at one of the short ends, roll the pasta up tightly. Rest the roll on its seam to keep it from unrolling, or secure the roll with toothpicks. When all of the pasta sheets and filling have been used up, slice each roll into 1¼-inch-thick rounds. Place them in the baking dish, making sure to leave space between. Place the pan in the oven and bake until the rotolo are lightly browned on top and warmed through, 10 to 12 minutes.

8. Remove the rotolo from the oven and let it rest for 10 minutes. To serve, place 2 to 3 tablespoons of the sauce on each of the warm serving plates, arrange three rotolo slices on top of the sauce, and garnish with additional parsley.

PASTA ALL'UOVO (SEE PAGE 47)

ALL-PURPOSE FLOUR, AS NEEDED

5 TABLESPOONS EXTRA-VIRGIN OLIVE OIL, PLUS MORE AS NEEDED

10 SCALLIONS, TRIMMED AND SLICED THIN

SALT, TO TASTE

1 LB. CREMINI MUSHROOMS, STEMMED AND MINCED

1 LB. EXTRA-FIRM TOFU, DRAINED AND CUT INTO ½-INCH SLICES

4 CUPS SHREDDED CABBAGE

4 CARROTS, PEELED AND GRATED

3 TABLESPOONS WATER

2 TABLESPOONS CASTER (SUPERFINE) SUGAR

1 TEASPOON WHITE PEPPER

4 TEASPOONS CORNSTARCH

2 HANDFULS OF FRESH PARSLEY, CHOPPED, PLUS MORE FOR GARNISH

2 CUPS MARINARA SAUCE (SEE PAGE 480), WARMED

Baked Rigatoni with Mushrooms, Leeks & Sausage

YIELD: 6 SERVINGS / **ACTIVE TIME:** 1 HOUR AND 30 MINUTES / **TOTAL TIME:** 2 HOURS AND 30 MINUTES

1. Bring water to a boil in a large saucepan. Add salt, let the water return to a full boil, and add the pasta. Cook until it is just starting to soften, 5 to 7 minutes. Drain the rigatoni, rinse it under cold water, and drain it again. Transfer the rigatoni to a bowl, add ½ tablespoon of the olive oil, toss to coat, and set the pasta aside.

2. Preheat the oven to 350°F. Place the porcini mushrooms in a small bowl, cover with warm water, and soak until they have softened, about 15 minutes. Lightly run your fingers across all the pieces to dislodge any dirt or debris.

3. Gather the porcini mushrooms in your hand and gently squeeze over the bowl to remove excess water. Chop them and set them aside. Strain the soaking liquid through a paper towel–lined fine-mesh sieve and reserve 1½ cups. Set aside.

4. Place 2 tablespoons of butter and 2 tablespoons of olive oil in a large skillet and warm the mixture over medium heat. Add the leeks, season with salt, and cook, stirring occasionally, until the leeks are tender, about 10 to 12 minutes. Remove the pan from heat, season the leeks with pepper, and stir in the nutmeg. Transfer the leeks to a bowl and set them aside.

5. Place 2 tablespoons of butter and 2 tablespoons of olive oil in the skillet and warm the mixture over medium heat. Add the porcini mushrooms, season with salt, and cook for 1 minute. Add the cremini mushrooms, raise the heat to medium-high, and cook, stirring occasionally, until the liquid the mushrooms release has evaporated, 10 to 15 minutes.

6. While the mushrooms are cooking, place the remaining olive oil in a medium skillet and warm it over medium-high heat. Add the bratwurst and cook until it is browned all over, stirring occasionally. Transfer the bratwurst to a bowl and set it aside.

7. Transfer the mushrooms to a large bowl and add the Béchamel Sauce and the reserved soaking water. Stir to combine, season to taste, and then stir in the leeks, sausage, ¾ cup of the Parmesan, and the rigatoni pasta. Transfer the mixture to a 13 x 9-inch baking dish, sprinkle the remaining Parmesan over the top, and place the dish in the oven.

8. Bake until the dish is bubbling, about 20 minutes. Remove it from the oven and let it rest for 10 minutes before serving.

SALT AND PEPPER, TO TASTE

1 LB. RIGATONI

5½ TABLESPOONS EXTRA-
VIRGIN OLIVE OIL

1 OZ. DRIED PORCINI
MUSHROOMS

4 TABLESPOONS UNSALTED
BUTTER

5 LARGE LEEKS, TRIMMED,
RINSED WELL, AND SLICED
THIN

2 TEASPOONS FRESHLY
GRATED NUTMEG

1 LB. CREMINI MUSHROOMS,
STEMMED AND CHOPPED

1 LB. BRATWURST, CASINGS
REMOVED, CRUMBLED

2½ CUPS BÉCHAMEL SAUCE
(SEE PAGE 514)

1¼ CUPS GRATED
PARMESAN CHEESE

Angel Hair with Walnut, Black Garlic & Mascarpone

YIELD: 4 SERVINGS / **ACTIVE TIME:** 10 MINUTES / **TOTAL TIME:** 15 MINUTES

3 TABLESPOONS PINE NUTS

½ CUP WALNUT PIECES

2 BLACK GARLIC CLOVES

½ CUP MASCARPONE CHEESE

3½ TABLESPOONS WHOLE MILK

3 TABLESPOONS PARMESAN CHEESE, GRATED

SALT AND WHITE PEPPER, TO TASTE

14 OZ. ANGEL HAIR PASTA

3 TABLESPOONS UNSALTED BUTTER

1. Bring water to a boil in a large saucepan.

2. Warm a small skillet over medium-low heat for 2 minutes. Add the pine nuts and toast until they are browned all over, 2 to 3 minutes, shaking the pan frequently. Remove the pine nuts from the pan and set them aside.

3. Place the walnuts and black garlic in a food processor and pulse until the mixture is coarsely chopped. Transfer the mixture to a small saucepan and add the mascarpone, milk, and Parmesan. Season with salt and pepper and cook over medium-low heat until just before it starts to boil. Remove the pan from heat and cover it.

4. Add salt to the boiling water, let it return to a full boil, and add the pasta. Cook until it is very al dente, 5 to 7 minutes. Reserve ¼ cup of the pasta water and drain the pasta.

5. Place the large saucepan over high heat, add the butter and reserved pasta water and stir. Add the drained pasta and cook, tossing continually, until the pasta is al dente. Add the mascarpone sauce and toss to coat. Top the pasta with the toasted pine nuts and serve.

Fettuccine with Pancetta, Hazelnuts & Orange

YIELD: 4 SERVINGS / **ACTIVE TIME:** 10 MINUTES / **TOTAL TIME:** 25 MINUTES

1 CUP DRY WHITE WINE

2 TABLESPOONS EXTRA-VIRGIN OLIVE OIL

4 THICK-CUT SLICES OF PANCETTA, DICED

½ CUP BLANCHED HAZELNUTS, CHOPPED

4 TABLESPOONS UNSALTED BUTTER, CHILLED

6 FRESH SAGE LEAVES

ZEST OF ½ ORANGE

SALT AND PEPPER, TO TASTE

¾ LB. FETTUCCINE

¾ CUP CHICKEN STOCK (SEE PAGE 536), VERY HOT

1. Bring water to a boil in a large saucepan.

2. Place the wine in a small saucepan and bring to a gentle boil. Cook until it has reduced by half, about 5 minutes. Remove the pan from heat and let the wine cool.

3. Place the olive oil in a large skillet and warm it over medium heat. Add the pancetta and cook, stirring occasionally, until it is golden brown, about 8 minutes.

4. Add the hazelnuts and toast until they are golden brown, 2 to 3 minutes, shaking the pan frequently. Transfer the pancetta and hazelnuts to a small bowl.

5. Add the reduced wine to the skillet and cook for 5 minutes. Add the butter, sage leaves, and orange zest and bring to a gentle boil. Remove the pan from heat and cover it to keep the sauce warm.

6. Add salt to the boiling water, let it return to a full boil, and add the pasta. Cook until it is very al dente, 6 to 8 minutes. Drain the pasta.

7. Place the stock in the large saucepan. Add the pasta and toss until it has absorbed the broth. Add the pancetta, hazelnuts, and sauce, toss to combine, and serve.

Gnocchi alla Sorrentina

YIELD: 4 SERVINGS / **ACTIVE TIME:** 10 MINUTES / **TOTAL TIME:** 20 MINUTES

2 LBS. GNOCCHI
(SEE PAGE 42)

1½ LBS. SUGO AL BASILICO
(SEE PAGE 448)

¾ LB. FRESH MOZZARELLA
CHEESE, DRAINED AND
SHREDDED

⅔ CUP GRATED PARMESAN
CHEESE

1. Bring water to a boil in a large saucepan. Add the gnocchi and cook until they are floating on the surface.

2. Drain the gnocchi, place them in a large bowl with the tomato sauce, and gently stir to combine.

3. Transfer half of the gnocchi to a deep baking dish with high edges and cover them with half of the mozzarella and Parmesan. Repeat with the remaining gnocchi, mozzarella, and Parmesan.

4. Set the oven's broiler to high. Place the baking dish in the oven and broil until the mozzarella has melted, 5 to 8 minutes.

5. Remove the gnocchi from the oven and serve immediately.

Classic Buttered Linguine with Parmesan

YIELD: 4 SERVINGS / **ACTIVE TIME:** 10 MINUTES / **TOTAL TIME:** 20 MINUTES

SALT AND WHITE PEPPER, TO TASTE

¾ LB. LINGUINE

5½ TABLESPOONS UNSALTED BUTTER, SOFTENED

½ CUP GRATED PARMESAN CHEESE, PLUS MORE FOR GARNISH

HANDFUL OF FRESH PARSLEY, CHOPPED

1. Bring water to a boil in a large saucepan. Add salt to the boiling water, let it return to a full boil, and add the pasta. Cook until it is very al dente, 6 to 8 minutes. Reserve ¼ cup of pasta water and drain the pasta.

2. Place the pan over high heat. Add the pasta water and ½ tablespoon of the butter and stir to combine. Add the drained pasta and toss until it is al dente, about 2 minutes.

3. Add the remaining butter, the Parmesan, and parsley, season with salt and pepper, and toss until the cheese has melted. Transfer the pasta to a large bowl, sprinkle additional Parmesan over the top, and serve.

Rigatoni with Caramelized Onions & Chickpeas

YIELD: 4 SERVINGS / **ACTIVE TIME:** 20 MINUTES / **TOTAL TIME:** 1 HOUR

6 TABLESPOONS PLUS 1 TEASPOON EXTRA-VIRGIN OLIVE OIL

4 YELLOW ONIONS, SLICED THIN

SALT AND PEPPER, TO TASTE

1 TABLESPOON BALSAMIC VINEGAR

¾ LB. RIGATONI

1 (14 OZ.) CAN OF CHICKPEAS, DRAINED AND RINSED

1. Bring water to a boil in a large saucepan.

2. Place 6 tablespoons of olive oil in a large skillet and warm it over medium heat. Add the onions and cook, stirring occasionally, until they start to soften, about 5 minutes.

3. Reduce the heat to medium-low and cook, stirring frequently, until the onions are caramelized, about 40 minutes. Season with salt and pepper, stir in the balsamic vinegar, and remove the pan from heat.

4. Add salt to the boiling water, let it return to a full boil, and add the pasta. Cook until it is very al dente, 6 to 8 minutes. Reserve ¼ cup of pasta water and drain the pasta.

5. Place the pan over high heat. Add the pasta water and remaining olive oil and stir to combine. Add the drained pasta and chickpeas and toss until the rigatoni is al dente, about 2 minutes. Stir in the caramelized onions, toss to combine, and serve.

Spaghetti alla Serena

YIELD: 4 SERVINGS / **ACTIVE TIME:** 45 MINUTES / **TOTAL TIME:** 1 HOUR AND 15 MINUTES

⅔ CUP MADEIRA WINE

½ CUP PLUS ½ TEASPOON UNSALTED BUTTER

1 LB. CREMINI MUSHROOMS, QUARTERED

SALT AND WHITE PEPPER, TO TASTE

2 TABLESPOONS EXTRA-VIRGIN OLIVE OIL

1 SMALL YELLOW ONION, GRATED

1 RED BELL PEPPER, STEMMED, SEEDED, AND SLICED THIN

1 CUP WHOLE MILK

1½ CUPS GRATED GRUYÈRE CHEESE

2 CUPS COOKED CHICKEN BREAST, SHREDDED

HANDFUL OF FRESH PARSLEY LEAVES, CHOPPED, PLUS MORE FOR GARNISH

¾ LB. SPAGHETTI

PARMESAN CHEESE, GRATED, FOR GARNISH

1. Bring water to a boil in a large saucepan. Place the wine in a small saucepan, bring to a boil, and cook until it has reduced by half, about 5 minutes. Remove pan from the stove and let the wine cool.

2. Place 2 tablespoons of butter in a large skillet and melt it over medium-high heat. Add half of the mushrooms, season with salt, and cook, stirring occasionally, until they start to brown, about 12 minutes. Transfer the mushrooms to a bowl and set them aside.

3. Place another 2 tablespoons of the butter in the pan, add the remaining mushrooms, season them with salt, and cook until they start to brown. Transfer them to the bowl containing the other mushrooms.

4. Add the olive oil to the skillet, reduce the heat to medium, and warm it for 1 minute. Add the onion and cook, stirring occasionally, until it is translucent, about 3 minutes. Add the bell pepper and cook, stirring occasionally, until it is tender, about 10 minutes. Raise the heat to medium-high and cook until the bell pepper starts to brown, about 4 minutes.

5. Stir in the mushrooms, milk, and reduced wine, bring to a boil, and then reduce the heat to low. Stir in the remaining butter and the Gruyère and stir until they have melted. Add the chicken and parsley, season the sauce with salt and pepper, and cook, stirring occasionally, until the chicken is warmed through. Remove the pan from heat and cover it.

6. Add salt to the boiling water, let it return to a full boil, and add the pasta. Cook until it is very al dente, 6 to 8 minutes. Reserve ¼ cup of pasta water and drain the pasta.

7. Place the pan over high heat. Add the pasta water and pasta and cook, tossing continually, until the spaghetti is al dente, about 2 minutes. Transfer the pasta to the skillet and toss to combine. Garnish with Parmesan and additional parsley and serve.

Penne with Clams & Calamari

YIELD: 4 SERVINGS / **ACTIVE TIME:** 25 MINUTES / **TOTAL TIME:** 30 MINUTES

¾ LB. SQUID BODIES AND TENTACLES, CLEANED AND SLICED THIN

SALT AND PEPPER, TO TASTE

¼ CUP PLUS 1 TEASPOON EXTRA-VIRGIN OLIVE OIL

3 LARGE PLUM TOMATOES, PEELED, SEEDED, AND CHOPPED

2 GARLIC CLOVES, SLICED THIN

3½ LBS. SMALL HARD-SHELL CLAMS, SCRUBBED AND RINSED WELL

¾ LB. PENNE

FRESH PARSLEY, CHOPPED, FOR GARNISH

1. Bring water to a boil in a large saucepan.

2. Place the squid in a colander, rinse it, let it drain, and pat dry. Season with salt and pepper, toss to combine, and set it aside.

3. Place ¼ cup of olive oil in a large, deep skillet and warm it over medium-high heat. Add the tomatoes and garlic, season with salt, and cook, stirring occasionally, until the tomatoes start to collapse, about 5 minutes.

4. Add the squid and clams and cook, stirring occasionally, until a few of the clams open. Remove the pan from heat and cover it. Let it sit for 5 minutes, remove the cover, and discard any clams that did not open. Set the mixture aside.

5. Add salt to the boiling water, let it return to a full boil, and add the pasta. Cook until it is very al dente, 6 to 8 minutes. Reserve ½ cup of pasta water and drain the pasta.

6. Place the saucepan over high heat. Add the pasta water and pasta and cook, tossing continually, until the penne is al dente, about 2 minutes. Add the clam mixture and toss to combine. Garnish with parsley and serve.

Lagane e Ceci

YIELD: 4 SERVINGS / **ACTIVE TIME:** 15 MINUTES / **TOTAL TIME:** 24 HOURS

14 OZ. DRIED CHICKPEAS, SOAKED OVERNIGHT

1 SPRIG OF FRESH ROSEMARY

3 GARLIC CLOVES, HALVED

2 TABLESPOONS EXTRA-VIRGIN OLIVE OIL

11 OZ. WHOLE PEELED TOMATOES, LIGHTLY CRUSHED

2 BAY LEAVES

RED PEPPER FLAKES, TO TASTE

SALT, TO TASTE

1 LB. LAGANE (SEE PAGE 26) OR DRIED PAPPARDELLE OR FETTUCCINE

1. Drain the chickpeas, place them in a large saucepan, and cover them with cold water. Add the rosemary and 1 garlic clove, bring to a boil, and cook until the chickpeas are tender, about 45 minutes. Drain the chickpeas, reserve the cooking liquid, and set both aside.

2. Place the olive oil in a large skillet and warm it over medium heat. Add the remaining garlic and cook, stirring frequently, for 2 minutes.

3. Add the tomatoes and bay leaves and cook, stirring occasionally, until the tomatoes have collapsed, about 20 minutes.

4. Remove the garlic and discard it. Season the sauce with red pepper flakes and salt and stir in the chickpeas. Reduce the heat to low and cook the sauce for 20 minutes.

5. Bring water to a boil in a large saucepan. Add salt, let the water return to a full boil, and add the pasta. Cook until the pasta is al dente.

6. Reserve 1 cup pasta water, drain the pasta, and stir it into the sauce.

7. Toss to combine, adding pasta water as needed to get the right consistency. Serve immediately.

Lagane e Ceci
SEE PAGE 287

Pasta Primavera

YIELD: 4 TO 6 SERVINGS / **ACTIVE TIME:** 15 MINUTES / **TOTAL TIME:** 15 MINUTES

2 TABLESPOONS UNSALTED BUTTER

1 CUP PEAS

½ LB. ASPARAGUS, TRIMMED AND CHOPPED

3 SCALLIONS, TRIMMED AND CHOPPED

2 GARLIC CLOVES, MINCED

SALT AND PEPPER, TO TASTE

¾ LB. FETTUCCINE

½ CUP FULL-FAT GREEK YOGURT

⅔ CUP GRATED PARMESAN CHEESE, PLUS MORE FOR GARNISH

3 TABLESPOONS CHOPPED FRESH PARSLEY, FOR GARNISH

2 TABLESPOONS CHOPPED FRESH TARRAGON, FOR GARNISH

1. Bring water to a boil in a large saucepan.

2. Place the butter in a large skillet and melt it over medium heat. Add the peas, asparagus, scallions, and garlic, season with salt and pepper, and cook, stirring continually, until the asparagus is tender, about 4 minutes. Transfer the mixture to a large bowl.

3. Add salt to the boiling water, let it return to a full boil, and add the pasta. Cook until it is al dente, 8 to 10 minutes. Drain the pasta and add it to the large bowl.

4. Add the yogurt and Parmesan and toss to combine. Garnish the dish with the parsley and tarragon and serve.

Sweet Potato Gnocchi with Sage Brown Butter, Arugula & Walnuts

YIELD: 6 TO 8 SERVINGS / **ACTIVE TIME:** 25 MINUTES / **TOTAL TIME:** 2 HOURS

SWEET POTATO GNOCCHI (SEE PAGE 68)

1 STICK OF UNSALTED BUTTER

1 TABLESPOON FINELY CHOPPED FRESH SAGE

2 CUPS ARUGULA

½ CUP WALNUTS, TOASTED AND CHOPPED

1. Bring water to a boil in a large saucepan. Working in batches to avoid crowding the pan, add the gnocchi to the boiling water and stir to keep them from sticking to the bottom. The gnocchi will eventually float to the surface. Cook for 1 more minute, remove, and transfer them to a parchment-lined baking sheet to cool.

2. Place the butter in a skillet and warm it over medium heat until it begins to brown. Add the sage and cook until the bubbles start to dissipate. Place the arugula in a bowl and set it aside.

3. Working in batches, add the gnocchi to the skillet, stir to coat, and cook until they have a nice sear on one side. Transfer the gnocchi to the bowl of arugula and toss to combine. Top with the toasted walnuts and serve.

Spaghetti with Asparagus & Peas

YIELD: 4 SERVINGS / **ACTIVE TIME:** 15 MINUTES / **TOTAL TIME:** 25 MINUTES

1 BUNCH OF ASPARAGUS, TRIMMED AND CHOPPED

½ LB. SUGAR SNAP PEAS, TRIMMED AND CHOPPED

¾ LB. SPAGHETTI

4 TABLESPOONS UNSALTED BUTTER

¼ CUP FRESHLY GRATED PARMESAN CHEESE

½ TEASPOON RED PEPPER FLAKES

1. Bring water to a boil in a medium saucepan. Bring water to a boil in a large saucepan.

2. Add salt to the medium saucepan, let the water return to a full boil, and add the asparagus and peas. Cook for 1 minute, drain, and set the mixture aside.

3. Add salt to the large saucepan, let the water return to a full boil, and add the pasta. Cook until it is very al dente, 6 to 8 minutes. Reserve ½ cup of pasta water and drain the pasta.

4. Place the butter in a large skillet and melt it over medium heat. Add the pasta and vegetable mixture and toss to combine. Add the reserved pasta water, Parmesan, and red pepper flakes and toss until the pasta is al dente. Season to taste and serve.

Butternut Squash Cannelloni

YIELD: 8 SERVINGS / **ACTIVE TIME:** 1 HOUR / **TOTAL TIME:** 1 HOUR AND 30 MINUTES

FOR THE FILLING

2 LBS. BUTTERNUT SQUASH, HALVED AND SEEDED

5 TABLESPOONS EXTRA-VIRGIN OLIVE OIL

5 GARLIC CLOVES, MINCED

1½ CUPS RICOTTA CHEESE

1 CUP GRATED PARMESAN CHEESE

12 FRESH SAGE LEAVES, SLICED THIN

1 TEASPOON FRESHLY GRATED NUTMEG

SALT AND WHITE PEPPER, TO TASTE

FOR THE PASTA

PASTA ALL'UOVO (SEE PAGE 47)

SEMOLINA FLOUR, AS NEEDED

1½ TEASPOONS EXTRA-VIRGIN OLIVE OIL, PLUS MORE AS NEEDED

SALT, TO TASTE

1. To begin preparations for the filling, preheat the oven to 375°F. Brush the flesh of the squash with 1 tablespoon of olive oil and place the squash on a parchment-lined baking sheet, cut side down. Place the baking sheet in the oven and roast until the squash is fork-tender, 40 to 45 minutes. Remove the squash from the oven and let it cool. When it is cool enough to handle, scoop the flesh into a wide, shallow bowl and mash it until it is smooth.

2. Place the remaining olive oil in a large skillet and warm it over medium heat. Add the garlic and cook, stirring continually, for 1 minute. Remove the pan from heat and transfer the garlic and oil to the bowl with the mashed squash. Add the cheeses, half of the sage, and the nutmeg, season with salt and pepper, and stir to combine.

3. To begin preparations for the pasta, divide the dough into 3 pieces. Cover 2 pieces with plastic wrap and place the other on a flour-dusted work surface. Roll it into a ¹⁄₁₆-inch-thick sheet (you can also use a pasta maker to do this). Cut the sheet into 5-inch squares and place the squares on flour-dusted, parchment-lined baking sheets. Repeat with the remaining pieces of dough.

4. Bring water to a boil in a large saucepan. Add salt, let the water return to a full boil, and add the pasta. Cook until they just start to soften, about 2 minutes. Drain and rinse under cold water. Transfer the pasta to a bowl, add the olive oil, and toss to coat.

5. Generously coat a baking dish large enough to fit all the filled cannelloni in a single layer with olive oil. To fill the cannelloni, place a pasta square in front of you. Place ¼ cup of the squash mixture in the center of the square and shape the filling into a rough cylinder. Roll the pasta over the filling and transfer it to the baking dish, seam side down. Repeat with remaining pasta and filling. When the baking dish is filled, drizzle olive oil over the cannelloni and place the dish in the oven.

6. Bake until the cannelloni are golden brown, about 20 minutes. Remove the dish from the oven, top with the remaining sage, and serve.

Fettuccine Alfredo

YIELD: 4 SERVINGS / **ACTIVE TIME:** 15 MINUTES / **TOTAL TIME:** 20 MINUTES

SALT AND PEPPER, TO TASTE

¾ LB. FETTUCCINE

½ CUP HEAVY CREAM

2½ TABLESPOONS UNSALTED BUTTER, SOFTENED

1 CUP GRATED PARMESAN CHEESE, PLUS MORE FOR GARNISH

½ TEASPOON FRESHLY GRATED NUTMEG

FRESH PARSLEY, CHOPPED, FOR GARNISH

1. Bring water to a boil in a large saucepan. Add salt to the boiling water, let it return to a full boil, and add the pasta. Cook until it is very al dente, 6 to 8 minutes. Reserve ½ cup of pasta water and drain the pasta.

2. Place some of the reserved pasta water and heavy cream in a large skillet and bring it to a simmer. Add the butter and stir until it has emulsified. Gradually incorporate the Parmesan, making sure each addition has melted before adding the next.

3. Add the fettuccine to the skillet and toss to combine, adding more pasta water if desired. Sprinkle the nutmeg and parsley over the dish and serve.

Baked Ziti

YIELD: 6 SERVINGS / **ACTIVE TIME:** 40 MINUTES / **TOTAL TIME:** 1 HOUR AND 30 MINUTES

2 TABLESPOONS EXTRA-VIRGIN OLIVE OIL

½ CUP DICED PANCETTA

1 LARGE YELLOW ONION, CHOPPED

SALT, TO TASTE

2 TEASPOONS RED PEPPER FLAKES

1 TABLESPOON TOMATO PASTE

1 TABLESPOON FISH SAUCE

3 (14 OZ.) CANS OF CRUSHED TOMATOES

¼ TEASPOON SUGAR

1½ TABLESPOONS UNSALTED BUTTER

1 CUP BÉCHAMEL SAUCE (SEE PAGE 514)

1 LB. FRESH MOZZARELLA CHEESE, CHOPPED

1 LB. ZITI

2½ CUPS FRESHLY GRATED PARMESAN CHEESE

FRESH BASIL, CHOPPED, FOR GARNISH

1. Bring water to a boil in a large saucepan. Preheat the oven to 350°F.

2. Place the olive oil in a large skillet and warm it over medium heat. Add the pancetta and cook, stirring occasionally, until it starts to brown, about 6 minutes. Raise the heat to medium-high and add the onion, a couple pinches of salt, and red pepper flakes. Reduce the heat to low, cover the pan, and cook, stirring occasionally, until the onion has become very tender, about 15 minutes.

3. Raise the heat to medium-high, stir in the tomato paste and fish sauce, and cook, stirring constantly, until the mixture has darkened, about 2 minutes. Stir in the tomatoes and sugar, season with salt, and bring the sauce to a gentle boil. Reduce the heat to low and cook, stirring frequently, until the sauce has thickened slightly, about 30 minutes. Season to taste with salt and pepper.

4. Coat a 13 x 9–inch baking dish with the butter. Combine the Béchamel Sauce and the mozzarella in a large bowl and set it aside.

5. Add salt to the boiling water, let it return to a full boil, and add the pasta. Cook until the pasta has just softened, about 5 minutes. Drain the pasta and immediately add it to the bowl containing the Béchamel-and-mozzarella mixture. Add 1 cup of the Parmesan and toss to combine.

6. Add all but 1½ cups of the tomato sauce to the bowl and gently fold to incorporate.

7. Transfer the mixture to the baking dish and top it with the remaining tomato sauce and Parmesan. Place the dish in the oven and bake for 15 to 20 minutes.

8. Set the oven's broiler to high and broil the baked ziti until the top starts to brown, about 4 minutes. Remove the dish from the oven and let the baked ziti rest for 15 minutes before serving. Garnish each portion with basil.

Malloreddus with Sausage, Kale & Rosemary

YIELD: 4 SERVINGS / **ACTIVE TIME:** 45 MINUTES / **TOTAL TIME:** 1 HOUR AND 30 MINUTES

1 TABLESPOON EXTRA-VIRGIN OLIVE OIL, PLUS MORE AS NEEDED

6 OZ. PORK SAUSAGE, CASING REMOVED AND CRUMBLED

2 TABLESPOONS FINELY CHOPPED SHALLOT

½ CUP DRY WHITE WINE

3 LARGE KALE LEAVES, STEMMED AND SLICED THIN

MALLOREDDUS (SEE PAGE 34)

1 TEASPOON CHOPPED FRESH ROSEMARY LEAVES

⅓ CUP FRESHLY GRATED PARMESAN CHEESE, PLUS MORE FOR GARNISH

1. Bring water to a boil in a large saucepan.

2. Place the olive oil in a large skillet and warm it over medium heat. Add the sausage and cook, stirring occasionally, until it is browned all over, about 6 minutes. Transfer the sausage to a bowl and set it aside.

3. Add the shallot to the skillet and cook, stirring occasionally, until it is translucent, about 3 minutes. Deglaze the pan with the white wine, scraping up any browned bits from the bottom. Add the sliced kale and cook, stirring occasionally.

4. Add salt to the boiling water, let the water return to a boil, and add the Malloreddus. Let them rise to the surface and cook for 1 more minute.

5. Drain the Malloreddus and add them to the skillet. Add the rosemary and Parmesan, return the sausage to the pan, and toss to combine. Garnish with additional Parmesan and serve.

Pumpkin Gnocchi with Chorizo & Padrón

YIELD: 2 TO 4 SERVINGS / **ACTIVE TIME:** 20 MINUTES / **TOTAL TIME:** 30 MINUTES

2 CUPS DICED PADRÓN PEPPERS

1 VIDALIA ONION, SLICED THIN

1 TABLESPOON EXTRA-VIRGIN OLIVE OIL

SALT, TO TASTE

4 OZ. FRESH CHORIZO, SLICED

PUMPKIN GNOCCHI (SEE PAGE 57)

1 TEASPOON BLACK PEPPER

CREAMY LEEK SAUCE (SEE PAGE 511)

1. Bring water to a boil in a large saucepan. Preheat the oven to 425°F.

2. Place the peppers and onion in a bowl, add the olive oil, season with salt, and toss to combine. Spread the mixture on a baking sheet in an even layer and add the chorizo.

3. Place the pan in the oven and roast until the chorizo is cooked through and the peppers are charred all over, about 15 minutes, turning the peppers as needed.

4. While the chorizo and peppers are roasting, cook the gnocchi. Add salt to the boiling water, let the water return to a boil, and add the gnocchi. Let the gnocchi rise to the surface and cook for another minute once they do. Remove them with a pasta fork and transfer to a bowl.

5. Remove the baking sheet from the oven and transfer the mixture to the bowl containing the gnocchi. Add the black pepper and sauce, toss to combine, and serve.

Pasta con Mollica e Pepe Rosso

YIELD: 4 SERVINGS / **ACTIVE TIME:** 15 MINUTES / **TOTAL TIME:** 25 MINUTES

¼ CUP EXTRA-VIRGIN
OLIVE OIL

3 GARLIC CLOVES, HALVED

CAYENNE PEPPER, TO TASTE

7 OZ. STALE BREAD,
CRUSTLESS AND CRUMBLED

SALT, TO TASTE

1 LB. SPAGHETTI

1. Place three-quarters of the olive oil in a large skillet and warm it over medium heat. Add the garlic and cook, stirring frequently, for 2 minutes.

2. Stir in a generous amount of cayenne pepper, remove the pan from heat, and set it aside.

3. Place the remaining olive oil in a large skillet and warm it over medium heat. Add the bread crumbs and cook, stirring, until they are browned.

4. Bring water to a boil in a large saucepan. Add salt, let the water return to a full boil, and add the pasta. Cook until the pasta is al dente.

5. Drain the pasta and place it in a serving dish. Add the infused oil and bread crumbs, quickly toss to combine, and serve.

Cicelievitati with Roasted Prosciutto, Mushroom & Artichokes

YIELD: 4 SERVINGS / **ACTIVE TIME:** 25 MINUTES / **TOTAL TIME:** 1 HOUR AND 5 MINUTES

½ LB. CREMINI MUSHROOMS, SLICED

1 TABLESPOON EXTRA-VIRGIN OLIVE OIL

2 CUPS CHERRY TOMATOES

1 CUP HALVED ARTICHOKE HEARTS

4 OZ. PROSCIUTTO, SLICED

SALT, TO TASTE

CICELIEVITATI (SEE PAGE 59)

1 CUP BABY ARUGULA

1 CUP GRATED PARMESAN CHEESE

BLACK PEPPER, TO TASTE

FRESH BASIL, FOR GARNISH

1. Bring water to a boil in a large saucepan. Preheat the oven to 400°F.

2. Place the mushrooms on a baking sheet and drizzle the olive oil over them. Place them in the oven and roast until they start to brown, 5 to 8 minutes.

3. Remove the baking sheet from the oven and carefully arrange the tomatoes and artichokes on it. Return it to the oven and roast until the tomatoes have burst, about 20 minutes.

4. Remove the baking sheet from the oven and transfer the vegetables to a large bowl. Place the prosciutto on the baking sheet, place it in the oven, and roast until it has browned, about 10 minutes.

5. While the prosciutto is in the oven, cook the Cicelieviati. Add salt to the boiling water, let the water return to a full boil, and add the pasta. Cook until the pasta has the consistency of properly cooked gnocchi, light and slightly chewy, 3 to 5 minutes.

6. Drain the Cicelieviati and add them to the bowl with the vegetable mixture. Add the arugula and Parmesan, season with pepper, and toss to combine.

7. Remove the baking sheet from the oven and chop the prosciutto. Top the pasta with the prosciutto, garnish with basil, and serve.

Egg Noodles with Eggplant & Rhubarb

YIELD: 4 SERVINGS / **ACTIVE TIME:** 25 MINUTES / **TOTAL TIME:** 45 MINUTES

1 TABLESPOON MIRIN

1 TABLESPOON SESAME OIL

2 TABLESPOONS CANOLA OIL

3 TABLESPOONS SOY SAUCE

1 TABLESPOON RICE VINEGAR

½ TEASPOON BLACK PEPPER

¼ TEASPOON CORIANDER SEEDS

2 JAPANESE EGGPLANTS, CHOPPED

¼ CUP SLICED RHUBARB

SALT, TO TASTE

CHINESE EGG NOODLES (SEE PAGE 104)

FRESH THYME, FOR GARNISH

1. Bring water to a boil in a large saucepan.

2. Set the oven's broiler to high. Place the mirin, sesame oil, canola oil, soy sauce, vinegar, pepper, and coriander seeds in a bowl and stir to combine.

3. Arrange the eggplants and rhubarb on a baking sheet. Pour the sauce over the mixture. Place the baking sheet in the oven and broil until the vegetables are tender and starting to char, about 8 minutes.

4. While the eggplants and rhubarb are in the oven, add salt to the boiling water, let it return to a full boil, and add the noodles. Cook until they are al dente, 2 to 3 minutes. Drain the noodles and place them in a large bowl.

5. Remove the baking sheet from the oven, cover it loosely with aluminum foil, and let the eggplant mixture rest for 5 minutes.

6. Add the eggplant mixture to the bowl and toss to combine. Garnish with thyme and serve.

Roasted Tortellini with Chorizo and Mango & Tomato Sauce

YIELD: 4 SERVINGS / **ACTIVE TIME:** 20 MINUTES / **TOTAL TIME:** 35 MINUTES

1 (14 OZ.) CAN OF WHOLE PEELED TOMATOES, DRAINED AND CHOPPED

FLESH OF ½ SMALL MANGO, DICED

4 OZ. CHORIZO, SLICED

1 TEASPOON KOSHER SALT

1 TEASPOON BLACK PEPPER

1¼ LBS. TORTELLINI (SEE PAGE 56), FILLED WITH RICOTTA

FRESH BASIL, CHOPPED, FOR GARNISH

1. Preheat the oven to 400°F. Line a baking sheet with parchment paper.

2. Place all of the ingredients, except for the basil, on the baking sheet and stir to combine.

3. Place the baking sheet in the oven and roast until the tortellini are al dente, about 15 minutes. Remove the dish from the oven, garnish it with basil, and serve.

Baked Shells with Pumpkin & Mozzarella

YIELD: 4 TO 6 SERVINGS / **ACTIVE TIME:** 25 MINUTES / **TOTAL TIME:** 40 MINUTES

1½ TEASPOONS KOSHER SALT, PLUS MORE TO TASTE

1 LB. SMALL SHELL PASTA

1½ LBS. PUMPKIN, DICED INTO ½-INCH CUBES

¼ TEASPOON WHITE PEPPER

¼ TEASPOON FRESHLY GRATED NUTMEG

3 TABLESPOONS EXTRA-VIRGIN OLIVE OIL

¼ TEASPOON BLACK PEPPER

1 CUP RICOTTA CHEESE

1 CUP TORN MOZZARELLA CHEESE

FRESH ROSEMARY, CHOPPED, FOR GARNISH

1. Preheat the oven to 425°F. Bring water to a boil in a large saucepan. Add salt, let the water return to a full boil, and add the pasta. Cook until the pasta is very al dente, 6 to 8 minutes. Drain the pasta and set it aside.

2. Place the pumpkin in a mixing bowl, season it with the salt, white pepper, and nutmeg, add half of the olive oil and the pasta, and toss to coat. Transfer the mixture to a baking pan, place it in the oven, and bake until the pumpkin is tender, 15 to 20 minutes.

3. Remove the pan from the oven, drizzle the remaining olive oil over it, and toss to coat. Top the dish with the ricotta and mozzarella, garnish with rosemary, and serve.

Pasta with 'Nduja & Butternut Squash

YIELD: 4 SERVINGS / **ACTIVE TIME:** 30 MINUTES / **TOTAL TIME:** 50 MINUTES

3 TABLESPOONS EXTRA-VIRGIN OLIVE OIL

1 GARLIC CLOVE, HALVED

1 ONION, FINELY DICED

2 LBS. BUTTERNUT SQUASH, SKINLESS AND CUBED

2 TABLESPOONS 'NDUJA

SALT AND PEPPER, TO TASTE

1 LB. MACCHERONI AL FERRETTO (SEE PAGE 24)

PECORINO CHEESE, GRATED, FOR GARNISH

1. Place the olive oil in a large, deep skillet and warm it over medium-low heat. Add the garlic and onion and cook, stirring frequently, for 5 minutes.

2. Add the butternut squash, cover the pan, and cook until the squash is tender, about 20 minutes.

3. Remove the garlic and discard it. Add the 'nduja and mash it and the squash with a wooden spoon. Season with salt and pepper.

4. Bring water to a boil in a large saucepan. Add salt, let the water return to a full boil, and add the pasta. Cook until the pasta is al dente.

5. Drain the pasta, add it to the sauce, and toss to combine. Garnish the dish with pecorino and serve.

Pasta with 'Nduja & Butternut Squash
SEE PAGE 303

Baked Rigatoni with Easy Vegetable Ragù

YIELD: 6 SERVINGS / **ACTIVE TIME:** 35 MINUTES / **TOTAL TIME:** 2 HOURS AND 35 MINUTES

1 LB. GROUND BEEF

2 TABLESPOONS EXTRA-VIRGIN OLIVE OIL, PLUS MORE AS NEEDED

1 SMALL ONION, FINELY DICED

1 SMALL CARROT, PEELED AND FINELY DICED

2 CELERY STALKS, PEELED AND FINELY DICED

2 GARLIC CLOVES, MINCED

1¼ TEASPOONS KOSHER SALT, PLUS MORE TO TASTE

1 CUP RED WINE

1 (14 OZ.) CAN OF CRUSHED TOMATOES

1 CUP BEEF STOCK (SEE PAGE 538)

½ TEASPOON DRIED OREGANO

½ TEASPOON DRIED BASIL

½ TEASPOON BLACK PEPPER, PLUS MORE TO TASTE

1 LB. RIGATONI

BÉCHAMEL SAUCE (SEE PAGE 514)

1 CUP SHREDDED MOZZARELLA CHEESE

FRESH BASIL, FOR GARNISH

1. Place the beef in a large skillet and cook over medium heat, breaking it up with a wooden spoon, until it is browned all over, 6 to 8 minutes. Drain excess grease from the pan and set the browned beef aside.

2. Place the olive oil in the pan and warm it over medium heat. Add the onion, carrot, celery, garlic, and ½ teaspoon salt and cook, stirring frequently, until the vegetables are tender, about 8 minutes.

3. Stir in the wine and browned beef and cook until the liquid has almost completely evaporated. Stir in the tomatoes, stock, dried herbs, ½ teaspoon of salt, and pepper. Bring to a rapid simmer, reduce the heat so that the mixture gently simmers, and cook until the ragù has thickened, 40 to 45 minutes, stirring occasionally.

4. While the ragù is simmering, bring water to a boil in a large saucepan. Add salt, let the water return to a full boil, and add the rigatoni. Cook until it is very al dente, 5 to 7 minutes. Drain the pasta and place it in a baking dish.

5. Add the ragù to the dish and stir to combine. Top the dish with the Béchamel Sauce and mozzarella and place it in the oven.

6. Bake until the top is golden brown and the sauce is bubbling, 40 to 45 minutes. Remove the dish from the oven and let the baked rigatoni rest for 5 minutes. Garnish with basil and serve.

Baked Rigatoni with Mushrooms & Grape Tomatoes

YIELD: 2 TO 4 SERVINGS / **ACTIVE TIME:** 25 MINUTES / **TOTAL TIME:** 50 MINUTES

1 TEASPOON KOSHER SALT, PLUS MORE TO TASTE

½ LB. RIGATONI

½ CUP UNSALTED BUTTER, SOFTENED

5 GARLIC CLOVES, CRUSHED

¾ LB. BABY BELLA MUSHROOMS

¾ LB. WHITE MUSHROOMS

1 CUP HALVED RED GRAPE TOMATOES

1 CUP HALVED YELLOW GRAPE TOMATOES

½ CUP PINE NUTS

½ TEASPOON BLACK PEPPER

1 TABLESPOON FRESH LEMON JUICE

FRESH PARSLEY, CHOPPED, FOR GARNISH

1. Preheat the oven to 400°F. Bring water to a boil in a large saucepan. Add salt, let the water return to a full boil, and add the rigatoni. Cook until it is very al dente, 5 to 7 minutes. Drain the pasta and set it aside.

2. Place the butter and garlic in a mixing bowl and stir until combined. Add the mushrooms and stir to coat.

3. Place the tomatoes, pine nuts, and mushroom mixture in the baking dish, season with the salt and pepper, and sprinkle the lemon juice over the top. Stir to combine.

4. Place the dish in the oven and bake until the tomatoes start to collapse and the mushrooms start to brown, 20 to 25 minutes.

5. Remove the dish from the oven, add the pasta, and stir to combine. Return the dish to the oven and bake until the pasta is al dente, 10 to 15 minutes.

6. Remove the dish from the oven, garnish with fresh parsley, and serve.

Tagliatelle with Venison Meatballs

YIELD: 4 SERVINGS / **ACTIVE TIME:** 30 MINUTES / **TOTAL TIME:** 50 MINUTES

2 TABLESPOONS EXTRA-VIRGIN OLIVE OIL

1 ONION, FINELY DICED

2 GARLIC CLOVES, MINCED

1 LB. GROUND VENISON

1 CUP BREAD CRUMBS

1 EGG, BEATEN

SALT AND PEPPER, TO TASTE

4 TABLESPOONS UNSALTED BUTTER

2 CUPS WILD MUSHROOMS

½ TEASPOON SWEET SMOKED PAPRIKA

1 TABLESPOON TOMATO PASTE

1 TABLESPOON ALL-PURPOSE FLOUR

1½ CUPS BEEF STOCK (SEE PAGE 538)

½ CUP BRANDY

½ CUP SOUR CREAM

1 LB. TAGLIATELLE (SEE PAGE 52)

FRESH PARSLEY, CHOPPED, FOR GARNISH

1. Place 1 tablespoon of olive oil in a large skillet and warm it over medium-high heat. Add the onion and cook, stirring occasionally, until it has softened, about 5 minutes.

2. Add the garlic and cook, stirring continually, for 1 minute. Transfer the mixture to a large mixing bowl and let it cool slightly.

3. Add the venison, bread crumbs, and egg to the bowl, season the mixture with salt and pepper, and work the mixture with your hands until it is well combined. Form the mixture into approximately 30 small meatballs.

4. Place the remaining olive oil in a clean, large skillet and warm it over medium-high heat. Working in batches to avoid crowding the pan, add the meatballs and cook, until they are browned all over and completely cooked through, 8 to 10 minutes, turning them as necessary. Transfer the cooked meatballs to a plate and cover them with aluminum foil.

5. Add the butter to the skillet and raise the temperature to high. Add the mushrooms and cook until they start to brown, about 8 minutes, stirring once or twice.

6. Bring water to a boil in a large saucepan.

7. Stir the paprika, tomato paste, and flour into the mushrooms and cook for 1 minute. Add the stock and brandy and cook until the sauce thickens, about 5 minutes.

8. Return the meatballs to the pan and stir in the sour cream. Cook the sauce for another 5 to 8 minutes.

9. Add salt to the boiling water, let it return to a full boil, and add the Tagliatelle. Cook it until it is al dente, 2 to 4 minutes.

10. Drain the pasta, add it to the sauce, and toss to combine. Garnish the dish with parsley and enjoy.

Spaghetti All'assassina

YIELD: 4 SERVINGS / **ACTIVE TIME:** 30 MINUTES / **TOTAL TIME:** 50 MINUTES

¼ CUP EXTRA-VIRGIN OLIVE OIL, PLUS MORE TO TASTE

3 GARLIC CLOVES

HOT CHILE PEPPERS, STEMMED, SEEDED, AND MINCED, TO TASTE

19½ OZ. WHOLE PEELED TOMATOES, CHOPPED

SALT, TO TASTE

1 LB. SPAGHETTI

2 TABLESPOONS TOMATO PASTE

1. Place the olive oil in a large, deep skillet and warm it over medium heat. Add the garlic and chiles and cook, stirring frequently, for 2 minutes.

2. Remove the garlic and discard it. Add the tomatoes, season them with salt, and cook for 10 minutes.

3. Bring water to a boil in a large saucepan. Add salt, let the water return to a full boil, and add the pasta. Cook for half of the typical cooking time, 4 to 5 minutes.

4. Using a pasta fork, remove the spaghetti from the boiling water and place it in the tomato sauce.

5. Raise the heat to medium-high and stir in the tomato paste and more olive oil.

6. Stir in the spaghetti, making sure not to break the strands, and cook until it sticks to the pan and is slightly charred.

7. Turn the spaghetti over and cook until it is slightly charred all over. Serve immediately.

Spaghetti All'assassina
SEE PAGE 309

Wild Boar & Chestnut Ragù with Spätzle

YIELD: 4 SERVINGS / **ACTIVE TIME:** 45 MINUTES / **TOTAL TIME:** 3 HOURS

2 TABLESPOONS AVOCADO OIL

1 LB. WILD BOAR MEAT, CUBED

SALT AND PEPPER, TO TASTE

1 LARGE ONION, DICED

¼ CUP DICED BACON

¼ CUP DICED GREEN BELL PEPPER

¼ CUP DICED RED BELL PEPPER

¼ CUP DICED YELLOW BELL PEPPER

¼ CUP CHOPPED ROASTED CHESTNUTS (SEE PAGE 539)

2 TABLESPOONS TOMATO PASTE

¼ CUP SOY SAUCE

½ CUP RED WINE

1 CUP WATER

2 DRIED JUNIPER BERRIES

2 WHOLE CLOVES

1 LB. GREEN BEANS, TRIMMED

SPÄTZLE (SEE PAGE 112)

1. Place the avocado oil in a large skillet and warm it over medium-high heat. Season the boar with salt and pepper, add it to the pan, and sear it until it is browned all over.

2. Add the onion, bacon, peppers, and chestnuts and cook, stirring, until the vegetables and bacon start to brown, about 8 minutes.

3. Stir in the tomato paste, soy sauce, wine, juniper berries, and cloves, season the sauce with salt and pepper, and bring it to a simmer. Reduce the heat to low, cover the pan, and cook until the boar is very tender, about 2 hours, stirring occasionally.

4. When the sauce is close to finished, bring water to a boil in a large saucepan. Add salt, let the water return to a full boil, and add the green beans. Cook until they are tender, 2 to 3 minutes.

5. Drain the green beans. Stir the Spätzle into the ragù and cook until they are warmed through. Serve alongside the green beans.

Farfalle with Swordfish & Shrimp

YIELD: 4 SERVINGS / **ACTIVE TIME:** 15 MINUTES / **TOTAL TIME:** 20 MINUTES

1½ LBS. SWORDFISH FILLETS, SKIN REMOVED

SALT AND PEPPER, TO TASTE

20 LARGE SHRIMP, SHELLS REMOVED, DEVEINED

6 TABLESPOONS EXTRA-VIRGIN OLIVE OIL

½ CUP SUN-DRIED TOMATOES IN OLIVE OIL, DRAINED AND CHOPPED

5 GARLIC CLOVES, MINCED

FARFALLE (SEE PAGE 60)

12 FRESH BASIL LEAVES, FINELY CHOPPED

1. Bring water to a boil in a large saucepan.

2. Cut the swordfish into 3-inch strips and season both sides with salt and pepper. Season the shrimp with salt and pepper. Set the seafood aside.

3. Place half of the olive oil, the sun-dried tomatoes, and the garlic in a small bowl and stir to combine. Set the mixture aside.

4. Add salt to the boiling water, let it return to a full boil, and add the pasta. Cook until it is al dente, 2 to 4 minutes. Drain the pasta and set it aside.

5. Place the remaining olive oil in a large skillet and warm it over medium-high heat. Arrange the swordfish in a single layer in the pan. Top it with half of the sun-dried tomato mixture, cook for about 2 to 3 minutes, and turn the swordfish over. Cover it with the remaining sun-dried tomato mixture and add the shrimp to the pan. Cook until the swordfish is slightly firm and the shrimp are just cooked through, 3 to 5 minutes.

6. Add the pasta and basil to the pan, toss to combine, and serve.

Sea Bass & Shrimp over Stir-Fried Egg Noodles

YIELD: 4 SERVINGS / **ACTIVE TIME:** 25 MINUTES / **TOTAL TIME:** 35 MINUTES

SALT AND PEPPER, TO TASTE

¾ LB. CHINESE EGG NOODLES (SEE PAGE 104)

4 SEA BASS FILLETS, DEBONED

2 TABLESPOONS FRESH LIME JUICE

3 TABLESPOONS AVOCADO OIL

8 LARGE SHRIMP, SHELLS REMOVED, DEVEINED

2 TABLESPOONS SESAME OIL

1 SMALL GREEN BELL PEPPER, STEMMED, SEEDED, AND CHOPPED

1 RED CHILE PEPPER, STEMMED, SEEDED, AND CHOPPED

1 GARLIC CLOVE, MINCED

2 SCALLIONS, TRIMMED AND CHOPPED

2 TABLESPOONS SOY SAUCE

1. Bring water to a boil in a large saucepan. Add salt, let the water return to a full boil, and add the egg noodles. Cook until very al dente, about 2 minutes. Drain the noodles, run them under cold water, and let them drain again.

2. Season the sea bass with salt and sprinkle some of the lime juice over it. Let the sea bass sit for 5 minutes.

3. Place the avocado oil in a large skillet and warm it over medium-high heat. Add the sea bass and cook for 3 minutes. Turn the sea bass over, add the shrimp to the pan, and cook until the sea bass and the shrimp are cooked through, 3 to 5 minutes. Remove the pan from heat and cover it to keep the seafood warm.

4. Place the sesame oil in a wok and warm it over high heat. Add the peppers, garlic, and scallions and stir-fry for 30 seconds. Add the egg noodles and stir-fry until they are warmed through and golden brown. Season the noodles with salt and pepper and stir in the soy sauce and remaining lime juice.

5. Divide the noodles among the serving plates and top with the sea bass and shrimp.

Seafood Lasagna

YIELD: 4 SERVINGS / **ACTIVE TIME:** 20 MINUTES / **TOTAL TIME:** 1 HOUR AND 15 MINUTES

9 SHEETS OF NO-BOIL LASAGNA

¼ CUP EXTRA-VIRGIN OLIVE OIL, PLUS MORE AS NEEDED

1 SMALL RED ONION, CHOPPED

1 GARLIC CLOVE, MINCED

1 (14 OZ.) CAN OF DICED TOMATOES, DRAINED

½ CUP SUN-DRIED TOMATOES IN OLIVE OIL, DRAINED AND CHOPPED

½ CUP SUGO AL BASILICO (SEE PAGE 448)

¼ CUP CAPERS, DRAINED AND RINSED

1 TABLESPOON FRESH LEMON JUICE

1½ LBS. HADDOCK, SKIN REMOVED, DEBONED

SALT AND PEPPER, TO TASTE

30 CHERRY TOMATOES, HALVED

¼ CUP CHOPPED FRESH DILL

1 CUP GRATED CHEDDAR CHEESE

1. Place the lasagna sheets in a roasting pan, cover with cold water, and let them sit for 15 minutes.

2. Place 1 tablespoon of olive oil in a large skillet and warm it over medium heat. Add the onion and cook, stirring occasionally, until it has softened, about 5 minutes.

3. Add the garlic and cook, stirring continually, for 1 minute. Add the canned tomatoes, sun-dried tomatoes, sauce, and capers, bring the sauce to a simmer, and cook, stirring occasionally, until it has reduced slightly and the flavor has developed to your liking, 18 to 20 minutes.

4. Preheat the oven to 350°F. Coat a baking dish with olive oil. Drain the lasagna sheets and set them aside.

5. Sprinkle the lemon juice over the haddock and season it with salt and pepper. Cut the fish into 2-inch strips.

6. Place the remaining olive oil in a large skillet and warm it over medium-high heat. Add the haddock to the pan and cook for 2 minutes on each side. Remove the haddock from the skillet and set it aside.

7. Remove the sauce from heat and stir in the cherry tomatoes and dill. Season the sauce with salt and pepper and coat the bottom of the baking dish with some of it. Top with a layer of lasagna sheets, spread some sauce over them, and then sprinkle some of the haddock on top. Repeat this layering process until the lasagna has been assembled, finishing with a layer of the sauce.

8. Sprinkle the cheddar over the lasagna, place it in the oven, and bake until the fish is cooked through and the top is golden brown, about 20 minutes.

9. Remove the lasagna from the oven and let it rest for 10 minutes before slicing and serving.

Fried Noodles, Malaysian Style

YIELD: 2 SERVINGS / **ACTIVE TIME:** 10 MINUTES / **TOTAL TIME:** 20 MINUTES

1 LB. RICE NOODLES

1 TABLESPOON CANOLA OIL

1 TEASPOON SESAME OIL

2 GARLIC CLOVES, MINCED

2 SCALLIONS, TRIMMED AND CHOPPED

6 LARGE SHRIMP, SHELLS REMOVED, DEVEINED

2 TABLESPOONS KECAP MANIS

1 TABLESPOON SRIRACHA

1 TABLESPOON SOY SAUCE

4 FRESH BASIL LEAVES

¼ CUP BEAN SPROUTS

FRESH CILANTRO, CHOPPED, FOR GARNISH

CARROT, SHREDDED, FOR GARNISH

1. Place the noodles in a large baking dish. Cover them with hot water and let them soak for 10 minutes. Drain the noodles and set them aside.

2. Place the canola oil and sesame oil in a large wok and warm them over high heat. Add the garlic and scallions and stir-fry for 30 seconds.

3. Add the noodles, shrimp, kecap manis, sriracha, and soy sauce and stir to combine. Stir-fry until the noodles are warmed through and crispy and the shrimp turn pink and are cooked through, 3 to 4 minutes.

4. Stir in the basil and bean sprouts, garnish the dish with cilantro and shredded carrot, and enjoy.

Noodles & Cabbage

YIELD: 6 TO 8 SERVINGS / **ACTIVE TIME:** 30 MINUTES / **TOTAL TIME:** 2 HOURS AND 30 MINUTES

¾ CUP SALTED BUTTER

2 HEADS OF GREEN CABBAGE, CORED AND SLICED THIN

SALT AND WHITE PEPPER, TO TASTE

1 LB. WIDE EGG NOODLES

1. Place half of the butter in a Dutch oven and melt it over medium heat. Add the cabbage. If it doesn't all fit initially, push down what does fit in the pot and add more as that wilts. Cover the pot with a lid and cook for 10 minutes.

2. Remove the lid and add the remaining butter. Cover and cook for an additional 30 minutes, stirring occasionally.

3. Reduce the heat to low and cook until the cabbage is extremely soft and browned, about 1 hour. Season with white pepper to taste.

4. About 20 minutes before the cabbage will be finished cooking, bring water to a boil in a large saucepan. Add salt, let the water return to a boil, and add the egg noodles. Cook until they are al dente, about 8 minutes. Drain the noodles and transfer them to a large bowl.

5. Add the cabbage, toss to combine, and serve.

Vegetable Lo Mein

YIELD: 4 TO 6 SERVINGS / **ACTIVE TIME:** 15 TO 25 MINUTES / **TOTAL TIME:** 30 MINUTES

¼ CUP SESAME OIL

3 TABLESPOONS SOY SAUCE

2 TABLESPOONS BLACK VINEGAR

1 TABLESPOON BROWN SUGAR

3 TABLESPOONS FISH SAUCE

1 TABLESPOON CANOLA OIL

6 SCALLIONS, TRIMMED AND CHOPPED, WHITES AND GREENS SEPARATED

1 TABLESPOON MINCED FRESH GINGER

2 GARLIC CLOVES, MINCED

¼ LB. BUTTON MUSHROOMS, SLICED

½ WHITE ONION, SLICED

½ CUP BEAN SPROUTS

1 CARROT, PEELED AND CUT INTO MATCHSTICKS

1 LB. LO MEIN NOODLES

1. In a large mixing bowl, add the sesame oil, soy sauce, black vinegar, brown sugar, and fish sauce and whisk to combine. Set the mixture aside.

2. Place the canola oil, scallion whites, ginger, and garlic in a Dutch oven and cook over high heat for 2 minutes. Add the mushrooms, onion, bean sprouts, and carrot and cook, stirring frequently, for 2 to 3 minutes, until the vegetables are cooked but still crisp. Remove the mixture from the pan and set it aside.

3. Wipe out the pot, fill it with water, and bring to a boil. Add the noodles and cook until they are al dente, 5 to 7 minutes.

4. Drain the noodles and add them to the mixing bowl containing the dressing. Toss to coat, add the vegetable mixture and scallion greens, and toss to combine. Serve immediately.

Sukiyaki

YIELD: 2 SERVINGS / **ACTIVE TIME:** 5 MINUTES / **TOTAL TIME:** 15 MINUTES

SALT, TO TASTE

¾ LB. UDON NOODLES
(SEE PAGE 106)

1 TABLESPOON CANOLA OIL

3 TABLESPOONS BROWN
SUGAR

1 LB. RIB EYE, SLICED VERY THIN

½ CUP MIRIN

½ CUP SAKE

⅓ CUP SOY SAUCE

1 CUP DASHI STOCK
(SEE PAGE 540)

1 BUNCH OF SCALLIONS,
TRIMMED AND SLICED INTO
2-INCH PIECES

2 CUPS CHOPPED NAPA
CABBAGE

1 BUNCH OF ENOKI
MUSHROOMS

6 LARGE SHIITAKE MUSHROOMS

1 CUP FRESH SPINACH

½ LB. TOFU, DRAINED AND CUT
INTO ¼-INCH CUBES

1. Bring water to a boil in a large saucepan. Add salt, let the water return to a full boil, and add the noodles. Cook until they are very al dente, 1 to 2 minutes. Drain, rinse the noodles under cold water, and set the noodles aside.

2. Place the canola oil in a Dutch oven and warm it over medium-high heat. Add the sugar and steak and cook until the steak is browned all over, about 2 minutes, stirring as necessary.

3. Stir in the mirin, sake, soy sauce, and stock and bring it to a simmer.

4. Carefully arrange the scallions, cabbage, mushrooms, spinach, and tofu in the broth. Add the noodles, cover the pot, and cook until the cabbage has wilted. Ladle into warmed bowls and enjoy.

Korean Chicken Thighs with Sweet Potato Vermicelli

YIELD: 6 SERVINGS / **ACTIVE TIME:** 45 MINUTES / **TOTAL TIME:** 3 HOURS AND 30 MINUTES

1. To prepare the marinade, place all of the ingredients in a blender and puree until smooth.

2. To begin preparations for the chicken thighs, place the chicken in a bowl, pour the marinade over the top, and stir to coat. Marinate the chicken in the refrigerator for 2 hours.

3. Fill a Dutch oven with water and bring to a boil. Add the vermicelli and cook until al dente, 6 to 8 minutes. Drain, rinse the noodles with cold water, and set them aside.

4. Preheat the oven to 375°F. Remove the chicken from the refrigerator and place the pot back on the stove. Add the canola oil and warm it over medium-high heat. Remove the chicken from the marinade and place it, skin side down, in the Dutch oven. Reserve the marinade. Sear the chicken until a crust forms on the skin, 5 to 7 minutes.

5. Turn the chicken thighs over, add the reserved marinade, place the pot in the oven, and cook until the chicken is cooked through (the interior temperature is 165°F on an instant-read thermometer).

6. Remove the pot from the oven, remove the chicken, and set it aside. Drain the Dutch oven and wipe it clean. Return it to the stove, add the cabbage, mushrooms, shallot, onion, garlic, scallion whites, and ginger, and cook, stirring occasionally, until the cabbage has wilted, about 8 minutes.

7. Place the brown sugar, sesame oil, fish sauce, soy sauce, and rice vinegar in a small bowl and stir to combine. Add this sauce and the vermicelli to the pot, stir until the noodles are coated, and then return the chicken to the Dutch oven.

8. Top with the scallion greens and sesame seeds, return to the oven for 5 minutes, and cook until everything is warmed through. Remove from the oven and serve immediately.

FOR THE MARINADE

1 LEMONGRASS STALK, BOTTOM HALF ONLY

2 GARLIC CLOVES

1 TABLESPOON MINCED FRESH GINGER

1 SCALLION

¼ CUP BROWN SUGAR

2 TABLESPOONS GOCHUJANG

1 TABLESPOON SESAME OIL

1 TABLESPOON RICE VINEGAR

2 TABLESPOONS FISH SAUCE

1 TABLESPOON BLACK PEPPER

FOR THE CHICKEN THIGHS

6 BONE-IN, SKIN-ON CHICKEN THIGHS

10 OZ. SWEET POTATO VERMICELLI

2 TABLESPOONS CANOLA OIL

¼ HEAD OF NAPA CABBAGE, SHREDDED

4 OZ. SHIITAKE MUSHROOMS, SLICED THIN

1 SHALLOT, SLICED THIN

1 YELLOW ONION, SLICED THIN

2 GARLIC CLOVES, MINCED

2 SCALLIONS, TRIMMED AND CHOPPED, WHITES AND GREENS SEPARATED

2 TABLESPOONS MINCED FRESH GINGER

¼ CUP BROWN SUGAR

2 TABLESPOONS SESAME OIL

2 TABLESPOONS FISH SAUCE

¼ CUP SOY SAUCE

¼ CUP RICE VINEGAR

¼ CUP SESAME SEEDS

Thai Mussels

YIELD: 4 SERVINGS / **ACTIVE TIME:** 15 MINUTES / **TOTAL TIME:** 25 MINUTES

1 TABLESPOON CANOLA OIL

4 SHALLOTS, MINCED

2 GARLIC CLOVES, SLICED

½ CUP FRESH CILANTRO

1 LEMONGRASS STALK, CUT INTO 4 LARGE PIECES

1 BIRD'S EYE CHILE PEPPER, STEMMED, SEEDED, AND SLICED

1 (14 OZ.) CAN OF COCONUT MILK

1 TABLESPOON FISH SAUCE (OPTIONAL)

2 LBS. MUSSELS, RINSED WELL AND DEBEARDED

JUICE OF 1 LIME

RICE NOODLES, COOKED, FOR SERVING

1. Place the canola oil in a Dutch oven and warm it over medium-high heat. Add the shallots, garlic, cilantro, lemongrass, and chile and cook, stirring frequently, until the garlic is lightly browned, about 4 minutes.

2. Add the coconut milk and the fish sauce (if using) and bring to a boil. Add the mussels and immediately cover the pot.

3. Steam until the majority of the mussels have opened, about 5 minutes. Discard any unopened mussels.

4. Stir a few times to coat the mussels and add half of the lime juice. Taste and add more lime juice as necessary. Ladle into warmed bowls and serve with rice noodles.

Japchae

YIELD: 4 SERVINGS / **ACTIVE TIME:** 30 MINUTES / **TOTAL TIME:** 30 MINUTES

CANOLA OIL, AS NEEDED

2 LARGE EGGS, YOLKS AND WHITES SEPARATED

6 DRIED SHIITAKE MUSHROOMS, SOAKED AND DRAINED, STEMS REMOVED, SLICED THIN

1 CUP SHREDDED CABBAGE

1 ONION, SLICED THIN

½ CUP JULIENNED CARROTS

6 WOOD EAR MUSHROOMS, SOAKED AND DRAINED, STEMS REMOVED

½ RED BELL PEPPER, JULIENNED

SALT AND PEPPER, TO TASTE

½ CUP VEGETABLE STOCK (SEE PAGE 537), PLUS MORE AS NEEDED

¼ CUP SOY SAUCE

2 TABLESPOONS MIRIN

2 TABLESPOONS SESAME OIL

1 TABLESPOON SUGAR

4 GARLIC CLOVES, MINCED

4 OZ. SWEET POTATO STARCH NOODLES, SOAKED UNTIL PLIABLE AND DRAINED

3 SCALLIONS, TRIMMED AND SLICED

¼ CUP SPINACH

1 TABLESPOON TOASTED SESAME SEEDS, FOR GARNISH

1. Place a little canola oil in a nonstick pan and warm it over medium heat. Place the egg yolks in the pan in a thin layer and cook until they are just set. Roll the egg yolks up into a tube, slice them thin, and set aside.

2. Add a little more canola oil to the pan if it looks dry. Place the egg whites in the pan in a thin layer and cook until they are just set. Roll the egg whites up into a tube, slice them thin, and set them aside.

3. Add a little more canola oil to the pan, raise the heat to medium-high, and add the shiitake mushrooms, cabbage, and onion to the pan. Stir-fry for 2 minutes, add the carrots, wood ear mushrooms, and bell pepper and season with salt and pepper. Cook, stirring frequently, until the vegetables are just cooked through and still firm and crispy. Remove the pan from heat and set it aside.

4. Place the stock, soy sauce, mirin, sesame oil, sugar, and garlic in a bowl and stir until well combined. Add the mixture to a wok and bring it to a boil. Add the noodles, reduce the heat so that the sauce simmers, and cook the noodles until they have absorbed all of the liquid; if more liquid is needed, add more stock or water.

5. Add the cooked vegetables, scallions, and spinach to the wok and toss to combine. Remove the pan from heat, garnish with the sesame seeds and thinly sliced egg, and enjoy.

Japchae
SEE PAGE 323

Soba Noodles with Marinated Eggplant & Tofu

YIELD: 4 SERVINGS / **ACTIVE TIME:** 45 MINUTES / **TOTAL TIME:** 1 HOUR AND 45 MINUTES

FOR THE MARINADE

2 TABLESPOONS RICE VINEGAR

3 TABLESPOONS SOY SAUCE

1 TABLESPOON TOASTED SESAME OIL

½ TEASPOON SUGAR

2 GARLIC CLOVES, MINCED

FOR THE DRESSING

1 TABLESPOON RICE VINEGAR

1 TABLESPOON PEANUT OIL

1 TEASPOON SOY SAUCE

1 TABLESPOON TOASTED SESAME OIL

1-INCH PIECE OF FRESH GINGER, PEELED AND GRATED

FOR THE NOODLES

2 LBS. EGGPLANTS

½ LB. SOBA NOODLES

3 TABLESPOONS PEANUT OIL

SALT, TO TASTE

¾ LB. EXTRA-FIRM TOFU, DRAINED AND DICED

SCALLIONS, CHOPPED, FOR GARNISH

1. To prepare the marinade, place all of the ingredients in a small bowl and stir to combine. To prepare the dressing, place all of the ingredients in a separate small bowl and stir to combine. Set the marinade and the dressing aside.

2. To begin preparations for the noodles, trim both ends of the eggplants, slice them in half, and cut them into ½-inch pieces. Place in a mixing bowl, add the marinade, and toss to combine. Let the eggplants marinate for 1 hour at room temperature.

3. Bring water to a boil in a large saucepan. Add the noodles and cook until they are al dente, 3 to 5 minutes. Drain, rinse under cold water, and drain the noodles again. Place them in a large bowl, add the dressing, toss to coat, and set the noodles aside.

4. Place the peanut oil in a large wok or skillet and warm it over medium-high heat. Add the eggplants, season with salt, and stir-fry until the eggplant softens and starts to brown, 5 to 6 minutes. Using a slotted spoon, transfer the eggplant to a paper towel–lined plate.

5. Add the tofu and stir-fry until it is golden brown all over, 4 to 5 minutes. Using a slotted spoon, transfer the tofu to a separate paper towel–lined plate.

6. Divide the noodles among four bowls. Arrange the eggplant and tofu on top, garnish with scallions, and serve.

Soba Noodle Stir-Fry

YIELD: 4 SERVINGS / **ACTIVE TIME:** 25 MINUTES / **TOTAL TIME:** 25 MINUTES

¼ CUP SOY SAUCE

3 TABLESPOONS WATER

1½ TABLESPOONS RICE VINEGAR

3 TABLESPOONS TOASTED SESAME OIL

½ LB. SOBA NOODLES

3 TABLESPOONS CANOLA OIL

1 YELLOW ONION, SLICED THIN

2 CARROTS, PEELED AND JULIENNED

1 LB. ASPARAGUS, TRIMMED AND CHOPPED

6 SHIITAKE MUSHROOMS, STEMMED AND CHOPPED

1 TEASPOON KOSHER SALT

2 GARLIC CLOVES, MINCED

1 TEASPOON RED PEPPER FLAKES

⅓ CUP EDAMAME, SHELLED AND COOKED

1. Combine the soy sauce, water, rice vinegar, and 2 tablespoons of sesame oil in a bowl and set the sauce aside.

2. Bring water to a boil in a large saucepan. Add the noodles and cook until they are al dente, 3 to 5 minutes. Drain, rinse under cold water, and drain the noodles again. Place them in a large bowl, add the remaining sesame oil, toss to coat, and set the noodles aside.

3. Place the canola oil in a large wok or skillet and warm it over medium-high heat. Add the onion, carrots, asparagus, mushrooms, and salt and stir-fry until the vegetables are tender, 4 to 5 minutes.

4. Reduce the heat to medium, add the garlic and red pepper flakes, and stir-fry for 1 minute.

5. Add the noodles and edamame and cook, tossing to combine, until they are warmed through. Add the sauce, toss to coat, and serve.

Garden Sesame Noodles

YIELD: 6 SERVINGS / **ACTIVE TIME:** 15 MINUTES / **TOTAL TIME:** 30 MINUTES

1 LB. CHINESE EGG NOODLES (SEE PAGE 104)

2½ TABLESPOONS TOASTED SESAME OIL

2 TABLESPOONS TAHINI PASTE

1½ TABLESPOONS SMOOTH PEANUT BUTTER

¼ CUP SOY SAUCE

2 TABLESPOONS RICE VINEGAR

1 TABLESPOON LIGHT BROWN SUGAR

2 TEASPOONS CHILI GARLIC SAUCE, PLUS MORE FOR SERVING

2-INCH PIECE OF FRESH GINGER, PEELED AND GRATED

2 GARLIC CLOVES, MINCED

1 YELLOW OR ORANGE BELL PEPPER, STEMMED, SEEDED, AND SLICED THIN

2 CUPS CHOPPED LEFTOVER COOKED CHICKEN

1 CUCUMBER, PEELED, SEEDED, AND SLICED THIN

1 CUP SNOW PEAS, TRIMMED

½ CUP CHOPPED ROASTED PEANUTS

2 TABLESPOONS SESAME SEEDS, TOASTED

6 SCALLIONS, TRIMMED AND CHOPPED

1. Bring water to a boil in a large saucepan. Add the noodles and cook until they are al dente, 2 to 3 minutes. Drain, rinse under cold water, and drain the noodles again. Place them in a large bowl, add 1½ teaspoons of sesame oil, toss to coat, and set the noodles aside.

2. Place the tahini and peanut butter in a small bowl. Add the soy sauce, vinegar, the remaining sesame oil, the sugar, chili garlic sauce, ginger, and garlic and whisk until combined. Taste and adjust the seasoning as necessary.

3. Add the sauce to the noodles and toss to coat. Divide the noodles among the serving bowls and top with the pepper, chicken, cucumber, snow peas, peanuts, sesame seeds, and scallions. Serve with additional chili garlic sauce.

Singapore-Style Noodles with Shrimp & Curry

YIELD: 4 SERVINGS / **ACTIVE TIME:** 25 MINUTES / **TOTAL TIME:** 45 MINUTES

¾ LB. RICE STICK NOODLES

½ CUP PLUS 1½ TEASPOONS PEANUT OIL

5 LARGE EGGS, LIGHTLY BEATEN

SALT, TO TASTE

2 TABLESPOONS TOASTED SESAME OIL

1 LB. PORK TENDERLOIN

1 LB. SHRIMP, SHELLS REMOVED, DEVEINED

1 YELLOW ONION, CUT INTO HALF-MOONS

2 JALAPEÑO CHILE PEPPERS, STEMMED, SEEDED, AND MINCED

2-INCH PIECE OF FRESH GINGER, PEELED AND GRATED

6 BLACK GARLIC CLOVES, MINCED

2 RED BELL PEPPERS, STEMMED, SEEDED, AND SLICED THIN

½ CUP SHREDDED GREEN CABBAGE

½ LB. CREMINI MUSHROOMS, STEMMED AND SLICED THIN

5 SCALLIONS, TRIMMED AND CHOPPED

6 OZ. SNOW PEAS, TRIMMED

½ TEASPOON WHITE PEPPER

½ TEASPOON GROUND CORIANDER

½ TEASPOON TOASTED SESAME SEEDS

¼ CUP MAHARAJAH CURRY POWDER

1 CUP CHICKEN STOCK (SEE PAGE 536)

1. Place the noodles in a baking dish, cover them with warm water, and let them soak until they are al dente, about 20 minutes. Drain the noodles, place them in a bowl, and add 1½ teaspoons of peanut oil. Toss to coat and set them aside.

2. Place 1 tablespoon of peanut oil in a large wok or skillet and warm it over medium-high heat. Add the eggs, season with salt, and cook until they are set, 2 to 3 minutes. Transfer the eggs to a plate and slice them into thin, 2-inch-long pieces.

3. Add the sesame oil to the pan. Pat the pork dry with paper towels, season it with salt, add it to the pan, and reduce the heat to medium. Cook until the pork is cooked through (the internal temperature is 145°F), about 10 minutes, turning occasionally. Transfer the pork to a cutting board and cut it into strips.

4. Add 1 tablespoon of peanut oil to the pan and warm it over medium-high heat. Add the shrimp, season it with salt, and stir-fry until the shrimp are cooked through, 2 to 3 minutes. Transfer the shrimp to the cutting board with the pork.

5. Add 2 tablespoons of peanut oil to the pan. Add the onion, jalapeños, ginger, and garlic and stir-fry until the onion is translucent, about 6 minutes. Add the bell pepper, cabbage, mushrooms, scallions, snow peas, white pepper, coriander, and toasted sesame seeds, season with salt, and stir-fry for 1 minute.

6. Place the curry powder, stock, and the remaining peanut oil in a small bowl and stir to combine.

7. Pour the mixture over the vegetables in the pan and cook until everything is tender, 3 to 4 minutes. Stir in the pork, shrimp, eggs, and noodles, toss to combine, and serve.

Singapore-Style Noodles with Shrimp & Curry
SEE PAGE 329

Vietnamese Noodle Salad

YIELD: 6 SERVINGS / **ACTIVE TIME:** 25 MINUTES / **TOTAL TIME:** 45 MINUTES

1 LB. EXTRA-FIRM TOFU, DRAINED AND CUT INTO ½-INCH STRIPS

2 CUPS MUNG BEAN SPROUTS, PICKED OVER

½ LB. RICE STICK NOODLES

¼ CUP PEANUT OIL

SALT, TO TASTE

2½ CUPS SHREDDED ROMAINE LETTUCE

2 HANDFULS OF MIXED FRESH HERBS, CHOPPED (MINT, CILANTRO, BASIL RECOMMENDED)

2 SMALL CUCUMBERS, PEELED AND JULIENNED

2 TABLESPOONS SALTED, ROASTED PEANUTS, CHOPPED, FOR GARNISH

NUOC CHAM (SEE PAGE 540)

1. Place the tofu in a single layer on a paper towel–lined tray. Cover with paper towels and pat dry. Let them sit for 30 minutes, changing the paper towels after 15 minutes. Cut the dried strips into ½-inch cubes and set them aside.

2. Bring water to a boil in a large saucepan. Place the bean sprouts in a bowl of cold water and discard any hulls that float to the top. Rinse the remaining sprouts under cold water, add them to the boiling water, and cook for 1 minute. Remove them with a strainer and run them under cold water. Drain well, chop the sprouts, and set them aside.

3. Add the noodles to the boiling water and cook until they are al dente, 2 to 3 minutes. Drain, rinse the noodles under cold water, and drain again. Set the noodles aside.

4. Place the peanut oil in a large, deep skillet and warm it over medium-high heat. Season the tofu with salt, add it to the pan, and cook until it is browned all over, 4 to 6 minutes, turning as necessary. Transfer the tofu to a paper towel–lined plate to drain.

5. Divide the noodles among four shallow bowls. Arrange the lettuce, herbs, cucumber, sprouts, and tofu on top. Drizzle some Nuoc Cham over each portion, garnish with the peanuts, and enjoy.

Spicy Cellophane Noodles with Green Beans & Tofu

YIELD: 6 SERVINGS / **ACTIVE TIME:** 25 MINUTES / **TOTAL TIME:** 45 MINUTES

10 OZ. EXTRA-FIRM TOFU, DRAINED AND CUT INTO ¾-INCH PIECES

½ LB. WIDE CELLOPHANE NOODLES

¼ CUP PEANUT OIL, PLUS MORE AS NEEDED

3 LARGE SHALLOTS, MINCED

SALT, TO TASTE

2 GARLIC CLOVES, MINCED

1 TEASPOON RED PEPPER FLAKES

1 LB. GREEN BEANS, TRIMMED AND CHOPPED

2 TABLESPOONS LIGHT BROWN SUGAR

2 TABLESPOONS SOY SAUCE

2 TABLESPOONS FISH SAUCE

JUICE OF 2 LIMES

½ CUP THAI BASIL, CHOPPED

⅓ CUP ROASTED PEANUTS, CHOPPED, FOR GARNISH

1. Place the tofu in a single layer on a paper towel–lined tray. Cover with paper towels and pat dry. Let them sit for 30 minutes, changing the paper towels after 15 minutes. Cut the dried strips into ½-inch cubes and set them aside.

2. Place the noodles in a baking dish and cover them with hot water. Let the noodles sit until they are al dente, about 15 minutes. Drain the noodles, rinse them under cold water, and drain them again. Set the noodles aside.

3. Place half of the peanut oil in a large, deep skillet and warm it over medium-high heat. Working in three batches, add the tofu to the pan and cook until it is crispy and browned all over, 4 to 6 minutes, turning as necessary. Transfer the tofu to a paper towel–lined plate to drain. Add more peanut oil to the pan as necessary.

4. Add the shallots to the pan, season with salt, and stir-fry until they are tender and golden brown, 6 to 8 minutes. Add the garlic, red pepper flakes, and green beans and stir-fry until the green beans are tender, 3 to 4 minutes. Add the tofu and brown sugar and cook until the tofu is heated through, about 3 minutes.

5. Add the noodles, soy sauce, and fish sauce to the pan and toss to combine. Remove the pan from heat, add the lime juice and half of the herbs, and toss to combine. Top with the peanuts and remaining herbs and serve.

Pasta C'anciova e Muddica Atturrata

YIELD: 4 SERVINGS / **ACTIVE TIME:** 20 MINUTES / **TOTAL TIME:** 45 MINUTES

5 TABLESPOONS EXTRA-VIRGIN OLIVE OIL

1 CUP BREAD CRUMBS

SALT AND PEPPER, TO TASTE

½ ONION, FINELY DICED

2 GARLIC CLOVES

8 ANCHOVIES IN OLIVE OIL, DRAINED AND CHOPPED

⅓ CUP RAISINS, SOAKED IN WARM WATER

⅓ CUP PINE NUTS

1 CUP TOMATO PASTE

1 CUP WARM WATER

1 LB. LINGUINE

1. Place 1 tablespoon of olive oil in a small skillet and warm it over medium heat. Add the bread crumbs, season them with salt, and cook, stirring occasionally, until they have browned, about 4 minutes. Remove the pan from heat and set it aside.

2. Place the remaining olive oil in a large skillet and warm it over medium heat. Add the onion, garlic, and anchovies and cook, stirring occasionally, until the onion has softened and the anchovies have dissolved, about 5 minutes.

3. Drain the raisins, squeeze them to remove any excess liquid, and add them to the skillet along with the pine nuts. Cook for 5 minutes.

4. Combine the tomato paste and water and stir the mixture into the pan. Raise the heat to medium-high and cook until the sauce has thickened, 5 to 10 minutes.

5. Bring water to a boil in a large saucepan. Add salt, let the water return to a full boil, and add the pasta. Cook until the pasta is al dente.

6. Drain the pasta and add it to the sauce along with the bread crumbs. Toss to combine, season with salt and pepper, and serve.

Shrimp Pad Thai

YIELD: 4 SERVINGS / **ACTIVE TIME:** 25 MINUTES / **TOTAL TIME:** 25 MINUTES

½ LB. WIDE RICE NOODLES

2½ TABLESPOONS PEANUT OIL

1 CUP MUNG BEAN SPROUTS, PICKED OVER

2 GARLIC CLOVES, MINCED

2 THAI CHILE PEPPERS, STEMMED, SEEDED, AND SLICED THIN

⅓ CUP LIGHT BROWN SUGAR, FIRMLY PACKED

½ CUP TAMARIND PASTE

5 TABLESPOONS FISH SAUCE

JUICE OF ½ LIME

1 LB. LARGE SHRIMP, SHELLS REMOVED, DEVEINED

⅛ TEASPOON RED PEPPER FLAKES

SALT, TO TASTE

3 LARGE EGGS, LIGHTLY BEATEN

2 SCALLIONS, WHITE PARTS ONLY, THINLY SLICED

2 CARROTS, PEELED AND JULIENNED

FRESH CILANTRO, CHOPPED, FOR GARNISH

ROASTED CASHEWS, CHOPPED, FOR GARNISH

LIME WEDGES, FOR SERVING

1. Place the noodles in a baking pan, cover them with warm water, and let them soak until they are al dente, about 20 minutes. Drain the noodles, place them in a bowl, and add ½ tablespoon of the peanut oil. Toss to coat and set the noodles aside.

2. Bring water to a boil in a large saucepan. Place the bean sprouts in a bowl of cold water and discard any hulls that float to the top. Rinse the remaining sprouts under cold water, add them to the boiling water, and cook for 1 minute. Remove them with a strainer and run them under cold water. Drain well, chop the sprouts, and set them aside.

3. Place the garlic, chiles, brown sugar, tamarind paste, and fish sauce in a small saucepan and stir to combine. Cook over medium heat, stirring continually, until the sugar and paste have dissolved, 2 to 3 minutes. Remove the pan from heat and stir the lime juice into the sauce.

4. Place the remaining peanut oil in a large wok or skillet and warm it over medium heat. Add the shrimp and red pepper flakes, season with salt, and stir-fry until the shrimp are almost cooked through, about 2 minutes.

5. Add the eggs and scramble until they are just set, about 30 seconds. Stir in one-third of the sauce and the noodles and toss to combine. Add the bean sprouts, scallions, carrots, and the remaining sauce and cook, tossing to combine, until everything is warmed through.

6. Garnish with cilantro and cashews and serve with lime wedges.

Tofu San Bei

YIELD: 4 SERVINGS / **ACTIVE TIME:** 30 MINUTES / **TOTAL TIME:** 1 HOUR

1 LB. EXTRA-FIRM TOFU

3 TABLESPOONS PEANUT OIL

1½ TEASPOONS CORNSTARCH, PLUS MORE AS NEEDED

3 TABLESPOONS TOASTED SESAME OIL

8 GARLIC CLOVES, SMASHED

2-INCH PIECE OF FRESH GINGER, PEELED AND CHOPPED INTO 8 PIECES

10 SCALLIONS, TRIMMED AND CHOPPED

SALT, TO TASTE

3 TABLESPOONS SUGAR

¾ CUP PLUS 1 TABLESPOON WATER

¾ CUP SHAOXING RICE WINE

⅓ CUP SOY SAUCE

⅓ LB. RAMEN NOODLES

FRESH BASIL, SLICED THIN, FOR GARNISH

1. Drain the tofu and cut it into ½-inch slices. Arrange it in a single layer on a paper towel–lined tray. Cover with paper towels and pat dry. Let them sit for 30 minutes, changing the paper towels after 15 minutes.

2. Place the peanut oil in a large skillet and warm it over medium heat. Place cornstarch in a shallow bowl and dredge the tofu in it.

3. Working in batches to avoid crowding the pan, add the tofu, raise the heat to medium-high, and cook until the tofu is a deep golden brown, 4 to 6 minutes, turning it as necessary. Transfer the tofu to a paper towel–lined plate to drain.

4. Wipe out the skillet and add the sesame oil to the pan. Reduce heat to medium and add the garlic, ginger, and scallions. Season with salt and cook, stirring frequently, for 2 minutes. Add the sugar and stir until it has melted. Stir in the ¾ cup water, rice wine, and soy sauce, raise heat to medium-high, and bring to a boil. Reduce the heat to low, cover, and simmer, stirring occasionally, for 10 minutes.

5. Place the cornstarch and 1 tablespoon of water in a small bowl and stir until the mixture is smooth. Stir the slurry into the sauce and cook, stirring occasionally, until the sauce has thickened, about 5 minutes. Add the tofu slices and cook until warmed through, about 3 minutes.

6. As the sauce is simmering, bring water to a boil in a large saucepan. Add the noodles and cook until they are al dente, 5 to 7 minutes. Drain the noodles and divide them among the serving bowls.

7. Ladle the tofu and sauce over the noodles, garnish with basil, and serve.

Noodles with Gochujang Sauce

YIELD: 6 SERVINGS / **ACTIVE TIME:** 15 MINUTES / **TOTAL TIME:** 30 MINUTES

6 TABLESPOONS RICE VINEGAR

5 TABLESPOONS WATER

¼ CUP SUGAR

3 TABLESPOONS GOCHUJANG

2 TABLESPOONS RED PEPPER FLAKES

2 TABLESPOONS TOASTED SESAME OIL

2 TABLESPOONS TOASTED SESAME SEEDS

3 GARLIC CLOVES, MINCED

2 TEASPOONS KOSHER SALT, PLUS MORE TO TASTE

2 CUPS MUNG BEAN SPROUTS, PICKED OVER

1½ LB. FROZEN JJOLMYEON NOODLES, THAWED UNDER COLD RUNNING WATER

½ LB. CABBAGE, SHREDDED

1 LARGE CUCUMBER, PEELED AND JULIENNED

2 CARROTS, PEELED AND JULIENNED

2 LARGE HARD-BOILED EGGS, HALVED LENGTHWISE

1. Combine the rice vinegar, water, sugar, gochujang, red pepper flakes, sesame oil, sesame seeds, garlic, and salt in a medium bowl and whisk until combined. Set the sauce aside.

2. Bring water to a boil in a large saucepan. Place the bean sprouts in a bowl of cold water. Discard any hulls that float to the top. Rinse the remaining sprouts under cold water, add the sprouts to the boiling water, and cook for 1 minute. Remove them with a strainer and run them under cold water. Drain well and set the sprouts aside.

3. Place the noodles in the boiling water and cook until tender but chewy, 3 to 5 minutes. Drain and run them under cold water, rubbing the noodles to remove excess starch. Drain the noodles well.

4. Divide the noodles among the serving bowls and then arrange the sprouts, cabbage, cucumber, carrots, and a hard-boiled egg half on top of each portion. Drizzle the sauce over the top and serve.

Sopa de Fideo

YIELD: 6 SERVINGS / **ACTIVE TIME:** 15 MINUTES / **TOTAL TIME:** 30 MINUTES

4 PLUM TOMATOES

2 CHIPOTLES IN ADOBO, SEEDED TO TASTE AND MINCED

1 TABLESPOON ADOBO SAUCE

2 GARLIC CLOVES, CHOPPED

SALT AND PEPPER, TO TASTE

¼ CUP EXTRA-VIRGIN OLIVE OIL

½ LB. FIDEO NOODLES

1 LARGE YELLOW ONION, CHOPPED

2 CUPS CHICKEN STOCK (SEE PAGE 536)

FLESH OF 1 AVOCADO, CHOPPED

HANDFUL OF FRESH CILANTRO, FOR GARNISH

1. Bring water to a boil in a large saucepan and prepare an ice bath. Add the tomatoes to the boiling water, blanch for 1 minute, remove them with tongs, and plunge them in the ice bath. When the tomatoes are completely cool, peel them and place them in a food processor. Add the chipotles, adobo sauce, and garlic, season the mixture with salt and pepper, and blitz until smooth.

2. Place the olive oil in a large, deep skillet and warm it over medium heat. Add the noodles and cook, stirring occasionally, until they are a deep golden brown, 5 to 7 minutes. Transfer the noodles to a paper towel–lined plate to drain.

3. Add the onion to the pan, season it with salt, and cook, stirring occasionally, until it is translucent, about 3 minutes. Reduce the heat to medium-low and cook, stirring occasionally, until the onion is browned, about 20 minutes.

4. Stir in the stock, raise the heat to medium-high, and bring the mixture to a boil. Stir in the noodles, reduce the heat to the lowest setting, and cover the pan. Cook until the noodles have absorbed all of the liquid.

5. Remove the pan from heat and let the noodles sit for 5 minutes. Add the sauce and toss to coat. Garnish with the avocado and cilantro and serve.

Mac & Cheese with Browned Butter Bread Crumbs

YIELD: 6 SERVINGS / **ACTIVE TIME:** 30 MINUTES / **TOTAL TIME:** 1 HOUR

SALT, TO TASTE

1 LB. ELBOW MACARONI

7 TABLESPOONS UNSALTED BUTTER

2 CUPS PANKO

½ YELLOW ONION, MINCED

3 TABLESPOONS ALL-PURPOSE FLOUR

1 TABLESPOON YELLOW MUSTARD

1 TEASPOON TURMERIC

1 TEASPOON GARLIC POWDER

1 TEASPOON WHITE PEPPER

2 CUPS LIGHT CREAM

2 CUPS WHOLE MILK

1 LB. AMERICAN CHEESE, SLICED

10 OZ. BOURSIN CHEESE

½ LB. EXTRA-SHARP CHEDDAR CHEESE, SLICED

1. Preheat the oven to 400°F. Fill a Dutch oven with water and bring it to a boil. Add salt and the macaroni and cook until the macaroni is just shy of al dente, about 7 minutes. Drain and set aside.

2. Place the pot over medium heat and add 3 tablespoons of the butter. Cook until the butter starts to give off a nutty smell and brown. Add the panko, stir, and cook until it starts to look like wet sand, about 4 minutes. Remove the panko from the pan and set it aside.

3. Wipe out the Dutch oven, place it over medium-high heat, and add the onion and the remaining butter. Cook, stirring frequently, until the onion has softened, about 10 minutes. Gradually add the flour, stirring constantly to prevent lumps from forming. Add the mustard, turmeric, garlic powder, and white pepper and stir until combined.

4. Stir in the light cream and the milk, reduce the heat to medium, and bring the mixture to a simmer.

5. Add the cheeses one at a time, stirring to incorporate before adding the next one. When all of the cheeses have been incorporated and the mixture is smooth, cook until the flour taste is gone, about 10 minutes. Stir in the macaroni and top with the panko.

6. Place the Dutch oven in the oven and bake until the panko is crispy, 10 to 15 minutes. Remove the pot from the oven and serve immediately.

Pastitsio

YIELD: 8 SERVINGS / **ACTIVE TIME:** 1 HOUR AND 30 MINUTES / **TOTAL TIME:** 3 HOURS AND 30 MINUTES

2 TABLESPOONS EXTRA-VIRGIN OLIVE OIL

2 ONIONS, MINCED

SALT AND PEPPER, TO TASTE

4 LARGE GARLIC CLOVES, MINCED

2 LBS. GROUND LAMB

2 CUPS WHOLE MILK

1 (28 OZ.) CAN OF CRUSHED TOMATOES

4 SPRIGS OF FRESH THYME

1 TABLESPOON FRESHLY GRATED NUTMEG

1 TEASPOON CINNAMON

10 WHOLE CLOVES

1 LB. ZITI

BÉCHAMEL SAUCE (SEE PAGE 514)

BUTTER, AS NEEDED

1 CUP PANKO

1⅔ CUPS GRATED PARMESAN CHEESE

1. Place the olive oil in a large, deep skillet and warm it over medium heat. Add the onions, season with salt, reduce the heat to low, cover the pan, and cook, stirring occasionally, for about 20 minutes.

2. Add the garlic, cook for 1 minute, raise the heat to medium-high, and add the lamb, breaking it up with a fork as it browns. When the lamb is brown and cooked through, stir in the milk and cook until all of the liquid has evaporated, about 15 minutes.

3. Add the tomatoes, thyme, nutmeg, cinnamon, and cloves, season with salt and pepper, and bring the mixture to a boil. Reduce the heat to low, cover the pan, and cook, stirring occasionally, for 2 hours. If the sauce looks too watery after 1½ hours of cooking, let it cook uncovered for the last 30 minutes.

4. Remove the thyme, discard, and set the mixture aside.

5. Preheat the oven to 400°F. Butter the bottom and sides of a 13 x 9–inch baking dish and bring a large pot of water to a boil. Add salt, let it return to a boil, and add the pasta. Cook until the pasta is very al dente, 5 to 7 minutes.

6. Drain the pasta, transfer it to the baking dish along with 2 cups of the Béchamel Sauce, and toss to coat. Arrange the ziti so that they are lined up side by side.

7. Reduce the oven's temperature to 375°F. Place the baking dish in the oven and bake until the sauce is bubbling, 40 to 45 minutes.

8. Toss the panko and Parmesan together in a medium bowl. Remove the dish from the oven and sprinkle the panko-and-cheese mixture evenly over the top.

9. Return the dish to the oven and set the broiler to high. Broil until the crumb topping turns golden brown.

10. Remove the pastitsio from the oven and let it cool for 15 minutes.

11. While the dish is resting, reheat the meat sauce. To serve, ladle the meat sauce into the bottom of a warmed bowl and then top it with a slice of the pastitsio.

Nakji Bokkeum

YIELD: 4 SERVINGS / **ACTIVE TIME:** 30 MINUTES / **TOTAL TIME:** 30 MINUTES

FOR THE OCTOPUSES

8 BABY OCTOPUSES

2 TABLESPOONS SESAME OIL, PLUS MORE AS NEEDED

½ ONION, SLICED THIN

½ CUP THINLY SLICED CARROT

½ CUP THINLY SLICED ZUCCHINI

1 BELL PEPPER, STEMMED, SEEDED, AND SLICED THIN

1 PACKAGE OF SOMYEON NOODLES

4 SESAME LEAVES

2 SCALLIONS, TRIMMED AND CUT ON A BIAS

SALT, TO TASTE

FOR THE SAUCE

¼ CUP GOCHUJANG

2 TABLESPOONS GOCHUGARU

3 TABLESPOONS SOY SAUCE

2 TABLESPOONS SUGAR

1½ TABLESPOONS SHAOXING RICE WINE

2 GARLIC CLOVES, MINCED

2 TEASPOONS GRATED FRESH GINGER

3 TABLESPOONS CHOPPED SCALLIONS

1 TABLESPOON SESAME OIL

BLACK PEPPER, TO TASTE

1. To begin preparations for the octopuses, remove their outer skins and cut them into 2-inch pieces.

2. Bring a large saucepan of water to a boil. Add the octopuses and cook for 1 minute. Remove the octopuses from the pan, rinse them under cold water, and set them aside.

3. To prepare the sauce, place all of the ingredients in a mixing bowl and stir until well combined. Set the sauce aside.

4. Place half of the sesame oil in a large wok or skillet and warm it over medium-high heat. Add the onion, carrot, zucchini, and bell pepper and stir-fry until the vegetables are al dente, about 2 minutes. Transfer the vegetables to a plate and set them aside.

5. Bring water to a boil in a large saucepan. Add salt, let the water return to a full boil, and add the noodles. Cook until they are al dente, 3 to 5 minutes. Drain, rinse the noodles under cold water, and let them drain again.

6. Place the noodles in a bowl, season them with sesame oil, and toss to combine. Set the noodles aside.

7. Add the remaining sesame oil to the wok, add the octopuses, and stir-fry for 30 to 40 seconds. Add the sauce and stir-fry for 1 minute. Return the cooked vegetables to the pan and toss to combine.

8. Add the sesame leaves and scallions, toss to incorporate, and remove the pan from heat.

9. Place the noodles on a serving platter, arrange the octopuses and vegetables on top, and serve.

Trahana with Green Beans & Tomatoes

YIELD: 4 SERVINGS / **ACTIVE TIME:** 30 MINUTES / **TOTAL TIME:** 1 HOUR

6 PLUM TOMATOES

3 TABLESPOONS EXTRA-VIRGIN OLIVE OIL

1 ONION, MINCED

¼ TEASPOON KOSHER SALT, PLUS MORE TO TASTE

1 GARLIC CLOVE, MINCED

1½ LBS. FRESH GREEN BEANS, TRIMMED

1½ CUPS CHICKEN STOCK (SEE PAGE 536), PLUS MORE AS NEEDED

⅔ CUP TRAHANA (SEE PAGE 111)

¼ CUP FRESH BASIL LEAVES, SHREDDED

BLACK PEPPER, TO TASTE

1. Bring a water to a boil in a medium saucepan. Add the tomatoes and boil for 1 minute. Use tongs to transfer them to a cutting board and let them cool. When the tomatoes are cool enough to handle, peel them and discard the skins. Cut the flesh into quarters, remove the seeds and discard them, and then mince the flesh.

2. Place the olive oil in a large, deep skillet and warm it over medium heat. Add the onion, season it with salt, and cook, stirring occasionally, until the onion is translucent, about 3 minutes. Reduce the heat to low, cover the pan, and cook until the onion is very soft, about 15 minutes.

3. Add the garlic and cook for 1 minute. Stir in the tomatoes, season with salt, and raise the heat to medium-high. Once the sauce starts to simmer, reduce the heat to low, cover the pan, and cook, stirring occasionally, until the tomatoes start to collapse, about 10 minutes.

4. Add the green beans, stock, salt, and Trahana. Raise the heat to medium-high and bring the mixture to a gentle simmer. Reduce heat to medium-low and cook, stirring occasionally, until the green beans and Trahana are tender, 15 to 20 minutes, adding more stock if the pan starts to look dry.

5. Taste and adjust the seasoning as necessary. Stir in the basil, season the dish with pepper, and serve.

Lobster Mac & Cheese

YIELD: 8 SERVINGS / **ACTIVE TIME:** 25 MINUTES / **TOTAL TIME:** 1 HOUR AND 5 MINUTES

½ CUP UNSALTED BUTTER, PLUS MORE AS NEEDED

SALT AND PEPPER, TO TASTE

1 LB. MACARONI OR PENNE

2 CUPS HEAVY CREAM

½ CUP ALL-PURPOSE FLOUR

1 CUP LOBSTER STOCK (SEE PAGE 541)

1 CUP WHITE WINE

2 CUPS GRATED EXTRA-SHARP CHEDDAR CHEESE

3 CUPS GRATED GRUYÈRE CHEESE

1 CUP PECORINO CHEESE

PINCH OF FRESHLY GRATED NUTMEG

1½ LBS. COOKED LOBSTER MEAT

3 TABLESPOONS PANKO

1. Preheat the oven to 350°F. Coat a large baking dish with butter. Bring a large saucepan of water to a boil. Add salt, let the water return to a full boil, and add the pasta. Cook until it is very al dente, 6 to 8 minutes, drain, and set it aside.

2. Place the cream in a saucepan and bring it to a simmer. Remove the pan from heat and set it aside.

3. Place 6 tablespoons of butter in a large saucepan and melt it over low heat. Add the flour and cook, stirring continually, until the mixture is smooth and golden brown, about 2 minutes. Stir in the warm cream, stock, and wine and cook until the mixture thickens slightly, 2 to 3 minutes.

4. Gradually add the cheeses, stirring continually, until they have melted. Season the sauce with salt, pepper, and nutmeg, stir in the pasta and lobster, and transfer the mixture to the baking dish. Set it aside.

5. Place the remaining butter in a skillet and melt it over medium heat. Add the panko and stir until coated. Top the mac and cheese with the panko and place it in the oven.

6. Bake the mac and cheese until it is bubbling and browned, about 30 minutes. Remove the mac and cheese from the oven and serve immediately.

Lobster Mac & Cheese
SEE PAGE 347

Linguine & Clams in Lazy Man's Pesto

YIELD: 6 SERVINGS / **ACTIVE TIME:** 30 MINUTES / **TOTAL TIME:** 45 MINUTES

SALT AND PEPPER, TO TASTE

1 LB. LINGUINE

5 TABLESPOONS EXTRA-VIRGIN OLIVE OIL

3 GARLIC CLOVES, MINCED

2 LBS. CLAMS, SCRUBBED

¾ CUP WATER

½ CUP FISH STOCK
(SEE PAGE 542)

6 TABLESPOONS CHOPPED FRESH PARSLEY

6 TABLESPOONS CHOPPED FRESH BASIL

6 TABLESPOONS CHOPPED FRESH LEMON BALM

1. Bring water to a boil in a large saucepan. Add salt, let the water return to a full boil, and add the pasta. Cook until it is very al dente, 6 to 8 minutes. Reserve ¼ cup pasta water, drain the pasta, and set it aside.

2. Place ¼ cup of olive oil in a large skillet and warm it over medium heat. Add the garlic and cook, stirring continually, for 1 minute. Add the clams and cook for 3 minutes.

3. Add the water and stock, reduce the heat to low, and cook the clams until the majority of them have opened, about 4 minutes. Discard any clams that did not open and transfer the remaining clams to a bowl.

4. Strain the broth into a clean saucepan through a fine-mesh sieve. Add the pasta water and pasta and cook over high heat until the pasta is al dente. Add the clams, stir in the parsley, basil, lemon balm, and remaining olive oil and toss to combine.

5. Season the dish with salt and pepper and serve.

Lobster Fettuccine

YIELD: 4 SERVINGS / **ACTIVE TIME:** 20 MINUTES / **TOTAL TIME:** 30 MINUTES

SALT AND PEPPER, TO TASTE

1 LB. FETTUCCINE

2 TABLESPOONS EXTRA-VIRGIN OLIVE OIL

2 SHALLOTS, MINCED

½ RED BELL PEPPER, SLICED THIN

½ YELLOW BELL PEPPER, SLICED THIN

3 GARLIC CLOVES, MINCED

2½ CUPS COOKED LOBSTER MEAT

½ CUP DRY WHITE WINE

½ CUP FRESH BASIL, CHOPPED, PLUS MORE FOR GARNISH

½ CUP HEAVY CREAM

½ CUP GRATED PARMESAN CHEESE, PLUS MORE FOR GARNISH

1. Bring water to a boil in a large saucepan. Add salt, let the water return to a full boil, and add the pasta. Cook until it is very al dente, 2 to 3 minutes. Reserve ⅓ cup pasta water, drain the pasta, and set it aside.

2. Place the olive oil in a large skillet and warm it over medium-high heat. Add the shallots and bell peppers and cook, stirring occasionally, until they start to soften, about 5 minutes.

3. Add the garlic and lobster and cook, stirring continually, for 1 minute. Stir in the wine and cook for 1 minute.

4. Add the basil, cream, Parmesan, and pasta water and bring the sauce to a simmer. Cook until it thickens slightly.

5. Add the pasta and cook, tossing to combine, until it is al dente. Season the dish with pepper, garnish with additional basil and Parmesan, and serve.

Seafood Linguine

YIELD: 4 SERVINGS / **ACTIVE TIME:** 35 MINUTES / **TOTAL TIME:** 45 MINUTES

SALT AND PEPPER, TO TASTE

1 LB. LINGUINE

¼ CUP EXTRA-VIRGIN OLIVE OIL

1 ONION, DICED

3 GARLIC CLOVES, CRUSHED

1 (14 OZ.) CAN OF DICED TOMATOES, DRAINED

1 TEASPOON RED PEPPER FLAKES

7 TABLESPOONS DRY WHITE WINE

1 LB. MEDIUM SHRIMP, SHELLS REMOVED, DEVEINED

12 CLAMS, RINSED WELL AND SCRUBBED

½ LB. MUSSELS, RINSED WELL AND DEBEARDED

FRESH PARSLEY, CHOPPED, FOR GARNISH

½ CUP GRATED PARMESAN CHEESE, FOR GARNISH

LEMON WEDGES, FOR SERVING

1. Bring water to a boil in a large saucepan. Add salt, let the water return to a full boil, and add the pasta. Cook until it is al dente, 8 to 10 minutes. Drain the pasta and transfer it to a large bowl. Drizzle 1 tablespoon of olive oil over it, toss to coat, set the pasta aside.

2. Place the remaining olive oil in a large skillet and warm it over medium-high heat. Add the onion and cook, stirring occasionally, until it is translucent, about 3 minutes. Add the garlic and cook, stirring continually, for 1 minute.

3. Stir in the tomatoes, red pepper flakes, and dry white wine and simmer the sauce until it thickens slightly, about 5 minutes.

4. Add the shrimp and cook for 1 minute. Turn the shrimp over and cook until they turn pink, 2 to 3 minutes. Remove the shrimp from the pan and set them aside.

5. Add the clams and mussels to the skillet, cover the pan, and cook until the majority of them have opened, about 5 minutes. Discard any clams and/or mussels that did not open.

6. Add the shrimp, pasta, and reserved pasta water to the skillet, season the dish with salt and pepper, and cook until everything is warmed through.

7. Garnish with parsley and the Parmesan and serve with lemon wedges.

Maccheroni with Braised Octopus

YIELD: 4 SERVINGS / **ACTIVE TIME:** 30 MINUTES / **TOTAL TIME:** 2 HOURS

1 OCTOPUS (ABOUT 4 LBS.)

2 TABLESPOONS EXTRA-VIRGIN OLIVE OIL

1 ONION, CHOPPED

2 TABLESPOONS TOMATO PASTE

3 GARLIC CLOVES, MINCED

3 CUPS CLAM JUICE

1 SPRIG OF FRESH ROSEMARY

1 SPRIG OF FRESH THYME

1 BAY LEAF

2 CINNAMON STICKS

1 CUP DRY RED WINE

2 TABLESPOONS RED WINE VINEGAR

SALT AND PEPPER, TO TASTE

MACCHERONI AL FERRETTO (SEE PAGE 24)

FRESH PARSLEY, CHOPPED, FOR GARNISH

1. Place the octopus in a medium saucepan, cover it with water by 2 inches, and bring to a boil. Reduce the heat, cover the pan, and simmer for 1 hour.

2. Remove the octopus from the pan, cut off the tentacles, and set them aside.

3. Place the olive oil in a medium saucepan and warm it over medium heat. Add the onion and cook, stirring occasionally, until it has softened, about 5 minutes. Add the tomato paste and garlic and cook, stirring continually, for 1 minute. Add all of the remaining ingredients, except for the pasta and parsley, and bring to a boil. Reduce the heat and simmer for 20 minutes.

4. Strain the liquid into a clean saucepan. Add the octopus and simmer until it is tender and the braising liquid has thickened, about 20 minutes.

5. Bring water to a boil in a large saucepan. Add salt, let the water return to a full boil, and add the pasta. Let it float to the surface and cook for another 5 minutes. Drain the pasta and divide it among the serving bowls.

6. Top the maccheroni with some octopus and ladle some of the braising liquid over the top. Garnish with parsley and serve.

Pasta alla Norcina

YIELD: 4 SERVINGS / **ACTIVE TIME:** 20 MINUTES / **TOTAL TIME:** 35 MINUTES

3 TABLESPOONS EXTRA-VIRGIN OLIVE OIL

½ ONION, THINLY SLICED

1 GARLIC CLOVE, HALVED

11 OZ. ITALIAN SAUSAGE, CASING REMOVED AND CRUMBLED

½ CUP WHITE WINE

SALT AND PEPPER, TO TASTE

1 LB. PENNE

7 OZ. RICOTTA CHEESE

½ CUP GRATED PARMESAN CHEESE

TRUFFLES, SHAVED, FOR GARNISH

1. Bring water to a boil in a large saucepan. Place the olive oil in a large skillet and warm it over medium-high heat. Add the onion and garlic and cook, stirring frequently, until the onion is translucent, about 3 minutes.

2. Add the sausage and cook, stirring occasionally, until it starts to brown.

3. Deglaze the pan with the wine and cook until it has evaporated.

4. Add salt, let the water return to a full boil, and add the pasta. Cook the pasta until it is al dente. Reserve 1 cup pasta water and drain the pasta.

5. Add the ricotta and a few tablespoons of pasta water to the skillet and stir to combine.

6. Add the Parmesan and pasta, season with salt and pepper, and cook for 2 to 3 minutes, tossing to combine.

7. Garnish the dish with shaved truffle and serve.

Frutti di Mare with Penne

YIELD: 6 SERVINGS / **ACTIVE TIME:** 30 MINUTES / **TOTAL TIME:** 1 HOUR AND 30 MINUTES

¼ CUP EXTRA-VIRGIN OLIVE OIL

½ LB. LARGE SHRIMP, SHELLS REMOVED AND RESERVED, DEVEINED

1 CUP WHITE WINE

1 ONION, SLICED THIN

4 GARLIC CLOVES, MINCED

2 TABLESPOONS TOMATO PASTE

⅛ TEASPOON RED PEPPER FLAKES

PINCH OF SAFFRON THREADS

1 (28 OZ.) CAN OF CHOPPED TOMATOES, WITH THEIR LIQUID

2 CUPS CLAM JUICE

SALT AND PEPPER, TO TASTE

1 LB. PENNE

½ LB. MUSSELS, RINSED WELL AND DEBEARDED

8 SCALLOPS

½ LB. SQUID, CLEANED

¼ CUP CHOPPED FRESH PARSLEY, FOR GARNISH

1 CUP PANKO, TOASTED, FOR GARNISH

1. Place 2 tablespoons of the olive oil in a medium saucepan and warm it over medium heat. Add the reserved shrimp shells and cook for 4 minutes. Add the wine, reduce the heat, and simmer for 4 minutes, scraping up any browned bits up from the bottom of the pan. Strain the stock into a bowl and set it aside.

2. Place the remaining olive oil in a large skillet and warm it over medium heat. Add the onion and cook, stirring occasionally, until it has softened, about 5 minutes. Add the garlic, tomato paste, red pepper flakes, and saffron and cook, stirring continually, for 1 minute.

3. Add the stock, tomatoes, and clam juice and bring the mixture to a boil. Reduce the heat and simmer the sauce for 20 minutes.

4. Bring water to a boil in a large saucepan. Add salt, let the water return to a full boil, and add the penne. Cook until it is al dente, 8 to 10 minutes. Reserve ½ cup of the pasta water and drain the pasta.

5. Add the mussels, hinges facing down, to the sauce and cover the pan. Cook until the majority of the mussels have opened, about 5 minutes. Remove the mussels using a slotted spoon, discarding any that didn't open.

6. Add the scallops and shrimp to the sauce and cook until cooked through, about 2 minutes. Remove the pan from heat, add the squid, and cover the pan. Let the pan sit until the squid is cooked through, about 2 minutes.

7. Add the mussels and penne to the sauce and toss to combine, adding pasta water as needed to get the desired consistency. Season with salt and pepper, garnish with the parsley and toasted panko, and enjoy.

Creamy Pappardelle with Crab

YIELD: 8 SERVINGS / **ACTIVE TIME:** 1 HOUR AND 15 MINUTES / **TOTAL TIME:** 1 HOUR AND 40 MINUTES

1 LB. FRESH PAPPARDELLE

1 LB. LUMP CRABMEAT

1 CUP FRESHLY GRATED PARMESAN CHEESE

3 TABLESPOONS CHOPPED FRESH PARSLEY

CREAMY BALSAMIC & MUSHROOM SAUCE (SEE PAGE 530), FOR SERVING

1. Bring water to a boil in a large saucepan. Add salt, let the water return to a full boil, and add the pasta. Cook until it is al dente, 2 to 4 minutes.

2. Reserve ¼ cup of the pasta water and then drain the pasta.

3. Return the pasta to the saucepan, add the crab, Parmesan, parsley, and sauce, and toss to coat, adding pasta water as needed to get the desired consistency. Serve immediately.

Spaghetti al Tonno

YIELD: 4 TO 6 SERVINGS / **ACTIVE TIME:** 20 MINUTES / **TOTAL TIME:** 1 HOUR

2 TABLESPOONS EXTRA-VIRGIN OLIVE OIL

3 GARLIC CLOVES, MINCED

1 SMALL YELLOW ONION, MINCED

⅛ TEASPOON RED PEPPER FLAKES

3 CUPS TOMATO PASSATA

SALT AND PEPPER, TO TASTE

1 LB. SPAGHETTI

6 OZ. TUNA IN OLIVE OIL, DRAINED

FRESH PARSLEY, CHOPPED, FOR GARNISH

1. Place the olive oil in a medium saucepan and warm it over medium-low heat. Add the garlic and onion and cook, stirring frequently, until the onion just starts to soften, about 5 minutes.

2. Add the red pepper flakes and passata, season with salt and pepper, and stir until well combined.

3. Add about 2 cups of water to the sauce and bring it to a boil. Cover the pan, reduce the heat to medium-low, and cook until the sauce has thickened, about 45 minutes.

4. While the sauce is simmering, bring a large pot of water to a boil. Add salt, let the water return to a full boil, and add the pasta. Cook until it is al dente, 8 to 10 minutes.

5. Add the drained tuna to the tomato sauce and continue to simmer for about 5 minutes.

6. Drain the pasta, place it in a bowl, add some of the tomato sauce, and toss to coat. To serve, top each serving of pasta with more of the sauce and garnish with parsley.

Farfalle, Tuna & Peas in Tomato Sauce

YIELD: 4 SERVINGS / **ACTIVE TIME:** 25 MINUTES / **TOTAL TIME:** 35 MINUTES

SALT AND PEPPER, TO TASTE

FARFALLE (SEE PAGE 60)

2 TABLESPOONS EXTRA-VIRGIN OLIVE OIL

1 SMALL ONION, FINELY DICED

1 GARLIC CLOVE, FINELY DICED

1 (14 OZ.) CAN OF DICED TOMATOES, WITH THEIR LIQUID

2 CANS OF TUNA IN OLIVE OIL, DRAINED

1 CUP FROZEN PEAS

1 TABLESPOON FRESH LEMON JUICE

FRESH BASIL, CHOPPED FOR GARNISH

1. Bring a large saucepan of water to a boil. Add salt, let the water return to a full boil, and add the Farfalle. Cook until it is very al dente, 2 to 3 minutes. Drain the pasta and set it aside.

2. Place the olive oil in a large skillet and warm it over medium-high heat. Add the onion and cook, stirring occasionally, until it is translucent, about 3 minutes. Add the garlic and cook, stirring continually, for 1 minute.

3. Raise the heat to high and stir in the tomatoes and tuna. Season the mixture with salt and pepper and cook, stirring occasionally, about 20 minutes.

4. Add the pasta, frozen peas, and lemon juice and stir to incorporate. Cook until the pasta is al dente and everything is warmed through, about 3 minutes. Garnish the dish with basil and serve.

American Chop Suey

YIELD: 4 SERVINGS / **ACTIVE TIME:** 15 MINUTES / **TOTAL TIME:** 15 MINUTES

SALT AND PEPPER, TO TASTE

1 LB. ELBOW MACARONI

1 LB. GROUND BEEF

1 ONION, DICED

1 (14 OZ.) CAN OF DICED TOMATOES

1. Bring water to a boil in a large saucepan. Add salt, let the water return to a full boil, and add the macaroni. Cook until the macaroni is very al dente, 6 to 8 minutes.

2. While the water for the macaroni is coming to a boil, place the beef in a large skillet, season it with salt and pepper, and cook over mediumh heat, breaking the beef up with a fork, until it starts to brown, about 5 minutes. Stir in the onion and cook, stirring frequently, until the beef is cooked through and the onion is translucent, about 3 minutes. Add the tomatoes and cook for about 3 minutes, stirring frequently.

3. Drain the macaroni and stir it into the pan. Season with salt and pepper and serve.

Spaghetti alla Carbonara

YIELD: 4 SERVINGS / **ACTIVE TIME:** 20 MINUTES / **TOTAL TIME:** 25 MINUTES

6½ OZ. GUANCIALE, CUT INTO 1-INCH-LONG AND ¼-INCH-THICK STRIPS

5 EGG YOLKS

⅔ CUP GRATED PECORINO CHEESE

SALT AND PEPPER, TO TASTE

1 LB. SPAGHETTI

1. Place the guanciale in a large skillet and warm it over medium-low heat. Cook until the guanciale has rendered most of its fat and is lightly browned. Remove the guanciale from the pan and set it aside.

2. Place the egg yolks and pecorino in a large bowl and lightly beat to combine. Season the mixture with a generous amount of pepper and set it aside.

3. Bring water to a boil in a large saucepan. Add salt, let the water return to a full boil, and add the pasta. Cook the pasta until it is al dente.

4. Drain the pasta and add it to the bowl containing the egg-and-cheese mixture along with the guanciale. Toss to combine and serve immediately.

Spaghetti alla Carbonara
SEE PAGE 359

Spaghetti with Zucchini & Pesto

YIELD: 4 SERVINGS / **ACTIVE TIME:** 15 MINUTES / **TOTAL TIME:** 15 MINUTES

SALT, TO TASTE

1 LB. SPAGHETTI

3 ZUCCHINI, SLICED VERY
THIN WITH A MANDOLINE

BASIL PESTO (SEE PAGE 482)

1. Bring water to a boil in a large saucepan. Add salt, let the water return to a full boil, and add the pasta. Cook until it is very al dente, 6 to 8 minutes. When the pasta has 1 minute left to cook, add the zucchini, and stir to combine.

2. Reserve ¼ cup of pasta water and then drain the pasta and zucchini. Return them to the pot, add the reserved pasta water, and cook over high heat, tossing continually, until all of the water has been absorbed, about 1 minute.

3. Divide the pasta and zucchini between the plates and top each portion with the pesto.

Weeknight Garganelli

YIELD: 4 SERVINGS / **ACTIVE TIME:** 20 MINUTES / **TOTAL TIME:** 40 MINUTES

1 TABLESPOON EXTRA-VIRGIN OLIVE OIL

6 OZ. UNSMOKED HAM, CUT INTO 1-INCH PIECES

4½ TABLESPOONS UNSALTED BUTTER

3 SHALLOTS, MINCED

SALT AND WHITE PEPPER, TO TASTE

¾ LB. GARGANELLI (SEE PAGE 64)

1½ CUPS PEAS

¾ CUP HEAVY CREAM

1 TEASPOON FRESHLY GRATED NUTMEG

PARMESAN CHEESE, GRATED, FOR GARNISH

1. Place the olive oil in a large, deep skillet and warm it over medium-high heat. Add the ham and cook, stirring occasionally, until it starts to brown, about 5 minutes. Transfer the ham to a small bowl and set it aside.

2. Add 4 tablespoons of the butter to the skillet and melt it over medium heat. Add the shallots and a pinch of salt and reduce the heat to low. Cover the pan and cook, stirring occasionally, until the shallots are very soft and golden brown, about 15 minutes.

3. While the shallots are cooking, bring water to a boil in a large saucepan. Add salt, let the water return to a full boil, and add the pasta. Cook for 5 minutes and then add the peas. Cook until the pasta is very al dente, 2 to 3 more minutes. Reserve ½ cup pasta water and drain the pasta and peas.

4. Stir the cream and nutmeg into the skillet and season the mixture with salt and pepper. Bring to a simmer, cook for 3 minutes, and then remove the skillet from heat.

5. Return the saucepan to the stove. Add the remaining butter and reserved pasta water, raise the heat to high, add the drained pasta and peas, and toss to combine. Add the contents of the skillet and cook, tossing to combine, for 2 minutes. Top the dish with the ham, garnish with Parmesan, and serve.

SOUPS

Harira

YIELD: 6 SERVINGS / **ACTIVE TIME:** 30 MINUTES / **TOTAL TIME:** 1 HOUR

3 TABLESPOONS UNSALTED BUTTER

1½ LBS. BONELESS, SKINLESS CHICKEN THIGHS

SALT AND PEPPER, TO TASTE

1 LARGE ONION, FINELY DICED

5 GARLIC CLOVES, MINCED

1-INCH PIECE OF FRESH GINGER, PEELED AND GRATED

2 TEASPOONS TURMERIC

1 TEASPOON CUMIN

½ TEASPOON CINNAMON

⅛ TEASPOON CAYENNE PEPPER

¾ CUP FINELY CHOPPED FRESH CILANTRO

½ CUP FINELY CHOPPED FRESH PARSLEY

4 CUPS CHICKEN STOCK (SEE PAGE 536)

4 CUPS WATER

1 (14 OZ.) CAN OF CHICKPEAS, DRAINED AND RINSED

1 CUP BROWN LENTILS, PICKED OVER AND RINSED

1 (28 OZ.) CAN OF CRUSHED TOMATOES

2 OZ. VERMICELLI, BROKEN INTO 2-INCH PIECES

2 TABLESPOONS FRESH LEMON JUICE, PLUS MORE TO TASTE

1. Place the butter in a Dutch oven and melt it over medium-high heat. Season the chicken thighs with salt and pepper, place them in the pot, and cook until browned on both sides, about 8 minutes. Remove the chicken from the pot and set it on a plate.

2. Add the onion and cook, stirring occasionally, until it starts to brown, about 8 minutes. Add the garlic and ginger and cook until fragrant, about 1 minute. Stir in the turmeric, cumin, cinnamon, and cayenne pepper and cook for 1 minute. Add ½ cup of the cilantro and ¼ cup of the parsley and cook for 1 minute.

3. Stir in the stock, water, chickpeas, and lentils and bring the soup to a simmer. Return the chicken to the pot, reduce the heat to medium-low, partially cover the Dutch oven, and gently simmer, stirring occasionally, until the lentils are just tender, about 20 minutes.

4. Add the tomatoes and vermicelli and simmer, stirring occasionally, until the pasta is tender, about 10 minutes.

5. Stir in the lemon juice and the remaining cilantro and parsley. Taste, adjust the seasoning as necessary, and enjoy.

Vietnamese Noodle Soup

YIELD: 6 SERVINGS / **ACTIVE TIME:** 15 MINUTES / **TOTAL TIME:** 35 MINUTES

1 LB. RICE NOODLES

2 TABLESPOONS EXTRA-VIRGIN OLIVE OIL

2-INCH PIECE OF FRESH GINGER, PEELED AND SLICED THIN

3 JALAPEÑO CHILE PEPPERS, STEMMED, SEEDED, AND SLICED

4 SCALLIONS, TRIMMED AND CHOPPED

1 LEMONGRASS STALK, BRUISED AND CHOPPED

1 TABLESPOON FISH SAUCE

2 TEASPOONS CHILI GARLIC SAUCE

1 TEASPOON SOY SAUCE

4 CUPS CHICKEN STOCK (SEE PAGE 536)

½ LB. MUSHROOMS, SLICED

1 TEASPOON WHITE PEPPER

1 CUP FRESH BASIL

1 CUP FRESH MINT

SALT AND PEPPER, TO TASTE

5 OZ. FRESH SPINACH, CHOPPED

1 CUP CHOPPED FRESH CILANTRO

2 CUPS BEAN SPROUTS

1 LB. MEDIUM SHRIMP, SHELLS REMOVED, DEVEINED

1. Place the rice noodles in a bowl and cover with boiling water. Soak until they are al dente. Drain the noodles and set them aside.

2. Place the olive oil in a Dutch oven and warm it over medium heat. Add the ginger, jalapeños, scallions, and lemongrass and cook, stirring occasionally, for 4 minutes. Reduce the heat to medium-low and add the remaining ingredients, except for the spinach, cilantro, bean sprouts, and shrimp. Bring to a simmer and cook for about 10 minutes.

3. Stir in the spinach, cilantro, bean sprouts, and shrimp and cook until the shrimp turn pink and are cooked through, 3 to 5 minutes.

4. Divide the rice noodles among the serving bowls, ladle the soup over them, and enjoy.

Noodle Soup with Crab Balls

YIELD: 6 SERVINGS / **ACTIVE TIME:** 15 MINUTES / **TOTAL TIME:** 1 HOUR AND 40 MINUTES

FOR THE CRAB BALLS

1 LB. FRESH LUMP CRABMEAT, PICKED OVER

¾ CUP BREAD CRUMBS

½ CUP CHOPPED FRESH CILANTRO

1 LARGE EGG, BEATEN

2 TEASPOONS FRESH LEMON JUICE

1 TEASPOON KOSHER SALT

½ TEASPOON BLACK PEPPER

FOR THE SOUP

¼ CUP AVOCADO OIL

6 GARLIC CLOVES, SLICED

1-INCH PIECE OF FRESH GINGER, PEELED AND GRATED

1 LEMONGRASS STALK, TRIMMED AND BRUISED

½ LB. MUSHROOMS, SLICED

PINCH OF SALT

6 CUPS CHICKEN STOCK (SEE PAGE 536)

¾ LB. RICE NOODLES

2 TABLESPOONS SOY SAUCE

FRESH CILANTRO, CHOPPED, FOR GARNISH

1. To prepare the crab balls, place all of the ingredients a mixing bowl and work the mixture with your hands until well combined. Form heaping tablespoons of the mixture into balls, place the crab balls on a plate, and cover them with plastic wrap. Chill the crab balls in the refrigerator for 1 hour.

2. To begin preparations for the soup, place 2 tablespoons of avocado oil in a large saucepan and warm it over medium heat. Add the garlic, ginger, lemongrass, mushrooms, and a pinch of salt and stir-fry until the garlic and mushrooms are golden brown, about 4 minutes.

3. Add the stock, bring the soup to a boil, and then reduce the heat so that it simmers. Add the rice noodles and cook until they are tender, about 6 minutes.

4. While the noodles are cooking, place the remaining avocado oil in a large skillet and warm it over medium heat. Add the crab balls to the skillet and cook until they are golden brown, 4 to 6 minutes, turning them as necessary.

5. Add the crab balls to the soup along with the soy sauce and cook until they are cooked through, about 3 minutes.

6. Ladle the soup into warmed bowls, garnish each portion with cilantro, and enjoy.

Miso Ramen with Shrimp

YIELD: 4 SERVINGS / **ACTIVE TIME:** 10 MINUTES / **TOTAL TIME:** 35 MINUTES

2 TABLESPOONS AVOCADO OIL

9 OZ. CREMINI MUSHROOMS, SLICED

SALT, TO TASTE

2 TEASPOONS SESAME OIL

2 GARLIC CLOVES, MINCED

1-INCH PIECE OF FRESH GINGER, PEELED AND MINCED

2 TABLESPOONS RED MISO PASTE

6 CUPS CHICKEN STOCK (SEE PAGE 536)

2 TABLESPOONS RICE VINEGAR

2 TABLESPOONS SAKE

3 TABLESPOONS SOY SAUCE

2 TEASPOONS CHILI OIL

11 OZ. RAMEN NOODLES

1 LB. BOK CHOY, TRIMMED, RINSED WELL, AND CHOPPED

11 OZ. SHRIMP, SHELLS REMOVED, DEVEINED

3 TABLESPOONS SESAME SEEDS, TOASTED

FRESH CILANTRO, CHOPPED, FOR GARNISH

2 RED THAI CHILE PEPPERS, STEMMED, SEEDED, AND SLICED, FOR GARNISH

LIME WEDGES, FOR SERVING

1. Place the avocado oil in a Dutch oven and warm it over medium heat. Add the mushrooms and a pinch of salt and cook, stirring occasionally, until the mushrooms are golden brown, about 10 minutes. Transfer the mushrooms to a bowl and set them aside.

2. Add the sesame oil and warm it over medium heat. Add the garlic and ginger and stir-fry for 45 seconds.

3. Stir in the miso paste, stock, vinegar, sake, soy sauce, and chili oil and bring the broth to a steady simmer. Cook for 5 minutes, stirring occasionally.

4. Add the noodles and bok choy and cook until the noodles are al dente, 8 to 10 minutes.

5. Stir in the shrimp and mushrooms and simmer until the shrimp are cooked through. Taste, adjust the seasoning as necessary, and ladle the soup into warmed bowls.

6. Garnish with the sesame seeds, cilantro, and Thai chiles and serve with lime wedges.

Chicken Meatball Soup with Farfalle & Spinach

YIELD: 8 SERVINGS / **ACTIVE TIME:** 35 MINUTES / **TOTAL TIME:** 1 HOUR

FOR THE MEATBALLS

1 CUP FRESH BREAD
CRUMBS

1 LB. GROUND CHICKEN

1 CUP FRESHLY GRATED
PARMESAN CHEESE

3 TABLESPOONS TOMATO
PASTE

1 HANDFUL OF FRESH
PARSLEY, CHOPPED

3 LARGE EGGS

SALT AND PEPPER, TO TASTE

2 TABLESPOONS EXTRA-
VIRGIN OLIVE OIL

FOR THE SOUP

2 TABLESPOONS EXTRA-
VIRGIN OLIVE OIL

2 LEEKS, TRIMMED, RINSED
WELL, AND CHOPPED

SALT AND PEPPER, TO TASTE

5 GARLIC CLOVES, SLICED
THIN

8 CUPS CHICKEN STOCK
(SEE PAGE 536)

5 CARROTS, PEELED AND
SLICED

½ LB. FARFALLE
(SEE PAGE 60)

2 HANDFULS OF BABY
SPINACH LEAVES

¼ CUP GRATED PARMESAN
CHEESE, PLUS MORE FOR
GARNISH

1. To begin preparations for the meatballs, place the bread crumbs, chicken, Parmesan, tomato paste, parsley, and eggs in a mixing bowl, season with salt and pepper, and work the mixture with your hands until thoroughly combined. Working with wet hands, form the mixture into ½-inch balls.

2. Place the olive oil in a large skillet and warm it over medium heat. Working in batches to avoid crowding the pan, add the meatballs and cook, turning occasionally, until they are browned all over. Transfer the browned meatballs to a paper towel–lined plate to drain.

3. To begin preparations for the soup, place the olive oil in a Dutch oven and warm it over medium heat. Add the leeks, season with salt and pepper, and cook, stirring frequently, until they are translucent, about 3 minutes. Reduce the heat to low, cover the pot, and cook, stirring occasionally, until the leeks are very soft, about 15 minutes.

4. Add the garlic, cook for 1 minute, and then stir in the stock, carrots, and meatballs. Raise the heat to medium-high and bring the soup to a gentle boil. Reduce the heat to medium-low and simmer the soup until the meatballs are cooked through and the carrots are tender, about 15 minutes.

5. Add the Farfalle and cook until tender, about 8 minutes. Remove the Dutch oven from heat and stir in the spinach and Parmesan. Cover the pot and let it rest until the spinach has wilted, about 5 minutes.

6. Ladle the soup into warmed bowls, garnish each portion with additional Parmesan, and serve.

Elk Soup with Gnocchi

YIELD: 4 SERVINGS / **ACTIVE TIME:** 1 HOUR / **TOTAL TIME:** 3 HOURS

2 TABLESPOONS EXTRA-VIRGIN OLIVE OIL

3 LBS. ELK BONES (NECK OR BACK BONES)

5 CUPS WATER

2 BAY LEAVES

3 ALLSPICE BERRIES

½ TEASPOON KOSHER SALT, PLUS MORE TO TASTE

2 TABLESPOONS BREAD CRUMBS

¾ LB. GROUND ELK SHOULDER

1 EGG

BLACK PEPPER, TO TASTE

PAPRIKA, TO TASTE

½ CELERIAC, PEELED AND DICED

3 CARROTS, PEELED AND DICED

3 CUPS MUSHROOMS

1 ONION, DICED

4 ROMA TOMATOES, DICED

GNOCCHI (SEE PAGE 42)

FRESH PARSLEY, CHOPPED, FOR GARNISH

1. Place the olive oil in a large saucepan and warm it over medium-high heat. Add the elk bones and cook, stirring occasionally, until they are starting to brown.

2. Add the water, bay leaves, allspice, and salt and bring the mixture to a simmer. Cook for 2 hours, skimming off any impurities that rise to the top.

3. Strain the stock into a clean saucepan and bring it to a simmer.

4. Place the bread crumbs, elk, and egg in a bowl, season the mixture with salt, pepper, and paprika, and work the mixture with your hands until it is thoroughly combined. Form the mixture into small balls and add them to the stock along with the celeriac, carrots, mushrooms, onion, and tomatoes. Bring the soup to a simmer and cook for 10 minutes.

5. Add the Gnocchi to the soup and cook until the meatballs and Gnocchi are cooked through, 5 to 7 minutes.

6. Ladle the soup into warmed bowls, garnish each portion with parsley, and serve.

Chicken Parm Soup

YIELD: 4 SERVINGS / **ACTIVE TIME:** 20 MINUTES / **TOTAL TIME:** 1 HOUR

2 TABLESPOONS EXTRA-VIRGIN OLIVE OIL

2 BONELESS, SKINLESS CHICKEN BREASTS, DICED

1 ONION, CHOPPED

2 GARLIC CLOVES, MINCED

1 TEASPOON RED PEPPER FLAKES

¼ CUP TOMATO PASTE

1 (14 OZ.) CAN OF DICED TOMATOES, WITH THEIR LIQUID

6 CUPS CHICKEN STOCK (SEE PAGE 536)

½ LB. PENNE

2 CUPS SHREDDED MOZZARELLA CHEESE

1 CUP FRESHLY GRATED PARMESAN CHEESE, PLUS MORE FOR GARNISH

SALT AND PEPPER, TO TASTE

FRESH BASIL, CHOPPED, FOR GARNISH

1. Place the olive oil in a medium saucepan and warm it over medium-high heat. Add the chicken and cook, stirring occasionally, until it is browned all over, about 6 minutes.

2. Add the onion and cook, stirring frequently, until it starts to soften, about 5 minutes. Stir in the garlic, red pepper flakes, tomato paste, tomatoes, and stock and bring the soup to a boil. Reduce the heat so that the soup simmers and cook for 10 minutes.

3. Add the penne and cook until it is al dente, 8 to 10 minutes. Stir in the mozzarella and Parmesan and cook until they have melted.

4. Season the soup with salt and pepper, ladle it into bowls, and garnish each portion with the basil and additional Parmesan.

Broccoli & Anchovy Soup

YIELD: 4 SERVINGS / **ACTIVE TIME:** 20 MINUTES / **TOTAL TIME:** 45 MINUTES

1 TABLESPOON EXTRA-VIRGIN OLIVE OIL

1 TABLESPOON UNSALTED BUTTER

1 ONION, CHOPPED

1 GARLIC CLOVE, MINCED

1½ CUPS CHOPPED PORTOBELLO MUSHROOMS

1 CHILE PEPPER, STEMMED, SEEDED, AND CHOPPED

2 WHITE ANCHOVY FILLETS, MINCED

2 TOMATOES, PEELED, SEEDED, AND CHOPPED

¼ CUP WHITE WINE

4 CUPS VEGETABLE STOCK (SEE PAGE 537)

2 CUPS BROCCOLI FLORETS

½ LB. ORECCHIETTE (SEE PAGE 30)

SALT AND PEPPER, TO TASTE

PARMESAN CHEESE, GRATED, FOR GARNISH

1. Place the olive oil and butter in a saucepan and warm over low heat. When the butter has melted, add the onion, garlic, mushrooms, chile, and anchovies and cook, stirring frequently, until the onion starts to soften, about 5 minutes.

2. Stir in the tomatoes and the white wine and simmer, stirring occasionally, for 10 minutes.

3. Add the stock, raise the heat to medium-high, and bring the soup to a boil. Reduce the heat so that the soup simmers. Add the broccoli florets and pasta cook until they are tender, about 10 minutes.

4. Season with salt and pepper, ladle the soup into warmed bowls, and garnish with Parmesan cheese.

Broken Pasta Soup

YIELD: 4 SERVINGS / **ACTIVE TIME:** 20 MINUTES / **TOTAL TIME:** 45 MINUTES

1 TABLESPOON EXTRA-VIRGIN OLIVE OIL

1 ONION, CHOPPED

2 GARLIC CLOVES, MINCED

2 CARROTS, PEELED AND CHOPPED

1 ZUCCHINI, CHOPPED

4 CELERY STALKS, PEELED AND CHOPPED

1 (28 OZ.) CAN OF DICED TOMATOES, WITH THEIR LIQUID

4 CUPS VEGETABLE STOCK (SEE PAGE 537)

1 CUP BROKEN SPAGHETTI

2 TABLESPOONS CHOPPED FRESH PARSLEY

SALT AND PEPPER, TO TASTE

1. Place the olive oil in a large saucepan and warm it over medium heat. Add the onion and cook, stirring frequently, until it starts to soften, about 5 minutes.

2. Add the garlic, carrots, zucchini, and celery and cook for 5 minutes. Add the tomatoes and stock and bring the soup to a boil. Reduce heat so that the soup simmers and cook for 15 minutes.

3. Add the spaghetti and cook until the pasta is al dente, 8 to 10 minutes.

4. Stir in the parsley and season with salt and pepper. Ladle the soup into warmed bowls and serve.

Pasta e Fagioli

YIELD: 8 SERVINGS / **ACTIVE TIME:** 30 MINUTES / **TOTAL TIME:** 1 HOUR AND 15 MINUTES

2 TABLESPOONS EXTRA-VIRGIN OLIVE OIL

4 OZ. PANCETTA OR BACON, CHOPPED

1 ONION, MINCED

1 CELERY STALK, PEELED AND MINCED

3 CARROTS, PEELED AND CHOPPED

SALT AND PEPPER, TO TASTE

3 GARLIC CLOVES, SLICED THIN

3 ANCHOVY FILLETS IN OLIVE OIL, DRAINED

1 (28 OZ.) CAN OF WHOLE SAN MARZANO TOMATOES, WITH THEIR JUICES, CRUSHED BY HAND

1 PARMESAN CHEESE RIND

3 (14 OZ.) CANS OF CANNELLINI BEANS, DRAINED AND RINSED

6½ CUPS CHICKEN STOCK (SEE PAGE 536)

½ LB. SHORT-FORMAT PASTA

¼ CUP CHOPPED FRESH PARSLEY

1 CUP FRESHLY GRATED PARMESAN CHEESE

1. Place the olive oil in a Dutch oven and warm it over medium heat. Add the pancetta or bacon and cook, stirring occasionally, until it is crispy, about 8 minutes.

2. Add the onion, celery, and carrots, season with salt, and cook, stirring occasionally, until the onion is translucent, about 3 minutes. Reduce the heat to low, cover the pot, and cook, stirring occasionally, until the vegetables are very soft, about 20 minutes.

3. Stir in the garlic and anchovies and cook, stirring continually, until the anchovies dissolve, about 1 minute. Add the tomatoes and scrape up any browned bits from the bottom of the pot. Raise the heat to medium-high, add the Parmesan rind, beans, and stock and bring the soup to a boil.

4. Reduce the heat to low and simmer, stirring occasionally, until the flavors have developed to your liking, about 45 minutes.

5. Remove the Parmesan rind and discard it. Stir in the pasta and cook until it is al dente, about 10 minutes.

6. Remove the pot from heat, season the soup with salt and pepper, and top with the parsley and Parmesan. Ladle the soup into warmed bowls and serve.

Italian Wedding Soup

YIELD: 4 SERVINGS / **ACTIVE TIME:** 30 MINUTES / **TOTAL TIME:** 1 HOUR AND 15 MINUTES

FOR THE MEATBALLS

¾ LB. GROUND CHICKEN

⅓ CUP PANKO

1 GARLIC CLOVE, MINCED

2 TABLESPOONS CHOPPED
FRESH PARSLEY

¼ CUP FRESHLY GRATED
PARMESAN CHEESE

1 TABLESPOON MILK

1 EGG, BEATEN

⅛ TEASPOON FENNEL
SEEDS

⅛ TEASPOON RED PEPPER
FLAKES

½ TEASPOON PAPRIKA

SALT AND PEPPER, TO TASTE

FOR THE SOUP

2 TABLESPOONS EXTRA-
VIRGIN OLIVE OIL

1 ONION, CHOPPED

2 CARROTS, PEELED AND
MINCED

1 CELERY STALK, PEELED
AND MINCED

6 CUPS CHICKEN STOCK
(SEE PAGE 536)

¼ CUP WHITE WINE

½ CUP SMALL PASTA

2 TABLESPOONS CHOPPED
FRESH DILL

6 OZ. BABY SPINACH

SALT AND PEPPER, TO TASTE

PARMESAN CHEESE,
GRATED, FOR GARNISH

1. Preheat the oven to 350°F. To prepare the meatballs, place all of the ingredients in a mixing bowl and work the mixture with your hands until combined. Working with wet hands, form the mixture into 1-inch balls and place them on a parchment-lined baking sheet. Place the meatballs in the oven and bake for 12 to 15 minutes, until they are browned and cooked through. Remove the meatballs from the oven and set them aside.

2. To begin preparations for the soup, place the olive oil in a saucepan and warm it over medium heat. Add the onion, carrots, and celery and cook, stirring frequently, until they start to soften, about 5 minutes.

3. Stir in the stock and the wine and bring the soup to a boil. Reduce the heat so that the soup simmers, add the pasta, and cook until it is al dente, about 8 minutes.

4. Add the cooked meatballs and simmer for 5 minutes.

5. Stir in the dill and the spinach and cook until the spinach has wilted, about 2 minutes. Ladle the soup into warmed bowls, garnish with Parmesan, and serve.

Lamb Sharba

YIELD: 6 SERVINGS / **ACTIVE TIME:** 30 MINUTES / **TOTAL TIME:** 2 HOURS

2 TABLESPOONS EXTRA-VIRGIN OLIVE OIL

¾ LB. BONELESS LEG OF LAMB, CUT INTO 1-INCH CUBES

1 ONION, CHOPPED

1 TOMATO, QUARTERED, SEEDED, AND SLICED THIN

1 GARLIC CLOVE, MINCED

1 TABLESPOON TOMATO PASTE

1 BUNCH OF FRESH MINT, TIED WITH TWINE, PLUS MORE FOR GARNISH

2 CINNAMON STICKS

1¼ TEASPOONS TURMERIC

1¼ TEASPOONS PAPRIKA

½ TEASPOON CUMIN

8 CUPS CHICKEN STOCK (SEE PAGE 536)

1 (14 OZ.) CAN OF CHICKPEAS, DRAINED AND RINSED

¾ CUP ORZO

SALT AND PEPPER, TO TASTE

1. Place the olive oil in a Dutch oven and warm it over medium-high heat. Add the lamb and cook, turning it as necessary, until it is browned all over, about 5 minutes. Remove the lamb with a slotted spoon and place it on a paper towel–lined plate.

2. Add the onion to the pot and cook, stirring occasionally, until it starts to soften, about 5 minutes. Add the tomato, garlic, tomato paste, mint, cinnamon sticks, turmeric, paprika, and cumin and cook, stirring continually, for 1 minute.

3. Add the stock and bring the mixture to a boil. Return the seared lamb to the pot, reduce the heat, and simmer until the lamb is tender, about 30 minutes.

4. Add the chickpeas and orzo and cook until the orzo is tender, about 10 minutes.

5. Remove the mint and discard it. Season the soup with salt and pepper and ladle it into warmed bowls. Garnish with additional mint and enjoy.

Chicken Liver & Farfalle Soup

YIELD: 4 SERVINGS / **ACTIVE TIME:** 25 MINUTES / **TOTAL TIME:** 1 HOUR

1 TABLESPOON EXTRA-VIRGIN OLIVE OIL

1 TABLESPOON UNSALTED BUTTER

½ CUP CHOPPED CHICKEN LIVERS

4 GARLIC CLOVES, MINCED

2 TABLESPOONS WHITE WINE

2 TABLESPOONS CHOPPED FRESH PARSLEY

2 TABLESPOONS CHOPPED FRESH MARJORAM

2 TABLESPOONS CHOPPED FRESH SAGE

1 TEASPOON FRESH THYME

6 FRESH BASIL LEAVES, FINELY CHOPPED

6 CUPS CHICKEN STOCK (SEE PAGE 536)

2 CUPS PEAS

6 OZ. FARFALLE (SEE PAGE 60)

3 SCALLION WHITES, SLICED

SALT AND PEPPER, TO TASTE

1. Place the olive oil and butter in a medium saucepan and warm the mixture over medium-high heat. When the butter has melted, add the chicken livers and garlic and cook, stirring frequently, until the chicken livers are browned all over, about 5 minutes.

2. Add the wine and cook until it evaporates. Stir in the herbs and cook for 2 minutes. Remove pan from heat and set aside.

3. Place the stock in a large saucepan and bring it to a boil. Reduce the heat so that the stock simmers, add the peas, and cook for 5 minutes.

4. Return the stock to a boil and add the Farfalle. Reduce the heat so that the stock simmers and cook until the pasta is al dente.

5. Add the chicken liver mixture and scallions and simmer for 3 minutes.

6. Season the soup with salt and pepper, ladle it into warmed bowls, and serve.

Pantrucas in Broth

YIELD: 4 SERVINGS / **ACTIVE TIME:** 1 HOUR / **TOTAL TIME:** 1 HOUR AND 15 MINUTES

2 LARGE EGG YOLKS

2 TABLESPOONS WATER

8 CUPS CHICKEN STOCK
(SEE PAGE 536)

PANTRUCAS (SEE PAGE 100)

BLACK PEPPER, TO TASTE

FRESH CILANTRO, CHOPPED,
FOR GARNISH

1. Place the egg yolks and water in a small bowl and whisk to combine. Set the egg wash aside.

2. Place the stock in a large saucepan and bring it to a gentle boil.

3. Add the Pantrucas and cook until they are al dente, 4 to 6 minutes.

4. Remove the pan from heat and stir in the egg wash.

5. Ladle the soup into warmed bowls, garnish each portion with cilantro, and serve.

Meatball & Orzo Soup

YIELD: 4 SERVINGS / **ACTIVE TIME:** 45 MINUTES / **TOTAL TIME:** 1 HOUR AND 15 MINUTES

FOR THE MEATBALLS

2 SLICES OF WHITE BREAD, CRUSTS REMOVED, TORN INTO SMALL PIECES

6 TABLESPOONS MILK

¾ LB. GROUND CHICKEN

½ ONION, CHOPPED

3 TABLESPOONS FINELY CHOPPED FRESH PARSLEY

1 TABLESPOON ORANGE ZEST

2 GARLIC CLOVES, MINCED

1 EGG, BEATEN

SALT AND PEPPER, TO TASTE

2 TABLESPOONS EXTRA-VIRGIN OLIVE OIL

FOR THE SOUP

1 (14 OZ.) CAN OF CANNELLINI BEANS, DRAINED AND RINSED

4 CUPS CHICKEN STOCK (SEE PAGE 536)

2 TABLESPOONS EXTRA-VIRGIN OLIVE OIL

1 ONION, CHOPPED

1 GARLIC CLOVE, MINCED

1 BIRD'S EYE CHILE PEPPER, STEMMED, SEEDED, AND CHOPPED

1 CELERY STALK, CHOPPED

1 CARROT, PEELED AND CHOPPED

1 TABLESPOON TOMATO PASTE

1½ CUPS ORZO

SALT AND PEPPER, TO TASTE

PECORINO CHEESE, GRATED, FOR GARNISH

FRESH BASIL, FINELY CHOPPED, FOR GARNISH

1. To begin preparations for the meatballs, place the bread and milk in a bowl and let the bread soak for 10 minutes.

2. Add the chicken, onion, parsley, orange zest, garlic, and egg and work the mixture with your hands until thoroughly combined. Season with salt and pepper and form the mixture into 1-inch balls.

3. Place the olive oil in a large skillet and warm it over medium heat. When it starts to shimmer, add the meatballs and cook, turning them occasionally, until they are browned all over, about 8 minutes. Transfer the meatballs to a paper towel–lined plate to drain.

4. To begin preparations for the soup, place the cannellini beans and 1 cup of the stock in a food processor, blitz until pureed, and set the mixture aside.

5. Place the olive oil in a saucepan and warm it over medium heat. Add the onion, garlic, chile, celery, and carrot and cook, stirring occasionally, until the vegetables start to soften, about 5 minutes.

6. Stir in the tomato paste, the cannellini puree, and the remaining stock and bring the soup to a boil. Reduce the heat so that the soup simmers and cook for 10 minutes.

7. Add the orzo and cook until it is al dente, about 8 minutes.

8. Add the meatballs, cook until they are completely cooked through, and then season the soup with salt and pepper.

9. Ladle the soup into warmed bowls, garnish with the Pecorino and basil, and serve.

Avgolemono

YIELD: 4 TO 6 SERVINGS / **ACTIVE TIME:** 15 MINUTES / **TOTAL TIME:** 45 MINUTES

8 CUPS CHICKEN STOCK (SEE PAGE 536)

½ CUP ORZO

3 EGGS

JUICE OF 1 LEMON

1 TABLESPOON COLD WATER

SALT AND PEPPER, TO TASTE

1 LEMON, SLICED THIN, FOR GARNISH

FRESH DILL, CHOPPED, FOR GARNISH

1. Place the stock in a large saucepan and bring it to a boil. Reduce the heat so that the stock simmers. Add the orzo and cook until tender, about 5 minutes.

2. Strain the stock and orzo over a large bowl. Set the orzo aside. Return the stock to the pan and bring it to a simmer.

3. Place the eggs in a mixing bowl and beat until scrambled and frothy. Stir in the lemon juice and cold water. While stirring constantly, add approximately ½ cup of the stock to the egg mixture. Stir another cup of stock into the egg mixture and then stir the tempered eggs into the saucepan. Reduce the heat to low and be careful not to let the stock come to boil once you add the egg mixture.

4. Return the orzo to the soup. Cook, stirring continually, until everything is warmed through, about 2 minutes. Season with salt and pepper, ladle the soup into warmed bowls, and garnish each portion with slices of lemon and dill.

Beet Soup with Mushroom Ravioli

YIELD: 4 SERVINGS / **ACTIVE TIME:** 1 HOUR / **TOTAL TIME:** 1 HOUR AND 45 MINUTES

FOR THE RAVIOLI

1 TABLESPOON UNSALTED BUTTER

2 CUPS CHOPPED PORTOBELLO MUSHROOMS

1 SHALLOT, MINCED

1 GARLIC CLOVE, MINCED

LEAVES FROM 1 SPRIG FRESH THYME, CHOPPED

2 TABLESPOONS MASCARPONE CHEESE

SALT AND PEPPER, TO TASTE

RAVIOLI (SEE PAGE 40), UNCUT

FOR THE SOUP

1 TABLESPOON EXTRA-VIRGIN OLIVE OIL

1 ONION, CHOPPED

2 GARLIC CLOVES, MINCED

1 TEASPOON FENNEL SEEDS

1 LARGE BEET, PEELED AND MINCED

6 CUPS VEGETABLE STOCK (SEE PAGE 537)

¼ CUP ORANGE JUICE

SALT AND PEPPER, TO TASTE

1. To begin preparations for the ravioli, place the butter in a medium saucepan and melt it over medium heat. Add the mushrooms and cook until they start to release their liquid, about 6 minutes.

2. Add the shallot, garlic, and thyme and cook, stirring frequently, until the shallot starts to soften, about 5 minutes.

3. Remove the pan from heat and strain the mixture to remove any excess liquid. Let the mixture cool. Once it is cool, place in a small bowl and add the mascarpone. Stir to combine, season with salt and pepper, and set the filling aside.

4. Make the ravioli as instructed, filling the depressions with the mushroom mixture. Set the ravioli aside.

5. To begin preparations for the soup, place the olive oil in a large saucepan and warm it over medium heat. Add the onion, garlic, and fennel seeds and cook, stirring occasionally, until the onion starts to soften, about 5 minutes.

6. Add the beet and cook for 5 minutes. Add the stock and orange juice, bring the soup to a boil, and then reduce the heat so that it simmers. Cook until the beet is tender, about 15 minutes.

7. Transfer the soup to a food processor and blitz until it is pureed.

8. Place the soup in a clean saucepan, season it with salt and pepper, and bring to a boil. Drop the ravioli into the pan and cook until they are al dente, 2 to 4 minutes.

9. Ladle the soup into warmed bowls, garnish with fennel fronds, and serve.

Tip: Once you get some practice with making ravioli, try making some into heart shapes to serve a loved one—they'll look great against the vibrant color of the soup.

Cream of Mushroom with Fusilli

YIELD: 4 SERVINGS / **ACTIVE TIME:** 20 MINUTES / **TOTAL TIME:** 50 MINUTES

4 TABLESPOONS UNSALTED BUTTER

1 ONION, CHOPPED

2 GARLIC CLOVES, CHOPPED

⅓ CUP MADEIRA WINE

¾ LB. MUSHROOMS

4 CUPS VEGETABLE STOCK (SEE PAGE 537)

1½ CUPS DRIED FUSILLI

1 CUP HEAVY CREAM

SALT AND PEPPER, TO TASTE

FRESH PARSLEY, FINELY CHOPPED, FOR GARNISH

1. Place the butter in a large saucepan and melt it over medium heat. Add the onion and garlic and cook, stirring frequently, until the onion starts to soften, about 5 minutes.

2. Stir in the Madeira and cook until it has evaporated, about 5 minutes. Add the mushrooms and cook until they have released all of their liquid and start to brown, about 10 minutes.

3. Add the stock and bring the soup to a boil. Reduce the heat so that it simmers and cook for 10 minutes.

4. Transfer the soup to a blender, puree until smooth and creamy, and then strain through a fine-mesh sieve.

5. Return the soup to a clean saucepan and bring it to a simmer. Add the fusilli and cook until it is al dente, 8 to 10 minutes.

6. Add the heavy cream and simmer for 2 minutes, stirring continually. Season with salt and pepper, ladle the soup into warmed bowls, and garnish with parsley.

Pea Soup with Pasta & Ricotta Salata

YIELD: 4 SERVINGS / **ACTIVE TIME:** 25 MINUTES / **TOTAL TIME:** 40 MINUTES

8 VERY RIPE PLUM TOMATOES

3 TABLESPOONS EXTRA-VIRGIN OLIVE OIL

1 LARGE YELLOW ONION, CHOPPED

SALT, TO TASTE

3 CUPS PEAS

¼ TEASPOON SUGAR

4 CUPS VEGETABLE STOCK (SEE PAGE 537)

1½ CUPS SHORT-FORMAT PASTA (SHELLS OR DITALINI PREFERRED)

SALT AND PEPPER, TO TASTE

½ CUP CRUMBLED RICOTTA SALATA CHEESE, FOR GARNISH

FRESH BASIL, SHREDDED, FOR GARNISH

1. Bring water to a boil in a small saucepan. Add the tomatoes and cook for 1 minute. Use tongs to remove the tomatoes, transfer them to a cutting board, and let them cool. When they are cool enough to handle, peel the tomatoes, cut them into quarters, and remove the seeds. Chop the tomatoes and set them aside.

2. Place the olive oil in a medium saucepan and warm it over medium heat. Add the onion, season with salt, and cook, stirring occasionally, until the onion is translucent. Reduce the heat to low, cover the pan, and cook, stirring occasionally, until the onion is very soft, about 15 minutes.

3. Add the peas, season with salt, raise the heat to medium-high, and cook, stirring frequently, for about 3 minutes. Add the tomatoes and any juices that have accumulated, sugar, and stock and bring to a boil.

4. Season with salt and pepper, add the pasta, and cook until it is al dente, 6 to 8 minutes.

5. Ladle the soup into warmed bowls, garnish with the ricotta salata and basil, and serve.

Zuppa Imperiale

YIELD: 6 SERVINGS / **ACTIVE TIME:** 1 HOUR / **TOTAL TIME:** 24 HOURS

1½ CUPS GRATED PARMESAN CHEESE

5 LARGE EGGS

½ CUP UNSALTED BUTTER, SOFTENED

1½ CUPS PLUS 3 TABLESPOONS ALL-PURPOSE FLOUR

1 TEASPOON FRESHLY GRATED NUTMEG, PLUS MORE FOR GARNISH

1 TEASPOON KOSHER SALT

½ TEASPOON WHITE PEPPER

8 CUPS CHICKEN STOCK (SEE PAGE 536)

1. Place the Parmesan, eggs, butter, flour, nutmeg, salt, and pepper in a large bowl and work the mixture with your hands until it comes together as a smooth dough.

2. Place the dough on a large piece of cheesecloth and shape the dough into a 2-inch-wide rope. Wrap the cheesecloth tightly around the dough and tie the cheesecloth closed at both ends with kitchen twine.

3. Place the stock and dough in a large saucepan and bring to a boil. Reduce the heat to low, cover the pan, and simmer for 3 hours.

4. Remove the dough from the broth and place it on a baking sheet. Place another baking sheet on top of the dough and weigh it down with several heavy books; this helps eliminate any broth or air bubbles trapped inside the dough. Let the dough and the broth cool for an hour at room temperature.

5. Transfer the dough—with the baking sheets and books—and broth to the refrigerator and chill them overnight.

6. Bring the broth to a gentle boil over medium heat. While the broth is warming up, remove the cheesecloth from the pasta imperiale and cut it into ½ inch cubes.

7. Stir the cubes into the broth and cook until the broth begins to gently simmer, 7 to 10 minutes.

8. Ladle the soup into warmed bowls, garnish with additional nutmeg, and serve.

Sour & Spicy Fish Soup

YIELD: 4 SERVINGS / **ACTIVE TIME:** 40 MINUTES / **TOTAL TIME:** 1 HOUR AND 30 MINUTES

¾ LB. SWORDFISH, CHOPPED

½ CUP FISH SAUCE

2 GARLIC CLOVES, MINCED

1 OZ. DRIED SQUID, SOAKED FOR 30 MINUTES

3 OZ. RICE NOODLES

1 TABLESPOON AVOCADO OIL

4 SCALLIONS, TRIMMED AND SLICED

2 SHALLOTS, MINCED

2 TABLESPOONS GRATED FRESH GINGER

2 LEMONGRASS STALKS, BRUISED

4 CUPS FISH STOCK (SEE PAGE 542)

2 TABLESPOONS TAMARIND PASTE

2 BIRD'S EYE CHILE PEPPERS, STEMMED, SEEDED, AND SLICED

¾ LB. PINEAPPLE, DICED

4 PLUM TOMATOES, CHOPPED

3 OZ. CANNED SLICED BAMBOO SHOOTS, DRAINED

½ LB. CALAMARI, CLEANED, BODIES SLICED INTO ¼-INCH-THICK PIECES, TENTACLES LEFT WHOLE

2 TABLESPOONS CHOPPED FRESH CILANTRO, PLUS MORE FOR GARNISH

SALT AND PEPPER, TO TASTE

BEAN SPROUTS, FOR GARNISH

ALFALFA SPROUTS, FOR GARNISH

LIME WEDGES, FOR SERVING

1. Place the swordfish, 2 tablespoons of fish sauce, and the garlic in a bowl. Toss until the swordfish is coated and let it marinate.

2. Drain and rinse the dried squid.

3. Place the rice noodles in a bowl and cover with boiling water. Soak until they are al dente. Drain the noodles and set them aside.

4. Place the avocado oil in a medium saucepan and warm it over medium heat. Add the dried squid, scallions, shallots, ginger, and lemongrass and cook, stirring frequently, for 2 minutes. Add the stock, bring the soup to a boil, and then reduce the heat so that it simmers. Cook for 10 minutes.

5. Strain the soup into a clean saucepan through a fine-mesh sieve and bring it to a boil. Stir in the remaining fish sauce, tamarind paste, and chiles and simmer for 3 minutes.

6. Add the pineapple, tomatoes, bamboo shoots, and calamari and cook for 3 minutes. Stir in the marinated swordfish and the cilantro and cook until the swordfish is cooked through, 3 to 5 minutes.

7. Season the soup to taste and divide the noodles among warmed bowls. Ladle the soup over the noodles, garnish with bean sprouts, alfalfa sprouts, and additional cilantro, and serve with lime wedges.

Vegetable Soup with Menietti

YIELD: 6 SERVINGS / **ACTIVE TIME:** 1 HOUR / **TOTAL TIME:** 1 HOUR AND 30 MINUTES

2½ TABLESPOONS EXTRA-VIRGIN OLIVE OIL, PLUS MORE FOR DRIZZLING

2 LARGE LEEKS, TRIMMED, RINSED WELL, AND DICED

2 CARROTS, DICED

3 CELERY STALKS, DICED

SALT AND PEPPER, TO TASTE

8 CUPS CHICKEN STOCK (SEE PAGE 536)

2 BAY LEAVES

1 SPRIG OF FRESH ROSEMARY

MENIETTI (SEE PAGE 110)

PARMESAN CHEESE, GRATED, FOR GARNISH

1. Place the olive oil in a large saucepan and warm it over medium-high heat. Add the leeks, carrots, and celery, season with salt, and cook, stirring occasionally, until the vegetables start to soften, about 5 minutes. Reduce the heat to medium-low, cover the pan, and cook, stirring occasionally, until the vegetables are very tender, about 15 minutes.

2. Add the stock, bay leaves, and rosemary, turn the heat to medium-high, and bring the soup to a boil. Reduce the heat so that the soup simmers and cook for 10 minutes.

3. Season the soup with salt and pepper, remove the bay leaves and rosemary, and discard them.

4. Bring the soup to a boil and add the pasta. Cook until it is al dente, 2 to 4 minutes, and ladle the soup into warmed bowls. Drizzle olive oil over the top of each portion, garnish with Parmesan, and serve.

Spinach, Cannellini & Fregola Soup

YIELD: 4 SERVINGS / **ACTIVE TIME:** 45 MINUTES / **TOTAL TIME:** 1 HOUR AND 20 MINUTES

4 VERY RIPE PLUM TOMATOES

¼ CUP EXTRA-VIRGIN OLIVE OIL, PLUS MORE FOR DRIZZLING

2 GARLIC CLOVES, CRUSHED

2 MEDIUM LEEKS, TRIMMED, RINSED WELL, AND DICED

1 SMALL RED ONION, MINCED

4 CELERY STALKS, MINCED

SALT AND PEPPER, TO TASTE

1 (14 OZ.) CAN OF CANNELLINI BEANS, DRAINED AND RINSED

1 TABLESPOON TOMATO PASTE

6 CUPS CHICKEN STOCK (SEE PAGE 536)

5 OZ. FREGOLA (SEE PAGE 32)

½ LB. FRESH BABY SPINACH

PECORINO CHEESE, GRATED, FOR GARNISH

1. Bring water to a boil in a large saucepan. Add the tomatoes and boil them for 2 minutes. Drain the tomatoes and let them cool. When they are cool enough to handle, peel the tomatoes, remove the seeds, and chop the remaining flesh. Set the tomatoes aside.

2. Place the olive oil in a large saucepan and warm it over medium-high heat. Add the garlic and cook, pressing it into the bottom of the pan, for 2 minutes. Remove the garlic and discard it.

3. Add the leeks, onion, and celery, season with salt, and cook, stirring occasionally, until the vegetables start to soften, about 5 minutes. Reduce the heat to medium-low, cover the pan, and cook, stirring occasionally, until the vegetables are very tender, about 15 minutes.

4. Raise the heat to medium-high and add the beans and tomato paste. Cook, stirring frequently, until the beans begin to brown, about 8 minutes.

5. Add the tomatoes and stock, season the soup with salt and pepper, and bring it to a boil. Reduce the heat to low, cover the pan, and simmer the soup for 30 minutes.

6. Add the Fregola and cook until it is al dente, about 15 minutes. When the pasta is close to being done, stir in the spinach.

7. Ladle the soup into warmed bowls, drizzle olive oil over the top, garnish with pecorino, and serve.

Pasta, Chickpea & Swiss Chard Soup

YIELD: 6 SERVINGS / **ACTIVE TIME:** 45 MINUTES / **TOTAL TIME:** 1 HOUR AND 30 MINUTES

3 TABLESPOONS EXTRA-VIRGIN OLIVE OIL, PLUS MORE FOR DRIZZLING

6 OZ. PANCETTA, CHOPPED

3 LEEKS, TRIMMED, RINSED WELL, AND DICED

SALT AND PEPPER, TO TASTE

4 LARGE GARLIC CLOVES, MINCED

2 CARROTS, PEELED AND CHOPPED

8 CUPS CHICKEN STOCK (SEE PAGE 536)

2 (14 OZ.) CANS OF CHICKPEAS, DRAINED AND RINSED

1 (14 OZ.) CAN OF PEELED WHOLE TOMATOES, CRUSHED BY HAND

1 LB. SWISS CHARD, STEMMED AND SLICED

½ LB. SMALL SHELL PASTA

FRESH BASIL, CHOPPED, FOR GARNISH

PECORINO CHEESE, GRATED, FOR GARNISH

1. Place the olive oil in a large saucepan and warm it over medium-high heat. Add the pancetta and cook, stirring occasionally, until it is golden brown, 6 to 8 minutes.

2. Add the leeks, season with salt, and cook, stirring occasionally, until they start to soften, about 5 minutes. Reduce the heat to medium-low, cover the pan, and cook, stirring occasionally, until the vegetables are very tender, about 15 minutes.

3. Raise the heat to medium-high, add the garlic, and cook, stirring frequently, until it is fragrant, about 1 minute. Add the carrots, season with salt, and cook, stirring occasionally, for 3 minutes.

4. Add the stock, chickpeas, and tomatoes, season the soup with salt and pepper, and bring the soup to a boil. Reduce the heat to medium-low, cover the pan, and simmer the soup for 20 minutes.

5. Bring water to a boil in a large saucepan.

6. Remove 2 cups of the chickpeas and vegetables from the soup, place the mixture in a blender, and blitz until smooth. Stir the puree into the soup and add the chard. Cook until it is tender, about 6 minutes.

7. Add salt to the boiling water, let it return to a full boil, and add the pasta. Cook until it is al dente, 8 to 10 minutes.

8. Drain the pasta, stir it into the soup, and ladle the soup into warmed bowls. Drizzle olive oil over each portion, garnish with basil and pecorino, and serve.

Pisarei & Cranberry Bean Soup

YIELD: 6 SERVINGS / **ACTIVE TIME:** 25 MINUTES / **TOTAL TIME:** 24 HOURS

½ LB. LARDO OR PANCETTA, MINCED

1 TABLESPOON FRESH ROSEMARY

1 YELLOW ONION, CHOPPED

2 CELERY STALKS, CHOPPED

SALT AND PEPPER, TO TASTE

1 CUP RED WINE

2½ CUPS DRIED CRANBERRY BEANS, SOAKED OVERNIGHT AND DRAINED

2 CUPS CRUSHED TOMATOES

2 CARROTS, PEELED AND DICED

16 CUPS BEEF STOCK (SEE PAGE 538)

¼ TEASPOON FRESHLY GRATED NUTMEG

5 WHOLE CLOVES

1 BAY LEAF

PISAREI (SEE PAGE 107)

1¼ CUPS FRESHLY GRATED PARMESAN CHEESE, PLUS MORE FOR GARNISH

HANDFUL OF FRESH PARSLEY, CHOPPED

1. Place the lardo or pancetta and rosemary in a food processor and pulse until the mixture is a paste.

2. Place the paste in a large saucepan and warm it over medium heat. Add the onion and celery, season with salt and pepper, and cook, stirring occasionally, until they start to soften, about 5 minutes.

3. Add the wine and cook until half of it has evaporated.

4. Add the beans, tomatoes, carrots, stock, nutmeg, cloves, and bay leaf, season with salt, and bring the soup to a boil. Reduce the heat so that it simmers and cook until the beans are tender, about 45 minutes.

5. Raise the heat to medium-high, stir in the Pisarei, Parmesan, and parsley, stir, and cook until the pasta is cooked through, about 5 minutes.

6. Ladle the soup into warmed bowls, garnish with Parmesan, and serve.

Tomato Soup with Chickpeas & Ditalini

YIELD: 4 SERVINGS / **ACTIVE TIME:** 20 MINUTES / **TOTAL TIME:** 35 MINUTES

2 TABLESPOONS EXTRA-VIRGIN OLIVE OIL

1 ONION, CHOPPED

2 GARLIC CLOVES, MINCED

2 (28 OZ.) CANS OF WHOLE TOMATOES, PUREED

2 TABLESPOONS FINELY CHOPPED FRESH THYME

4 CUPS CHICKEN STOCK (SEE PAGE 536)

½ CUP DITALINI

1 (14 OZ.) CAN OF CHICKPEAS, DRAINED AND RINSED

¼ CUP CHOPPED FRESH PARSLEY

¼ CUP FRESHLY GRATED PARMESAN CHEESE, PLUS MORE FOR GARNISH

SALT AND PEPPER, TO TASTE

FRESH BASIL, CHOPPED, FOR GARNISH

1. Place the olive oil in a large saucepan and warm over medium heat. Add the onion and cook, stirring occasionally, until it starts to soften, about 5 minutes. Add the garlic, cook for 1 minute, and then stir in the pureed tomatoes, thyme, and stock.

2. Bring the soup to a boil, reduce the heat so that the soup simmers, and add the pasta. Cook until it is tender, about 8 minutes.

3. Stir in the chickpeas, parsley, and Parmesan and cook for 3 minutes. Season with salt and pepper, ladle into warmed bowls, and garnish with additional Parmesan and the basil.

Virtù Teramane

YIELD: 4 SERVINGS / **ACTIVE TIME:** 1 HOUR AND 30 MINUTES / **TOTAL TIME:** 24 HOURS

SALT, TO TASTE

3 CUPS FRESH SPINACH

1 SMALL ZUCCHINI, CHOPPED

1 HEAD OF ENDIVE, CHOPPED

1 CARROT, PEELED AND CHOPPED

1 CELERY STALK, CHOPPED

¾ CUP DRIED CHICKPEAS, SOAKED OVERNIGHT AND DRAINED

¾ CUP LENTILS

1 CUP DRIED FAVA BEANS, SOAKED OVERNIGHT AND DRAINED

⅔ CUP DRIED SPLIT PEAS

2 OZ. LARD, CHOPPED

1 ONION, FINELY DICED

1 GARLIC CLOVE

5 OZ. PANCETTA, CUBED

1 TEASPOON CHOPPED FRESH PARSLEY

2 TOMATOES, CHOPPED

8 CUPS CHICKEN STOCK (SEE PAGE 536)

½ LB. SHORT-FORMAT PASTA

PECORINO CHEESE, GRATED, FOR GARNISH

1. Bring water to a boil in a large saucepan. Add salt, the spinach, zucchini, endive, carrot, and celery and cook for 5 minutes. Drain the vegetables and let them cool. When they are cool enough to handle, squeeze them to remove as much water as possible and set them aside.

2. Place the chickpeas, lentils, beans, and split peas in separate saucepans, cover them with water, and cook until they just start to soften—the cook times will differ for each legume. Drain the legumes and set them aside.

3. Place the lard in a large saucepan and warm it over medium heat. Add the onion, garlic, and pancetta and cook, stirring frequently, until the pancetta's fat starts to render.

4. Remove the garlic from the pan and discard it. Add the parsley and tomatoes and cook, stirring occasionally, until the tomatoes start to collapse, about 15 minutes.

5. Add the stock and cooked vegetables to the pan and cook for 10 minutes.

6. Add the legumes and cook until they are tender, about 30 minutes.

7. Add the pasta and cook until it is al dente, 8 to 10 minutes.

8. Ladle the soup into warmed bowls, garnish each portion with pecorino, and serve.

Zuppa di Asparagi e Uova

YIELD: 4 SERVINGS / **ACTIVE TIME:** 30 MINUTES / **TOTAL TIME:** 45 MINUTES

8 CUPS WATER

1 LB. ASPARAGUS, TRIMMED

SALT, TO TASTE

2 EGGS

2 EGG WHITES

¼ CUP GRATED PECORINO OR PARMESAN CHEESE

¼ CUP EXTRA-VIRGIN OLIVE OIL

1. Place the water in a large saucepan and bring it to a boil. Separate the asparagus into stems and tips. Chop the stems and set the tips aside.

2. Add salt and the asparagus stems to the water and boil for 5 minutes.

3. Add the tips to the boiling water and boil until they are just tender.

4. Place the eggs, egg whites, and pecorino in a bowl and whisk to combine.

5. Stir the mixture into the broth and serve immediately.

Pasta e Lattuga

YIELD: 4 SERVINGS / **ACTIVE TIME:** 10 MINUTES / **TOTAL TIME:** 25 MINUTES

8 CUPS WATER

SALT, TO TASTE

½ LB. MACARONI OR OTHER SHORT-FORMAT PASTA

1 HEAD OF ROMAINE LETTUCE, RINSED AND CHOPPED

2 TABLESPOONS EXTRA-VIRGIN OLIVE OIL, FOR DRIZZLING

1. Bring the water to a boil in a large saucepan. Add salt—less than you would for a typical pasta dish.

2. Add the pasta and lettuce and cook until the pasta is al dente, 8 to 10 minutes.

3. Ladle the soup into warmed bowls, top each portion with some of the olive oil, and enjoy.

Zuppa di Castagne Sarda

YIELD: 4 SERVINGS / **ACTIVE TIME:** 1 HOUR / **TOTAL TIME:** 3 HOURS

1 LB. CHESTNUTS

6 OZ. LARD, CHOPPED

1 ONION, FINELY DICED

6 CUPS WATER, PLUS MORE AS NEEDED

SALT, TO TASTE

¾ LB. SHORT-FORMAT PASTA

1. Preheat the oven to 350°F. Peel the chestnuts, place them on a baking sheet, and roast them for 20 minutes. Remove the chestnuts from the oven, remove the nuts, and set them aside.

2. Place the lard in a large saucepan and warm it over medium heat. Add the onion and cook, stirring occasionally, until it starts to soften, about 5 minutes.

3. Add the chestnuts and water, season with salt, and partially cover the pan. Bring the soup to a simmer, reduce the heat to low, and cook for 1½ hours.

4. Add the pasta and cook until it is al dente, 8 to 10 minutes, adding more water to the pan if needed.

5. Ladle the soup into warmed bowls and serve.

Meatball & Conchiglie Soup

YIELD: 4 SERVINGS / **ACTIVE TIME:** 45 MINUTES / **TOTAL TIME:** 1 HOUR AND 15 MINUTES

FOR THE MEATBALLS

2 SLICES OF WHITE BREAD, CRUSTS REMOVED, TORN INTO SMALL PIECES

6 TABLESPOONS MILK

¾ LB. GROUND VEAL

½ ONION, CHOPPED

3 TABLESPOONS FINELY CHOPPED FRESH PARSLEY

1 TABLESPOON ORANGE ZEST

2 GARLIC CLOVES, MINCED

1 EGG, BEATEN

SALT AND PEPPER, TO TASTE

2 TABLESPOONS EXTRA-VIRGIN OLIVE OIL

FOR THE SOUP

1 (14 OZ.) CAN OF CANNELLINI BEANS, DRAINED AND RINSED

4 CUPS BEEF STOCK (SEE PAGE 538)

2 TABLESPOONS EXTRA-VIRGIN OLIVE OIL

1 ONION, CHOPPED

1 GARLIC CLOVE, MINCED

1 THAI CHILE PEPPER, STEMMED, SEEDED, AND CHOPPED

1 CELERY STALK, CHOPPED

1 CARROT, PEELED AND CHOPPED

1 TABLESPOON TOMATO PASTE

½ LB. CONCHIGLIE

SALT AND PEPPER, TO TASTE

PECORINO CHEESE, GRATED, FOR GARNISH

FRESH BASIL, FINELY CHOPPED, FOR GARNISH

1. To begin preparations for the meatballs, place the bread and milk in a bowl and let the bread soak for 10 minutes.

2. Add the veal, onion, parsley, orange zest, garlic, and egg, season it with salt and pepper, and work the mixture with your hands until well combined. Working with wet hands, form the mixture into balls that are about the size of a grape.

3. Place the olive oil in large skillet and warm it over medium heat. Working in batches to avoid crowding the pan, add the meatballs and cook until they are browned all over, turning them as necessary. Transfer the meatballs to a paper towel–lined plate to drain.

4. Place the cannellini beans and 1 cup of stock in a food processor, blitz until smooth, and set the mixture aside.

5. Place the olive oil in a medium saucepan and warm it over medium heat. Add the onion, garlic, chile, celery, and carrot and cook, stirring frequently, until they start to soften, about 5 minutes.

6. Add the tomato paste, cannellini puree, and remaining stock and bring to a boil. Reduce the heat so that the soup simmers and cook for 10 minutes.

7. Add the meatballs and cook until they are cooked through, about 5 minutes.

8. Add the pasta and cook until it is al dente, 8 to 10 minutes.

9. Season the soup with salt and pepper and ladle it into warmed bowls. Garnish with pecorino and basil and serve.

Leftover Turkey & Orzo Soup

YIELD: 4 SERVINGS / **ACTIVE TIME:** 20 MINUTES / **TOTAL TIME:** 45 MINUTES

1 TABLESPOON EXTRA-VIRGIN OLIVE OIL

1 ONION, CHOPPED

2 CELERY STALKS, CHOPPED

2 CARROTS, PEELED AND CHOPPED

6 CUPS CHICKEN STOCK (SEE PAGE 536)

1 BAY LEAF

1 TEASPOON FINELY CHOPPED FRESH ROSEMARY

½ CUP ORZO

2 CUPS CHOPPED COOKED TURKEY

1 TEASPOON CHOPPED FRESH PARSLEY

SALT AND PEPPER, TO TASTE

1. Place the olive oil in a medium saucepan and warm it over medium heat. Add the onion, celery, and carrots and cook, stirring occasionally, until they start to soften, about 5 minutes.

2. Add the stock, bay leaf, and rosemary and bring the soup to a boil. Reduce the heat so that the soup simmers and cook for 10 minutes.

3. Add the orzo and simmer until it is very al dente, about 8 minutes.

4. Stir in the turkey and parsley and cook until it is warmed through and the pasta is al dente, about 2 minutes. Season with salt and pepper, ladle the soup into warmed bowls, and serve.

Macaroni & Cheese Soup

YIELD: 4 SERVINGS / **ACTIVE TIME:** 15 MINUTES / **TOTAL TIME:** 40 MINUTES

1½ CUPS ELBOW MACARONI

¼ CUP UNSALTED BUTTER

1 ONION, PEELED AND CHOPPED

2 CARROTS, PEELED AND CHOPPED

2 CELERY STALKS, CHOPPED

2 TABLESPOONS ALL-PURPOSE FLOUR

4 CUPS CHICKEN STOCK (SEE PAGE 536)

2 CUPS WHOLE MILK

4 CUPS SHREDDED SHARP CHEDDAR CHEESE

SALT AND PEPPER, TO TASTE

1. Bring water to a boil in a large saucepan. Add salt, let the water return to a full boil, and add the pasta. Cook until it is al dente, 8 to 10 minutes, drain, and set it aside.

2. Place the butter in a medium saucepan and melt it over medium heat. Add the onion, carrots, and celery and cook, stirring occasionally, until they start to soften, about 5 minutes.

3. Add the flour and cook, stirring frequently, for 5 minutes.

4. Add the stock and milk and bring the soup to a boil. Reduce the heat so that the soup simmers and cook for 10 minutes.

5. Remove the pan from heat, add the cheddar, and stir until it has melted.

6. Season with salt and pepper, stir in the pasta, and serve.

Minestrone with Pasta

YIELD: 4 SERVINGS / **ACTIVE TIME:** 20 MINUTES / **TOTAL TIME:** 45 MINUTES

2 TABLESPOONS EXTRA-VIRGIN OLIVE OIL

1 ONION, CHOPPED

1 LEEK, TRIMMED, RINSED WELL, AND CHOPPED

2 CELERY STALKS, CHOPPED

2 CARROTS, PEELED AND CHOPPED

2 (14 OZ.) CANS OF DICED TOMATOES, WITH THEIR LIQUID

2 GARLIC CLOVES, MINCED

4 CUPS VEGETABLE STOCK (SEE PAGE 537)

2 CUPS CHOPPED GREEN CABBAGE

2 TEASPOONS FRESH OREGANO

1 BAY LEAF

¼ CUP TOMATO PASTE

½ CUP SMALL SHELLS OR OTHER SHORT-FORMAT PASTA

SALT AND PEPPER, TO TASTE

PARMESAN CHEESE, GRATED, FOR GARNISH

1. Place the olive oil in a medium saucepan and warm it over medium heat. Add the onion, leek, celery, and carrots and cook, stirring occasionally, until they start to soften, about 5 minutes.

2. Stir in the tomatoes and garlic and cook, stirring occasionally, for 10 minutes.

3. Add the stock, cabbage, oregano, bay leaf, and tomato paste and bring the soup to a boil. Reduce the heat so that the soup simmers and cook for 10 minutes.

4. Add the pasta and cook until it is al dente, 8 to 10 minutes.

5. Season the soup with salt and pepper and ladle it into warmed bowls. Garnish with Parmesan and serve.

Minestrone with Pasta
SEE PAGE 411

Wagon Wheel Soup

YIELD: 4 SERVINGS / **ACTIVE TIME:** 15 MINUTES / **TOTAL TIME:** 30 MINUTES

2 TABLESPOONS EXTRA-VIRGIN OLIVE OIL

1 CUP CHOPPED ONION, CHOPPED

1 LB. GROUND BEEF

4 CUPS SUGO AL BASILICO (SEE PAGE 448)

½ TEASPOON GROUND FRESH OREGANO

2 CUPS BEEF STOCK (SEE PAGE 538)

2 CUPS CANNED KIDNEY BEANS, DRAINED AND RINSED

SALT AND PEPPER, TO TASTE

1 CUP WAGON WHEEL PASTA

1. Bring water to a boil in a large saucepan.

2. Place the olive oil in a medium saucepan and warm it over medium heat. Add the onion and cook, stirring occasionally, until it starts to soften, about 5 minutes.

3. Add the beef and cook, breaking it up with a wooden spoon, until it starts to brown, about 5 minutes.

4. Add the tomato sauce, oregano, stock, and kidney beans and bring the soup to a boil. Reduce the heat so that the soup simmers and cook for 10 minutes.

5. Add salt to the boiling water, let it return to a full boil, and add the pasta. Cook until it is al dente, 6 to 8 minutes. Drain the pasta and add it to the soup.

6. Season with salt and pepper, ladle the soup into warmed bowls, and serve.

Seafood & Sausage Gumbo

YIELD: 4 TO 6 SERVINGS / **ACTIVE TIME:** 30 MINUTES / **TOTAL TIME:** 1 HOUR

½ CUP AVOCADO OIL

½ CUP ALL-PURPOSE FLOUR

¼ CUP UNSALTED BUTTER

1 ONION, FINELY DICED

1 GREEN BELL PEPPER, STEMMED, SEEDED, AND CHOPPED

1 RED BELL PEPPER, STEMMED, SEEDED, AND CHOPPED

2 CELERY STALKS, CHOPPED

1 LB. ANDOUILLE SAUSAGE, SLICED

2 GARLIC CLOVES, MINCED

1 BAY LEAF

¼ TEASPOON FRESH THYME

½ TEASPOON CAYENNE PEPPER

3 CUPS LOBSTER STOCK (SEE PAGE 541)

1 CUP CHOPPED TOMATO

1 CUP CHOPPED OKRA

1½ CUP ORZO

1½ LBS. SHRIMP, SHELLS REMOVED, DEVEINED

½ LB. CRABMEAT, PICKED OVER AND COOKED

½ LB. CALAMARI, CLEANED, TENTACLES LEFT WHOLE, BODIES HALVED AND SCORED

SALT AND PEPPER, TO TASTE

TABASCO, TO TASTE

1. Place the avocado oil in a medium saucepan and warm it over medium heat. Add the flour a little at a time, stirring until all of it has been incorporated and the mixture is a smooth paste.

2. Cook the roux, stirring constantly, until it is the color of peanut butter, 5 to 10 minutes. Remove the pan from heat and let the roux cool.

3. Place the butter in a clean medium saucepan and melt it over medium heat. Add the onion, peppers, and celery and cook, stirring occasionally, until the onion starts to soften, about 5 minutes.

4. Add the sausage and cook, stirring occasionally, for 5 minutes. Add the garlic, bay leaf, thyme, and cayenne and cook, stirring continually, for 5 minutes.

5. Stir in the stock, tomatoes, and okra and bring the soup to a boil. Reduce the heat so that the soup simmers and cook for 10 minutes.

6. Whisk the roux and the orzo into the soup and return it to a boil, stirring continually. Reduce the heat and simmer the soup for 5 minutes.

7. Stir in the shrimp, crab, and calamari and cook until the shrimp turns pink and the orzo is al dente, 3 to 4 minutes. Season the soup with salt, pepper, and Tabasco.

8. Ladle the gumbo into warmed bowls and serve.

Seafood & Sausage Gumbo
SEE PAGE 415

Sole & Pasta Soup

YIELD: 4 SERVINGS / **ACTIVE TIME:** 30 MINUTES / **TOTAL TIME:** 1 HOUR AND 30 MINUTES

1 RED BELL PEPPER

1 EGG YOLK

4 GARLIC CLOVES, MASHED

1 TABLESPOON WHITE WINE VINEGAR

1½ TEASPOONS WATER

½ TEASPOON MUSTARD POWDER

1 CUP AVOCADO OIL

1 TEASPOON FRESH LEMON JUICE

⅛ TEASPOON CHILI POWDER

SALT AND PEPPER, TO TASTE

2 TABLESPOONS EXTRA-VIRGIN OLIVE OIL

1 ONION, SLICED

1 GARLIC CLOVE, MINCED

½ LEEK, WHITE PART ONLY, RINSED WELL AND SLICED

4 CUPS VEGETABLE STOCK (SEE PAGE 537)

1 (14 OZ.) CAN OF DICED TOMATOES, DRAINED

1 TEASPOON HERBES DE PROVENCE

⅛ TEASPOON SAFFRON THREADS

2 CUPS FARFALLE (SEE PAGE 60)

1½ LBS. SOLE FILLETS, HALVED LENGTHWISE

16 MUSSELS, RINSED WELL AND DEBEARDED

CRUSTY BREAD, FOR SERVING

1. Over an open flame, on a grill, or in the oven, roast the red pepper until it is lightly charred all over. Place the pepper in a bowl, cover it with plastic wrap, and let it steam for 10 minutes. Remove the skin, stem, and seeds from the pepper and finely chop the flesh.

2. Place the egg yolk, garlic, vinegar, water, and mustard powder in a mixing bowl and whisk until the mixture is foamy. While whisking continually, gradually add the avocado oil in a thin stream until it has emulsified. Stir the lemon juice, chili powder, and one-quarter of the roasted red pepper into the rouille, season it with salt and pepper, and store it in the refrigerator.

3. Place the olive oil in a large saucepan and warm it over medium heat. Add the onion, garlic, and leek and cook, stirring frequently, until the onion is translucent, about 3 minutes.

4. Add the stock, tomatoes, fresh herbs, and saffron and bring the soup to a boil.

5. Add the pasta, sole, mussels, and remaining roasted red pepper, reduce the heat so that the soup simmers, and cook until the majority of the mussels have opened, the sole is cooked through, and the pasta is al dente, 5 to 8 minutes. Discard any mussels that did not open.

6. Season the soup with salt and pepper, ladle it into warmed bowls, and serve with the rouille and crusty bread.

Seafood Minestrone

YIELD: 4 TO 6 SERVINGS / **ACTIVE TIME:** 45 MINUTES / **TOTAL TIME:** 1 HOUR AND 30 MINUTES

½ CUP WHITE WINE

30 MUSSELS, RINSED WELL AND DEBEARDED

1 TABLESPOON EXTRA-VIRGIN OLIVE OIL

4 SLICES OF THICK-CUT BACON, CHOPPED

1 GARLIC CLOVE, MINCED

1 ONION, CHOPPED

2 CELERY STALKS, CHOPPED

1 TABLESPOON TOMATO PASTE

1 TEASPOON CHOPPED FRESH ROSEMARY

1 TEASPOON FRESH THYME

1 BAY LEAF

1 TEASPOON FRESH LEMON JUICE

6 TABLESPOONS CANNED KIDNEY BEANS, DRAINED AND RINSED

⅔ CUP CHOPPED TOMATO

6 CUPS FISH STOCK (SEE PAGE 542)

½ CUP ORZO

6 OZ. SHRIMP, SHELLS REMOVED, DEVEINED

12 OYSTERS, SHUCKED, JUICES RESERVED

SALT AND PEPPER, TO TASTE

FRESH BASIL, CHOPPED, FOR GARNISH

PARMESAN CHEESE, SHAVED, FOR GARNISH

BASIL PESTO (SEE PAGE 482), FOR SERVING

1. Place the wine and mussels in a large saucepan, cover the pan, and cook the mussels over medium heat until the majority of them have opened, about 5 minutes. Discard any mussels that did not open.

2. Strain the mussels through a fine-mesh sieve and reserve the cooking liquid. Remove the mussels from their shells and set them aside.

3. Place the olive oil in a medium saucepan and warm it over medium heat. Add the bacon and cook, stirring occasionally, until it starts to brown, about 4 minutes. Add the garlic, onion, and celery and cook, stirring frequently, until the celery and onion start to soften, about 5 minutes.

4. Add the tomato paste, rosemary, thyme, bay leaf, lemon juice, kidney beans, and tomato and cook for 2 minutes.

5. Add the stock and bring the soup to a boil. Reduce the heat so that the soup simmers and cook until the beans and rice are tender, 12 to 15 minutes.

6. Add the orzo and cook for 4 minutes. Add the mussels, shrimp, and oysters and simmer until the orzo is al dente and the shrimp and oysters are cooked through, about 4 minutes.

7. Season the soup with salt and pepper and ladle it into warmed bowls. Garnish each portion with basil and Parmesan and serve with pesto.

Pho

YIELD: 8 SERVINGS / **ACTIVE TIME:** 1 HOUR / **TOTAL TIME:** 5 HOURS AND 30 MINUTES

1. Set the oven's broiler to high. Place the onions and ginger on a parchment-lined baking sheet and broil until they are lightly blackened on all sides, turning the pieces every 30 seconds; it should take about 3 minutes all together. Remove from the oven and let the onions and ginger cool. When cool enough to handle, remove the charred skin and discard it. Set the onions and ginger aside.

2. Place the beef shin and chuck in a large saucepan and cover with water. Bring to a boil and cook for 20 minutes. Drain the beef and then thoroughly wash the pan. Once the meat and bones are cool enough to handle, rinse them under cold water, wiping away any debris.

3. While the beef is cooling, place the cloves, star anise, cinnamon stick, and fennel seeds in a small skillet and toast over medium heat until they are fragrant, 3 to 4 minutes, shaking the pan frequently. Transfer the toasted aromatics to a piece of cheesecloth and tie it closed with kitchen twine.

4. Add 16 cups water to the pan and bring to a boil. Add the beef and bones, onions, ginger, toasted spice sachet, scallions, fish sauce, sugar, and salt and return to a boil. Reduce the heat to low and simmer for 1½ hours, skimming the pho as needed to remove any impurities from the surface.

5. Remove the beef chuck from the pho, transfer it to a small plate, and let it cool. Continue to simmer the pho until the flavor has developed to your liking, at least another 3 hours, skimming as needed.

6. While the pho simmers, place the noodles in a baking dish, cover with lukewarm water, and let them soak until they are al dente, 20 to 30 minutes. Drain the noodles, rinse them under cold water, and set them aside.

7. Taste the stock and adjust the seasoning as necessary. Divide the noodles among the serving bowls. Slice the beef chuck thinly and divide it among the bowls. Bring the stock to a rolling boil, ladle it into the bowls, and serve alongside the cilantro, basil, chiles, scallions, bean sprouts, peanuts, and lime wedges.

THE ENCYCLOPEDIA OF PASTA

2 SMALL ONIONS, HALVED

2-INCH PIECE OF FRESH GINGER, HALVED LENGTHWISE

4 LBS. BEEF SHIN BONES, WITH SOME MEAT ATTACHED

1 LB. BONELESS BEEF CHUCK

8 WHOLE CLOVES

6 STAR ANISE PODS

1 CINNAMON STICK

2 TEASPOONS FENNEL SEEDS

5 SCALLIONS, TRIMMED AND CHOPPED

¼ CUP FISH SAUCE

2½ TABLESPOONS SUGAR

1 TABLESPOON SALT

¾ LB. RICE NOODLES

FRESH CILANTRO, CHOPPED, FOR SERVING

FRESH THAI BASIL, CHOPPED, FOR SERVING

THAI CHILE PEPPERS, SLICED THIN, FOR SERVING

SCALLION GREENS, CHOPPED, FOR SERVING

MUNG BEAN SPROUTS, PICKED OVER, FOR SERVING

ROASTED PEANUTS, FOR SERVING

LIME WEDGES, FOR SERVING

Sweet & Sour Egg Drop Soup

YIELD: 6 SERVINGS / **ACTIVE TIME:** 30 MINUTES / **TOTAL TIME:** 45 MINUTES

1 LB. EXTRA-FIRM TOFU, DRAINED AND CUBED

10 OZ. BLACK RICE RAMEN NOODLES

2½ TABLESPOONS TOASTED SESAME OIL

3 GARLIC CLOVES, PEELED AND MINCED

2-INCH PIECE OF FRESH GINGER, PEELED AND GRATED

6 SCALLIONS, TRIMMED AND SLICED THIN, WHITES AND GREENS SEPARATED

SALT, TO TASTE

½ LB. GROUND PORK

8 CUPS CHICKEN STOCK (SEE PAGE 536)

8 CREMINI MUSHROOMS, SLICED

¼ CUP RICE VINEGAR

3 TABLESPOONS SOY SAUCE

2 TEASPOONS SUGAR

1 TABLESPOON SPICY CHILI OIL (OPTIONAL)

2 LARGE EGGS, BEATEN

SESAME SEEDS, TOASTED, FOR GARNISH

1. Place the tofu in a single layer on a paper towel–lined tray. Cover with paper towels and pat dry. Let them sit for 30 minutes, changing the paper towels after 15 minutes. Cut the dried strips into ½-inch cubes and set them aside.

2. While the tofu drains, bring water to a boil in a large saucepan. Add the noodles and cook until al dente, 3 to 5 minutes. Drain, rinse the noodles under cold water, and drain again. Transfer the noodles to a medium bowl, add ½ tablespoon of sesame oil, and toss to coat. Set the noodles aside.

3. Place 1 tablespoon of sesame oil in a large saucepan and warm it over medium heat. Add the garlic, ginger, and scallion whites, season with salt, and cook, stirring frequently, until the scallions start to soften, about 5 minutes.

4. Add the pork and cook, breaking it up with a wooden spoon, until it has browned, 8 to 10 minutes.

5. Add the stock and bring the soup to a gentle boil. Add the tofu, mushrooms, vinegar, soy sauce, sugar, the remaining sesame oil, and the chili oil (if desired). Return the soup to a gentle boil, reduce the heat so that it simmers and cook for 5 minutes.

6. Taste the soup and adjust the seasoning as necessary. While whisking continually, slowly add the eggs into the soup and bring the soup back to a simmer.

7. Divide the noodles among the serving bowls and ladle the soup over them. Garnish with the scallion greens and toasted sesame seeds.

Miso Soup with Udon Noodles

YIELD: 4 SERVINGS / **ACTIVE TIME:** 20 MINUTES / **TOTAL TIME:** 35 MINUTES

¾ LB. UDON NOODLES
(SEE PAGE 106)

6 CUPS VEGETABLE STOCK
(SEE PAGE 537)

3 TABLESPOONS SAKE

2-INCH PIECE OF FRESH
GINGER, PEELED AND
SLICED THIN

4 CREMINI MUSHROOMS,
TRIMMED AND SLICED THIN

1 CARROT, PEELED AND
SLICED VERY THIN WITH A
MANDOLINE

1½ TABLESPOONS RED MISO
PASTE

4 OZ. SILKEN TOFU,
DRAINED AND CUT INTO ½-
INCH CUBES

SCALLIONS, CHOPPED FOR
GARNISH

1. Bring water to a boil in a large saucepan. Add the noodles and cook until they are al dente, 2 to 3 minutes.

2. While the water is coming to a boil, place the stock, sake, and ginger in a medium saucepan and bring to a boil. Reduce the heat to medium-low and simmer for 5 minutes. Remove the ginger with a slotted spoon and discard it. Add the mushrooms and carrot and simmer until the carrot just starts to soften, about 4 minutes.

3. Drain the noodles and divide them among four warmed bowls.

4. Place the miso in a small bowl and add ¼ cup of the hot broth. Stir until the miso dissolves and the liquid looks creamy. Pour the mixture into the broth.

5. Warm up the tofu by placing it in a fine-mesh sieve and running a slow stream of hot tap water over it for 1 minute. Divide the tofu among the serving bowls and ladle the hot broth over it. Garnish with the scallions and serve.

Tomato Alphabet Soup

YIELD: 4 SERVINGS / **ACTIVE TIME:** 15 MINUTES / **TOTAL TIME:** 30 MINUTES

¼ CUP UNSALTED BUTTER

2 ONIONS, CHOPPED

4 CARROTS, PEELED AND CHOPPED

2 CELERY STALKS, CHOPPED

3 CUPS VEGETABLE STOCK (SEE PAGE 537)

4 (14 OZ.) CANS OF DICED TOMATOES, DRAINED

SALT AND PEPPER, TO TASTE

1 CUP ALPHABET PASTA

2 TEASPOONS FRESH BASIL, CHOPPED

1. Bring water to a boil in a large saucepan.

2. Place the butter in a medium saucepan and melt it over medium heat. Add the onion, carrots, and celery and cook, stirring occasionally, until they start to soften, about 5 minutes.

3. Add the stock and tomatoes and bring the soup to a boil. Reduce the heat so that the soup simmers and cook for 10 minutes.

4. Add salt to the boiling water, let it return to a full boil, and add the pasta. Cook until it is al dente, 6 to 8 minutes. Drain the pasta and set it aside.

5. Stir the basil into the soup and transfer it to a food processor. Puree until smooth.

6. Place the soup in a clean pan and bring to a simmer. Stir in the pasta. Season with salt and pepper, ladle the soup into warmed bowls, and serve.

Udon Noodle Soup with Baby Bok Choy & Poached Eggs

YIELD: 4 SERVINGS / **ACTIVE TIME:** 10 MINUTES / **TOTAL TIME:** 25 MINUTES

8 CUPS CHICKEN STOCK
(SEE PAGE 536)

3 STAR ANISE PODS

2 CINNAMON STICKS

8 SHIITAKE MUSHROOMS,
STEMMED AND CHOPPED

4 LARGE EGGS

4 BABY BOK CHOY, CUT
INTO BITE-SIZE PIECES

1 LB. UDON NOODLES
(SEE PAGE 106)

6 TABLESPOONS SOY SAUCE

5 SCALLIONS, TRIMMED AND
SLICED THIN

2 RED CHILE PEPPERS,
STEMMED, SEEDED, AND
SLICED THIN, FOR GARNISH

1. Place the stock in a large saucepan and bring it to a simmer over medium-high heat. Add the star anise and cinnamon sticks, reduce the heat to low, and simmer for 10 minutes. Remove the star anise and cinnamon stick with a slotted spoon and discard them.

2. Stir the mushrooms into the simmering broth. Working with 1 egg at a time, crack it into a small, shallow bowl and then slide it into the broth. Cook for 2 minutes.

3. Add the bok choy, gently pushing down to submerge them in the broth while being careful not to break the eggs. Cook until the egg whites are set, about 2 minutes. Cook for another 2 minutes if you desire firm yolks.

4. While the broth is simmering, bring water to a boil in a large saucepan and add the noodles. Cook until they are al dente, 2 to 3 minutes. Drain and divide the noodles between four warmed bowls.

5. Remove the broth from heat and gently stir in the soy sauce and scallions. Taste, adjust the seasoning as necessary, and divide the soup among the serving bowls, making sure each portion gets an egg and an even amount of the bok choy. Garnish with the chiles and serve.

Cold Noodle Soup

YIELD: 4 SERVINGS / **ACTIVE TIME:** 35 MINUTES / **TOTAL TIME:** 3 HOURS

FOR THE BROTH

8 CUPS BEEF STOCK

⅓ CUP RICE VINEGAR

1½ TABLESPOONS SOY SAUCE

2 GARLIC CLOVES, SLICED THIN

2-INCH PIECE OF FRESH GINGER, PEELED AND SLICED THIN

4 SCALLIONS, TRIMMED AND CHOPPED

2½ TABLESPOONS SUGAR

FOR THE SOUP

2 SMALL CUCUMBERS, PEELED AND JULIENNED

5 RADISHES, TRIMMED AND SLICED VERY THIN WITH A MANDOLINE

1½ TEASPOONS KOSHER SALT

1 TEASPOON SUGAR

1 TEASPOON RICE VINEGAR

2 SMALL ASIAN PEARS, CORED AND JULIENNED

½ LB. DOTORI GUKSU (KOREAN ACORN NOODLES)

1 CUP CRUSHED ICE

2 LARGE HARD-BOILED EGGS, PEELED AND HALVED LENGTHWISE

SESAME SEEDS, FOR GARNISH

SPICY MUSTARD, FOR SERVING

1. To prepare the broth, place all of the ingredients in a large saucepan and bring to a boil over medium heat. Reduce the heat so that the broth simmers and cook until it has reduced by one-quarter, about 30 minutes. Strain the broth through a fine-mesh sieve and let cool to room temperature. When it is cool, chill the broth in the refrigerator for at least 2 hours.

2. To prepare the soup, place the cucumbers in a bowl and the radishes in another bowl. Sprinkle ½ teaspoon of salt, sugar, and vinegar over each of them and toss to coat. Place the pears in another bowl, sprinkle the remaining salt over them, and toss to coat. Let the cucumbers, radishes, and pears rest for 15 minutes.

3. Bring water to a boil in a large saucepan. Add the noodles and cook until they are al dente, 5 to 7 minutes. Drain, rinse the noodles under cold water, and drain again.

4. Divide the noodles among the serving bowls. Ladle about 1¾ cups of broth into each bowl. Add the crushed ice and arrange the radish, cucumber, hard-boiled eggs, and pears on top of the noodles. Garnish with sesame seeds and serve with spicy mustard.

Cold Noodle Soup
SEE PAGE 427

Coconut Curry Chicken Noodle Soup

YIELD: 4 SERVINGS / **ACTIVE TIME:** 30 MINUTES / **TOTAL TIME:** 45 MINUTES

1 LEMONGRASS STALK

1 CUP BEAN SPROUTS, PICKED OVER

2 TABLESPOONS CANOLA OIL

1 SMALL ONION, MINCED

2-INCH PIECE OF FRESH GINGER, PEELED AND GRATED

SALT, TO TASTE

2 GARLIC CLOVES, MINCED

1 TEASPOON SAMBAL OELEK, PLUS MORE FOR SERVING

1 LB. BONELESS, SKINLESS CHICKEN THIGHS, CHOPPED

2½ TABLESPOONS CURRY POWDER

4 CUPS CHICKEN STOCK (SEE PAGE 536)

1 (14 OZ.) CAN OF UNSWEETENED COCONUT MILK

⅓ CUP HEAVY CREAM

2½ TABLESPOONS FISH SAUCE

1½ TABLESPOONS SUGAR, MORE TO TASTE

½ TEASPOON GROUND TURMERIC

½ LB. THIN VERMICELLI RICE NOODLES

FRESH CILANTRO, CHOPPED, FOR GARNISH

SCALLIONS, TRIMMED AND SLICED THIN, FOR GARNISH

LIME WEDGES, FOR SERVING

1. Trim the top and base of the lemongrass stalk and use only the bottom 4 inches or so, as it is the most tender part. Peel off the dry or tough outer layer and then mince the tender inner core. Set the lemongrass aside.

2. Bring water to a boil in a large saucepan. Place the bean sprouts in a bowl of cold water and discard any hulls that float to the top. Rinse the remaining sprouts under cold water, add them to the boiling water, and cook for 1 minute. Remove them with a strainer and run them under cold water. Drain well, chop the sprouts, and set them aside. Keep the water at a gentle simmer.

3. Place the canola oil in a Dutch oven and warm it over medium-high heat. Add the lemongrass, onion, and ginger, season with salt and cook until the mixture starts to gently sizzle. Reduce the heat to low, cover the pot, and cook, stirring occasionally, until the lemongrass has softened, about 10 minutes.

4. Add the garlic and sambal oelek, raise the heat to medium-high, and stir-fry for 1 minute. Add the chicken, season with salt, and stir-fry for 1 minute. Add the curry powder, stir to coat the chicken, and then add the stock, coconut milk, cream, fish sauce, sugar, and turmeric. Stir to combine and bring the soup to a boil. Reduce the heat to low and simmer the soup until the chicken is cooked through, 6 to 8 minutes.

5. While the chicken is cooking, bring the large pot of water to a rolling boil, add the noodles, and cook until they are al dente, 2 to 4 minutes. Drain, rinse the noodles under hot water, and drain again.

6. Divide the noodles among the serving bowls. Ladle the soup over the noodles, making sure every portion gets an equal amount of the chicken. Garnish with cilantro, scallions, and the bean sprouts and serve with lime wedges and additional sambal oelek.

Shrimp Laksa Curry

YIELD: 6 SERVINGS / **ACTIVE TIME:** 20 MINUTES / **TOTAL TIME:** 40 MINUTES

2 LEMONGRASS STALKS

3 CUPS MUNG BEAN SPROUTS, PICKED OVER

4 BOK CHOY, CHOPPED

SALT AND WHITE PEPPER, TO TASTE

⅓ CUP PLUS 1½ TEASPOONS PEANUT OIL

3 GARLIC CLOVES, MINCED

5 LARGE SHALLOTS, MINCED

1-INCH PIECE OF FRESH GINGER, PEELED AND GRATED

6 TABLESPOONS LAKSA PASTE

2 CINNAMON STICKS

3 CUPS UNSWEETENED COCONUT MILK

8 CUPS CHICKEN STOCK (SEE PAGE 536)

2 TABLESPOONS FISH SAUCE

1 LB. RICE NOODLES

1 LB. MEDIUM SHRIMP, SHELLS REMOVED, DEVEINED

FRESH MINT, FOR SERVING

LIME WEDGES, FOR SERVING

SAMBAL OELEK OR SRIRACHA, FOR SERVING

1. Trim the top and base of the lemongrass stalk and use only the bottom 4 inches or so, as it is the most tender part. Peel off the dry or tough outer layer and then mince the tender inner core. Set the lemongrass aside.

2. Bring water to a boil in a large saucepan. Place the bean sprouts in a bowl of cold water and discard any hulls that float to the top. Rinse the remaining sprouts under cold water, add them to the boiling water, and cook for 1 minute. Remove them with a strainer and run them under cold water. Drain well, chop the sprouts, and set them aside. Keep the water at a gentle simmer.

3. Warm a large skillet over medium heat for 2 to 3 minutes. Add the bok choy and 2 cups water, season with salt, and bring to a boil. Cover the pan and steam the bok choy for 2 minutes. Remove the skillet from the heat and set it aside.

4. Place ⅓ cup of peanut oil in a Dutch oven and warm it over medium-high heat. Add the garlic, shallots, and ginger, season with salt, and stir-fry for 1 minute. Reduce the heat to low, cover the pot, and cook, stirring occasionally, for 15 minutes.

5. Raise the heat to medium, add the laksa paste, and stir-fry for 1 minute. Add the lemongrass and cinnamon sticks, stir, and cook for 5 minutes.

6. Add the coconut milk, stock, and fish sauce, season with salt and pepper, and stir to combine. Bring to a boil, reduce the heat to medium-low, cover the pot, and simmer the soup until the flavor has developed to your liking, at least 20 minutes.

7. While the soup is simmering, bring the large pot of water to a rolling boil, add the noodles, and cook until they are al dente, 2 to 4 minutes. Drain, rinse the noodles under hot water, and drain again. Place them in a bowl, add the remaining peanut oil, and toss to coat. Set the noodles aside.

8. Add the shrimp to the soup and cook until they turn pink and are cooked through, about 3 to 4 minutes.

9. Divide the noodles among warmed bowls and place the bok choy on top of them. Ladle the hot soup over the top, making sure everyone gets an equal amount of shrimp. Top with the bean sprouts, garnish with mint, and serve with lime wedges and sambal oelek.

Spicy Chicken Ramen

YIELD: 4 SERVINGS / **ACTIVE TIME:** 15 MINUTES / **TOTAL TIME:** 45 MINUTES

6 CUPS CHICKEN STOCK (SEE PAGE 536)

4 GARLIC CLOVES, MINCED

2-INCH PIECE OF FRESH GINGER, PEELED AND GRATED

½ CUP SOY SAUCE

2 TEASPOONS WORCESTERSHIRE SAUCE

1 TEASPOON FIVE-SPICE POWDER

⅛ TEASPOON CHILI POWDER

1 TABLESPOON SUGAR

SALT AND PEPPER, TO TASTE

½ LB. RAMEN NOODLES

2 TABLESPOONS SESAME OIL

2 BONELESS, SKINLESS CHICKEN BREASTS, CHOPPED

1 CUP CANNED CORN, DRAINED

1 CUP SPINACH

4 HARD-BOILED EGGS, HALVED, FOR GARNISH

SCALLION GREENS, CHOPPED, FOR GARNISH

1 SHEET OF NORI, SHREDDED, FOR GARNISH

1. Place the stock, garlic, ginger, soy sauce, Worcestershire sauce, five-spice powder, and chili powder in a medium saucepan and bring to a boil. Reduce the heat so that the soup simmers and cook for 5 minutes.

2. Turn off the heat and stir in the sugar. Season the soup with salt and pepper and let it stand for 5 minutes.

3. Bring water to a boil in a medium saucepan. Add the noodles and cook until they are al dente, 3 to 5 minutes. Drain, rinse the noodles under cold water, and set them aside.

4. Place the sesame oil in a medium skillet and warm it over medium heat. Add the chicken and cook until it is browned all over, about 8 minutes, stirring as necessary.

5. Add the corn and cook until it is warmed through, about 2 minutes. Add the noodles and the spinach and cook for 1 minute. Remove the pan from heat and set it aside.

6. Strain the broth through a fine-mesh sieve and discard the solids. Place the broth in a clean saucepan and bring it to a boil.

7. Divide the chicken-and-noodle mixture among the serving bowls. Ladle the broth over the top, garnish with the hard-boiled eggs, scallions, and nori, and serve.

Fast Pho

YIELD: 4 SERVINGS / **ACTIVE TIME:** 15 MINUTES / **TOTAL TIME:** 30 MINUTES

3 OZ. RICE NOODLES

2 TABLESPOONS EXTRA-VIRGIN OLIVE OIL

1 SMALL YELLOW ONION, CHOPPED

1-INCH PIECE OF FRESH GINGER, UNPEELED

2 CINNAMON STICKS

3 STAR ANISE PODS

SEEDS FROM 2 CARDAMOM PODS, CRUSHED

6 CUPS BEEF STOCK (SEE PAGE 538)

1 TABLESPOON FISH SAUCE

1 TABLESPOON HOISIN SAUCE

1 TEASPOON SRIRACHA

1 JALAPEÑO CHILE PEPPER, STEMMED, SEEDED, AND SLICED, FOR GARNISH

BEAN SPROUTS, PICKED OVER, FOR GARNISH

FRESH THAI BASIL, CHOPPED, FOR GARNISH

LIME WEDGES, FOR SERVING

1. Place the rice noodles in a baking dish and cover with boiling water. Let them soak until they are al dente, about 15 minutes.

2. Place the olive oil in a medium saucepan and warm it over medium heat. Add the onion and ginger and cook, stirring occasionally, until the onion has softened, about 8 minutes.

3. Place the cinnamon sticks, star anise, and cardamom seeds in a dry skillet and toast over medium heat until they are very fragrant, about 3 minutes, shaking the pan frequently.

4. Add the toasted aromatics to the saucepan. Add the stock and bring the broth to a boil. Reduce the heat so that the broth simmers and cook for 10 minutes.

5. Strain the soup into a clean saucepan. Stir in the fish sauce, hoisin sauce, and sriracha and bring it to a simmer.

6. Drain the noodles and divide them among the serving bowls. Ladle the broth over the top, garnish with jalapeño, bean sprouts, and Thai basil, and serve with lime wedges.

Chicken Noodle Soup

YIELD: 4 SERVINGS / **ACTIVE TIME:** 20 MINUTES / **TOTAL TIME:** 30 MINUTES

1 TABLESPOON EXTRA-VIRGIN OLIVE OIL

½ ONION, MINCED

1 CARROT, PEELED AND MINCED

1 CELERY STALK, MINCED

1 TEASPOON FRESH THYME

4 CUPS CHICKEN STOCK (SEE PAGE 536)

SALT AND PEPPER, TO TASTE

1½ CUPS EGG NOODLES

1 COOKED CHICKEN BREAST, CHOPPED

1. Place the olive oil in a medium saucepan and warm it over medium heat. Add the onion and cook, stirring occasionally, until it starts to soften, about 5 minutes. Add the carrot and celery and cook, stirring occasionally, until they start to soften, about 5 minutes.

2. Add the thyme and stock and bring the soup to a boil. Reduce the heat so that the soup simmers and cook for 20 minutes.

3. Season the soup with salt and pepper, add the egg noodles, and cook until they are al dente, 8 to 10 minutes. Stir in the chicken and cook until it is warmed through.

4. Ladle the soup into warmed bowls and serve.

Chicken Noodle Soup
SEE PAGE 435

OVER THE TOP: SAUCES & PERFECT PARTNERS

Roasted Grapes & Sausage

YIELD: 4 SERVINGS / **ACTIVE TIME:** 10 MINUTES / **TOTAL TIME:** 45 MINUTES

1½ LBS. SPICY ITALIAN SAUSAGE

1 BUNCH OF MUSCAT GRAPES

6 OZ. FRESH MOZZARELLA CHEESE, TORN

2 TABLESPOONS BALSAMIC GLAZE (SEE PAGE 542)

1. Preheat the oven to 500°F. Cut the sausage into ¼-inch-thick slices, place them in a large cast-iron skillet, and add the grapes. Toss to evenly distribute and place the pan over medium-high heat. Cook, stirring occasionally, until the sausage starts to brown, about 5 minutes.

2. Add the mozzarella to the pan, place it in the oven, and cook until the sausage is well browned and cooked through, the grapes have collapsed, and the mozzarella is melted, 15 to 20 minutes.

3. Remove the pan from the oven, drizzle the Balsamic Glaze over the top, and serve over pasta.

Pork Milanesa

YIELD: 4 SERVINGS / **ACTIVE TIME:** 15 MINUTES / **TOTAL TIME:** 15 MINUTES

2 CUPS FINE BREAD CRUMBS

4 LARGE EGGS

1 CUP EXTRA-VIRGIN OLIVE OIL

2 LBS. PORK CUTLETS (¼ INCH THICK)

SALT, TO TASTE

1. Place the bread crumbs in a shallow bowl. Place the eggs in a separate bowl and beat them.

2. Place the olive oil in a large cast-iron skillet and warm it over medium-high heat until it is hot enough that a bread crumb sizzles gently when added.

3. Season the pork cutlets with salt, dredge them in the beaten eggs, and then in the bread crumbs until they are coated all over. Gently press down on the bread crumbs so that they adhere to the pork.

4. Gently slip the cutlets into the hot oil and fry until golden brown on both sides and cooked through, 8 to 10 minutes. Transfer the milanesa to a paper towel–lined plate to drain briefly before serving it over pasta.

Pork Milanesa
SEE PAGE 441

General Tso's Chicken

YIELD: 4 SERVINGS / **ACTIVE TIME:** 1 HOUR AND 30 MINUTES / **TOTAL TIME:** 2 HOURS

1 EGG WHITE

1½ TEASPOONS TOASTED SESAME OIL

¼ CUP PLUS 1 TABLESPOON LOW-SODIUM SOY SAUCE

¼ CUP PLUS 1 TABLESPOON CORNSTARCH

1 LB. BONELESS, SKINLESS CHICKEN THIGHS, CUT INTO BITE-SIZE PIECES

1 TABLESPOON CANOLA OIL, PLUS MORE AS NEEDED

2 TABLESPOONS MINCED FRESH GINGER

3 GARLIC CLOVES, MINCED

1 CUP CHICKEN STOCK (SEE PAGE 536)

2 TEASPOONS SRIRACHA

3 TABLESPOONS SUGAR

3 SCALLIONS, TRIMMED AND SLICED THIN

1. Place the egg white in a mixing bowl. Add the sesame oil, 1 tablespoon of soy sauce, and ¼ cup of cornstarch and whisk to combine. Add the chicken, stir to coat, and let it marinate for 30 minutes.

2. Place the canola oil in a saucepan and warm it over medium-high heat. Add the ginger and garlic and cook, stirring continually, for 1 minute. Add the stock, sriracha, sugar, and remaining soy sauce and cornstarch, and whisk until the sauce gets thick and glossy. Reduce the heat to low and cover the sauce to keep it warm.

3. Place a large, deep cast-iron skillet over medium-high heat and add canola oil until it is about ½ inch deep. When the oil is hot, gently slip the chicken into it and cook until they are crispy and cooked through, 6 to 8 minutes, turning them as necessary. Transfer the fried chicken to a paper towel–lined plate to drain.

4. Stir the fried chicken and scallions into the sauce and serve over noodles.

Sugo al Peperoni

YIELD: 8 CUPS / **ACTIVE TIME:** 25 MINUTES / **TOTAL TIME:** 40 MINUTES

¼ CUP EXTRA-VIRGIN OLIVE OIL

1 GARLIC CLOVE

½ ONION, MINCED

2 MEDIUM RED BELL PEPPERS, STEMMED, SEEDED, AND SLICED THIN

SALT, TO TASTE

1.8 LBS. WHOLE PEELED TOMATOES, CRUSHED BY HAND

DRIED OREGANO, TO TASTE

RED PEPPER FLAKES, TO TASTE

1. Place the olive oil in a medium saucepan and warm it over medium heat. Add the garlic and onion and cook until the onion is translucent, about 3 minutes.

2. Add the peppers, season with salt, and cook, stirring frequently, until they have softened, about 10 minutes.

3. Add the tomatoes, partially cover the pan, and cook the sauce for 20 minutes, stirring occasionally.

4. Remove the garlic and season the sauce with salt, oregano, and red pepper flakes.

5. Cook until the taste has developed to your liking and the sauce has the desired consistency, 5 to 10 minutes. During this last phase, leave the pan uncovered if the sauce is too liquid, or reduce the heat and add a splash of water if it is too thick. To serve, ladle the sauce over pasta.

Sugo al Soffritto

YIELD: 8 CUPS / **ACTIVE TIME:** 25 MINUTES / **TOTAL TIME:** 40 MINUTES

¼ CUP EXTRA-VIRGIN OLIVE OIL

½ CARROT, PEELED AND CHOPPED

½ ONION, CHOPPED

½ CELERY STALK WITH ITS LEAVES, CHOPPED

½ GARLIC CLOVE, MINCED

1.8 LBS. WHOLE PEELED TOMATOES, CRUSHED BY HAND

SALT, TO TASTE

RED PEPPER FLAKES, TO TASTE

1. Place the olive oil in a medium saucepan and warm it over low heat. Add the carrot, onion, celery, and garlic and cook, stirring frequently, until the vegetables have softened, about 5 minutes, making sure that they do not brown.

2. Add the tomatoes, season the sauce with salt and red pepper flakes (the latter is optional, but will benefit the sauce), and partially cover the pan. Raise the heat to medium and cook the sauce for 20 minutes, stirring occasionally.

3. Cook until the taste has developed to your liking and the sauce has the desired consistency, 5 to 10 minutes. During this last phase, leave the pan uncovered if the sauce is too liquid, or reduce the heat and add a splash of water if it is too thick. To serve, ladle the sauce over pasta.

Sugo al Basilico

YIELD: 8 CUPS / **ACTIVE TIME:** 25 MINUTES / **TOTAL TIME:** 40 MINUTES

¼ CUP EXTRA-VIRGIN OLIVE OIL

2 GARLIC CLOVES

1.8 LBS. WHOLE PEELED TOMATOES, CRUSHED BY HAND

SALT, TO TASTE

RED PEPPER FLAKES, TO TASTE

HANDFUL OF FRESH BASIL, TORN

1. Place the olive oil in a medium saucepan and warm it over medium heat. Add the garlic and cook until it starts to brown.

2. Add the tomatoes, partially cover the pan, and cook the sauce for 20 minutes, stirring occasionally. Remove the garlic, season the sauce with salt and red pepper flakes, and add the basil.

3. Cook until the taste has developed to your liking and the sauce has the desired consistency, 5 to 10 minutes. During this last phase, leave the pan uncovered if the sauce is too liquid, or reduce the heat and add a splash of water if it is too thick. To serve, ladle the sauce over pasta.

Ragù Ricco

YIELD: 8 CUPS / **ACTIVE TIME:** 25 MINUTES / **TOTAL TIME:** 2 HOURS AND 30 MINUTES

3 TABLESPOONS EXTRA-VIRGIN OLIVE OIL

1 ONION, FINELY DICED

1 CARROT, PEELED AND FINELY DICED

½ CELERY STALK, FINELY DICED

11 OZ. STEW BEEF, FINELY DICED

11 OZ. CHICKEN OR VEAL LIVER, FINELY DICED

1 TEASPOON FINELY CHOPPED FRESH ROSEMARY

1 BAY LEAF

½ CUP RED WINE

11 OZ. WHOLE PEELED TOMATOES, CRUSHED BY HAND

½ CUP BEEF STOCK (SEE PAGE 538), HOT

SALT AND PEPPER, TO TASTE

1. Place the olive oil in a large, deep skillet and warm it over medium heat. Add the onion, carrot, and celery and cook, stirring occasionally, until they have softened, about 5 minutes.

2. Add the beef, chicken liver, rosemary, and bay leaf, and cook, stirring occasionally, until the meat is browned, about 8 minutes.

3. Add the wine and cook until it has evaporated.

4. Remove the bay leaf and discard it. Add the tomatoes, reduce the heat to low, partially cover the pan, and cook for about 2 hours, stirring occasionally and seasoning the ragù with salt and pepper halfway through. If the ragù becomes too thick, add the stock as needed.

5. When the taste has developed to your liking and the ragù has the desired consistency, ladle the sauce over pasta.

Ragù Bianco

YIELD: 8 CUPS / **ACTIVE TIME:** 1 HOUR / **TOTAL TIME:** 2 HOURS AND 30 MINUTES

3 TABLESPOONS EXTRA-VIRGIN OLIVE OIL

1 LARGE CARROT, PEELED AND FINELY DICED

½ WHITE ONION, FINELY DICED

1 CELERY STALK, FINELY DICED

1 GARLIC CLOVE, MINCED

2 OZ. PANCETTA, FINELY DICED

14 OZ. GROUND BEEF

14 OZ. GROUND PORK

2 BAY LEAVES

1 TEASPOON FINELY CHOPPED FRESH ROSEMARY

HANDFUL OF FRESH MARJORAM, FINELY CHOPPED

½ CUP DRY WHITE WINE

2 CUPS BEEF STOCK (SEE PAGE 538), HOT

PINCH OF GROUND CLOVES

PINCH OF CINNAMON

SALT AND PEPPER, TO TASTE

½ CUP WHOLE MILK

1. Place the olive oil in a large, deep skillet and warm it over medium heat. Add the carrot, onion, celery, and garlic and cook, stirring occasionally, until they have softened, about 5 minutes.

2. Add the pancetta and cook, stirring occasionally, until it starts to brown, about 4 minutes.

3. Add the beef, pork, bay leaves, rosemary, and marjoram, and cook, stirring occasionally, until the meat starts to brown, about 5 minutes.

4. Add the wine and cook until it has evaporated.

5. Reduce the heat to low and add 2 ladles of the stock. Partially cover the pan and cook for about 2 hours, stirring occasionally and seasoning the ragù with the cloves, cinnamon, salt, and pepper halfway through. If the ragù becomes too thick, add the remaining stock as needed.

6. Stir in the milk, uncover the pan, and cook until the ragù has the desired consistency. To serve, ladle the sauce over pasta.

Ragù di Cinghiale

YIELD: 8 CUPS / **ACTIVE TIME:** 1 HOUR / **TOTAL TIME:** 2 HOURS AND 30 MINUTES

3 TABLESPOONS EXTRA-VIRGIN OLIVE OIL

1 CARROT, PEELED AND FINELY DICED

½ WHITE ONION, FINELY DICED

1 CELERY STALK, FINELY DICED

1 GARLIC CLOVE, MINCED

3½ OZ. PANCETTA, FINELY DICED

14 OZ. WILD BOAR SHOULDER, FINELY DICED

1 TEASPOON FINELY CHOPPED FRESH THYME

5 DRIED JUNIPER BERRIES

½ CUP RED WINE

1.8 LBS. WHOLE PEELED TOMATOES, CRUSHED BY HAND

1 CUP WATER

SALT AND PEPPER, TO TASTE

1. Place the olive oil in a large, deep skillet and warm it over medium heat. Add the carrot, onion, celery, and garlic and cook, stirring occasionally, until they have softened, about 5 minutes.

2. Add the pancetta and cook, stirring occasionally, until it has browned, about 4 minutes.

3. Add the boar, thyme, and juniper berries and cook, stirring occasionally, until the meat starts to brown, about 5 minutes.

4. Add the wine and cook until it has evaporated.

5. Add the tomatoes and water, season with salt and pepper, and reduce the heat to low. Partially cover the pan and cook for about 2 hours, stirring occasionally.

6. When the taste has developed to your liking and the ragù has the desired consistency, ladle it over pasta.

Ragù di Cinghiale
SEE PAGE 453

Salsa di Noci

YIELD: 3 CUPS / **ACTIVE TIME:** 5 MINUTES / **TOTAL TIME:** 15 MINUTES

1 SLICE OF WHITE BREAD, CRUST REMOVED

7 OZ. WHOLE MILK

1⅔ CUPS WALNUTS

½ GARLIC CLOVE

HANDFUL OF FRESH MARJORAM

1 TABLESPOON GRATED PARMESAN CHEESE

2 PINCHES OF FINE SEA SALT

5 TABLESPOONS EXTRA-VIRGIN OLIVE OIL

2 TABLESPOONS LUKEWARM WATER

1. Place the bread and milk in a bowl and let the bread soak for 10 minutes. Drain the bread and squeeze it to remove any excess liquid.

2. Place the bread in a blender, add the walnuts, garlic, marjoram, Parmesan, and salt and puree until the mixture is a paste.

3. With the blender running, add the olive oil and water and blend until the sauce is thick and creamy. When using this sauce for pasta, dilute it with pasta water until it has the desired consistency and toss with pasta.

Salsa al Cren

YIELD: 4 CUPS / **ACTIVE TIME:** 5 MINUTES / **TOTAL TIME:** 5 MINUTES

11 OZ. HORSERADISH, FINELY GRATED

1 CUP FRESH BREAD CRUMBS

⅓ CUP WHITE WINE VINEGAR

3 TABLESPOONS EXTRA-VIRGIN OLIVE OIL

2 PINCHES OF FINE SEA SALT

2½ TEASPOONS SUGAR

1. Place all of the ingredients in a food processor and blitz until the sauce is creamy and spreadable. To serve, ladle the sauce over pasta.

Bagnet Ross

YIELD: 10 CUPS / **ACTIVE TIME:** 5 MINUTES / **TOTAL TIME:** 3 HOURS AND 30 MINUTES

SALT AND PEPPER, TO TASTE

2.2 LBS. RIPE TOMATOES

2 CELERY STALKS, FINELY DICED

2 CARROTS, PEELED AND FINELY DICED

1 LARGE ONION, FINELY DICED

2 GARLIC CLOVES, MINCED

½ SMALL FRESH CHILE PEPPER, MINCED

1 LARGE RED BELL PEPPER, STEMMED, SEEDED, AND FINELY DICED

1 TABLESPOON FINELY CHOPPED FRESH PARSLEY

1 TABLESPOON FINELY CHOPPED FRESH SAGE

1 CUP EXTRA-VIRGIN OLIVE OIL

1 TABLESPOON RED WINE VINEGAR

CINNAMON, TO TASTE

MUSTARD POWDER, TO TASTE

1. Bring water to a boil in a large saucepan. Add salt and the tomatoes and cook for 30 minutes.

2. Drain the tomatoes and let them cool.

3. Peel the tomatoes and puree them in a blender or with a food mill. If using a blender, strain the puree to remove the seeds.

4. Place the tomato puree in a saucepan, add the celery, carrots, onion, garlic, chile, bell pepper, parsley, and sage, and cover the pan. Cook the sauce over low heat until the flavor has developed to your liking, about 2 hours.

5. Pass the sauce through a sieve or a food mill. If it is too thin for your liking, return it to the pan and cook it over medium heat until it has the desired consistency.

6. Let the sauce cool and then add the olive oil and vinegar. Season the sauce with salt, pepper, cinnamon, and mustard powder and toss it with pasta.

Bolognese Sauce

YIELD: 10 SERVINGS / **ACTIVE TIME:** 20 MINUTES / **TOTAL TIME:** 4 HOURS AND 30 MINUTES

3 TABLESPOONS EXTRA-VIRGIN OLIVE OIL

1 YELLOW ONION, GRATED

2 CELERY STALKS, GRATED

SALT, TO TASTE

2 LBS. GROUND MEAT (BLEND OF PORK, VEAL, AND BEEF)

2 CUPS WHOLE MILK

2 (28 OZ.) CANS OF CRUSHED TOMATOES

2 BAY LEAVES

7 WHOLE CLOVES OR 1 TEASPOON GROUND CLOVES

1. Place the olive oil in a Dutch oven and warm it over medium heat. Add the onion and celery, season with salt, and cook, stirring occasionally, for 2 minutes. Reduce the heat to low, cover the pot, and cook for 30 minutes, stirring occasionally.

2. Raise the heat to medium-high and add the ground meat. Cook, breaking it up with a wooden spoon, until it has browned, about 5 minutes. Add the milk and cook, stirring occasionally, until the milk has completely evaporated.

3. Add the tomatoes, bay leaves, and cloves, season with salt and bring to a boil. Reduce the heat to low and cook until the sauce has visibly thickened and the fat has separated from the sauce, about 4 hours, stirring every 30 minutes or so. Remove the bay leaves and discard them before ladling the sauce over pasta.

Garlic & Basil Baked Cod

YIELD: 4 SERVINGS / **ACTIVE TIME:** 10 MINUTES / **TOTAL TIME:** 1 HOUR AND 20 MINUTES

2 LBS. COD FILLETS

SALT AND PEPPER, TO TASTE

2 TABLESPOONS FINELY CHOPPED FRESH OREGANO

1 TEASPOON CORIANDER

1 TEASPOON PAPRIKA

10 GARLIC CLOVES, MINCED

15 FRESH BASIL LEAVES, SHREDDED

6 TABLESPOONS EXTRA-VIRGIN OLIVE OIL

2 TABLESPOONS FRESH LEMON JUICE

2 SHALLOTS, SLICED

2 TOMATOES, SLICED

1. Place the cod in a mixing bowl and add all of the remaining ingredients, except for the shallots and tomatoes. Stir to combine, place the mixture in the refrigerator, and let the cod marinate for 1 hour, stirring occasionally.

2. Preheat the oven to 425°F, remove the cod from the refrigerator, and let it come to room temperature. Cover the bottom of a baking dish with the shallots, place the cod on top, and top with the tomatoes. Pour the marinade over the mixture, place it in the oven, and bake for about 15 minutes, until the fish is flaky. Remove from the oven and let the cod rest briefly before serving over pasta.

Broccolini & Sausage Meatballs

YIELD: 4 SERVINGS / **ACTIVE TIME:** 40 MINUTES / **TOTAL TIME:** 1 HOUR AND 35 MINUTES

6 OZ. HICKORY-SMOKED BACON

6 GARLIC CLOVES, 2 LEFT WHOLE; 4 SLICED THIN

2 TEASPOONS KOSHER SALT, PLUS MORE TO TASTE

2 TEASPOONS APPLE CIDER VINEGAR

1 LB. GROUND PORK

½ CUP CHOPPED FRESH PARSLEY

1 TEASPOON FRESHLY GRATED NUTMEG

1 TEASPOON RED PEPPER FLAKES

5 TABLESPOONS EXTRA-VIRGIN OLIVE OIL

1 LB. BROCCOLINI, TRIMMED

1. Place the bacon in a food processor and pulse until it is finely ground. Set the bacon aside. Using a mortar and pestle, grind the whole garlic cloves and half of the salt until the mixture is a paste. Add the vinegar and stir until well combined.

2. Place the pork in a mixing bowl, add the bacon, garlic paste, parsley, nutmeg, half of the red pepper flakes, and remaining salt until well mixed. Form the mixture into balls the size of cherry tomatoes.

3. Place 2 tablespoons of olive oil in a large, deep skillet and warm it over medium heat. Working in batches to avoid crowding the pan, add the meatballs and cook until they are browned all over, turning them as needed. Transfer the meatballs to a paper towel–lined plate to drain.

4. Bring water to a boil in a large saucepan. Add salt, let the water return to a full boil, and add the broccolini. Cook for 2 minutes, drain, and rinse the broccolini under cold water. Drain again and set the broccolini aside.

5. Place the remaining olive oil in a clean large skillet and warm it over medium heat. Add the sliced garlic and remaining red pepper flakes and cook for 1 minute. Add the broccolini and meatballs and cook, stirring occasionally, until the meatballs are cooked through.

6. To serve, toss the broccolini and meatballs with your cooked pasta and some pasta water.

Baked Lamb & Tomato Sauce

YIELD: 6 SERVINGS / **ACTIVE TIME:** 45 MINUTES / **TOTAL TIME:** 1 HOUR AND 30 MINUTES

2 LBS. PLUM TOMATOES

3 LBS. LAMB CHOPS

3 TABLESPOONS EXTRA-VIRGIN OLIVE OIL

SALT AND PEPPER, TO TASTE

5 GARLIC CLOVES, SLICED THIN

1 TEASPOON FRESH OREGANO

2 TEASPOONS TOMATO PASTE

1. Preheat the oven to 350°F.

2. Bring water to a boil in a large saucepan. Add the tomatoes and boil them for 2 minutes. Drain the tomatoes and let them cool. When they are cool enough to handle, peel the tomatoes, remove the seeds, and chop the remaining flesh. Set the tomatoes aside.

3. Pat the lamb chops dry with paper towels and season with salt. Place the olive oil in a large skillet and warm it over medium-high heat. Add the lamb chops and cook until they are browned on each side, about 5 minutes, turning them over once. Transfer the lamb chops to a large baking dish.

4. Add the tomatoes to the pan, season with salt and pepper, and cook, scraping up any browned bits from the bottom, until they start to collapse, about 6 minutes.

5. Stir in the garlic, oregano, and tomato paste and cook for 1 minute. Pour the tomato mixture over the lamb chops, cover the dish with aluminum foil, and place it in the oven.

6. Bake for 15 minutes and remove the dish from the oven. Remove the foil and discard it. Turn the lamb chops over, return the dish to the oven, and bake for 15 minutes.

7. Remove the sauce from the oven and ladle it over pasta.

Tomato, Veal & Roasted Butternut Squash Sauce

YIELD: 6 SERVINGS / **ACTIVE TIME:** 1 HOUR / **TOTAL TIME:** 2 HOURS AND 45 MINUTES

6½ TABLESPOONS EXTRA-VIRGIN OLIVE OIL

1 VIDALIA ONION, DICED

2 CELERY STALKS, MINCED

SALT, TO TASTE

2 GARLIC CLOVES, SLICED THIN

1½ LBS. LEAN, BONELESS VEAL, CUT INTO 1½-INCH CUBES

6 PLUM TOMATOES, DICED

1 SPRIG OF FRESH SAGE

3½ CUPS CHICKEN STOCK (SEE PAGE 536), WARM

2 LB. BUTTERNUT SQUASH, PEELED, HALVED, SEEDED, AND DICED

1. Preheat the oven to 400°F. Place ¼ cup of olive oil in a large, deep skillet and warm it over medium heat. Add the onion and celery, season with salt, and cook, stirring occasionally, until the onion is translucent, about 3 minutes.

2. Add the garlic and cook, stirring frequently, for 2 minutes. Remove the vegetables from the pot and set it aside.

3. Pat the veal dry with paper towels and season it with salt. Working in batches to avoid crowding the pan, add the veal and cook until it is browned all over, turning as necessary. Add the tomatoes, sage, stock, and the vegetable mixture, season with salt, and bring to a boil. Cover the pan, reduce the heat to low, and simmer, stirring occasionally, until the sauce is thick and glossy, about 1 hour.

4. While the sauce is simmering, place the squash in a bowl, add the remaining olive oil, season with salt, and toss to combine. Place the squash on a baking sheet, place it in the oven, and roast until it is tender, 25 to 35 minutes.

5. Remove the squash from the oven, stir it into the sauce, and serve over pasta.

Ratatouille

YIELD: 6 SERVINGS / **ACTIVE TIME:** 30 MINUTES / **TOTAL TIME:** 1 HOUR

¼ CUP EXTRA-VIRGIN OLIVE OIL

1 CUP CHOPPED ONION

4 GARLIC CLOVES, MINCED

2 TABLESPOONS TOMATO PASTE

1 CUP CHOPPED RED BELL PEPPER

1 CUP CHOPPED YELLOW BELL PEPPER

1 CUP CHOPPED ZUCCHINI

1 CUP CHOPPED EGGPLANT

½ CUP WATER

2 TABLESPOONS HERBES DE PROVENCE

SALT AND PEPPER, TO TASTE

¼ CUP FRESH BASIL LEAVES

½ CUP SHAVED PARMESAN CHEESE

1. Place the olive oil in a large, deep skillet and warm it over medium heat. Add the onion and cook, stirring occasionally, until it starts to soften, about 5 minutes. Add the garlic and tomato paste and cook, stirring continually, for 1 minute.

2. Add the bell peppers and cook, stirring occasionally, until they have softened, about 5 minutes.

3. Add the zucchini, eggplant, water, and herbes de Provence, cover the pot, and cook for 10 minutes. Remove the cover and cook until the liquid has reduced, about 5 minutes.

4. Season the ratatouille with salt and pepper, stir in the basil and Parmesan, and serve it over pasta.

Ratatouille
SEE PAGE 465

Swedish Meatballs

YIELD: 4 TO 6 SERVINGS / **ACTIVE TIME:** 1 HOUR / **TOTAL TIME:** 1 HOUR AND 20 MINUTES

5 SLICES OF WHITE SANDWICH BREAD, CRUSTS REMOVED

¾ CUP WHOLE MILK

½ CUP UNSALTED BUTTER

1 SMALL YELLOW ONION, MINCED

1½ LBS. GROUND BEEF

¾ LB. GROUND PORK

¼ LB. GROUND VEAL

2 LARGE EGGS

2 TEASPOONS KOSHER SALT, PLUS MORE TO TASTE

1 TEASPOON FRESHLY GRATED NUTMEG

1 TEASPOON ALLSPICE

1 TEASPOON WHITE PEPPER

¼ CUP ALL-PURPOSE FLOUR

4 CUPS BEEF STOCK (SEE PAGE 538), AT ROOM TEMPERATURE

½ CUP SOUR CREAM

1. Tear the slices of bread into strips and place them in a bowl with the milk. Let the bread soak for 10 minutes.

2. Place 2 tablespoons of the butter in a large skillet and melt it over medium heat. Add the onion and cook, stirring continually, until it is translucent, about 3 minutes. Remove the onion from the pan and let it cool slightly.

3. Place the meats, eggs, salt, nutmeg, allspice, and white pepper in a large bowl and use a wooden spoon or your hands to combine the mixture.

4. Remove the bread from the milk and squeeze to remove any excess liquid. Tear the bread into small pieces and stir it into the meat mixture.

5. Add the cooled onion to the meat mixture and stir to combine.

6. Form the meat mixture into golf ball–sized spheres and set them aside.

7. Place the remaining butter in a large skillet and melt it over medium heat. Working in batches if necessary to avoid crowding the pan, add the meatballs to the skillet and cook until they are browned all over, turning them as necessary. Remove the meatballs from the pan and set them aside.

8. Sprinkle the flour into the skillet and cook for 2 minutes, stirring continually. Add the stock 2 tablespoons at a time, stirring continually, until it has all been incorporated into the sauce.

9. Return the meatballs to the skillet, gently stir to coat them with the sauce, and reduce the heat to low. Cover the pan and simmer the meatballs until they are completely cooked through, about 10 minutes.

10. Stir in the sour cream and serve the meatballs and sauce over egg noodles.

Spicy Cauliflower & Chickpeas

YIELD: 4 SERVINGS / **ACTIVE TIME:** 25 MINUTES / **TOTAL TIME:** 45 MINUTES

FOR THE CAULIFLOWER & CHICKPEAS

1 (14 OZ.) CAN OF CHICKPEAS, DRAINED AND RINSED

3 CUPS CAULIFLOWER FLORETS, CHOPPED

3 GARLIC CLOVES, SLICED THIN

1 SHALLOT, SLICED THIN

⅓ CUP OLIVE OIL

½ TEASPOON CHILI POWDER

½ TEASPOON CHIPOTLE CHILE POWDER

½ TEASPOON BLACK PEPPER

½ TEASPOON ONION POWDER

½ TEASPOON GARLIC POWDER

¼ TEASPOON PAPRIKA

1 TABLESPOON KOSHER SALT

FOR THE DRESSING

2 SCALLIONS, TRIMMED AND SLICED THIN

2 FRESNO CHILE PEPPERS, STEMMED, SEEDED, AND SLICED THIN

3 TABLESPOONS SUGAR

¼ CUP RED WINE VINEGAR

½ TEASPOON DARK CHILI POWDER

½ TEASPOON CHIPOTLE CHILE POWDER

½ TEASPOON BLACK PEPPER

½ TEASPOON ONION POWDER

½ TEASPOON GARLIC POWDER

¼ TEASPOON PAPRIKA

½ TABLESPOON KOSHER SALT

1. Preheat the oven to 400°F. To begin preparations for the cauliflower and chickpeas, place all of the ingredients in a mixing bowl and toss to coat.

2. Place the mixture in a 13 x 9–inch baking pan, place the pan in the oven, and roast until the cauliflower is slightly charred and still crunchy, about 30 minutes.

3. Remove the pan from the oven and let the mixture cool slightly.

4. To prepare the dressing, place all of the ingredients in a food processor and blitz until combined.

5. To serve, top pasta with the cauliflower and chickpeas and drizzle some of the dressing over the top.

Eggplant Parmesan

YIELD: 4 SERVINGS / **ACTIVE TIME:** 20 MINUTES / **TOTAL TIME:** 1 HOUR

1 LARGE EGGPLANT

SALT, TO TASTE

2 TABLESPOONS EXTRA-VIRGIN OLIVE OIL

1 CUP ITALIAN BREAD CRUMBS

¼ CUP GRATED PARMESAN CHEESE

1 EGG, BEATEN

MARINARA SAUCE (SEE PAGE 480), AS NEEDED

2 GARLIC CLOVES, MINCED

½ LB. SHREDDED MOZZARELLA CHEESE

FRESH BASIL, FINELY CHOPPED, FOR GARNISH

1. Preheat the oven to 350°F. Trim the top and bottom off the eggplant and slice it into ¼-inch-thick slices. Put the slices on paper towels in a single layer, sprinkle salt over them, and let them rest for about 15 minutes. Turn the slices over, salt the other side, and let them rest for another 15 minutes. Rinse the eggplant and pat dry with paper towels.

2. Drizzle the olive oil over a baking sheet. In a shallow bowl, combine the bread crumbs and Parmesan cheese. Place the beaten egg in another shallow bowl. Dredge the eggplant in the egg and then in the bread crumb-and-cheese mixture until completely coated. Place the breaded slices on the baking sheet and place it in the oven.

3. Bake the eggplant for 10 minutes. Remove, turn the eggplant over, and bake for another 10 minutes. Remove the eggplant from the oven and let it cool slightly.

4. Spread some of the sauce over a square baking dish or a cast-iron skillet and stir in the garlic. Lay some of the eggplant on top of the sauce, top with more sauce, and then arrange the remaining eggplant on top. Sprinkle the mozzarella over the eggplant and place the dish in the oven.

5. Bake until the sauce is bubbling and the cheese is golden brown, about 30 minutes.

6. Remove the eggplant Parmesan from the oven and let it cool for 10 minutes before slicing and serving over pasta.

Eggplant Parmesan
SEE PAGE 471

Chicken with 40 Cloves

YIELD: 6 SERVINGS / **ACTIVE TIME:** 35 MINUTES / **TOTAL TIME:** 1 HOUR AND 15 MINUTES

2 TABLESPOONS EXTRA-VIRGIN OLIVE OIL

8 BONELESS, SKINLESS CHICKEN THIGHS

SALT AND PEPPER, TO TASTE

8 WHITE OR BABY BELLA MUSHROOMS, QUARTERED

40 GARLIC CLOVES

⅓ CUP DRY VERMOUTH

¾ CUP CHICKEN STOCK (SEE PAGE 536)

1 TABLESPOON UNSALTED BUTTER

1 TABLESPOON FINELY CHOPPED FRESH TARRAGON

1. Preheat the oven to 350°F. Place the olive oil in a Dutch oven and warm it over medium-high heat. Generously season the chicken with salt and pepper and place it in the pot, working in batches if necessary to avoid crowding the pan. Cook until the chicken is browned on both sides, about 6 minutes, turning them over halfway through. Transfer the chicken to a plate and set it aside.

2. Add the mushrooms to the pot and cook, stirring occasionally, until they are browned all over, about 12 minutes.

3. Add the garlic and cook, stirring frequently, for 1 minute.

4. Add the vermouth and stock and scrape any browned bits form the bottom of the pot. Return the chicken to the pot, cover it, and place it in the oven.

5. Braise until the chicken is tender and cooked through (the interior is 165°F), about 25 minutes.

6. Remove the pot from the oven and transfer the chicken and mushrooms to a plate. Using a fork or large spoon, mash about half of the garlic and stir to incorporate it into the sauce. If the sauce is too thin for your liking, place the pot over medium-high heat and cook until it has reduced to the desired consistency. Return the chicken and mushrooms to the pot, reduce the heat, and cook until warmed through.

7. Stir in the butter and tarragon and serve over pasta or egg noodles.

Veal Scallopini

YIELD: 4 SERVINGS / **ACTIVE TIME:** 15 MINUTES / **TOTAL TIME:** 20 MINUTES

½ CUP ALL-PURPOSE FLOUR

½ TEASPOON FRESHLY GRATED NUTMEG

SALT AND PEPPER, TO TASTE

2 TABLESPOONS UNSALTED BUTTER

1 LB. VEAL CUTLETS, POUNDED VERY THIN

½ CUP BEEF STOCK (SEE PAGE 538)

¼ CUP GREEN OLIVES, SLICED

ZEST AND JUICE OF 1 LEMON

1. Warm a large cast-iron skillet over medium heat for 5 minutes.

2. Place the flour, nutmeg, salt, and pepper in a shallow bowl and stir to combine.

3. Place the butter in the pan. When it starts to sizzle, dredge the veal in the seasoned flour until it is coated lightly on both sides. Working in batches if necessary to avoid crowding the pan, place the veal in the skillet and cook until it is browned on both sides and the juices run clear—which means that it is cooked through—about 2 minutes, turning it over just once. Remove the veal from the pan and let it rest.

4. Deglaze the pan with the stock, scraping up any browned bits from the bottom. Add the olives, lemon zest, and lemon juice, stir to combine, and cook until the sauce is warmed through.

5. Serve the veal scallopini over pasta and drizzle the pan sauce over each portion.

Chicken Bolognese

YIELD: 6 SERVINGS / **ACTIVE TIME:** 45 MINUTES / **TOTAL TIME:** 2 HOURS

2 TABLESPOONS EXTRA-VIRGIN OLIVE OIL

½ LB. BACON, CHOPPED

1½ LBS. GROUND CHICKEN

SALT AND PEPPER, TO TASTE

1 CUP DICED CARROTS

1 CUP DICED CELERY

2 CUPS DICED ONIONS

3 GARLIC CLOVES, MINCED

1 TABLESPOON FRESH THYME

2 CUPS SHERRY

8 CUPS CRUSHED TOMATOES

1 CUP WATER

1 CUP HEAVY CREAM

2 TABLESPOONS CHOPPED FRESH SAGE

1 CUP GRATED PARMESAN CHEESE

1. Place the olive oil and bacon in a cast-iron Dutch oven and cook over medium heat until the bacon is crispy, about 8 minutes, turning it as necessary.

2. Add the chicken, season with salt and pepper, and cook until it is browned and cooked through, breaking it up with a wooden spoon, about 8 minutes. Remove the mixture from the pan and set it aside.

3. Reduce the heat to medium and add the carrots, celery, onions, and garlic. Season with salt and cook until the carrots are tender, about 10 minutes, stirring occasionally.

4. Return the bacon and chicken to the pan, add the thyme and sherry, and cook until the sherry has nearly evaporated. Add the tomatoes and water, reduce the heat to low, and cook until the sauce has thickened, stirring frequently, about 45 minutes.

5. Add the cream and sage and cook for an additional 15 minutes.

6. Add the Parmesan to the sauce and stir until it has melted. Serve the sauce over noodles, or use it in a baked pasta dish.

Caprese Chicken

YIELD: 6 SERVINGS / **ACTIVE TIME:** 15 MINUTES / **TOTAL TIME:** 45 MINUTES

1 GARLIC CLOVE, MINCED

1 TEASPOON DRIED OREGANO

1 TEASPOON GRANULATED GARLIC

SALT AND PEPPER, TO TASTE

2 TABLESPOONS EXTRA-VIRGIN OLIVE OIL

2 LBS. BONELESS, SKINLESS CHICKEN BREASTS, HALVED ALONG THEIR EQUATOR

2 LBS. ROMA OR PLUM TOMATOES, SLICED INTO ¼-INCH-THICK ROUNDS

1 LB. FRESH MOZZARELLA CHEESE, SLICED INTO ¼-INCH-THICK PIECES

LEAVES FROM 1 BUNCH OF FRESH BASIL

BALSAMIC GLAZE (SEE PAGE 542), FOR DRIZZLING

1. Preheat the oven to 375°F. Combine the fresh garlic, oregano, granulated garlic, salt, and pepper in a bowl. Place 1 tablespoon of olive oil and the chicken in a bowl and toss to coat. Dredge the chicken in the garlic-and-spice mixture and set aside.

2. Place the remaining olive oil in a large cast-iron skillet and warm it over medium-high heat. Working in batches, add the chicken to the pan and sear for 1 minute per side.

3. Place half of the chicken in an even layer on the bottom of the skillet. Top with two-thirds of the tomatoes and mozzarella and half of the basil. Place the remaining chicken on top and cover with the remaining tomatoes, mozzarella, and basil.

4. Place the skillet in the oven and cook until the cheese is melted and bubbling and the chicken is cooked through (the interior is 165°F), about 10 minutes.

5. Remove the skillet from the oven and let the chicken rest for 10 minutes before drizzling balsamic glaze over the top and serving it over pasta.

Sicilian Meatballs

YIELD: 4 SERVINGS / **ACTIVE TIME:** 20 MINUTES / **TOTAL TIME:** 45 MINUTES

2 TABLESPOONS EXTRA-VIRGIN OLIVE OIL

½ SMALL RED ONION, CHOPPED

2 GARLIC CLOVES, MINCED

1 LARGE EGG

2 TABLESPOONS WHOLE MILK

½ CUP ITALIAN BREAD CRUMBS

¼ CUP FRESHLY GRATED PARMESAN CHEESE

¼ CUP PINE NUTS, TOASTED

3 TABLESPOONS MINCED DRIED CURRANTS

2 TABLESPOONS FINELY CHOPPED FRESH OREGANO

2 TABLESPOONS FINELY CHOPPED FRESH PARSLEY

¾ LB. GROUND PORK

½ LB. SWEET OR SPICY GROUND ITALIAN SAUSAGE

SALT AND PEPPER, TO TASTE

2 CUPS ROMESCO SAUCE (SEE PAGE 543)

1. Preheat the broiler to high, position a rack so that the tops of the meatballs will be approximately 6 inches below the broiler, and line a rimmed baking sheet with aluminum foil.

2. Place the olive oil in a large skillet and warm over medium-high heat. When it starts to shimmer, add the onion and garlic and cook, stirring frequently, until the onion is translucent, about 3 minutes. Remove the pan from heat and set it aside.

3. Place the egg, milk, bread crumbs, Parmesan, pine nuts, currants, oregano, and parsley in a mixing bowl and stir until combined. Add the pork, sausage, and onion mixture, season with salt and pepper, and stir until thoroughly combined. Working with wet hands, form the mixture into 1½-inch meatballs, arrange them on the baking sheet, and spray the tops with cooking spray.

4. Place the meatballs in the oven and broil until browned all over, turning them as they cook. Remove the meatballs from the oven and set them aside.

5. Place the sauce in the skillet and warm it over medium heat. Add the meatballs to the sauce, reduce the heat to low, cover the pan, and simmer, turning the meatballs occasionally, until they are cooked through, about 15 minutes.

6. Season with salt and pepper and serve them over pasta.

Marinara Sauce

YIELD: 8 CUPS / **ACTIVE TIME:** 30 MINUTES / **TOTAL TIME:** 2 HOURS

4 LBS. TOMATOES, PEELED, SEEDED, AND CHOPPED

1 YELLOW ONION, SLICED

15 GARLIC CLOVES, CRUSHED

2 TEASPOONS FRESH THYME

2 TEASPOONS FRESH OREGANO

2 TABLESPOONS EXTRA-VIRGIN OLIVE OIL

1½ TABLESPOONS KOSHER SALT, PLUS MORE TO TASTE

1 TEASPOON BLACK PEPPER, PLUS MORE TO TASTE

2 TABLESPOONS FINELY CHOPPED FRESH BASIL

1 TABLESPOON FINELY CHOPPED FRESH PARSLEY

1. Place all of the ingredients, except for the basil and parsley, in a large saucepan and cook, stirring constantly, over medium heat until the tomatoes begin to collapse, about 10 minutes.

2. Reduce the heat to low and cook, stirring occasionally, for about 1½ hours, or until the flavor is to your liking.

3. Stir in the basil and parsley and season the sauce to taste. The sauce will be chunky. If you prefer a smoother texture, transfer the sauce to a food processor and blitz before serving it over pasta.

Basil Pesto

YIELD: 1 CUP / **ACTIVE TIME:** 10 MINUTES / **TOTAL TIME:** 25 MINUTES

¼ CUP PINE NUTS

3 GARLIC CLOVES

SALT AND PEPPER, TO TASTE

2 CUPS FIRMLY PACKED FRESH BASIL LEAVES

½ CUP EXTRA-VIRGIN OLIVE OIL

¼ CUP FRESHLY GRATED PARMESAN CHEESE

1 TEASPOON FRESH LEMON JUICE

1. Warm a small skillet over low heat for 1 minute. Add the pine nuts and cook, shaking the pan frequently, until they begin to give off a toasty fragrance, 2 to 3 minutes. Transfer the pine nuts to a plate and let them cool completely.

2. Place the garlic, salt, and pine nuts in a food processor or blender and pulse until the mixture is a coarse meal. Add the basil and pulse until finely minced. Transfer the mixture to a medium bowl and, while whisking to incorporate, add the oil in a thin stream.

3. Add the cheese and stir until thoroughly incorporated. Stir in the lemon juice, taste, and adjust the seasoning as necessary. To serve, toss pasta in the pesto.

Note: You can also make this pesto using a mortar and pestle, which will give it more texture.

Lamb Ragù

YIELD: 8 CUPS / **ACTIVE TIME:** 40 MINUTES / **TOTAL TIME:** 3 HOURS

2 TABLESPOONS EXTRA-VIRGIN OLIVE OIL

2 SMALL ONIONS, MINCED

2 CELERY STALKS, PEELED AND MINCED

SALT, TO TASTE

2 LBS. GROUND LAMB

1 CUP DRY RED WINE

2 TEASPOONS FRESH THYME

2 TEASPOONS CHOPPED FRESH MARJORAM

1 TEASPOON RED PEPPER FLAKES

2 (28 OZ.) CANS OF PEELED WHOLE SAN MARZANO TOMATOES, WITH THEIR LIQUID, CRUSHED BY HAND

1. Place the olive oil in a Dutch oven and warm it over medium-high heat. Add the onions and celery, season with salt, and stir to combine. When the mixture starts to sizzle, reduce the heat to low, cover the pot, and cook, stirring occasionally, until the vegetables are very tender and a deep golden brown, about 30 minutes.

2. Add the ground lamb to the pot and cook, breaking it up with a wooden spoon, until it is no longer pink. Raise the heat to medium-high, add the wine, and cook until it has reduced by half, about 5 minutes.

3. Stir in the thyme, marjoram, and red pepper flakes and cook for 2 minutes. Add the tomatoes, season the sauce with salt and pepper, stir, and bring to a boil.

4. Reduce the heat to medium-low and simmer, stirring occasionally, until the sauce has visibly thickened and the fat has separated and is bubbling on the surface, about 2 hours. Serve the ragù over pasta.

Rose Sauce

YIELD: 8 CUPS / **ACTIVE TIME:** 15 MINUTES / **TOTAL TIME:** 30 MINUTES

4 LBS. VERY RIPE PLUM
TOMATOES, PEELED,
SEEDED, AND CHOPPED

¼ CUP UNSALTED BUTTER

½ WHITE OR VIDALIA
ONION, QUARTERED

SALT AND PEPPER, TO TASTE

2 CUPS HEAVY CREAM

1. Place the tomatoes in a food processor and blitz until pureed.

2. Warm a medium saucepan over medium-low heat for 2 minutes. Add the butter and raise the heat to medium. Once the butter melts and stops foaming, add the onion, season with salt, and cook until it begins to sizzle. Reduce the heat to low, cover the pan, and cook, stirring occasionally, until the onion is soft, about 10 minutes.

3. Add the pureed tomatoes and season with salt. Bring the sauce to a boil, reduce the heat to low, and simmer until it has thickened and the flavor is to your liking, about 20 minutes.

4. As the tomato sauce cooks, place the cream in a small saucepan and cook over low heat until it has reduced by about half. Remove the pan from heat and set the reduced cream aside.

5. Using a slotted spoon, remove as much of the onion from the sauce as you can. Stir the reduced cream into the tomato sauce, season it with salt and pepper, and toss it with pasta.

Fontina Sauce

YIELD: 3 CUPS / **ACTIVE TIME:** 40 MINUTES / **TOTAL TIME:** 1 HOUR AND 15 MINUTES

FLORETS FROM 1 HEAD OF CAULIFLOWER

6½ TABLESPOONS EXTRA-VIRGIN OLIVE OIL

SALT AND PEPPER, TO TASTE

1 LB. CREMINI MUSHROOMS, STEMMED AND CHOPPED

1 TABLESPOON FRESH THYME

6 OZ. BACON, CHOPPED

1 LARGE YELLOW ONION, GRATED

½ CUP CHICKEN STOCK (SEE PAGE 536)

1 CUP GRATED FONTINA CHEESE

¾ CUP HEAVY CREAM

1½ TEASPOONS WORCESTERSHIRE SAUCE

1. Preheat the oven to 450°F. Place the cauliflower and 2 tablespoons of olive oil in a large bowl and toss to coat. Transfer the cauliflower to a baking pan, season with salt and pepper, cover the pan with aluminum foil, and place it in the oven.

2. Bake for 15 minutes, remove from the oven, remove the foil and discard it, and turn the cauliflower over. Return the pan to the oven, uncovered, lower the oven's temperature to 400°F, and roast the cauliflower until it is tender and its edges are browned, about 40 minutes.

3. While the cauliflower is roasting, place the mushrooms in a large bowl with 2 tablespoons of olive oil and toss to coat. Transfer to a parchment-lined baking sheet, season with salt and pepper, and sprinkle the thyme over the top.

4. Place the baking sheet in the 400°F oven, roast for 15 minutes, and remove from oven. Carefully drain the liquid, return to the oven, and roast until the mushrooms are tender and lightly browned, about 25 minutes.

5. Place 2 tablespoons of olive oil in a large skillet and warm it over medium heat. Add the bacon and cook, stirring occasionally, until it is browned and crispy, about 8 minutes. Transfer the bacon to a small bowl and set it aside.

6. Add the onion to the pan, season it with salt, and raise the heat to medium-high. Cook until the onion starts to sizzle. Reduce the heat to low, cover the pan, and cook, stirring occasionally, until the onion becomes very soft, about 15 minutes.

7. Raise the heat to medium-high, stir in the stock, cheese, and cream, and cook until the mixture starts to bubble. Stir in the Worcestershire sauce, bacon, and roasted vegetables and toss the sauce with pasta.

Calamari Fra Diavolo

YIELD: 6 CUPS / **ACTIVE TIME:** 40 MINUTES / **TOTAL TIME:** 1 HOUR

1 CUP DRY RED WINE

2 LBS. SQUID, BODIES CUT INTO RINGS, TENTACLES HALVED LENGTHWISE

3½ TABLESPOONS EXTRA-VIRGIN OLIVE OIL

4 GARLIC CLOVES, MINCED

1 TEASPOON RED PEPPER FLAKES

SALT, TO TASTE

3 ANCHOVY FILLETS PACKED IN OLIVE OIL

2 HANDFULS OF FRESH PARSLEY, CHOPPED

1 (28 OZ.) CAN OF PEELED WHOLE SAN MARZANO TOMATOES, WITH THEIR LIQUID, PUREED

½ CUP CLAM JUICE

1. Place the wine in a small saucepan, bring it to a boil, and cook until it has reduced by half, about 5 minutes. Remove the pan from heat and set it aside.

2. Thoroughly rinse the squid thoroughly and transfer it to a paper towel–lined plate. Blot the squid with paper towels to remove as much surface moisture as possible.

3. Place the olive oil in a large, deep skillet and warm it over medium heat. Add the garlic and half of the red pepper flakes, season with salt, and cook until the garlic starts to brown, about 1 minute.

4. Raise the heat to medium-high and add the squid, anchovies, and half of the parsley. Cook, stirring occasionally, until the anchovies dissolve and the calamari is golden brown, about 4 minutes.

5. Add the reduced wine and continue to cook until the liquid in the mixture has reduced by one-third, about 5 minutes.

6. Stir in the tomatoes, the clam juice, and remaining red pepper flakes, season with salt, and bring the sauce to a boil. Reduce the heat to medium-low and simmer the sauce until it has thickened slightly, about 20 minutes. Serve over pasta.

Aromatic Walnut Sauce

YIELD: 2 CUPS / **ACTIVE TIME:** 20 MINUTES / **TOTAL TIME:** 50 MINUTES

1 CUP DAY-OLD BREAD PIECES

1 CUP WALNUTS

1 GARLIC CLOVE, SLICED THIN

¼ CUP BREAD CRUMBS

HANDFUL OF FRESH PARSLEY, CHOPPED

2 TABLESPOONS FINELY CHOPPED FRESH MARJORAM

3 TABLESPOONS WALNUT OIL

3 TABLESPOONS HEAVY CREAM

5 TABLESPOONS UNSALTED BUTTER, AT ROOM TEMPERATURE

SALT, TO TASTE

1. Place the bread in a small bowl, cover it with warm water, and let it soak for 30 minutes.

2. Drain, squeeze the bread to remove as much water from it as possible, and set it aside.

3. Bring water to a boil in a small saucepan, add the walnuts, and cook for 2 minutes. Drain and let them cool. When cool enough to handle, rub off their skins and place them on paper towels to dry. When dry, chop the walnuts.

4. Place the bread, walnuts, garlic, bread crumbs, parsley, and half of the marjoram in a food processor and pulse until the mixture is a smooth paste.

5. Transfer the mixture to a bowl and slowly add the walnut oil, whisking until it has emulsified.

6. Stir in the cream and butter, season the sauce with salt, and serve it over pasta.

Roasted Tomato & Garlic Sauce

YIELD: 6 CUPS / **ACTIVE TIME:** 15 MINUTES / **TOTAL TIME:** 2 HOURS

3 LBS. TOMATOES, HALVED

¼ CUP EXTRA-VIRGIN OLIVE OIL

5 LARGE GARLIC CLOVES, UNPEELED

SALT AND PEPPER, TO TASTE

HANDFUL OF FRESH BASIL LEAVES

1. Preheat the oven to 350°F. Place the tomatoes in a baking dish and drizzle the olive oil over them. Stir to ensure the tomatoes are coated evenly, place them in the oven, and lower the oven's temperature to 325°F. Roast the tomatoes for 1 hour.

2. Remove the baking dish from the oven, add the garlic, return it to the oven, and roast for another 30 minutes.

3. Remove the baking dish from the oven and let the tomatoes and garlic cool slightly.

4. When the garlic is cool enough to handle, peel it and place it in a large bowl. Add the tomatoes, season the mixture with salt and pepper, and let cool completely.

5. Place the roasted tomato mixture and basil in a food processor and blitz until smooth.

6. Place the puree in a medium saucepan and bring to a simmer over medium heat, stirring occasionally, until it has the desired consistency.

7. Taste, adjust the seasoning as necessary, and serve over pasta.

Shrimp & Pistou Sauce

YIELD: 5 CUPS / **ACTIVE TIME:** 35 MINUTES / **TOTAL TIME:** 1 HOUR

1½ LBS. SHRIMP, SHELLS REMOVED, DEVEINED

4 GARLIC CLOVES

5 TABLESPOONS TOMATO PASTE

SALT AND PEPPER, TO TASTE

½ CUP FRESHLY GRATED PARMESAN CHEESE

2 HANDFULS OF FRESH BASIL LEAVES, TORN

6½ TABLESPOONS EXTRA-VIRGIN OLIVE OIL

3 CUPS SUGO AL BASILICO (SEE PAGE 448)

½ CUP WATER

1. Place the shrimp on a paper towel–lined plate and let them come to room temperature.

2. Place the garlic, tomato paste, and a generous pinch of salt in a food processor and pulse until thoroughly combined. Add the Parmesan and pulse to incorporate. Add the basil and pulse once. Transfer the mixture to a small bowl and whisk in ¼ cup of the olive oil. Set the pistou aside.

3. Place the remaining olive oil in a large, deep skillet and warm it over medium heat. Pat the shrimp dry with paper towels and add it to the pan. Cook until the shrimp just turns pink, 2 to 3 minutes, turning it over once. Remove the shrimp from the pan and set it aside.

4. Place the sauce and water in the skillet and bring to a simmer over medium-high heat. Stir in the pistou, taste, and season the sauce with salt and pepper. Add the shrimp, cook until it is cooked through, and serve over pasta.

Chicken Cacciatore

YIELD: 6 SERVINGS / **ACTIVE TIME:** 25 MINUTES / **TOTAL TIME:** 1 HOUR AND 45 MINUTES

2 LBS. BONE-IN, SKIN-ON CHICKEN THIGHS

SALT AND PEPPER, TO TASTE

2 TABLESPOONS EXTRA-VIRGIN OLIVE OIL

1 LARGE ONION, CHOPPED

1 LB. PEELED WHOLE SAN MARZANO TOMATOES, WITH THEIR LIQUID, CRUSHED BY HAND

2 CARROTS, PEELED AND GRATED

4 OZ. BUTTON MUSHROOMS, STEMMED AND CHOPPED

1 CUP SUGO AL BASILICO (SEE PAGE 448)

½ CUP DRY WHITE WINE

1 BAY LEAF

1 TEASPOON FRESH THYME

1 TEASPOON MARJORAM

4 GARLIC CLOVES, MINCED

1. Season the chicken with salt and pepper. Place the olive oil in a large skillet and warm it over medium heat. Add the chicken, skin side down, and cook until it is browned on both sides, about 8 minutes.

2. Add the remaining ingredients and stir to combine. Let the cacciatore simmer until the chicken is very tender and the flavor is to your liking, at least 1 hour.

3. Remove the bay leaf, discard it, and serve the cacciatore over pasta.

Chicken Parmesan

YIELD: 6 SERVINGS / **ACTIVE TIME:** 25 MINUTES / **TOTAL TIME:** 1 HOUR AND 30 MINUTES

2 LBS. BONELESS, SKINLESS CHICKEN CUTLETS, POUNDED THIN

SALT AND PEPPER, TO TASTE

½ CUP ALL-PURPOSE FLOUR

3 LARGE EGGS

2 CUPS PANKO

½ CUP EXTRA-VIRGIN OLIVE OIL

5 CUPS MARINARA SAUCE (SEE PAGE 480)

1 CUP FRESHLY GRATED PARMESAN CHEESE

½ LB. FRESH MOZZARELLA CHEESE, CHOPPED

1. Preheat the oven to 400°F. Season the chicken breasts with salt and pepper. Place the flour, eggs, and panko in separate shallow bowls. Dredge the cutlets in the flour, then the eggs, and then the panko until they are completely coated.

2. Place the olive oil in a large skillet and warm it over medium-high heat. Working in batches to avoid crowding the pan, add the breaded chicken and cook until it is browned on both sides, about 8 minutes, turning it over once. Transfer the browned cutlets to a paper towel–lined plate.

3. Coat the bottom of a 13 x 9–inch baking pan with a thin layer of sauce. Sprinkle one-third of the Parmesan over the sauce, place half of the cutlets over the cheese, and top them with half of the mozzarella. Spread half of the remaining sauce over the mozzarella, sprinkle another third of the Parmesan over the sauce, and repeat the layering process, ending with a layer of Parmesan on top.

4. Place the pan in the oven and bake until the chicken is cooked through (the interior is 165°F) and the cheese is golden brown, about 40 minutes. Remove from the oven and let the chicken Parmesan cool briefly before serving it over pasta.

Spiced Pork Sauce

YIELD: 4 CUPS / **ACTIVE TIME:** 20 MINUTES / **TOTAL TIME:** 1 HOUR AND 30 MINUTES

6 TABLESPOONS UNSALTED BUTTER

1 YELLOW ONION, GRATED

2 CELERY STALKS, PEELED AND GRATED

SALT, TO TASTE

1½ LBS. GROUND PORK

1 CUP MILK

½ TEASPOON GROUND CLOVES

1 CUP CHICKEN STOCK (SEE PAGE 536)

2 TABLESPOONS TOMATO PASTE

2 BAY LEAVES

6 FRESH SAGE LEAVES

1. Place half of the butter in a large saucepan and melt it over medium-high heat. Add the onion and celery, season with salt, and cook, stirring continually, until the onion is translucent, about 3 minutes. Reduce the heat to low, cover the pan, and cook, stirring occasionally, until the vegetables are very tender, about 30 minutes.

2. Add the ground pork to the pan and raise the heat to medium-high. Season the pork with salt and cook, using a wooden spoon to break it up, until it is browned.

3. Stir in the milk and cook until it has completely evaporated, about 10 minutes.

4. Stir in the cloves, cook for 2 minutes, and then add the stock, tomato paste, and bay leaves. Bring the sauce to a boil, reduce the heat to low, and let the sauce simmer, stirring occasionally, until the flavor has developed to your liking, about 45 minutes.

5. Place the remaining butter in a small skillet and melt it over medium-low heat. Add the sage leaves and cook until the leaves are slightly crispy. Remove the sage leaves and discard them. Stir the seasoned butter into the sauce and serve it over pasta.

Spiced Pork Sauce
SEE PAGE 495

Slow-Cooker Chicken & Sausage Cacciatore

YIELD: 6 SERVINGS / **ACTIVE TIME:** 10 MINUTES / **TOTAL TIME:** 6 HOURS AND 15 MINUTES

6 BONELESS, SKINLESS CHICKEN THIGHS

1 LB. ITALIAN SAUSAGE

1 (28 OZ.) CAN OF WHOLE SAN MARZANO TOMATOES, DRAINED

1 (28 OZ.) CAN OF DICED TOMATOES, WITH THEIR JUICE

⅔ CUP DRY RED WINE

4 SHALLOTS, CHOPPED

3 GARLIC CLOVES, MINCED

1 GREEN BELL PEPPER, STEMMED, SEEDED, AND CHOPPED

1 YELLOW BELL PEPPER, STEMMED, SEEDED, AND CHOPPED

1 CUP BUTTON MUSHROOMS, CHOPPED

1½ TEASPOONS DRIED OREGANO

1 TABLESPOON GARLIC POWDER

1 TABLESPOON SUGAR

1 TABLESPOON KOSHER SALT, PLUS MORE TO TASTE

½ TEASPOON RED PEPPER FLAKES

BLACK PEPPER, TO TASTE

PARMESAN CHEESE, GRATED, FOR GARNISH

FRESH PARSLEY, FINELY CHOPPED, FOR GARNISH

1. Place all of the ingredients, except for the Parmesan and parsley, in a slow cooker and cook on low until the chicken is very tender, about 5½ hours. The cooking time may vary depending on your slow cooker, so be sure to check after about 4½ hours to avoid overcooking.

2. Serve the cacciatore over pasta and garnish each portion with Parmesan and parsley.

Sheet Pan Veal Caprese

YIELD: 4 TO 6 SERVINGS / **ACTIVE TIME:** 35 MINUTES / **TOTAL TIME:** 1 HOUR

2 LARGE EGGS

3 CUPS ITALIAN BREAD CRUMBS

6 VEAL CUTLETS, POUNDED TO ⅛ INCH THICK

3 TABLESPOONS UNSALTED BUTTER

¼ CUP EXTRA-VIRGIN OLIVE OIL

1 TEASPOON KOSHER SALT

½ TEASPOON BLACK PEPPER

1 CUP BASIL PESTO (SEE PAGE 482)

1 HEIRLOOM TOMATO, SLICED

½ LB. MOZZARELLA CHEESE, CUT INTO THICK SLICES

HANDFUL OF FRESH BASIL

1. Preheat the oven to 400°F. Place the eggs in a shallow bowl and whisk until scrambled. Place the bread crumbs in a separate shallow bowl. Dredge the veal in the eggs and then in the bread crumbs until it is coated all over. Set the breaded veal aside.

2. Place the butter and olive oil on a baking sheet, place the pan in the oven, and melt the butter. Carefully remove the pan from the oven and gently tilt the pan to spread the butter and olive oil over it evenly.

3. Arrange the breaded veal in the pan, season with the salt and pepper, and return the pan to the oven. Bake for 15 minutes, turning the veal over halfway through.

4. Remove the pan from the oven and set the oven's broiler to high. Spread the pesto over the veal and arrange the tomato and mozzarella around it. Top with half of the basil leaves and return the pan to the oven.

5. Broil until the veal is completely cooked through and the mozzarella has melted, about 5 minutes.

6. Remove the pan from the oven, top the dish with the remaining basil, and serve the veal caprese over pasta.

Easy Chicken Saltimbocca

YIELD: 4 SERVINGS / **ACTIVE TIME:** 30 MINUTES / **TOTAL TIME:** 50 MINUTES

1 LB. BONELESS, SKINLESS CHICKEN BREASTS

1 TEASPOON KOSHER SALT

½ TEASPOON BLACK PEPPER

12 FRESH SAGE LEAVES

8 SLICES OF PROSCIUTTO

CLOVES FROM 1 GARLIC BULB, SEPARATED AND UNPEELED

½ LEMON, CUT INTO WEDGES

1 TABLESPOON EXTRA-VIRGIN OLIVE OIL

1. Preheat the oven to 425°F. Coat a baking sheet with nonstick cooking spray.

2. Season the chicken breasts with salt and pepper, lay 2 sage leaves on top of each chicken breast, then wrap each one with 2 slices of prosciutto, covering the entire breast.

3. Carefully place the chicken on the pan and arrange the garlic cloves around it. Squeeze the lemon over the chicken and drizzle the olive oil over it.

4. Scatter the remaining sage around the chicken and place the pan in the oven. Bake until the chicken is cooked through (the internal temperature is 165°F), 20 to 25 minutes.

5. Remove the pan from the oven and let the chicken rest for 3 minutes before serving it over pasta.

Lemon & Pesto Chicken

YIELD: 4 SERVINGS / **ACTIVE TIME:** 30 MINUTES / **TOTAL TIME:** 1 HOUR AND 5 MINUTES

8 CHICKEN DRUMSTICKS

1 TABLESPOON UNSALTED BUTTER, MELTED

2 LEMONS, 1 ZESTED AND JUICED; 1 SLICED

SALT AND PEPPER, TO TASTE

BASIL PESTO (SEE PAGE 482)

1. Preheat the oven to 425°F. Place the chicken in a baking pan. Place the butter, lemon zest, and lemon juice in a small bowl and stir to combine.

2. Rub the lemon butter over the chicken and season with salt and pepper. Spoon half of the pesto over the chicken and add the sliced lemon to the pan.

3. Place the pan in the oven and bake for 25 minutes.

4. Set the oven's broiler to high and broil until the chicken is cooked through (the internal temperature is 165°F) and browned, 5 to 10 minutes.

5. Remove the chicken from the oven, top it with the remaining pesto, and serve.

Chicken with Zucchini & Eggplant

YIELD: 4 TO 6 SERVINGS / **ACTIVE TIME:** 30 MINUTES / **TOTAL TIME:** 1 HOUR AND 10 MINUTES

1 LARGE ZUCCHINI, SLICED THIN

1 SMALL EGGPLANT, SLICED THIN

8 CHICKEN DRUMSTICKS

2 MEDIUM RUSSET POTATOES, PEELED AND CUT INTO 1-INCH CUBES

2 TABLESPOONS EXTRA-VIRGIN OLIVE OIL

1 TEASPOON KOSHER SALT

½ TEASPOON BLACK PEPPER

½ TEASPOON GARLIC POWDER

½ TEASPOON PAPRIKA

1. Set the oven's broiler to high. Coat a baking sheet with nonstick cooking spray. Place the zucchini and eggplant on the baking sheet, place it in the oven, and broil until the vegetables are charred all over and cooked through, 8 to 10 minutes, turning them as necessary.

2. Remove the pan from the oven, remove the vegetables from the pan, and set them aside.

3. Preheat the oven to 425°F. Place the remaining ingredients in a mixing bowl and toss to coat. Transfer the chicken and potatoes to a baking pan and spread them into an even layer.

4. Place the pan in the oven and roast until the chicken is almost cooked through (the internal temperature is 160°F) and the potatoes are tender, about 35 minutes, turning the chicken over halfway through.

5. Remove the pan from the oven, add the zucchini and eggplant to the pan, and return it to the oven. Roast until the zucchini and eggplant are warmed through and the chicken is cooked through, about 5 minutes.

6. Remove the pan from the oven and serve the chicken and potatoes over pasta.

Pea Shoot Pesto

YIELD: 2 CUPS / **ACTIVE TIME:** 15 MINUTES / **TOTAL TIME:** 15 MINUTES

2 CUPS PEA SHOOTS

1 CUP FRESH BASIL

2 TABLESPOONS FRESH LEMON JUICE

½ TEASPOON RED PEPPER FLAKES

¼ CUP PINE NUTS

¼ CUP FRESHLY GRATED PARMESAN CHEESE

¼ CUP EXTRA-VIRGIN OLIVE OIL

SALT AND PEPPER, TO TASTE

1. Place the pea shoots, basil, lemon juice, red pepper flakes, pine nuts, and Parmesan in a food processor and pulse until you have a rough paste.

2. With the food processor running, add the olive oil in a slow stream until it has emulsified. Season the pesto with salt and toss it with pasta.

Chipotle & Pistachio Pesto

YIELD: 2 CUPS / **ACTIVE TIME:** 5 MINUTES / **TOTAL TIME:** 5 MINUTES

4 CANNED CHIPOTLES IN ADOBO, SEEDED

3 GARLIC CLOVES

⅔ CUP SHELLED SALTED PISTACHIOS, SHELLS REMOVED

⅓ CUP EXTRA-VIRGIN OLIVE OIL

1 CUP FRESHLY GRATED MANCHEGO CHEESE

SALT, TO TASTE

1. Place the chipotles and garlic in a food processor and blitz until smooth. Add the pistachios and pulse until they are slightly crushed. Transfer the mixture to a medium bowl.

2. While whisking continually, add the olive oil in a slow, steady stream until it has emulsified.

3. Stir in the cheese, season the sauce with salt, and toss it with pasta.

Roasted Red Pepper, Corn & Herb Sauce

YIELD: 3 CUPS / **ACTIVE TIME:** 30 MINUTES / **TOTAL TIME:** 1 HOUR

2 LARGE RED BELL PEPPERS

2 TABLESPOONS UNSALTED BUTTER

5 SCALLIONS, TRIMMED AND SLICED THIN

SALT AND PEPPER, TO TASTE

KERNELS FROM 4 EARS OF CORN

ANCHO CHILE POWDER, TO TASTE

2 TABLESPOONS EXTRA-VIRGIN OLIVE OIL

2 HANDFULS OF FRESH PARSLEY, CHOPPED

2 HANDFULS OF FRESH CILANTRO, CHOPPED

¼ CUP HEAVY CREAM

¾ CUP CRUMBLED COTIJA CHEESE

1. Preheat the oven to 400°F. Place the peppers on a baking sheet, place them in the oven, and roast until they are charred all over, turning them as necessary. Remove the peppers from the oven, place them in a bowl, and cover it with plastic wrap. Let the peppers steam for 10 minutes.

2. Remove the stems, seeds, and skins from the peppers and chop the remaining flesh.

3. Place the butter in a large skillet and melt it over medium heat. Add the scallions, season with salt, and cook, stirring occasionally, until they are translucent, about 4 minutes.

4. Add two-thirds of the corn, season the mixture with ancho chile powder, and cook, stirring occasionally, until the corn is tender, about 4 minutes. Transfer the mixture to a food processor and pulse until it is a chunky puree.

5. Place the olive oil in a clean skillet and warm it over medium-high heat. Add the peppers and the remaining corn, season the mixture with salt and pepper, and cook, stirring occasionally, until the corn turns golden brown, about 6 minutes.

6. Stir in half of the parsley and half of the cilantro and cook for 30 seconds. Add the puree, cream, and cheese, reduce the heat to low, and bring the sauce to a gentle simmer.

7. Season the sauce with salt, pepper, and ancho chile powder and toss it with pasta to serve.

Roasted Poblano & Caramelized Onion Sauce

YIELD: 3 CUPS / **ACTIVE TIME:** 1 HOUR / **TOTAL TIME:** 1 HOUR AND 30 MINUTES

3 POBLANO PEPPERS

3 TABLESPOONS EXTRA-VIRGIN OLIVE OIL, PLUS MORE AS NEEDED

2 LARGE ONIONS, SLICED THIN

SALT AND PEPPER, TO TASTE

KERNELS FROM 3 EARS OF CORN

1 CUP CREMA

¾ CUP FRESHLY GRATED MANCHEGO CHEESE

1. Preheat the oven to 500°F. Place the peppers on a baking sheet, place them in the oven, and roast until they are charred all over, turning them as necessary. Remove the peppers from the oven, place them in a bowl, and cover it with plastic wrap. Let the peppers steam for 10 minutes.

2. Remove the stems, seeds, and skins from the peppers and chop the remaining flesh.

3. Place the olive oil in a large skillet and warm it over medium-low heat. Add the onions, season them with salt, and cook, stirring occasionally, until the onions are caramelized and very tender, about 40 minutes.

4. Add the corn, raise the heat to medium, and cook, stirring occasionally, until the corn starts to brown, about 10 minutes. Remove the pan from heat.

5. Place the roasted poblanos, crema, and cheese in a food processor and blitz until smooth. Transfer the mixture to a bowl, stir in the caramelized onion mixture, and toss it with pasta to serve.

Brown Butter & Sage Sauce

YIELD: ¾ CUP / **ACTIVE TIME:** 5 MINUTES / **TOTAL TIME:** 10 MINUTES

¾ CUP UNSALTED BUTTER, CUT INTO SMALL PIECES

16 FRESH SAGE LEAVES

SALT AND PEPPER, TO TASTE

1. Place the butter in a large skillet and melt it over medium heat.

2. Add the sage and cook, stirring occasionally, until the butter begins to brown and give off a nutty fragrance and the sage leaves become crispy. You will need to be very attentive during this step, as butter can burn in a blink of an eye.

3. Remove the pan from heat, remove the sage leaves from the butter, and season the sauce with salt and pepper. To serve, either toss cut pasta in the sauce or ladle it over gnocchi and filled pastas.

Brown Butter & Sage Sauce
SEE PAGE 507

Gingery Red Pepper Sauce

YIELD: 2 CUPS / **ACTIVE TIME:** 10 MINUTES / **TOTAL TIME:** 30 MINUTES

2 RED BELL PEPPERS, STEMMED, SEEDED, AND CHOPPED

1-INCH PIECE OF FRESH GINGER, PEELED AND CHOPPED

4 GARLIC CLOVES, MINCED

3 TABLESPOONS SUGAR

2 TABLESPOONS TOMATO PASTE

1 TABLESPOON EXTRA-VIRGIN OLIVE OIL

1 TABLESPOON APPLE CIDER VINEGAR

1 TABLESPOON SOY SAUCE

1. Place all of the ingredients in a food processor and blitz until smooth.

2. Transfer the mixture to a small saucepan and cook over medium heat, stirring occasionally, until it has reduced and thickened, about 15 minutes.

3. Taste, adjust the seasoning as necessary, and serve the sauce over pasta.

Smoked Salmon & Asparagus Sauce

YIELD: 4 CUPS / **ACTIVE TIME:** 20 MINUTES / **TOTAL TIME:** 3 HOURS AND 45 MINUTES

4 OZ. SMOKED SALMON, SLICED

¾ CUP HEAVY CREAM

1 TEASPOON FRESHLY GRATED NUTMEG

SALT, TO TASTE

1 LB. ASPARAGUS, TRIMMED

1½ TABLESPOONS UNSALTED BUTTER

2 LEEKS, TRIMMED, RINSED WELL, AND SLICED THIN

1. Place the salmon, cream, and nutmeg in a small bowl, stir to combine, and let the mixture steep for 3 hours in the refrigerator.

2. Bring water to a boil in a large saucepan. Add salt, let the water return to a full boil, and add the asparagus. Cook until it is just tender, about 3 minutes. Drain and let the asparagus cool slightly. When the asparagus is cool enough to handle, chop it.

3. Place the butter in a large skillet and warm it over medium heat. Add the asparagus and cook, stirring occasionally, until it is golden brown. Remove the asparagus from the pan and set it aside.

4. Add the leeks to the skillet, season them with salt, and cook, stirring occasionally, until they are very soft, about 15 minutes.

5. Add the asparagus and salmon-and-cream mixture to the pan, reduce the heat to low, and cook the sauce until it is warmed through, about 5 minutes. Serve the sauce over pasta.

Broccoli Rabe & Ham Sauce

YIELD: 4 CUPS / **ACTIVE TIME:** 25 MINUTES / **TOTAL TIME:** 40 MINUTES

2 TABLESPOONS KOSHER SALT, PLUS MORE TO TASTE

1½ LBS. BROCCOLI RABE, TRIMMED

¼ CUP EXTRA-VIRGIN OLIVE OIL

1 SMALL YELLOW ONION, MINCED

3 GARLIC CLOVES, MINCED

1 TABLESPOON CAPERS, DRAINED AND RINSED

4 OZ. SLICED HAM, JULIENNED

1. Bring water to a boil in a large saucepan. Add the salt, let the water return to a full boil, and add the broccoli rabe. Cook until it is tender, about 6 minutes. Drain and rinse it under cold water. Squeeze the broccoli rabe to remove as much water from it as possible, chop it, and set it aside.

2. Place the olive oil in a large skillet and warm it over medium heat. Add the onion and garlic and cook, stirring frequently, until the onion is translucent, about 3 minutes.

3. Stir in the capers and ham and cook until the mixture becomes very tender, about 6 minutes.

4. Add the broccoli rabe, season the sauce with salt, and cook for 5 minutes. Serve the sauce over pasta.

Creamy Leek Sauce

YIELD: 2 CUPS / **ACTIVE TIME:** 20 MINUTES / **TOTAL TIME:** 40 MINUTES

2½ TABLESPOONS UNSALTED BUTTER

4 LEEKS, TRIMMED, RINSED WELL, AND CHOPPED

SALT, TO TASTE

1 CUP HEAVY CREAM

¼ CUP WHOLE MILK

½ TEASPOON WHITE PEPPER

1. Warm a large skillet over low heat for 2 to 3 minutes. Add 2 tablespoons of the butter, raise the heat to medium, and melt the butter. Add the leeks, season with salt, and cook until the leeks begin to gently sizzle. Reduce the heat to low, cover the pan, and cook the leeks, stirring occasionally, until they are very soft and turn a slightly darker shade of green, about 20 minutes.

2. Raise heat to medium-high, stir in the cream, milk, white pepper, and remaining butter, season the sauce with salt, and bring it to a boil. Reduce the heat to low and simmer the sauce until it has reduced slightly, about 5 minutes. To serve, toss the sauce with pasta.

Romanesco Broccoli Cream

YIELD: 4 CUPS / **ACTIVE TIME:** 15 MINUTES / **TOTAL TIME:** 25 MINUTES

SALT AND PEPPER, TO TASTE

1 LB. ROMANESCO BROCCOLI FLORETS

1 TABLESPOON EXTRA-VIRGIN OLIVE OIL, PLUS MORE AS NEEDED

½ SMALL ONION, SLICED THIN

1 OZ. PARMESAN CHEESE, GRATED

3 FRESH BASIL LEAVES

1. Bring water to a boil in a large saucepan. Add salt, let the water return to a full boil, and add the broccoli. Cook until it starts to feel tender, drain, and pat it dry.

2. Coat the bottom of a skillet with olive oil and warm it over medium-high heat. Add the onion and broccoli and cook, stirring occasionally, until the onion starts to soften, about 5 minutes. Transfer the mixture to a food processor, add the remaining ingredients, and blitz until smooth.

3. If the sauce is not as thick as you would like, place it in a saucepan and cook over medium heat until it has reduced to the desired consistency. To serve, toss the sauce with pasta.

Pistachio Pesto

YIELD: 2 CUPS / **ACTIVE TIME:** 5 MINUTES / **TOTAL TIME:** 5 MINUTES

½ LB. SHELLED UNSALTED PISTACHIOS

2 OZ. PARMESAN CHEESE, GRATED

ZEST OF ½ LEMON

½ GARLIC CLOVE

½ CUP WATER

1 GENEROUS HANDFUL OF FRESH BASIL

SALT AND PEPPER, TO TASTE

½ CUP EXTRA-VIRGIN OLIVE OIL

1. Place the pistachios in a food processor and pulse until they are coarsely ground.

2. Add the remaining ingredients and pulse until the mixture is a slightly chunky paste. To serve, toss the pesto with pasta.

Zucchini Cream

YIELD: ½ CUP / **ACTIVE TIME:** 20 MINUTES / **TOTAL TIME:** 20 MINUTES

2 TABLESPOONS EXTRA-VIRGIN OLIVE OIL

1 ZUCCHINI, CHOPPED

½ ONION, CHOPPED

SALT AND PEPPER, TO TASTE

1. Coat the bottom of a large skillet with half of the olive oil and warm it over medium heat. Add the zucchini and onion and cook, stirring occasionally, until they are tender, about 10 minutes.

2. Season the vegetables with salt and pepper, raise the heat to medium-high, and cook until all of the liquid in the pan has evaporated.

3. Place the sautéed vegetables in a food processor, add the remaining olive oil, and puree until smooth. To serve, toss the pesto with pasta.

Parsley Pesto

YIELD: 1 CUP / **ACTIVE TIME:** 20 MINUTES / **TOTAL TIME:** 20 MINUTES

1 BUNCH OF FRESH PARSLEY

¼ CUP BREAD CRUMBS

6 TABLESPOONS EXTRA-VIRGIN OLIVE OIL, PLUS MORE TO TASTE

DASH OF WATER

3 ANCHOVIES IN OLIVE OIL, DRAINED

SALT, TO TASTE

1. Place all of the ingredients in a food processor and blitz until smooth. To serve, toss the pesto with pasta.

Béchamel Sauce

YIELD: 2 CUPS / **ACTIVE TIME:** 30 MINUTES / **TOTAL TIME:** 45 MINUTES

4 CUPS WHOLE MILK

2 BAY LEAVES

½ WHITE ONION

10 BLACK PEPPERCORNS

½ CUP UNSALTED BUTTER

½ CUP ALL-PURPOSE FLOUR

SALT AND WHITE PEPPER, TO TASTE

1. Place the milk, bay leaves, onion, and peppercorns in a medium saucepan and warm over medium heat. Cook, stirring occasionally, until the mixture is just about to come to a boil, about 6 minutes. Remove the pan from heat, let the mixture steep for 20 minutes, and then strain. Discard the solids and set the liquid aside.

2. Place the butter in a medium saucepan and melt it over medium heat. Add the flour and stir until the mixture is smooth. Cook, stirring continually, until the mixture is golden brown, about 5 minutes.

3. Pour in ½ cup of the milk mixture and stir vigorously until you've thinned out the flour mixture. Add the remaining milk and cook, stirring continually, until the mixture thickens.

4. Season the sauce with salt and pepper and toss it with pasta or use it in a layered pasta dish. Béchamel sauce is also a wonderful way to add moisture when reheating pasta.

Sausage Ragù

YIELD: 4 CUPS / **ACTIVE TIME:** 30 MINUTES / **TOTAL TIME:** 4 TO 6 HOURS

2 LBS. ITALIAN SAUSAGE

2 TABLESPOONS EXTRA-VIRGIN OLIVE OIL

1 SWEET ONION, DICED

2 GREEN BELL PEPPERS, STEMMED, SEEDED, AND DICED

1 (28 OZ.) CAN OF SAN MARZANO TOMATOES, WITH THEIR LIQUID

1 CUP CHOPPED FRESH BASIL

2 TEASPOONS RED PEPPER FLAKES

1 TABLESPOON ITALIAN SEASONING

1 CUP WATER, PLUS MORE AS NEEDED

SALT AND PEPPER, TO TASTE

1. Working in batches to avoid crowding the pan, place the sausage in a large saucepan and cook it over medium-high heat, stirring occasionally, until it is browned and cooked through. Remove the sausage from the pan and set it aside.

2. Add the olive oil and onion to the pan and cook over medium heat, stirring occasionally, until the onion translucent, about 3 minutes. Add the peppers and cook, stirring occasionally, for 5 minutes.

3. Chop the sausage and add it to the pan along with the remaining ingredients. Bring the sauce to a boil, reduce the heat, and partially cover the pan.

4. Simmer the sauce until the flavor has developed to your liking, at least 2 hours. Add water as needed so that the sauce doesn't burn.

5. To serve, ladle the ragù over pasta.

Peppercorn Cream Sauce

YIELD: 1 CUP / **ACTIVE TIME:** 20 MINUTES / **TOTAL TIME:** 20 MINUTES

2 TABLESPOONS PEPPERCORNS

1 CUP HEAVY CREAM

SALT, TO TASTE

1. Using a mortar and pestle, roughly grind the peppercorns. Place them in a dry skillet and toast for 1 minute, shaking the pan occasionally.

2. Add the cream and a pinch of salt, reduce the heat to medium-low, and cook the sauce, stirring constantly, for 2 minutes. To serve, toss the sauce with pasta.

Sun-Dried Tomato Pesto

YIELD: 2 CUPS / **ACTIVE TIME:** 5 MINUTES / **TOTAL TIME:** 5 MINUTES

12 SUN-DRIED TOMATOES IN OLIVE OIL, DRAINED

½ CUP FRESH BASIL LEAVES

¼ SMALL SHALLOT

¼ CUP PINE NUTS

1 GARLIC CLOVE

1 TABLESPOON BLACK PEPPER

1 TEASPOON SEA SALT

½ CUP EXTRA-VIRGIN OLIVE OIL

1. Place all of the ingredients, except for the olive oil, in a food processor and pulse until the mixture is a thick paste.

2. With the food processor running, add the olive oil in a slow stream until it has emulsified. To serve, toss the pesto with pasta.

Broccoli Rabe Pesto

YIELD: 3 CUPS / **ACTIVE TIME:** 10 MINUTES / **TOTAL TIME:** 25 MINUTES

SALT AND PEPPER, TO TASTE

1 BUNCH OF BROCCOLI RABE, TRIMMED

1 CUP PINE NUTS

4 GARLIC CLOVES

1 CUP FRESH BASIL

1 CUP FRESHLY GRATED PARMESAN CHEESE

ZEST OF 1 LEMON

1 CUP EXTRA-VIRGIN OLIVE OIL

1. Preheat the oven to 325°F.

2. Bring water to a boil in a large saucepan and prepare an ice bath. Add salt to the boiling water, let it return to a full boil, and add the broccoli rabe. Cook for 1 minute. Drain the broccoli rabe and plunge it into the ice bath until it has cooled completely. Drain the broccoli rabe again and set it aside.

3. Place the pine nuts on a baking sheet, place the pan in the oven, and toast until the pine nuts are slightly browned, about 8 minutes.

4. Remove the pine nuts from the oven and transfer them to a food processor. Add the broccoli rabe and remaining ingredients and blitz until the pesto has the desired texture. To serve, toss the pesto with pasta.

Arugula Pesto

YIELD: 1 CUP / **ACTIVE TIME:** 10 MINUTES / **TOTAL TIME:** 10 MINUTES

2 CUPS ARUGULA

1 GARLIC CLOVE, MINCED

½ TEASPOON KOSHER SALT

¼ CUP WALNUTS

1 TEASPOON LEMON ZEST

⅓ CUP EXTRA-VIRGIN OLIVE OIL

1 TEASPOON FRESH LEMON JUICE

1. Place the arugula, garlic, salt, walnuts, and lemon zest in a food processor and pulse until the mixture is smooth.

2. With the food processor running, drizzle in the olive oil until it has emulsified. Add the lemon juice and pulse to incorporate.

3. Taste, adjust the seasoning as necessary, and toss the pesto with pasta to serve.

Radicchio Cream Sauce

YIELD: 3 CUPS / **ACTIVE TIME:** 15 MINUTES / **TOTAL TIME:** 30 MINUTES

3 TABLESPOONS UNSALTED BUTTER

1 LARGE HEAD OF RADICCHIO, CORED AND GRATED

SALT AND WHITE PEPPER, TO TASTE

3 TABLESPOONS WARM WATER

1½ CUPS HEAVY CREAM

1. Warm a large skillet over medium heat for 2 to 3 minutes and then add the butter. When it melts and stops foaming, add the radicchio, season with salt and white pepper, and cook, stirring occasionally, until the radicchio wilts, about 5 minutes.

2. Add the warm water and cook until the radicchio has softened, another 4 to 5 minutes. Using a slotted spoon, transfer the radicchio to a bowl and cover it to keep warm.

3. Add the cream to the skillet and bring it to a simmer. Reduce heat to low and cook until the cream has reduced, about 15 minutes.

4. Add the reduced cream to the bowl containing the radicchio, stir to combine, and serve the sauce over pasta.

Radicchio Cream Sauce
SEE PAGE 519

Red Bell Pepper & Shallot Pesto

YIELD: 2 CUPS / **ACTIVE TIME:** 20 MINUTES / **TOTAL TIME:** 45 MINUTES

3 RED BELL PEPPERS

3 TABLESPOONS EXTRA-VIRGIN OLIVE OIL

3 SHALLOTS, DICED

SALT, TO TASTE

1 TABLESPOON WORCESTERSHIRE SAUCE

¾ CUP CRUMBLED FETA CHEESE

1. Preheat the oven to 400°F. Place the peppers on a baking sheet, place them in the oven, and roast the peppers until they are tender and charred all over. Remove the peppers from the oven, place them in a mixing bowl, and let them cool.

2. When the peppers are cool enough to handle, remove the skins, stems, and seeds and discard them. Set the flesh of the roasted peppers aside.

3. Place the olive oil in a small skillet and warm it over medium heat. Add the shallots and cook, stirring occasionally, until they are browned, about 10 minutes.

4. Place the peppers, shallots, and the remaining ingredients in a food processor and pulse until the pesto has the desired texture. To serve, toss the pesto with pasta.

Mascarpone Sauce

YIELD: 2 CUPS / **ACTIVE TIME:** 15 MINUTES / **TOTAL TIME:** 30 MINUTES

3 TABLESPOONS PINE NUTS

⅛ TEASPOON KOSHER SALT

½ CUP WALNUT PIECES

2 BLACK GARLIC CLOVES

½ CUP MASCARPONE CHEESE

3½ TABLESPOONS WHOLE MILK

3 TABLESPOONS FRESHLY GRATED PARMESAN CHEESE

WHITE PEPPER, TO TASTE

1. Warm a small skillet over medium-low heat for 2 minutes. Add the pine nuts and cook until they begin to brown in spots, 3 to 4 minutes, shaking the pan frequently. Remove the pan from heat and season the pine nuts with the salt. Set the pine nuts aside.

2. Place the walnuts and black garlic in a food processor and blitz until the mixture is coarse crumbs.

3. Transfer the mixture to a small saucepan and add the mascarpone, milk, and Parmesan. Season with pepper and warm the mixture over medium-low heat until it comes to a simmer.

4. Remove the pan from heat and stir in the toasted pine nuts. To serve, toss the sauce with pasta.

Gorgonzola Cream Sauce

YIELD: 3 CUPS / **ACTIVE TIME:** 15 MINUTES / **TOTAL TIME:** 15 MINUTES

2 CUPS HEAVY CREAM

4 OZ. GORGONZOLA DOLCE CHEESE, CHOPPED

⅔ CUP FRESHLY GRATED PARMESAN CHEESE

1 TEASPOON FRESHLY GRATED NUTMEG

SALT AND WHITE PEPPER, TO TASTE

1. Place the cream and cheeses in a medium saucepan and cook the mixture over medium heat, stirring occasionally, until it is gently simmering and the sauce is smooth, about 5 minutes. Continue to simmer the sauce until it is thick enough to coat the back of a wooden spoon, about 8 minutes.

2. Stir in the nutmeg and season the sauce with salt and white pepper. To serve, toss the sauce with pasta.

Peanut Sauce

YIELD: 1 CUP / **ACTIVE TIME:** 10 MINUTES / **TOTAL TIME:** 10 MINUTES

2 GARLIC CLOVES, MINCED

2 SHALLOTS, MINCED

2 TABLESPOONS AVOCADO OIL

½ CUP COCONUT MILK

¼ CUP SMOOTH PEANUT BUTTER

1 TABLESPOON TAMARIND PASTE

1½ TABLESPOONS KECAP MANIS

2 TEASPOONS FISH SAUCE

2 TEASPOONS FRESH LIME JUICE

2 TEASPOONS SWEET CHILI SAUCE

1. Using a mortar and pestle, grind the garlic and shallots into a paste.

2. Place the paste and the avocado oil in a small saucepan and warm the mixture over low heat, stirring frequently, for 2 minutes.

3. Stir in the remaining ingredients and cook until the sauce starts to bubble. Remove the pan from heat, taste the sauce, and adjust the seasoning as necessary. To serve, toss the sauce with noodles.

Oxtail Ragù

YIELD: 6 CUPS / **ACTIVE TIME:** 30 MINUTES / **TOTAL TIME:** 3 TO 4 HOURS

1 TABLESPOON EXTRA-VIRGIN OLIVE OIL

1½ LBS. OXTAILS

SALT AND PEPPER, TO TASTE

1 ONION, CHOPPED

4 GARLIC CLOVES, MINCED

1 TEASPOON FRESH THYME

2 CINNAMON STICKS

½ TEASPOON GROUND CLOVES

⅓ CUP RED WINE

4 CUPS BEEF STOCK (SEE PAGE 538)

1 (28 OZ.) CAN OF DICED TOMATOES, WITH THEIR LIQUID

1. Preheat the oven to 300°F. Place the olive oil in a Dutch oven and warm it over medium heat. Season the oxtails with salt and pepper, place them in the pot, and sear until golden brown all over, about 6 minutes, turning them as necessary. Remove the oxtails from the pot and set them aside.

2. Add the onion and cook, stirring occasionally, until it starts to soften, about 5 minutes. Add the garlic, thyme, cinnamon sticks, and cloves and cook, stirring continually, for 1 minute.

3. Add the red wine and cook for 4 minutes. Add the stock and tomatoes and bring the mixture to a boil. Return the seared oxtails to the pot, cover the pot, and place it in the oven.

4. Braise until the oxtails are falling off the bone, 3 to 4 hours.

5. Remove the ragù from the oven, remove the oxtails from the sauce, and place them on a cutting board. Let them cool slightly and then use two forks to shred the meat.

6. Remove the cinnamon sticks from the sauce, stir in the shredded oxtails, and ladle the sauce over pasta.

Chile & Garlic Sauce

YIELD: 1 CUP / **ACTIVE TIME:** 15 MINUTES / **TOTAL TIME:** 30 MINUTES

1 CUP CHOPPED FRESNO CHILE PEPPERS

8 GARLIC CLOVES, CHOPPED

¼ CUP WHITE VINEGAR

2 TABLESPOONS SUGAR

1 TEASPOON KOSHER SALT, PLUS MORE TO TASTE

BLACK PEPPER, TO TASTE

1. Place the chiles, garlic, and vinegar in a small saucepan and bring to a simmer over medium heat, stirring occasionally. Cook for 10 minutes.

2. Transfer the mixture to a blender and puree until smooth.

3. Strain the puree through a fine-mesh sieve into a clean saucepan. Add the sugar and salt and bring the sauce to a simmer. Season the sauce with salt and pepper, remove the pan from heat, and let the sauce cool slightly. To serve, toss the sauce with noodles.

Cilantro Pesto

YIELD: 1½ CUPS / **ACTIVE TIME:** 5 MINUTES / **TOTAL TIME:** 5 MINUTES

1 CUP FRESH CILANTRO

1 GARLIC CLOVE

¼ CUP ROASTED AND SHELLED SUNFLOWER SEEDS

¼ CUP SHREDDED QUESO ENCHILADO

1 TEASPOON FRESH LEMON JUICE

SALT AND PEPPER, TO TASTE

¼ CUP EXTRA-VIRGIN OLIVE OIL

1. Place all of the ingredients, except for the olive oil, in a food processor and blitz until smooth.

2. With the food processor running, add the olive oil in a slow stream until it has emulsified. To serve, toss the pesto with pasta.

Charred Scallion Sauce

YIELD: 1 CUP / **ACTIVE TIME:** 10 MINUTES / **TOTAL TIME:** 10 MINUTES

3 SCALLIONS

2 GARLIC CLOVES, MINCED

2 BIRD'S EYE CHILE PEPPERS, STEMMED, SEEDED, AND MINCED

¼ CUP CHOPPED FRESH CILANTRO

1 TABLESPOON GRATED FRESH GINGER

1 TABLESPOON SESAME OIL

½ CUP SOY SAUCE

1 TABLESPOON SAMBAL OELEK

2 TABLESPOONS FRESH LIME JUICE

1 TEASPOON SUGAR

1 TABLESPOON SESAME SEEDS

SALT AND PEPPER, TO TASTE

1. On a grill or over an open flame on a gas stove, char the scallions all over. Remove the charred scallions from heat and let them cool.

2. Slice the charred scallions, place them in a mixing bowl, and add the remaining ingredients. Stir to combine, taste the sauce, and adjust the seasoning as necessary. To serve, toss the sauce with noodles.

Charred Scallion Sauce
SEE PAGE 527

Creamy Balsamic & Mushroom Sauce

YIELD: 2 CUPS / **ACTIVE TIME:** 30 MINUTES / **TOTAL TIME:** 30 MINUTES

¼ CUP UNSALTED BUTTER

2 CUPS SLICED MUSHROOMS

2 ONIONS, DICED

2 TEASPOONS TOMATO PASTE

1 CUP VEGETABLE STOCK (SEE PAGE 537)

1 CUP HEAVY CREAM

SALT AND PEPPER, TO TASTE

2 TEASPOONS BALSAMIC VINEGAR

2 TEASPOONS DRIED THYME

¼ CUP CHOPPED FRESH PARSLEY

2 TABLESPOONS CORNSTARCH

1. Place 2 tablespoons of the butter in a large skillet and melt it over medium heat. Add the mushrooms and cook, stirring one or two times, until browned all over, about 10 minutes. Remove the mushrooms from the pan and set them aside.

2. Place the remaining butter in the pan, add the onions, and cook, stirring occasionally, until they have softened, about 5 minutes. Add the tomato paste and cook, stirring continually, for 2 minutes.

3. Deglaze the pan with the stock and heavy cream, scraping up any browned bits from the bottom of the pan. Cook until the liquid has been reduced by half.

4. Add the mushrooms back to the pan and season the sauce with salt and pepper. Stir in the vinegar, thyme, and parsley and let the mixture simmer.

5. Place the cornstarch in a small bowl and add a splash of water. Whisk to combine and then whisk the slurry into the sauce. Continue whisking until the sauce has thickened, about 2 minutes. Serve the sauce over pasta.

Lemon & Caper Sauce

YIELD: ½ CUP / **ACTIVE TIME:** 5 MINUTES / **TOTAL TIME:** 5 MINUTES

6 TABLESPOONS EXTRA-VIRGIN OLIVE OIL

SALT AND PEPPER, TO TASTE

2 TABLESPOONS CHOPPED FRESH PARSLEY

1 TABLESPOON CAPERS, DRAINED AND CHOPPED

ZEST AND JUICE OF 1 LEMON

1. Place the ingredients in a bowl and whisk to combine. To serve, toss the sauce with pasta.

Eggplant & Pine Nut Ragù

YIELD: 2 CUPS / **ACTIVE TIME:** 20 MINUTES / **TOTAL TIME:** 40 MINUTES

1 TABLESPOON EXTRA-VIRGIN OLIVE OIL

1 EGGPLANT, TRIMMED AND CHOPPED (¾-INCH CUBES)

½ TEASPOON RAS EL HANOUT

1 TABLESPOON RAISINS

2 TABLESPOONS PINE NUTS, TOASTED

1 TEASPOON LEMON ZEST

SALT AND PEPPER, TO TASTE

1. Place the olive oil in a large saucepan and warm it over medium heat. Add the eggplant, cover the pan, and cook the eggplant, stirring occasionally, for 5 minutes. Remove the cover and cook, stirring occasionally, until the eggplant is browned, about 10 minutes.

2. Stir in the remaining ingredients and cook, stirring occasionally, until the eggplant has collapsed and the flavor has developed to your liking, 10 to 15 minutes. To serve, ladle the ragù over pasta.

Venison Ragù

YIELD: 4 TO 6 SERVINGS / **ACTIVE TIME:** 1 HOUR / **TOTAL TIME:** 2 HOURS AND 45 MINUTES

2½ LBS. VENISON, TRIMMED AND CUBED

SALT AND PEPPER, TO TASTE

3 TABLESPOONS ALL-PURPOSE FLOUR

¼ CUP EXTRA-VIRGIN OLIVE OIL

4 STRIPS OF BACON, CHOPPED

2 ONIONS, FINELY DICED

3 LARGE CARROTS, PEELED AND FINELY DICED

2 CELERY STALKS, FINELY DICED

2 GARLIC CLOVES, MINCED

⅔ CUP DRY WHITE WINE

½ TEASPOON DRIED OREGANO

½ TEASPOON DRIED BASIL

2 BAY LEAVES

3 CUPS BEEF STOCK (SEE PAGE 538)

½ CUP HEAVY CREAM

1. Season the venison with salt and pepper. Place the flour in a shallow bowl and dredge the venison in it.

2. Place 2 tablespoons of olive oil in a Dutch oven and warm it over medium heat. Working in batches to avoid crowding the pot, add the venison and sear it until it is browned all over, turning it as necessary. If the pan starts to look dry, add more of the remaining olive oil. Remove the seared venison from the pot and set it aside.

3. Add the bacon to the pot and cook, stirring occasionally, until it is crispy and golden brown, about 8 minutes. Remove the bacon from the pot and set it aside.

4. Add the remaining olive oil to the pot and warm it. Add the onion, carrot, celery, season the mixture with salt, and cook, stirring occasionally, until the vegetables are golden brown and tender, about 10 minutes.

5. Stir in the garlic and cook for 1 minute. Add the wine, bring the mixture to a simmer, and cook until the liquid has reduced by three-quarters.

6. Add the dried herbs and bay leaves, return the venison and bacon to the pot, and stir to combine. Pour in the stock and bring the sauce to a boil. Partially cover the pot, reduce the heat to low, and cook, stirring occasionally, until the venison is so tender it can be pulled apart with your fingers, 1½ to 2 hours.

7. Stir the cream into the ragù and bring it to a simmer. Season it with salt and pepper before serving over pasta.

APPENDIX

Chicken Stock

YIELD: 16 CUPS / **ACTIVE TIME:** 1 HOUR / **TOTAL TIME:** 10 HOURS

4 LBS. LEFTOVER CHICKEN BONES

32 CUPS COLD WATER

¼ CUP WHITE WINE

1 ONION, CHOPPED

1 CELERY STALK, CHOPPED

1 CARROT, CHOPPED

2 BAY LEAVES

10 SPRIGS OF FRESH PARSLEY

10 SPRIGS OF FRESH THYME

1 TEASPOON BLACK PEPPERCORNS

SALT, TO TASTE

1. Preheat the oven to 400°F. Place the chicken bones on a baking sheet, place them in the oven, and roast them until they are caramelized, about 1 hour.

2. Remove the chicken bones from the oven and place them in a stockpot. Cover them with the water and bring to a boil, skimming to remove any impurities that rise to the surface.

3. Deglaze the baking sheet with the white wine, scraping up any browned bits from the bottom. Stir the liquid into the stock, add the remaining ingredients, and reduce the heat so that the stock simmers. Simmer the stock until it has reduced by three-quarters and the flavor is to your liking, about 6 hours, skimming the surface as needed.

4. Strain the stock and either use immediately or let it cool completely and store it in the refrigerator.

Marinated Artichokes

YIELD: 4 SERVINGS / **ACTIVE TIME:** 30 MINUTES / **TOTAL TIME:** 1 HOUR

2 CUPS EXTRA-VIRGIN OLIVE OIL, PLUS MORE AS NEEDED

4 TO 8 GLOBE ARTICHOKES, PEELED AND QUARTERED

JUICE OF 1 LEMON

6 GARLIC CLOVES

¼ TEASPOON RED PEPPER FLAKES

2 SPRIGS OF FRESH THYME

1 SHALLOT, SLICED THIN

FRESH BASIL, CHOPPED, FOR GARNISH

1. Place the olive oil and artichokes in a medium saucepan. The artichokes need to be completely covered by the oil, as any contact with the air will cause them to turn brown. Add more oil to cover the artichokes, if necessary.

2. Add the remaining ingredients, except for the basil, and bring the mixture to a simmer over medium heat. Reduce the heat to the lowest setting and cook the artichokes until they are tender, about 30 minutes.

3. Remove the pan from heat and let the artichokes cool. Remove them from the oil, garnish with basil, and enjoy.

Vegetable Stock

YIELD: 6 CUPS / **ACTIVE TIME:** 20 MINUTES / **TOTAL TIME:** 3 HOURS

2 TABLESPOONS EXTRA-VIRGIN OLIVE OIL

2 LARGE LEEKS, TRIMMED AND RINSED WELL

2 LARGE CARROTS, PEELED AND SLICED

2 CELERY STALKS, SLICED

2 LARGE YELLOW ONIONS, SLICED

3 GARLIC CLOVES, UNPEELED BUT SMASHED

2 SPRIGS OF FRESH PARSLEY

2 SPRIGS OF FRESH THYME

1 BAY LEAF

8 CUPS WATER

½ TEASPOON BLACK PEPPERCORNS

SALT, TO TASTE

1. Place the olive oil and the vegetables in a large stockpot and cook over low heat until the liquid they release has evaporated. This will allow the flavor of the vegetables to become concentrated.

2. Add the garlic, parsley, thyme, bay leaf, water, peppercorns, and salt. Raise the heat to high and bring to a boil. Reduce the heat so that the stock simmers and cook for 2 hours, while skimming to remove any impurities that float to the surface.

3. Strain through a fine-mesh sieve, let the stock cool slightly, and place in the refrigerator, uncovered, to chill. Remove the fat layer and cover the stock. The stock will keep in the refrigerator for 3 to 5 days, and in the freezer for up to 3 months.

Beef Stock

YIELD: 8 CUPS / **ACTIVE TIME:** 1 HOUR / **TOTAL TIME:** 10 HOURS

2 LBS. YELLOW ONIONS, CHOPPED

1 LB. CARROTS, CHOPPED

1 LB. CELERY, CHOPPED

5 LBS. BEEF BONES

2 TABLESPOONS TOMATO PASTE

16 CUPS WATER

1 CUP RED WINE

1 TABLESPOON BLACK PEPPERCORNS

2 BAY LEAVES

3 SPRIGS OF FRESH THYME

3 SPRIGS OF FRESH PARSLEY

1. Preheat the oven to 375°F. Divide the onions, carrots, and celery between two baking sheets in even layers. Place the beef bones on top, place the pans in the oven, and roast the vegetables and beef bones for 45 minutes.

2. Spread the tomato paste over the beef bones and then roast for another 5 minutes.

3. Remove the pans from the oven, transfer the vegetables and beef bones to a stockpot, and cover with the water. Bring to a boil.

4. Reduce the heat so that the stock simmers. Deglaze the pans with the red wine, scraping up any browned bits from the bottom. Stir the liquid into the stock, add the remaining ingredients, and cook, skimming any impurities that rise to the surface, until the stock has reduced by half and the flavor is to your liking, about 6 hours.

5. Strain the stock and either use immediately or let it cool completely before storing in the refrigerator.

Roasted Chestnuts

YIELD: 8 SERVINGS / **ACTIVE TIME:** 5 MINUTES / **TOTAL TIME:** 1 HOUR

1 LB. CHESTNUTS

½ TEASPOON KOSHER SALT

¼ TEASPOON BLACK PEPPER

2 TABLESPOONS UNSALTED BUTTER, MELTED

1 TABLESPOON EXTRA-VIRGIN OLIVE OIL

3 SPRIGS OF FRESH THYME

1 CINNAMON STICK

2 WHOLE CLOVES

1. Preheat the oven to 425°F. Carve an "X" on the rounded side of each chestnut and place them in a bowl of hot water. Soak for about 10 minutes.

2. Drain the chestnuts and create an aluminum foil pouch. Place the chestnuts in the pouch, sprinkle salt and pepper over them, drizzle the butter and olive oil over the top, and add the thyme, cinnamon stick, and cloves to the pouch. Close the pouch, leaving an opening so that steam can escape.

3. Place the chestnuts in the oven and roast until tender, 40 to 45 minutes. Remove the chestnuts from the oven and serve them warm.

Dashi Stock

YIELD: 6 CUPS / **ACTIVE TIME:** 10 MINUTES / **TOTAL TIME:** 40 MINUTES

8 CUPS COLD WATER

2 OZ. KOMBU

1 CUP BONITO FLAKES

1. Place the water and the kombu in a medium saucepan. Soak the kombu for 20 minutes, remove it, and score it gently with a knife.

2. Return the kombu to the saucepan and bring to a boil. Remove the kombu as soon as the water boils, so that the stock doesn't become bitter.

3. Add the bonito flakes to the water and return it to a boil. Turn off the heat and let the mixture stand.

4. Strain the stock through a fine-mesh sieve. Use immediately or let it cool before using or storing.

Nuoc Cham

YIELD: 1 CUP / **ACTIVE TIME:** 10 MINUTES / **TOTAL TIME:** 10 MINUTES

¼ CUP FISH SAUCE

⅓ CUP WATER

2 TABLESPOONS SUGAR

¼ CUP FRESH LIME JUICE

1 GARLIC CLOVE, MINCED

2 BIRD'S EYE CHILIES, STEMS AND SEEDS REMOVED, SLICED THIN

1 TABLESPOON CHILI GARLIC SAUCE

1. Place all of the ingredients in a mixing bowl and stir until the sugar has dissolved and the mixture is well combined.

2. Taste, adjust the seasoning as necessary, and use as desired.

Lobster Stock

YIELD: 8 CUPS / **ACTIVE TIME:** 30 MINUTES / **TOTAL TIME:** 4 HOURS AND 30 MINUTES

5 LBS. LOBSTER SHELLS AND BODIES

2 TABLESPOONS EXTRA-VIRGIN OLIVE OIL

½ LB. CARROTS, PEELED AND CHOPPED

½ LB. ONIONS, CHOPPED

10 TOMATOES, CHOPPED

1 CUP V8

5 SPRIGS OF FRESH THYME

5 SPRIGS OF FRESH PARSLEY

5 SPRIGS OF FRESH TARRAGON

5 SPRIGS OF FRESH DILL

1 GARLIC CLOVE

2 CUPS WHITE WINE

1. Preheat the oven to 350°F. Arrange the lobster bodies and shells on two baking sheets, place them in the oven, and roast them for 30 to 45 minutes. Remove the roasted bodies and shells from the oven and set them aside.

2. While the lobster bodies and shells are in the oven, place the olive oil in a stockpot and warm it over medium heat. Add the carrots and onions and cook, stirring occasionally, until the onions start to brown, about 10 minutes. Remove the pan from heat.

3. Add the lobster bodies and shells and the remaining ingredients to the stockpot. Add enough water to cover the mixture, raise the heat to high, and bring to a boil. Reduce the heat and simmer the stock for at least 2 hours, occasionally skimming to remove any impurities that rise to the surface.

4. When the flavor of the stock has developed to your liking, strain it through a fine-mesh sieve or a colander lined with cheesecloth. Place the stock in the refrigerator and chill until it is completely cool.

5. Remove the fat layer from the top of the cooled stock. The stock will keep in the refrigerator for 3 to 5 days and in the freezer for up to 3 months.

Fish Stock

YIELD: 6 CUPS / **ACTIVE TIME:** 20 MINUTES / **TOTAL TIME:** 4 HOURS

¼ CUP EXTRA-VIRGIN OLIVE OIL

1 LEEK, TRIMMED, RINSED WELL, AND CHOPPED

1 LARGE YELLOW ONION, UNPEELED, ROOT CLEANED, CHOPPED

2 LARGE CARROTS, PEELED AND CHOPPED

1 CELERY STALK, CHOPPED

¾ LB. WHITEFISH BODIES

4 SPRIGS OF FRESH PARSLEY

3 SPRIGS OF FRESH THYME

2 BAY LEAVES

1 TEASPOON BLACK PEPPERCORNS

1 TEASPOON KOSHER SALT

8 CUPS WATER

1. Place the olive oil in a stockpot and warm it over low heat. Add the vegetables and cook until the liquid they release has evaporated.

2. Add the whitefish bodies, the aromatics, peppercorns, salt, and water to the pot, raise the heat to high, and bring to a boil. Reduce the heat so that the stock simmers and cook for 3 hours, skimming to remove any impurities that float to the surface.

3. Strain the stock through a fine-mesh sieve, let it cool slightly, and place in the refrigerator, uncovered, to chill. When the stock is completely cool, remove the fat layer from the top and cover. The stock will keep in the refrigerator for 3 to 5 days and in the freezer for up to 3 months.

Balsamic Glaze

YIELD: ½ CUP / **ACTIVE TIME:** 10 MINUTES / **TOTAL TIME:** 25 MINUTES

1 CUP BALSAMIC VINEGAR

¼ CUP BROWN SUGAR

1. Place the vinegar and sugar in a small saucepan and bring the mixture to a boil.

2. Reduce the heat to medium-low and simmer for 8 to 10 minutes, stirring frequently, until the mixture has thickened.

3. Remove the pan from heat and let the glaze cool for 15 minutes before using.

Romesco Sauce

YIELD: 2 CUPS / **ACTIVE TIME:** 5 MINUTES / **TOTAL TIME:** 20 MINUTES

¾ CUP DAY-OLD BREAD PIECES (½-INCH CUBES), CRUST REMOVED

2 TABLESPOONS SLIVERED ALMONDS

¾ CUP ROASTED RED PEPPERS IN OLIVE OIL, DRAINED AND CHOPPED

1 PLUM TOMATO, SEEDED AND CHOPPED

1 TABLESPOON EXTRA-VIRGIN OLIVE OIL

2 TEASPOONS RED WINE VINEGAR

1 GARLIC CLOVE, MINCED

2 PINCHES OF CAYENNE PEPPER

SALT AND PEPPER, TO TASTE

1. Preheat the oven to 350°F. Place the bread and almonds on separate sections of a baking sheet, place the pan in the oven, and toast until the bread and almonds are golden brown, 5 to 7 minutes. Remove from the oven and let them cool.

2. Place the toasted bread and almonds in a food processor and pulse until they are finely ground.

3. Add the peppers and pulse until combined. Add the remaining ingredients and blitz until smooth.

4. Taste, adjust the seasoning as necessary, and use as desired.

Mostarda Mantovana

YIELD: 4 CUPS / **ACTIVE TIME:** 40 MINUTES / **TOTAL TIME:** 2 DAYS

1.1 LBS. QUINCE, PEELED, CORED, AND THINLY SLICED

1¼ CUPS SUGAR

6 TO 8 DROPS MUSTARD ESSENCE

1. Place the quince and sugar in a bowl, cover it with plastic wrap, and let the mixture macerate for 1 day.

2. Collect the juice from the quince and place it in a saucepan. Cook over low heat until it has thickened, about 10 minutes.

3. Add the juice back to the mixture, toss to combine, and cover the bowl. Let the mixture macerate for 1 day.

4. Repeat Steps 2 and 3.

5. Place the mixture in a saucepan and cook until it has caramelized, about 10 minutes.

6. Remove the pan from heat and let the mixture cool.

7. Add the mustard essence and transfer the mostarda to sterilized mason jars. Use immediately or store in the refrigerator.

METRIC CONVERSION CHART

Weights

1 oz. = 28 grams

2 oz. = 57 grams

4 oz. (¼ lb.) = 113 grams

8 oz. (½ lb.) = 227 grams

16 oz. (1 lb.) = 454 grams

Volume Measures

⅛ teaspoon = 0.6 ml

¼ teaspoon = 1.23 ml

½ teaspoon = 2.5 ml

1 teaspoon = 5 ml

1 tablespoon (3 teaspoons) = ½ fluid oz. = 15 ml

2 tablespoons = 1 fluid oz. = 29.5 ml

¼ cup (4 tablespoons) = 2 fluid oz. = 59 ml

⅓ cup (5⅓ tablespoons) = 2.7 fluid oz. = 80 ml

½ cup (8 tablespoons) = 4 fluid oz. = 120 ml

⅔ cup (10⅔ tablespoons) = 5.4 fluid oz. = 160 ml

¾ cup (12 tablespoons) = 6 fluid oz. = 180 ml

1 cup (16 tablespoons) = 8 fluid oz. = 240 ml

Temperature Equivalents

°F	°C	Gas Mark
225	110	¼
250	130	½
275	140	1
300	150	2
325	170	3
350	180	4
375	190	5
400	200	6
425	220	7
450	230	8
475	240	9
500	250	10

Length Measures

1/16 inch = 1.6 mm

⅛ inch = 3 mm

¼ inch = 6.35 mm

½ inch = 1.25 cm

¾ inch = 2 cm

1 inch = 2.5 cm

INDEX

ABOUT CIDER MILL PRESS BOOK PUBLISHERS

Good ideas ripen with time. From seed to harvest, Cider Mill Press brings fine reading, information, and entertainment together between the covers of its creatively crafted books. Our Cider Mill bears fruit twice a year, publishing a new crop of titles each spring and fall.

"Where Good Books Are Ready for Press"

501 Nelson Place
Nashville, TN 37214
cidermillpress.com